Flash® Professional CS5 & Flash® Catalyst™ CS5

FOR

DUMMIES®

by Ellen Finkelstein,
Gurdy Leete, and Mary Leete

WILEY

Wiley Publishing, Inc.

Flash® Professional CS5 & Flash® Catalyst™ CS5 For Dummies®

Published by
Wiley Publishing, Inc.
111 River Street
Hoboken, NJ 07030-5774

www.wiley.com

WILEY

About the Authors

Ellen Finkelstein has written numerous bestselling computer books on PowerPoint, AutoCAD, and Flash. She also writes articles for Web sites, e-zines, magazines, and her own Web site (www.ellenfinkelstein.com). The ten editions of her *AutoCAD Bible* have sold more than 125,000 copies in the United States and abroad. She writes at home so that she can take the bread out of the oven on time.

Gurdy Leete has been working as a computer animator, computer animation software engineer, and teacher of computer animation since 1981. He has been teaching Flash and other computer animation programs for 18 years at Maharishi University of Management, where he is an Assistant Professor of Art and the Co-Chair of the Department of Communications and Media. He writes a blog at www.peaceloveandhappiness.org.

Mary Leete wrote most of the Flash code for *50 Fast Flash MX Techniques*. She is also the author of *Free Software For Dummies* and co-wrote *Microsoft Expression Blend Bible* and *OpenOffice.org For Dummies*. She has a B.S. in Computer Science and a master's degree in Professional Writing. She has worked as a screenwriter under contract and on producer-approved script-writing projects for television.

Dedication

To MMY, for explaining that life is meant to be lived in happiness and teaching us how to realize that reality in daily life.

Authors' Acknowledgments

Ellen Finkelstein: This book was very much a group effort. First, I'd like to thank my co-author, Gurdy Leete, without whom I could not have completed this book nor even thought of writing it. Gurdy is always a pleasure to work with, always in a good mood, and helpful. He's a brilliant artist and a programmer, too, while I am neither. I've been quite impressed.

I'd also like to thank Mary Leete, who wrote some of the more difficult new chapters and updated others. Mary is an amazing programmer who loves to figure out problems; she's also an excellent writer. It's been great working with her.

At Wiley, I'd like to thank Steve Hayes, our acquisitions editor, for his ongoing support. Great kudos go to Nicole Sholly, our project editor, for a great job of organizing and keeping us on track. And special thanks to Teresa Artman for whipping the text into shape. Also, I'd like to thank our technical editor, Jon McFarland, for painstakingly following all our steps and flushing out the flaws. He did an outstanding job.

Personally, I'd like to thank my husband, Evan, and my kids, Yeshayah and Eliyah, who helped out and managed as I wrote every day, evening, and weekend. I love you all.

Thanks to Adobe, for supporting Flash authors while we were learning the new features of Flash CS5, testing Flash and Catalyst, and writing, all at the same time.

And now, a few comments from Gurdy.

Gurdy Leete: I'd like to echo all of Ellen's words and to thank her and my wife, Mary, for being such great collaborators. I'd like to thank our son Porter Leete for the excellent help he gave us in reviewing our work. I'd also like to thank my brilliant former students Alek Lisefski (www.bluesheepstudios.com) and Benek Lisefski (www.benekdesign.com); as well as my intrepid research assistants Nutthawut Chandhaketh, of Thailand; Radim Schreiber, of the Czech Republic; Burcu Cenberci, of Turkey; and Praveen Mishra, of Nepal; whose research activities on the Web were so helpful in writing this book. Thanks to my omnitalented former student Mike Zak for the wonderful collection of clip art drawings that he created in Flash for the companion Web site. And thanks to my adorable daughter Jacqueline for not minding too much the many hours that Mary and I spent working on this book.

Publisher's Acknowledgments

We're proud of this book; please send us your comments at http://dummies.custhelp.com. For other comments, please contact our Customer Care Department within the U.S. at 877-762-2974, outside the U.S. at 317-572-3993, or fax 317-572-4002.

Some of the people who helped bring this book to market include the following:

Acquisitions, Editorial, and Media Development

Project Editor: Nicole Sholly

Executive Editor: Steve Hayes

Senior Copy Editor: Teresa Artman

Technical Editor: Jon McFarland

Editorial Manager: Kevin Kirschner

Media Development Project Manager: Laura Moss-Hollister

Media Development Assistant Project Manager: Jenny Swisher

Media Development Associate Producers: Josh Frank, Marilyn Hummel, Douglas Kuhn, and Shawn Patrick

Editorial Assistant: Amanda Graham

Senior Editorial Assistant: Cherie Case

Cartoons: Rich Tennant (www.the5thwave.com)

Composition Services

Project Coordinator: Kristie Rees

Layout and Graphics: Samantha K. Cherolis, Joyce Haughey

Proofreaders: Jacqui Brownstein, John Greenough

Indexer: Potomac Indexing, LLC

Publishing and Editorial for Technology Dummies

Richard Swadley, Vice President and Executive Group Publisher

Andy Cummings, Vice President and Publisher

Mary Bednarek, Executive Acquisitions Director

Mary C. Corder, Editorial Director

Publishing for Consumer Dummies

Diane Graves Steele, Vice President and Publisher

Composition Services

Debbie Stailey, Director of Composition Services

Contents at a Glance

Table of Contents

Part VI: Building Web Sites Fast with Flash Catalyst ... 361

Part VII: The Part of Tens 401

Chapter 16: Ten Frequently Asked Questions 403

Chapter 17: Ten Best Flash Resources 417

Chapter 18: Ten Flash Designers to Watch .423

Introduction

*W*elcome to *Flash Professional CS5 & Flash Catalyst CS5 For Dummies,* your friendly Web animation companion. In this book, we explain in plain English how to make the most of Flash and Catalyst to create stunning, animated Web sites. We aim to give you all the information you need to start using Flash and Catalyst right away — with no hassle.

About This Book

As though you hadn't guessed, *Flash Professional CS5 & Flash Catalyst CS5 For Dummies* covers the powerful animation product Flash CS5 Professional, from Adobe. (The preceding version was Adobe Flash CS4. You're holding the seventh edition of this book.) Flash CS5 is the latest version of the popular software used on some of the coolest Web sites on the planet. We also cover Adobe Flash Catalyst, a brand new program that offers a new way to create Web sites.

We comprehensively explain the Flash features, including

- Working with the Flash screen, toolbars, and menus
- Creating graphics and text in Flash
- Adding sound and video
- Using layers to organize your animation
- Creating *symbols,* which are objects that you save for repeated use and animation
- Animating graphics (the key to Flash)
- Creating interactive Web sites

We also cover Flash Catalyst, including:

- Importing artwork from Adobe Photoshop and Illustrator
- Defining Web pages in Catalyst
- Working with buttons and other user interface components
- Creating artwork and text in Catalyst
- Importing sound, video, and SWF files
- Publishing your Web site

How to Use This Book

You don't have to read this book from cover to cover. We provide just the information you need, when you need it. Start with the first three chapters. Then play around with graphics until you create what you need for your Web site. You might want to check out Chapter 6, on layers, to help you organize it all, and Chapter 7, which covers symbols. Then feel free to jump right to Chapter 9, on animation, to create your first real Flash movie. Chapter 13 tells you how to get your movie on your Web site. Then fire up your browser, sit back, and marvel.

You'll want to check out other chapters when you need them so that you can create text and buttons, add sound and video, and build an interactive Web site. Chapter 12 provides some ideas for putting all the Flash features together for your best Web site ever.

Are you a designer, first and foremost? Do you love Adobe Photoshop? Then check out Chapters 14 and 15, which introduce you to Flash Catalyst. This new program lets you create Flash Web sites in Adobe Photoshop or Illustrator and use Catalyst to convert your artwork to a fully functioning Web site.

Keep *Flash Professional CS5 & Flash Catalyst CS5 For Dummies* by your computer while you work. You'll find that it's a loyal helper.

Foolish Assumptions

We assume that you're not a master Flash developer. If you want to use Flash to create high-quality Web sites and you're not an expert animator, you'll find this book to be a great reference. *Flash Professional CS5 & Flash Catalyst CS5 For Dummies* is ideal for beginners who are just starting to use Flash or for current Flash users who want to further hone their skills.

Because people usually add Flash movies to Web sites, we also assume that you know some of the basics of Web site creation. You should know what HyperText Markup Language (HTML) is and understand the process of creating and structuring HTML pages as well as uploading them to a Web site.

If you want some help on the topic of Web sites, you might want to take a look at *Web Design For Dummies,* 2nd Edition, by Lisa Lopuck or *Building Web Sites All-in-One For Dummies,* 2nd Edition, by Claudia Snell and Doug Sahlin.

Conventions Used in This Book

Sometimes it helps to know why some text is bold and other text is italic so that you can figure out what we're talking about. (A typographic convention is *not* a convention of typographers meeting to discuss the latest typography techniques.)

New terms are in *italics* to let you know that they're new. When we suggest that you type something, we show you what we want you to type in **bold.** Messages and other text that come from Flash, including programming code, are in a `special typeface, like this.`

When we say something like "Choose File⇨Save As," it means to click the File menu at the top of your screen and then choose Save As from the menu that opens. When we want you to use a toolbar or panel button (or tool), we tell you to click it.

The Flash interface features an item for changing values that's like a combo text box and slider, except that there isn't any text box when you first see it. If you click the value, a box appears in which you can type and then press Enter (Windows) or Return (Mac). Alternatively, you can also click and drag upward or downward, like a traditional slider even though no slider is visible. Calling it a text box seems misleading because you don't see a text box. For this book, this is how we generally describe this way of doing things: "Click the value, type a new value, and then press Enter (Windows) or Return (Mac), or drag to specify a new value."

How This Book Is Organized

We start by presenting an overview of the Flash universe and then continue in the general order that you would use to create a Flash movie. More basic material is at the beginning of the book, and more advanced material (but not too advanced!) comes later.

To be more specific, this book is divided into seven parts (to represent the seven states of consciousness — okay, we don't have to get too cosmic here). Each part contains two or more chapters that relate to that part. Each chapter thoroughly covers one topic so that you don't have to go searching all over the cosmos to get the information you need.

Part I: A Blast of Flash

Part I contains important introductory information about Flash. In Chapter 1, we tell you what Flash is all about, show you what the Flash screen looks like, and explain how to get help when you need it most. You also find instructions for starting a new movie and opening an existing movie, and we give you a list of steps for creating your first animation. If you're new to Flash, running through these steps will give you a great overview. Chapter 2 explains in more detail the steps for creating a Flash movie. We also explain some basic concepts that all Flash users need to know.

Part II: 1,000 Pictures and 1,000 Words

Part II explains all the tools available for creating graphics in Flash. Chapter 3 explains the unique drawing tools included in Flash. We also explain how to import graphics if you don't feel like creating your own. Chapter 4 shows you how to edit and manipulate graphic objects, and Chapter 5 is all about creating text. Chapter 6 explains *layers,* which help you organize your graphics so that they don't interfere with each other.

Part III: Getting Symbolic

Symbols are graphical objects that you save to use again and again. Whenever you want to place an object on a Web page more than once, you can save the object as a symbol. You can also group together many individual objects, making them useful when you want to manipulate, edit, or animate them all at one time. Chapter 7 explains creating and editing symbols. Chapter 8 describes how to create buttons — not the kind that you sew, but rather the kind that you click with your mouse.

Part IV: Total Flash-o-Rama

Part IV explains how to put all of your graphics together and make them move. Chapter 9 covers animation in detail — from frame-by-frame animation to *tweening,* where Flash calculates the animation between your first and last frames. Tween movement to make your objects move or morph into new shapes. You can also tween color and transparency.

Chapter 10 shows how to create interactive Web sites that react to your viewers. For example, when a viewer clicks a button, Flash can jump to a different part of a movie or go to a different Web page entirely. To create interactivity, you use *ActionScript,* Flash's JavaScript-like programming language. We tell you how to put ActionScript to work.

Chapter 11 is about adding multimedia — sound, music, and video — to your Flash movies and buttons.

Part V: The Movie and the Web

This part helps you put all your animated graphics and cool buttons together and publish your work on the Web. Chapter 12 outlines the various techniques that you can use to create a great Web site by using only Flash.

Chapter 13 explains how to test your animation for speed and suitability for all browsers and systems. Then we cover the details of publishing movies as well as the other available formats, such as HTML and GIF. You can also create *projectors* — movies that play themselves.

Part VI: Building Web Sites Fast with Flash Catalyst

For designers who like to design Web sites, Catalyst is a dream come true. Chapter 14 explains how to build Web sites in Photoshop or Illustrator, import the file into Catalyst, and add elements such as buttons and check boxes. We also show you how to add animation to the user interface. Chapter 15 covers adding art, text, audio, video, and more.

Part VII: The Part of Tens

What's a *For Dummies* book without The Part of Tens? Chapter 16 answers some frequently asked questions about Flash and introduces some special techniques, such as synchronizing sound with motion and rescaling the size of your entire movie. Chapter 17 provides you with the ten best resources for Flash (besides this book, of course). Chapter 18 points you to the work of ten fabulous Flash Web designers

Icons Used in This Book

Icons help point out special information. For example, sometimes they tell you that you don't care about this information and can skip over it without fear.

This icon flags new features in Flash CS5. If you have been using Flash CS4 or even an earlier version, you may want to skim through this book and look for this icon to help you quickly get up to speed in the new version.

Look for this icon to find all the goodies on the companion Web site, at www. dummies.com/go/flashCS5fd. We include supporting files for many of our examples so that you can try them out.

This icon alerts you to information that you need to keep in mind to avoid wasting time or falling on your face.

Flash has some advanced features you might want to know about — or skip entirely. This icon lets you know when we throw the heavier stuff at you.

Tips help you finish your work more easily, quickly, or effectively. Don't miss out on these.

Uh-oh! "Watch out here!" is what this icon is telling you. If you skip this icon, you never know what might happen.

Where to Go from Here

If you haven't already installed Flash, check out the complete instructions for installing Flash on this book's companion Web site, www.dummies.com/go/flashCS5fd. Then open Flash, open this book, and plunge in.

Here's some of the other cool stuff that you can find on the *Flash Professional CS5 & Flash Catalyst CS5 For Dummies* companion Web site:

- ✔ A library of geometric, fanciful, and artistic vector graphics ready to be instantly opened in any Flash movie
- ✔ Flash movies that you can dissect

Your own personal library of vector graphics

We created for you more than 50 vector graphics that you can use in your Flash movies. Some are geometric shapes that are hard to create in Flash. We added fun shapes . . . some practical and others whimsical, such as our thought bubble and explosion. Finally, we included some art drawings of everyday objects. We hope you like them! (Please keep in mind that these files are provided for your personal use and are not to be sold or redistributed.)

To download the library of graphics, point your Web browser to www.dummies.com/go/flashCS5fd and click the download link to download the zip file for this book. When you unzip the file, you'll see a file named Flash CS5 For Dummies Library.fla. All that you see when you open this file in Flash is a blank screen. To see the graphics, choose Window⇨Library. To use these shapes in another Flash file, choose File⇨Import to Library and choose the file named Flash CS5 For Dummies Library.fla from the location where you saved it on your computer.

An even better idea is to copy the FLA file from wherever it is on your computer to the Libraries subfolder of your Flash CS5 folder. (In Windows, you find this at `Program Files\Adobe\Adobe Flash CS5\en_US\ Configuration\Libraries` on your hard drive. On a Mac, you find it in `Applications/Adobe Flash CS5/en_US/Configuration/Libraries` on your hard drive.) (The en_US subfolder refers to the language, and may differ for your installation.) Then you can access this file at any time by choosing Window⇨Common Libraries.

Flash movies galore

Throughout this book, we refer you to the companion Web site to look at Flash movies as examples of the features we are explaining. These movies are organized by chapter. They help you understand some of the more complex capabilities of Flash that are hard to explain or show in a figure. Some of these movies are real-world Flash movies that come from active Web sites. Others are examples that we created for you to isolate a Flash feature. Either way, we hope that you can use them to further your understanding of Flash.

To examine and use these movie files, you need to first download them to your hard drive. Point your Web browser to `www.dummies.com/go/ flashCS5fd` and download the zipped file. When you unzip it, you can open the file you want. Here are a few troubleshooting tips to keep in mind when you use the Flash movie files provided on the Web site:

✔ **The Flash movie doesn't play.** Sometimes when you open a Flash movie and try to play the animation, nothing happens. Choose Control⇨Test Movie⇨In Flash Professional to see the animation.

✔ **The fonts look different.** If some of the fonts required by the Flash files aren't available on your system, you might see less-than-satisfactory substitutions when you play the Flash Player files. You might also see a message asking you to substitute fonts. You can click Default or choose any fonts you want.

We would love to hear your comments about this book. You can contact Gurdy Leete at `gleete@mum.edu` or Ellen Finkelstein at `ellen@ellen finkelstein.com`. Please note that we can't provide technical support on Flash. (If you need technical support, check out the resources we list in Chapter 17.)

Enough of all this talk. It's time to move into the real part of this book and start creating cool Flash movies! Enjoy!

Part I
A Blast of Flash

The 5th Wave — By Rich Tennant

"You know, I've asked you a dozen times <u>not</u> to animate the torches on our Web page."

In this part . . .

1 n this part, you discover what Flash can and can't do and start to make your way around the Flash world. In Chapter 1, we introduce you to Flash, show you what it looks like, and explain how to use its toolbars, menus, and panels. You find out about the Stage and the Timeline, two central Flash concepts. Play your way through your first animation to get firsthand experience in the power of Flash.

In Chapter 2, you get an overview of the entire process of creating a Flash animated movie, from developing your concept to publishing your movie in the format a browser can display. We explain how to set properties that affect your movie as a whole and how Flash works with various kinds of graphics. We close with the steps for printing your movie on paper. This part provides the foundation for future success.

Resources · Rainbow

2009-2010 Season

The Box Office is Now Open!

Individual concert tickets are now on sale for the 2009-2010 season. Order online, by phone, or come to the box office.

BUY TICKETS

Getting Acquainted with Flash CS5

In This Chapter

▶ Introducing Flash

▶ Figuring out what you can create with Flash CS5

▶ Knowing when not to use Flash CS5

▶ Starting Flash

▶ Perusing the screen

▶ Using Help

▶ Creating your first animation

▶ Closing Flash

*O*nce upon a time in a galaxy that seems far, far away by now, there was the Internet, which contained only plain, unformatted text. Then came the Web, and we gained text formatting and graphics. Then the Web grew up a little, and Web page graphics got fancier with things such as small animations in banner ads. But people, being used to movies and TV, wanted an even more animated and interactive Web experience. Along came Flash.

Flash is the software that runs some of the coolest Web sites around. When you surf the Web and see sites that contain animation across the entire page or buttons that do spectacular stunts when you click them, you're probably seeing some Flash magic. If you create a Web site, you can use Flash to rev up the basics and actively respond to users' choices so that your viewers will say, "Wow!" Even a lot of video that you see on the Internet, such as at YouTube.com, uses a compressed Flash video format (FLV).

In this chapter, you find out what Flash is all about, what the Flash screen looks like, and how to use Help. Then you create your first, simple animation so that all the rest of this book makes sense.

Rainbow Resources

Want a great new way to create a Flash Web site without using Flash? Yes, it's possible! You can design the site in Adobe Photoshop or Illustrator and then use Adobe Flash Catalyst to create the site. For more information, see Part VI.

Discovering Flash

Flash offers a powerful system for creating animation for the Web. In a nutshell, here's an overview of how you use the system:

1. Create a Flash movie by creating graphics and animating them over the duration of the movie.

   Besides animated graphics, you can add navigational buttons, check boxes, and other user interface elements. You can add a few Flash components to a Web site or create an entire Web site.

2. Use the Publish command in Flash to publish the movie into a Flash Player file that a browser can display.

   At the same time, Flash creates the appropriate HyperText Markup Language (HTML) code that you need for your Web page.

3. Insert HTML code into your HTML document that references the Flash Player file.

   This is similar to adding a graphic to a Web page. Or you can use the HTML code alone as a new Web page for a fully Flashed page.

4. Upload the new or edited HTML document and the Flash Player file to the location where you keep other files for your Web pages.

5. Open your browser, navigate to your Web page, and presto! — there's your cool animation, navigation, or other Flash element on your Web page.

You need Flash Player to see the effects that Flash creates. These days, Flash Player comes installed with most computer systems and browsers, so most people can view Flash-driven Web sites immediately without any special download or preparation. When you display a Web site that contains Flash effects, your system uses Flash Player to play the animation. Users who don't have Flash Player can download it for free from Adobe at `www.adobe.com/go/flashplayer`.

Web sites continue to grow more and more sophisticated. By using animation, special effects, and interactive techniques, you can distinguish your Web site from the also-rans. Creating animation isn't hard, and you don't have to be a professional graphic artist, either. Anyone can create simple animations to enhance a Web site; it just takes a little time.

To find great Web sites that use Flash, check out the Adobe site at www.
adobe.com/cfusion/showcase/index.cfm and look at some examples.
Don't get discouraged by seeing some truly sophisticated results at these
sites. You can start with a simple, animated site and go from there. (Chapter
18 lists ten great Flash designers and where you can find their work.)

Understanding What You Can Create with Flash CS5

You can use Flash CS5 to create simple animation to add to your Web page.
Or you can create an entire Web page or site with Flash and incorporate text,
graphics, interactive buttons, user interface components, and animation.

This book helps you use Flash to create a simple or complex Web site. The
following list describes some ways that you can manipulate text, graphics,
and sound by using Flash CS5:

- **Create still or animated text on your Web page.** You can choose to
  stop the animation after a few seconds or repeat it while your viewers
  view the page.

- **Use Flash tools to create your own graphics for your Web page or to
  import graphics.** You can lay out an entire Web page graphically or add
  graphics to only a part of a Web page, as shown in Figure 1-1.

Thanks to the New York Philharmonic, www.nyphil.org, for permission. Photo by Chris Lee

Figure 1-1: The New York Philharmonic Web site uses Flash to
create an ever-changing display on its home page.

✔ **Animate graphics and make objects appear and disappear by using the transparency feature.** Objects can move, get bigger or smaller, or rotate. Flash also lets you *morph* — that is, transform — shapes into new shapes.

✔ **Fill shapes and text with *gradients*, which are colors that gradually change into new colors.** You can even fill shapes and text with bitmap images that you import into Flash. For example, you could fill the letters of your name with dozens of flowers. (You aren't a flower child any more?)

✔ **Create Web page buttons that not only lead your viewers wherever you want them to go but also change shape or color at the same time.** You can make buttons change when you pass your mouse over them. People who view your page can click a button to display a movie (animation) or start a small application.

✔ **Add sound or video to your movie.** It's easy to add sound effects in Flash. You can control how long the sound or music plays and whether it loops to play continuously. You can play video files as well.

✔ **Create menus that viewers can use to navigate your site.** You can create navigation tools as well as forms, check boxes, and other interface elements that look a lot more stylish than plain HTML ones.

As you can see, you can go far with Flash if you want. And why not? It's great fun!

Determining When Not to Use Flash CS5

If Flash CS5 is so wonderful, why doesn't every Web site designer use it? Why aren't most Web sites created completely with Flash?

Here's the other side of the story.

Although the vector graphics and animation of Flash load quickly, they don't load as quickly as plain text and simple graphics. Adding a movie to your Web page adds to its loading time. There's no point in using Flash if you want simple pages consisting of mostly text and a few graphics that you want to stay put and not move.

You can create certain graphic effects more easily by using bitmap graphics. Painted brush stroke and textured effects are examples. Artists create these types of graphics by using graphics editing software, and the results are bitmaps. Similarly, to add photographs to your Web page, you need to insert electronic image files. Flash creates *vector graphics* (defined mathematically), which are different from *bitmap graphics* (defined by lots of dots). However, you can import bitmap graphics into Flash. Find out more about bitmap and vector graphics in Chapter 2.

If you want simple animation, such as a few blinking dots or a marquee effect, animated *GIFs* (the animated bitmap graphics that you often see on the Web) might be smaller than Flash movies, so they load faster. You can create animated GIFs by using animated GIF editing software.

Some sites don't lend themselves to animation. Animation can distract from your content, and overdoing animation can make a serious site seem silly. Animation is great, but it has its place. Also, although Flash has some features that allow accessibility for people with disabilities, it still isn't as accessible as plain HTML. You need to determine whether animation is right for your Web site.

Getting the Right Start

Well begun is half done, as the saying goes. The easiest way to begin using Flash CS5 is with a shortcut or alias right on your desktop. Double-click the Flash icon, and you're on your way. (See the book's companion Web site for information on installing Flash.)

Starting Flash on a PC

Whether you installed Flash from the DVD or by downloading it from the Adobe Web site onto your PC, you might or might not have a shortcut on your desktop. To create one, choose Start⇨All Programs⇨Adobe Flash Professional CS5. With your desktop visible, press the Ctrl key and drag the Adobe Flash CS5 item onto the desktop.

To rename the shortcut, click the shortcut on your desktop. Then click the text beneath the icon. Type **Flash CS5** (or whatever you want) and press Enter. Just double-click the icon to open Flash.

Starting Flash on a Mac

You might find it handy to add the Flash CS5 icon to your Dock for easy launching. To do this, click the Finder icon on the extreme left of the Dock to bring up a new Finder window. Navigate in the Finder window to the Applications folder, and in the Applications folder, double-click the Adobe Flash Professional CS5 folder to open it. Click and drag the Flash CS5 application icon to the Dock. A copy of the Flash CS5 application icon appears on the Dock.

Creating a new movie

Files that you create by using Flash are commonly called *movies*. When you start Flash, the startup screen appears (by default), as shown in Figure 1-2. In the Create New section, click one of several options to immediately open a new movie file. These options let you create movies for various types of uses, such as mobile devices and further programming. For the purposes of this book, we assume that you want to create a general-use movie using the latest technology, which is the ActionScript 3.0 option. (ActionScript 3.0 is the latest version of Flash's programming language.)

If you already opened a movie and have the menus available, choose File⇨ New. In the New Document dialog box, select ActionScript 3.0 on the General tab and then click OK. You usually start by creating or importing some graphics. (To find out more about working with graphics, see Chapter 3.)

FL

ADOBE® FLASH® PROFESSIONAL CS5

Create from Template

- Advertising
- Animation
- Banners
- Media Playback
- Presentations
- Sample Files

Open a Recent Item

- ligature example.fla
- movie of the year.fla
- Open...

Create New

- ActionScript 3.0
- ActionScript 2.0
- Adobe AIR 2
- iPhone
- Flash Lite 4
- ActionScript File
- Flash JavaScript File
- Flash Project
- ActionScript 3.0 Class
- ActionScript 3.0 Interface

Extend

- Flash Exchange »

Learn

- 1. Introducing Flash »
- 2. Symbols »
- 3. Timelines and Animation »
- 4. Instance Names »
- 5. Simple Interactivity »
- 6. ActionScript »
- 7. Working with Data »
- 8. Building an Application »
- 9. Publishing for Mobile »
- 10. Publishing for AIR »
- 11. Adobe TV »

- Getting Started »
- New Features »
- Developers »
- Designers »
- Don't show again

Adobe® CS Live online services

Learn more about the new Adobe CS Live online services. (FL,en_US,11.0)

Figure 1-2: The Startup screen.

Opening an existing movie

If you want to work on a movie that you already created when you first open Flash, choose the movie from the Open a Recent Item section of the Startup screen, or click Open to find the file. If you already opened a movie and have the menus available, press Ctrl+O (Windows) or ⌘+O (Mac) or choose File➪Open; then double-click the movie to open it. The first frame appears on your screen, and you can edit the movie any way you want.

When you open more than one movie, you see a tab at the top for each movie. You can click the tabs to move from movie to movie. The tabs appear in the order you created or opened the movies.

Taking a Look Around

The Flash screen is different from screens in other programs that you might be used to, so take the time to get to know it. You can also customize the Flash screen. Figure 1-3 shows one possible display.

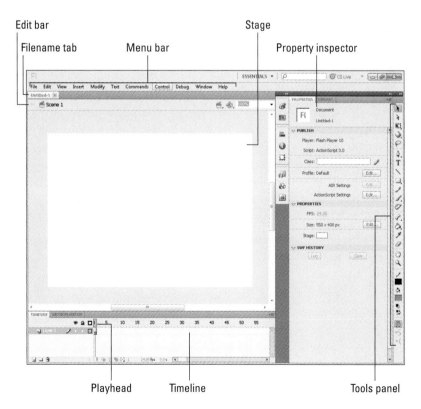

Figure 1-3: The Flash screen.

If your screen opens with several rectangular panels strewn about or docked on various sides, don't worry about them now. We explain how to open and use these panels throughout this book, but you don't need them for this chapter. If they drive you crazy, right-click (Windows) or Control-click (Mac) each panel's title bar and choose Close or Close Group in the menu that appears.

Tooling around the toolbars

Flash contains two toolbars in the Mac version: the Edit bar and the Controller. In Windows, Flash also offers the Main toolbar. To display or hide these toolbars, choose Window➪Toolbars and click the toolbar that you want to display or hide. Here is a description of the toolbars:

- **Main toolbar (Windows only):** Contains commonly used commands, such as Open, Save, and Print. By default, Flash does *not* display the Main toolbar.

- **Controller:** Lets you control the playback of movies. For more information, see Chapter 9.

- **Edit bar:** Helps you work with the symbols, scenes, and the user interface (UI). The bar, shown in Figure 1-3, appears below the menu. It includes a button to access symbols (which we cover in Part III), a button for editing scenes, and a zoom control. We discuss the Timeline later in the chapter, in the "Following a timeline" section. For detailed information about the Timeline and scenes, see Chapter 9.

Using panels

Panels give you access to the many Flash tools and settings. You access the panels from the Window menu. We discuss the specific panels throughout this book. In this section, we explain how to keep control over your panels.

Most panels are *dockable,* which means they can sit at the side or bottom of your Flash window without covering up your work and they fit together in a group with other panels. You can also stack undocked panels on top of each other. You control panels by doing the following:

- **Dock a panel.** Drag it by its title bar to the side or bottom of your screen. When you see a blue bar highlight, release the mouse button.

 ✔ **Undock a panel.** Drag it by its title bar.

 ✔ **Open or close a panel.** Choose it from the Window menu.

 ✔ **Close an undocked panel.** Click its Close button.

 ✔ **Close a docked panel.** Right-click (Windows) or Control-click (Mac) its title bar and choose Close.

 ✔ **Collapse a group of panels to icons.** Click the double right arrow at the top of the group of docked panels.

Color

Swatches

Align

Info

Transform

Actions

Figure 1-4: The icon panels look like toolbar buttons. Use them to open and close panels.

You can also stack panels. Drag a panel (by its title bar) to another panel to stack it below the first one. You can also collapse or expand panels: A *collapsed* panel displays only its title bar, so it doesn't take up much space. Just click its title bar. Repeat the process to expand the panel again.

A set of *icon panels,* shown in Figure 1-4, provides shortcuts to often-used panels. You click the button to both open and close its panel.

The Tools panel contains all the tools you need to draw and edit objects. At the bottom of the Tools panel are options that modify how the tools function. (See Chapters 3 and 4 for a complete description of the Tools panel.)

The Property inspector, shown in Figure 1-5, is another important panel. This panel displays information about selected objects, such as size, name, and location. You can modify objects in the Property inspector as well. It's *context sensitive,* which means that its contents change according to what you're doing. For example, if you select a graphic object, the Property inspector provides settings relating to that object, and you can use the Property inspector to edit that object.

By default, the Property inspector is grouped with the Library (which we explain in Chapter 2).

The Property inspector has several controls for changing its configuration:

- **Tab:** Double-click the tab at the top (which reads `Properties`) to collapse the Property inspector completely (you see just the tab); click the tab to restore it to its full glory.

- **Collapse to Icons button:** Click the small double arrows at the top of the Property inspector to switch between an icon and the open state.

- **Title bar:** Click the gray bar at the top to minimize or maximize the Property inspector. In the default configuration, the top bar also applies to the Library.

Discovering the Flash menus

Most drawing functions are available only from the Tools panel. You often use the Timeline for creating animation, as we discuss in the "Following a timeline" section, later in this chapter. Almost every other function in Flash is on a menu somewhere. You just need to find it. In general, we discuss the specific menu functions where appropriate throughout this book. Table 1-1 offers an overview of the menus.

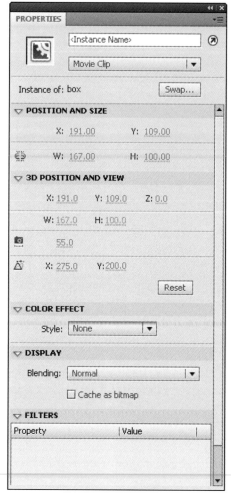

Figure 1-5: The Property inspector.

Table 1-1	Flash Menus
Menu	*Use It To*
Flash	(Mac only) Set preferences, create keyboard shortcuts, and quit Flash.
File	Open and close files, save files, import and export files, print, publish movies for the Web, send a movie via e-mail, and quit Flash.

Menu	Use It To
Edit	Undo and redo commands; cut, copy, and paste to and from the Clipboard; delete, duplicate, select, and deselect objects; find and replace; copy and paste entire frames and motions on the Timeline; edit symbols (see Chapter 7); set preferences (Windows only); customize the Tools panel; map fonts; and create keyboard shortcuts for commands (Windows only).
View	Zoom in and out; show or hide the ruler, grid, and guides; choose a preview mode; and specify snapping preferences for objects for easy placement.
Insert	Insert symbols (see Chapter 7); insert and delete Timeline features, such as frames and keyframes (see Chapter 9); insert layers (see Chapter 6); and add scenes (see Chapter 9).
Modify	Modify symbols, bitmaps, shapes, frames, Timeline features and effects, scenes, or the entire movie (the *document*). Transform, align, group, and ungroup objects; arrange objects; and break objects apart.
Text	Format text , check spelling, and embed fonts.
Commands	Reuse and manage saved commands. A *command* is any action that you take in Flash, such as drawing or editing an object. You can save commands from the History panel. (See Chapter 4.)
Control	Control the playing of movies, test movies and scenes, access certain interactive functions, and mute sounds.
Debug	Debug ActionScript code. (See Chapter 10.)
Window	Open lots of things, including a duplicate window, panels that help you control objects, the Library (see Chapter 2), windows for creating interactive controls (see Chapter 10), workspaces, and the Movie Explorer (to help manage your movie — see Chapter 12).
Help	You can find a wide variety of help resources, including Adobe online forums.

Many menu commands offer keyboard shortcuts. You can also create your own keyboard shortcuts. (See the bonus chapter, available at the book's companion Web site, www.dummies.com/go/flashcs5fd, for instructions.) The shortcuts are displayed on the menus, next to the command name. Here are some of the most commonly used keyboard shortcuts.

- **Ctrl+N (Windows) or ⌘+N (Mac):** Open the New Document dialog box so you can start a new movie.

- **Ctrl+O (Windows) or ⌘+O (Mac):** Open an existing movie.

- **Ctrl+S (Windows) or ⌘+S (Mac):** Save your movie. Use this shortcut often!

- **Ctrl+Q (Windows) or ⌘+Q (Mac):** Exit Flash.

- ✓ **Ctrl+X (Windows) or ⌘+X (Mac):** Cut to the Clipboard. Chapter 4 explains more about using the Clipboard.

- ✓ **Ctrl+C (Windows) or ⌘+C (Mac):** Copy to the Clipboard.

- ✓ **Ctrl+V (Windows) or ⌘+V (Mac):** Paste from the Clipboard. The copy goes at the center of the display.

- ✓ **Ctrl+Shift+V (Windows) or ⌘+Shift+V:** Paste in Place (the same location as the original).

- ✓ **Ctrl+Z (Windows) or ⌘+Z (Mac):** Undo. Would you believe that by default Flash remembers your last 100 actions and can undo them? What a relief! And if you choose Window➪Other Panels➪History, the History panel lists each action so you know what the next Undo will undo. Think of it as a journey into the long-forgotten past. (See Chapter 4 for more on the History panel, and see the Bonus Chapter at the book's companion Web site for details on customizing the number of Undos that Flash remembers.)

- ✓ **Ctrl+Y (Windows) or ⌘+Y (Mac):** Redo. This redoes actions that you undid by using the Undo command. (Got that?) This button remembers just as many actions as the Undo command. If you undo more actions than you want, Redo until you're back where you want to be. Using the Undo and Redo commands is like traveling through Flash time — and it gives you lots of slack while you're working.

We mention other keyboard shortcuts throughout this book when we discuss their corresponding commands.

Although it's not a shortcut, note that you can find the Zoom Control box in the upper-right corner of the Stage — that is, when the Edit bar is open. (Choose Window➪Toolbars➪Edit Bar if necessary.) Click the arrow and choose a zoom factor to zoom in and out. Zooming doesn't change the actual size of objects — it just makes them look bigger or smaller.

You aren't limited to the choices on the Zoom drop-down list. Type a number in the Zoom Control box and press Enter (Windows) or Return (Mac) to set your own zoom factor. For example, type **85** to set the zoom factor to 85%.

Customizing the workspace

For the best in customization, you can save any layout of panels you like. Set up the panels and choose Window➪Workspace➪New Workspace. In the New Workspace dialog box that opens, shown in Figure 1-6, give the layout a name and click OK. To restore that layout at any time, choose Window➪Workspace and choose your very own layout. Choose Window➪Workspace➪Manage Workspaces if you need to rename or delete a workspace.

New Workspace

Name: Default+color

[OK] [Cancel]

Figure 1-6. Make your very own workspace.

You can access the same workspace features on the right side of the Menu bar. It's easy to choose a new workspace by just clicking the Workspace drop-down list.

Staging your movies

The white box in the center of your screen is the *Stage*. Think of the Stage as a movie screen where you place objects. You can place graphics and text there and then animate them. Flash also plays back movies on the Stage.

Around the edge of the Stage is a gray area called the *Pasteboard*. You can use the Pasteboard to store graphics that you plan to use soon but don't want on the Stage just yet. (For more permanent storage, use the Library, as we explain in Chapter 2.) You can also store data and other nongraphical content on the Pasteboard. Content that you put on the Pasteboard doesn't appear in your Flash movie.

Following a timeline

The Timeline window divides your movie into *frames*. Each frame represents a tiny stretch of time, such as $\frac{1}{24}$ of a second. Creating a movie is simply a matter of assembling frames, which are then quickly played in order.

Chapter 9 explains in detail how to make using the Timeline completely pain-less. For now, you should just understand the essentials. See Figure 1-7 for the basic Timeline.

Figure 1-7: The Timeline is your key to managing animation.

On the left side of the Timeline is the layer list. When you open a new movie, you see only one layer, unimaginatively named Layer 1. A *layer* is like a sheet of transparent acetate on which you draw objects. Layers help you keep objects from running into each other, causing unfortunate, messy results. You organize your entire movie by using layers. For example, if you want to keep some text constant throughout the movie but animate a bouncing dot, you would give the dot its own layer and animate it on that layer. The layer list has room for more layers, and you can add as many layers as you want. (Chapter 6 gives you the lowdown on layers.)

You can drag the upper edge of the Timeline to make room for more layers. Hover the mouse cursor over the top of the Timeline's gray title bar until you see the two-headed arrow and then drag upward.

To the right of Layer 1, you see a bunch of rectangles, each representing a frame. (Actually, before you start using the Timeline, they're just potential frames, like unexposed frames on a roll of film.) By default, each frame lasts $\frac{1}{24}$ of a second. Each layer has its own row of frames because you can have different animations or objects on each layer.

A *keyframe* is a frame that defines some change in your animation. In some animations, every frame is a keyframe. Other animations need keyframes for only the first and last frames.

The *playhead* indicates the current frame in the animation and consists of a red rectangle as well as a vertical hairline that crosses a frame on all layers. Before you create any animation, the playhead is always on Frame 1,

You don't use the Timeline until you're ready to animate. While you work, however, you should organize your objects on separate layers. Don't worry — you can always move an object from one layer to another.

Next to the Timeline tab is the Motion Editor tab. We discuss the Motion Editor in Chapter 9. For now, it's good to know that the Motion Editor gives you detailed control over your animations.

Getting Help in a Flash

This book is all that you need to start creating great animations, but we would be remiss if we didn't tell you about the Flash Help system. To use Flash Help, choose Help⇨Flash Help.

Help's multiple manuals

Flash Help contains three sections:

- **Using Flash CS5 Professional** is the main Help manual.

- **ActionScript 3.0 Language and Components Reference** is a manual on the latest version of ActionScript, Flash's programming language. (See Chapter 10 to find out more.)

> You don't need to program Flash to use it, if you are interested only in graphics and animation.

> ✔ **Additional Resources (adobe.com)** brings you to the Adobe.com Search Community Help page, where you can search through discussion groups and other support resources.

To search for a term, click the Search button. Then type the term and click Search. You can then choose from the list of topics.

Finding more help on the Web

Adobe offers support on its Web site. Choose Help➪Flash Support Center. There, you can search the knowledge base and tutorials for answers to your questions.

Try It — You'll Like It

Perhaps by now you're getting impatient to try out Flash. Getting started is easy. You collect a few ideas, put together some art, add animation, save your movie, and publish it. Then you view it in a browser either online or offline. That's the gratifying part. In the following sections, you get to try out Flash by working through a basic animation. The rest of the book explains these concepts in more detail.

Conceiving your first animation

Suppose that you want to add an animated logo to a home page that you already set up. You want the animation to run when the page loads and then stop. Figure 1-8 shows the Rainbow Resources company logo — unanimated, of course — that you can find on this book's Web site, at www.dummies.com/go/flashcs5fd.

Figure 1-8: A company logo that could stand some animation.

Suppose that you want the word *Rainbow* to fly into your page from the right and the word *Resources* to fly in from the left. At the same time, you want the graphic to rotate 180 degrees. The following section shows you how to create this animation.

Creating flashy drawings

You can use Flash to create a company logo, but importing one from this book's Web site is simpler. Often, you import existing graphics (such as a company logo) from a file rather than create them from scratch. (Chapter 3 explains how to import and manipulate graphics.)

If you're going through the steps and make a mistake, choose Edit⟹Undo (or press Ctrl+Z or ⌘+Z) and try again. You can use Undo repeatedly to undo several steps, if necessary.

To import the Rainbow Resources logo into Flash, follow these steps. (The steps might vary if you're importing some other graphic in a different format.)

1. **Start Flash.**

   See the instructions in the section "Starting Flash on a PC" or "Starting Flash on a Mac," earlier in this chapter, if you need help.

2. **In the Create New section of the Startup screen, choose ActionScript 3.0.**

   You see a spanking-new movie on your screen.

3. **Go to www.dummies.com/go/flashcs5fd and download the Bonus Content, which contains the rainbow.gif image file.**

   You'll need to unzip the file and extract the image file. Extract this image file to the location where you plan to save your Flash movie.

4. **Choose File⟹Import⟹Import to Stage.**

   The Import dialog box opens.

5. **Browse the dialog box until you find rainbow.gif in the location where you saved it, and then double-click the file to open it.**

   You see the logo onscreen. You need to break the logo into pieces and make it a vector graphic so that you can animate sections of it separately.

6. **Choose Modify⟹Bitmap⟹Trace Bitmap.**

   The Trace Bitmap dialog box appears.

7. **In the Trace Bitmap dialog box, set the color threshold to 100, the minimum area to 1, the corner threshold to Many Corners, and the curve fit to Pixels. Click OK.**

   In our example, we chose to use settings that reproduce the bitmap as faithfully as possible. Flash creates a vector graphic and breaks the graphic into individual components. The entire graphic, however, is selected.

8. **Click anywhere outside the graphic to deselect it.**

You have your logo! Now you need to set it up for animation.

Turning your objects into symbols

In the logo that you imported in the preceding section, each letter is a separate object, which can get pretty confusing. Each line in the logo's design is also separate, but you want your words — and the little design — to stay together. So, you must combine each word and the logo into a symbol. A *symbol* helps keep objects together and is required for some kinds of animation. (See Chapter 7 for the scoop on symbols.)

To turn the words and the logo into symbols, follow these steps:

1. **To get a better view of your image, click the Zoom Control drop-down list (upper-right corner of the Stage area) and choose 200%.**

   If you don't see the Zoom Control drop-down list, choose Window⇨ Toolbars⇨Edit Bar to display it.

   Use the scroll bar to scroll the words of the logo into view, if necessary.

2. **Click the Selection tool on the Tools panel if it's not already selected.**

3. **Click the upper-right corner of the word *Rainbow* (just above and to the right of the *w*) and drag to the lower-left corner of the first letter, *R*.**

   Dragging from right to left makes it easier to avoid selecting the logo at the same time. The entire word should be selected. If it isn't, click outside the word and try again. Your screen should look like Figure 1-9.

   Figure 1-9: Selecting text to prepare it for animation.

4. **Choose Modify⇨Convert to Symbol.**

5. **In the Convert to Symbol dialog box, choose Graphic from the Type drop-down list, enter** Rainbow **in the Name text box, and then click OK.**

   When you click OK, Flash places a box around the word so you can see that it's one object.

6. **Repeat the procedure outlined in Steps 3–5 with the word *Resources*.**

   In this case, you might want to start clicking and dragging from the upper-left area of the word; then choose Modify⇨Convert to Symbol again, enter **Resources** in the Name text box, and click OK. Now all the letters of the word *Resources* are a single object.

7. **Click above and to the left of the logo and drag to the lower right to select the entire logo.**

8. **Hold down the Shift key and click each word to remove both words from the selection.**

   The design portion of the logo is selected.

9. **Choose Modify⇨Convert to Symbol.**

   The Convert to Symbol dialog box opens.

10. **Enter** Lines **in the Name text box, and then click OK in the Convert to Symbol dialog box.**

    Flash creates a symbol from the lines of the logo's design.

See Chapter 7 to find out more about what symbols are and how to use them. Symbols are important building blocks in Flash movies.

Putting your graphics on layers

You need to place different pieces on different layers when you're animating. You use layers to organize your movie and keep shapes separate so that they don't interfere with each other. (See Chapter 6 for the complete story on layers.)

To split your three symbols onto three separate layers, you can use a convenient feature of Flash CS5: Distribute to Layers. Follow these steps:

1. **Click the Selection tool on the Tools panel if it's not already selected.**

2. **Drag diagonally across the entire logo, including the two words, to select it.**

   You should see two rectangles inside one bigger rectangle. All three objects in the logo are selected.

3. **Choose Modify⇨Timeline⇨ Distribute to Layers.**

   You now have three new layers, named Rainbow, Resources, and Lines. The three objects of the logo have been distributed to the three new layers and removed from Layer 1. Your layer list should look like Figure 1-10.

4. **Click the Zoom Control drop-down list (at the upper-right corner of the Stage area) and choose 100%.**

5. **Click outside the Stage to dese-lect any objects.**

   Figure 1-10: In addition to the original Layer 1, you now have three new layers.

6. **To save the file, choose File⇨Save and choose the same location you used for the rainbow. gif image file.**

   We don't recommend saving the file in the Flash CS5 program folder because it might get lost among your Flash program files.

7. **Give your movie a name, such as *movie of the year*, and click Save.**

   Flash creates a file named movie of the year.fla. Flash adds .fla for you because that's the filename extension for Flash movies.

You're now ready for the animation process.

Making graphics move

We explain earlier in this chapter that your goal is to have the word *Rainbow* fly in from the right and the word *Resources* fly in from the left. You also want the graphic to rotate 180 degrees at the same time. What you see now is how the animation should end — the last frame of the movie.

Now go back and create the beginning of your movie. Flash can fill in all the blanks in between. This type of animation is called a *motion tween*. Follow these steps to create the animation:

1. **Right-click (Windows) or Control-click (Mac) the word *Rainbow* and choose Create Motion Tween.**

   Oops! The other two symbols disappear! That's okay. Flash created the motion tween and automatically set the length of the animation to 24 frames, or one second (using the default setting of 24 frames to a second). The playhead is now on Frame 24, but the other two symbols don't exist at the 24th frame yet. Note that the Rainbow row in the Timeline turns blue to indicate that it has a motion tween.

2. **Click Frame 1 on the Timeline.**

   You can click Frame 1 on any layer. Whew! The other two symbols reappear.

3. **Repeat Steps 1 and 2 for the word *Resources* and for the lines.**

   Your Timeline should now look like Figure 1-11. Be sure to click Frame 1 to place the playhead on that frame.

Figure 1-11: The Timeline indicates three motion tweens, each lasting 24 frames.

4. **To move the Rainbow symbol to its proper location for Frame 1, click the Rainbow symbol, then press and hold down the Shift key while you drag the word *Rainbow* to the right, just off the Stage into the gray area.**

You might need to use the horizontal scroll bar or choose a lower zoom percentage in the Zoom Control drop-down list to see the gray area. Pressing Shift keeps the object from moving up or down while you drag to the right. By clicking the first frame and moving the word, you set its position at the beginning of the animation.

5. **To move the Rainbow symbol to its proper location for Frame 24 (the end of the motion tween animation), click Frame 24 in the Rainbow layer. Then press the Shift key and drag the Rainbow symbol back to its original position.**

   You now see a dot in Frame 24 on the Rainbow layer. On the Stage, you see a magenta line indicating the movement of the Rainbow symbol. The motion tween is now complete.

6. **Click Frame 1 on the Resources layer.**

   The playhead is now on Frame 1, and the Resources symbol has a blue selection border.

7. **Press the Shift key and drag the Resources symbol to the left, just off the Stage.**

8. **Click in Frame 24 on the Resources layer, press Shift, and then drag the Resources symbol back to its original location.**

   You now see a dot in Frame 24 on the Resources layer and a horizontal line on the Stage showing the motion of the Resources symbol. The motion tween is now complete.

9. **To return to Frame 1 and select the Lines symbol, click in Frame 1 of the Lines layer.**

10. **Choose Modify⇨Transform⇨Rotate 90° CW to rotate the design 90 degrees clockwise.**

11. **Repeat the Modify⇨Transform⇨Rotate 90° CW command to rotate the design a total of 180 degrees.**

    This sets up the desired position of the Lines symbol at Frame 1.

12. **Click Frame 24 of the Lines layer.**

13. **Again, choose Modify⇨Transform⇨Rotate 90° CW twice to rotate the Lines symbol a total of 180 degrees.**

    Because you only rotated the Lines symbol — you didn't move it — you don't see a line on the Stage.

14. **If necessary, drag the horizontal scroll box until the Stage is in the center of your screen.**

    Otherwise, you won't be able to see the entire animation — and you don't want to miss this one!

15. **Click the first frame of any layer.**

    This takes you to the start of your movie. Your screen should look like the one shown in Figure 1-12.

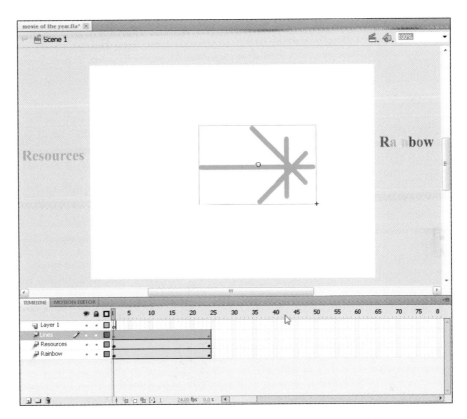

Figure 1-12: Before you run the animation, *Rainbow* appears to the right and *Resources* to the left, and the Lines symbol is rotated.

16. **Press Enter (Return) and watch the animation. (Start writing your Academy Award acceptance speech.)**

17. **Save your movie again by choosing File➪Save.**

Publishing your first animation for posterity

You can't watch the animation in a Web browser until you publish your movie and insert it into an HTML document. To do so, follow these steps:

1. **Click an empty area of the Stage to change the display of the Property inspector.**

    If the Property inspector isn't open, choose Window➪Properties. You may need to click the Property inspector's label to expand it or bring it to the forefront. You should see the Edit button in the Publish section.

2. **In the Property inspector, click the Edit button next to the Profile: Default label.**

   The Publish Settings dialog box opens. (We cover publish settings in detail in Chapter 13.)

3. **Click the HTML tab.**

4. **Deselect the Loop check box in the Playback section.**

   We want the animation to play only once.

5. **Click the Publish button, and then click OK to close the dialog box.**

   With scarcely a blip, Flash publishes your movie and creates two files, named `Movie of the Year.swf` (assuming you used that name) and `Movie of the Year.html`. They're in the same folder as your `.fla` movie file. `Movie of the Year.swf` is the file that your browser reads to play the animation. `Movie of the Year.html` contains the HTML code required to display your movie on a Web page.

6. **Open your Web browser.**

7. **Choose File⇨Open (or Open File) and find `Movie of the Year. html` (or whatever you named your movie file).**

   You might need to click Browse and navigate to the file.

8. **Double-click the file.**

   Your browser opens the HTML document and reads its instructions to play the Flash movie.

9. **Sit back and watch it roll.**

   Don't blink, or you'll miss it. (If you do miss it, click the Refresh or Reload Current Page button in your browser.) You can see the movie in Figure 1-13.

10. **When you finish watching the movie, close your browser.**

You can find the Movie of the Year files (`.fla`, `.html`, and `.swf`) on this book's Web site, `www.dummies.com/go/flashcs5fd`.

Exiting Flash

When you finish creating something in Flash, choose File⇨Exit (Windows) or Flash⇨Quit (Mac). If you see a message asking whether you want to save changes to the movie, click Yes if that's what you want to do.

Figure 1-13: The Movie of the Year animation in detail.

Your Basic Flash

*T*his chapter starts with an overview of the process of creating animation in Flash. We then discuss some tools and features that are fundamental to using Flash efficiently.

As you find out in this chapter, you can set the screen size and color, frame rate, and measurement units for the Flash movie as a whole. We also discuss the Library and how it's a storehouse for images, symbols, video, and sound. Templates enable you to create great movies without much work. Finally, near the end of this chapter, we explain how you can print a Flash movie.

Looking at the Big Picture

When you use Flash to create animation, you generally go through several steps of construction. The steps might vary in their order, depending on your situation. After you know the basics, you can start getting creative and make your Web site rock. Here's a typical path to add animation to an existing Web page:

1. **Think about it.** Noodle around, maybe make some doodles on a napkin, collect a few ideas, and choose one or all of them.

2. **Set up your movie.** Flash lets you choose the size and color of the Stage, the speed of animation (number of frames per second), and other general parameters that affect the entire Flash movie. See the next section of this chapter for details.

3. **Add some graphics.** You have to decide whether you want to create graphics in Flash, create them in another graphics software package, or import existing graphics. Your choice partly depends on how artistic you are, whether you have other software available to you, and whether you can find the right graphics elsewhere. You can also use a combination of sources, which is a common practice.

4. **Lay out your graphics the way you want your animation to start.** Here's where you might want to scale, rotate, or otherwise fiddle with your graphics. (Chapter 4 has more on transforming your graphics.)

5. **Add some text.** Using Flash is a great way to get terrific text onto your Web site. Add text (also called *type*); then reshape it, make it semi-transparent (if you don't want to be too obvious), add other effects, and move it where you want it. (Check out Chapter 5 for typography tips.)

6. **Organize your text and graphics by using layers.** Layers help you keep track of what each graphic and text object does while you organize everything into a powerful, coherent statement. Layers keep your animations from going bump in the night and getting entangled. After you have some objects, create as many layers as you need and transfer your existing graphics and text to those layers. Or create the layers first and then add your graphics and text on those layers. (See Chapter 6 for further details on layers.)

7. **Turn a graphic into a symbol and multiply it all over the Stage.** Converting objects into symbols is a way to keep them from merging with other objects. You also use symbols to keep the file size down, to enable animation, and for interactivity. (Turn to Chapter 7 for more info on symbols.)

8. **Design some buttons.** You know those buttons you click on Web sites all the time? The coolest ones are made in Flash. You can even create animated buttons. (Chapter 8 has more on buttons.)

9. **Animate!** You can create your animation frame by frame or let Flash fill in the animation between your first and last frames, which is called *tweening.* Flash can tween motion, shapes, colors, and transparency, which means that you can create some real magic. (See Chapter 9 for more on animation and the section in Chapter 1 where we step you through your first animation.)

10. **Get interactive.** You want to start a relationship with your viewers, so you can create buttons, frames, and symbols that respond to your viewers' actions. This is probably the most complex functionality of Flash, but we make most of it seem easy. (Turn to Chapter 10 for additional info on interactivity.)

11. **Make it louder! Make it move!** Who wants a quiet Web site? Add sound to your movies or your buttons. You can also add video. (Check out Chapter 11 for more on sound and video.)

12. **Publish your magnum opus.** Flash makes getting your movie to your Web site easy by creating both the Flash Player (.swf) file and the HyperText Markup Language (HTML) code for your Web page. Flash has other options, too, so you can publish to other formats if you want. (Chapter 12 explains how to put all the elements together, and Chapter 13 shows you how to publish your animation for the Web.)

Congratulations! You've completed your first Flash Web animation — in fantasy, at least. The following sections cover some details about how to get started.

Setting the Stage

Before you create graphics and animate them — all that fun stuff — you need to make some decisions about the structure of your entire movie. You should make these decisions before you start because changing midway can create problems.

The first step is to decide on the size and color of your Stage and other fundamental settings. Make sure that the Property inspector is open. (Choose Window⇨Properties.) When the Stage is active (just click the Stage), the Property inspector looks like Figure 2-1.

Choosing the Stage color

You can set the color of the Stage to create a colored background for your entire movie. As with other settings, you need to consider the context of the Web page that will contain the Flash movie. For example, you might want to match the color of your Web page's background. If your Flash movie will constitute the entire Web page, set the Stage color to the color you want for the Web page background.

Figure 2-1: You can change movie properties in the Property inspector.

To set the Stage color, click the Stage swatch in the Property inspector. Flash opens the Color palette. Click the color you want.

Specifying the frame rate

Next to the FPS (frames per second) label, click the current value, specify how many frames you want the Flash movie to play each second, and then press Enter (Windows) or Return (Mac). A faster rate allows for smoother animation but might present a performance problem on slower computers. Chapter 9 explains more about this setting. The Flash default is 24 fps, which is a good starting point. Beware that changing the frame rate midstream in the creation process changes the rate of all the animation in your movie, which might not give you the results you want.

Setting the Stage size

The Size label displays the current size of the Stage. By default, Flash uses a Stage size of 550 pixels (px) wide x 400 px high. To determine the proper setting, you need to know how your Flash movie will fit into your Web page or site. The default fits on almost everyone's browser screen. However, you might want to fit your movie into a small corner of a Web page — for example, into an animated logo in a top corner of a page. In that case, make the Stage smaller.

To change the Stage size, click the Edit button in the Properties section to open the Document Settings dialog box, as shown in Figure 2-2. Type the dimensions that you want in the Width and Height text boxes.

Figure 2-2: The Document Settings dialog box sets the movie's overall parameters.

Flash offers three shortcuts for setting the Stage size in the Document Settings dialog box:

- ✔ **Match Default:** This option is the default and sets the size of the Stage to 550 px x 400 px.

- ✔ **Match Contents:** Select this option to set the Stage size to the contents of the Stage. Of course, for this to work, you need some objects on the Stage. Flash creates a Stage size by placing equal space around all sides of the entire contents of the Stage. If you want to create the smallest possible Stage, place your objects in the upper-left corner and then select Match Contents.

> ✔ **Match Printer:** Select this option to set the Stage size according to the paper size set in the Page Setup dialog box. (Choose File➪Page Setup.) On a Mac, the Print Margins dialog box (access by choosing File➪Print Margins) also affects the paper size. Flash sets the size of the Stage to the maximum possible area of the paper minus the margins. Later in this chapter, in the section "Printing Your Movie," we cover this dialog box in more detail.

To change the units used for measuring the screen and objects, choose a unit from the Ruler Units drop-down list.

Click the Make Default button to make your settings the default for all your new Flash movies. When you finish setting document properties, click OK to close the dialog box.

Adding Metadata

You can add metadata to your movies. *Metadata* — information embedded in the movie — provides a way to include useful tags for your collaborators.

Flash uses the Adobe eXtensible Metadata Platform (XMP), which enables you to embed the metadata into the file. Programmers can write software that accesses the data to help keep track of workflow, manage rights, and more.

To add metadata, choose File➪File Info. The dialog box that opens has the name of your movie in its title bar. You can use the various tabs to insert tags and descriptions relating to your movie file. For example, on the Description tab, you can include title, author, and description content. You can even click the stars to give your movie a rating from one to five stars. You can choose whether you want to include your metadata when you publish your movie. For more information, see the section on publishing to SWF in Chapter 13.

Grabbing a Graphic

The next step when creating animation for your Web site is usually to create or import graphics. Before you do that, however, you should know a little about the different kinds of graphics you can use in a Flash movie.

Understanding vectors and bitmaps

If you know enough about graphics to understand the difference between bitmap and vector graphics, feel free to skip this section. (We hope you always feel free.)

Bitmaps are created with lots of dots. Put them all together, and you get a picture. Onscreen, they're displayed as pixels. As you can imagine, it can take a large file to store the information about all the dots in a bitmap. Another problem with bitmaps is that they don't scale up well. If you try to enlarge a bitmap, it starts to look grainy because you see all those dots (as in the right example shown in Figure 2-3).

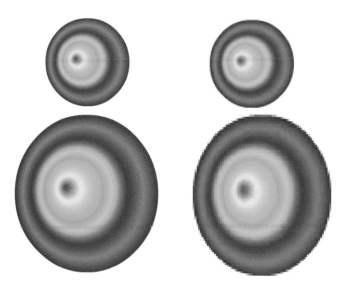

Figure 2-3: Vector graphics remain sharp and clear (left); bitmaps lose focus when enlarged (right).

Vector graphics are defined with equations that specify lines, shapes, and locations. Blank space doesn't have to be recorded, and the equations are particularly efficient at storing information. As a result, file sizes are usually smaller than bitmap file sizes.

Vector graphics are infinitely scalable, either up or down. No matter how big you make your graphic, it always looks perfect, as shown in the left example in Figure 2-3. In fact, your graphic might even look better when it's larger because the curves are smoother.

Flash creates vector-based graphics. The small size of the files means that Flash Player files load and play super-fast on a Web page. As you undoubtedly know, fast file loading means that your Web page viewers don't have to wait a long time to see your effects. That's the advantage of Flash. Nevertheless, you can create great graphics with bitmaps that you can't duplicate with vector graphics; we explain how to import bitmaps in Chapter 3.

Finding graphics

Okay, so you noodled and doodled and played around with some ideas for your Flash animation and perhaps jotted down a few notes or maybe even made a few sketches. You're ready to start building your Flash animation. A logical place to start is to collect some of the graphics that will serve as building blocks in this process.

Where do you get them? You have several choices:

- Create your graphics from scratch (if you feel artistic) by using the Flash drawing tools that we describe in detail in Chapter 3.
- Create graphics in another graphics software package, such as Adobe Fireworks, Photoshop, or Illustrator.
- Import graphics from archives of art available on this book's Web site, from other places on the Web, or from digital (or scanned) photographs — perhaps your own.
- Combine any or all of these approaches.

You can also import video files. If you want to add video to your Flash movies, see Chapter 11 for detailed instructions.

Going to the Library

Every graphic that you create in Flash is precious and deserves to be archived in style. Each movie file that you create has a Library. The Library saves the following types of objects so that they never get lost:

- Graphic, movie clip, and button symbols
- Sounds
- Imported bitmap graphics (but not vector graphics that you create in Flash)
- Imported video files

You'll find yourself going to the Library often. Figure 2-4 shows a Library containing symbols, video, a sound, and a bitmap.

To go to the Library of the current movie file, choose Window➪Library. You can also press Ctrl+L (Windows) or ⌘+L (Mac). When you open the Library, Flash creates a new window or adds the Library panel to the set of panels that are already open, usually next to the Property inspector.

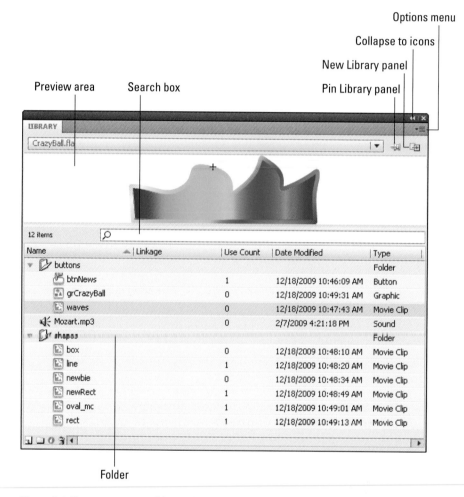

Options menu

Collapse to icons

New Library panel

Pin Library panel

Preview area   Search box

Figure 2-4: You can store graphics, animation, buttons, sounds, and video files in your current movie file's Library.

Folder

To use any object in the Library, follow these steps:

1. **Select the layer on which you want to put the object or create a new layer for the object.**

2. **Click the point on the Timeline where you want the object to start or appear.**

The point that you click on the Timeline must be a keyframe. Chapter 9 explains keyframes in detail.

   3. Click and drag the object from its listing in the Library to the Stage.

   You can also drag an object's image from the preview box.

You can drag items to the Pasteboard, the gray area around the edge of the Stage, until you're ready to use them.

Using folders

A Flash movie can contain dozens or even hundreds of symbols, so you need to keep them organized. Flash provides several features to keep you from tearing out your hair.

If you have more than a few symbols, you should organize them into folders. To create a new folder, follow these steps:

   1. Click the New Folder button at the bottom of the Library panel.

   Flash creates a new folder.

   2. Type a name that describes the type of symbols that you want to put into the folder.

   For example, you could create a folder named Intro and another one named Conclusion.

   3. Press Enter (Windows) or Return (Mac).

To put symbols into a folder, drag them to the folder. You can also move symbols from one folder to another — just drag them. Note that folders exist just to help keep you organized. You can move symbols from one folder to another without affecting your movie.

To keep your symbol list from getting unwieldy, you can collapse folders. A collapsed folder doesn't display its contents. As soon as you need to see what's inside, you can expand the folder. Double-click a folder to either collapse or expand it.

To quickly see the structure of your folders, click the Library's Options menu. Choose Collapse All Folders. You can also choose Expand All Folders to see everything in the Library.

More Library housekeeping

By default, Flash alphabetizes items in the Library by name. However, you might have different ideas. You can sort from A–Z (ascending) or from Z–A (descending). You can also sort by any of the columns in the Library. To change the direction of sorting (for any column in the Library), click the heading of the column that you want to sort by. You can click the column heading again to reverse the sort order.

You can reorder the columns in the Library. Just drag a column's name left or right to the desired location. You can resize any column by dragging the column heading's divider to the left or right.

If the Library panel is docked, you can resize it by dragging its left border. If the Library panel isn't docked, you can drag the right border to resize the panel.

To rename any Library item, double-click the item's name, type the new name, and press Enter or Return. Don't worry — the original filenames of imported files remain unchanged at their original locations.

To duplicate an item, select the item. Then right-click (Windows) or Control-click (Mac) and choose Duplicate. To delete an item, select the item and click the Trash can (Delete) icon.

If you want to find out which items in the Library you aren't using, look in the third column (Use Count) for items with a zero-use count. After you know which items you aren't using, you can delete them.

You can update imported bitmaps and sounds if the original files have changed. Select the file and choose Update in the Options menu of the Library panel.

Using the Libraries of other movies

After you place objects in a file's Library, you can use those objects in any other Flash movie that you create. Just open the movie and display its Library panel, and its Library's contents are available for you to use in your current movie.

Choose File➪Import➪Open External Library to open the Library of another Flash movie that isn't open. A new Library panel opens for the other Flash movie.

You can switch among the Libraries of open movies by using the drop-down list at the top of the Library panel.

When you have libraries open from more than one Flash file, you can copy symbols or anything else in a Library from one movie to another by simply dragging them from one Library to another. Choose the Library that you want to use, select an item, and drag it into the other Library. Easy!

To create a new symbol that goes directly into the Library (rather than on the Stage), choose New Symbol from the Library Options menu in the upper-right corner. (Refer to Figure 2-4.) The Create New Symbol dialog box opens where you can name your symbol. Click OK, and you're transported to symbol-editing mode, where you can create your symbol as you normally would. To return to your main movie, choose Edit➪Edit Document. For more information on creating and editing symbols, see Chapter 7.

Exploring the Flash stock Library

Flash comes with Libraries that contain an excellent assortment of button symbols and sounds. They are worth looking through. Choose Window⇨Common Libraries and choose Buttons or Sounds. (We cover using sounds in Chapter 11.)

Using a Template

To help you create Flash movies more easily, Flash CS5 comes with templates for common types of movies. Instructions are included on the templates. To create a Flash movie from a template, choose File⇨New and click the Templates tab. In the New from Template dialog box (see Figure 2-5), select a category, select one of the templates, and then click OK.

Figure 2-5: Use the New from Template dialog box to create a Flash movie from a template.

For example, the advertising category offers movie sizes suitable for Web-based ads. Here are a few of your options:

- **120 x 240 Vertical:** This is a tower ad, 120 pixels wide x 240 pixels tall.

- **120 x 60 Button2:** This is a small, vertical rectangular ad.

- **120 x 600 Skyscraper:** This is another tower ad.

- **120 x 90 Button1:** This is another vertical rectangular ad.

- **125 x 125 Square Button:** This is a small square ad.

- **160 x 600 Wide Skyscraper:** This is another tower ad but wider than the previous ones.

When you open a new movie from a template, you should save it as a movie. This way, the template is unchanged, and you are free to make any changes you want.

You can also save movies as templates. If you create a movie that you want to reuse in many variations, choose File⇨Save as Template to open the Save as Template dialog box, as shown in Figure 2-6. (You can ignore the warning that SWF history data will be cleared, and go ahead and click the Save as Template option.)

Figure 2-6: The Save as Template dialog box saves your movies as templates.

Type a name, choose a category, and enter a description for your template. Then click Save. From now on, you can open your template like any of the templates that come with Flash, just as we describe. Using templates can save you lots of work!

To create your own category for templates, type a category name in the Category list box instead of choosing one of the existing categories from the list.

Printing Your Movie

Usually, you don't print your movies — you publish them on the Web — but you might want to collaborate on a movie with others who don't have Flash. (How unenlightened of them!) Or you might just want to analyze a movie on paper, tack your animation frames on the wall, and rearrange their sequence. In this type of situation, you can print frame by frame.

To print a movie, follow these steps:

1. **To set page margins, choose File⇨Page Setup (Windows) or File⇨ Print Margins (Mac).**

   The Page Setup (Windows) or Print Margins (Mac) dialog box appears. See Figure 2-7.

2. **In the Margins section, set the margins.**

   You can probably keep the default margin settings.

3. **Select the Center check boxes to center the printing horizontally and vertically on the page.**

4. **(Windows only) In the Paper section, select the size of the paper; define the paper source.**

   Usually, you can leave this section as is because it's based on your printer's default settings.

5. **In the Layout section, click the Frames drop-down list and decide whether to print only the first frame or all frames.**

6. **In the Layout section, click the Layout drop-down list to choose from the following options:**

Page Setup

Margins (inches)

Left: 0.25   Right: 0.25

Top: 0.25   Bottom: 0.25

Center: ☑ Horizontal ☑ Vertical

Paper

Size: Letter

Source: Paper Feed Switch

Orientation

◉ Portrait

○ Landscape

Layout

Frames: First Frame Only   Scale: 100 %

Layout: Actual Size

OK   Cancel

Figure 2-7: Use the Page Setup dialog box to specify how to print your Flash movie.

- *Actual Size:* Lets you choose a scale. This option prints one frame to a page.

- *Fit on One Page:* Fits one frame on a page, scaling it to fit the paper.

- *Storyboard–Boxes:* Places several thumbnail sketches of your movie on a page. You can specify how many frames that you want in a row in the Frames Across text box. You might need to experiment to get the right result. In the Frame Margin text box, enter the space in pixels between the boxes. The Storyboard–Boxes option places each frame in a box.

- *Storyboard–Grid:* Creates a grid of lines for your storyboard rather than individual boxes around the frames. This option is just a matter of aesthetics — don't get too hung up over these choices.

- *Storyboard–Blank:* Leaves out the boxes or grid and just prints all your frames in the storyboard. You have the same Frames Across and Frame Margin settings as for the other storyboard options.

7. **(Windows only) If you chose a Storyboard option, select the Label Frames check box to give each frame a number.**

8. **(Mac only) When you finish setting your options, click OK; then choose File➪Page Setup.**

   In Windows, you skip this step because you already opened the Page Setup dialog box in Step 1.

9. **In the Orientation section, select Portrait (taller rather than wider) or Landscape (wider rather than taller).**

10. **(Mac only) In the Format section, choose your printer in the drop-down list.**

11. **(Mac only) In the Paper Size section, select the size of the paper.**

12. **When you finish setting your options, click OK.**

13. **To print, choose File⇨Print.**

    Alternatively, you can press Ctrl+P (Windows) or ⌘+P (Mac). In Windows, you choose the printer in the Name drop-down list in the Print dialog box.

Figure 2-8 shows an example of the storyboard with the box option. The storyboard shows four frames across with a portrait orientation and includes frame labels. You can find out more about the Flash Player's special printing capabilities in Chapter 13.

Figure 2-8: You can print a storyboard of your movie that displays a thumbnail sketch of each frame.

Part II
1,000 Pictures and 1,000 Words

The 5th Wave By Rich Tennant

"I'm not sure— I like the mutual funds with rotating dollar signs, although the dancing stocks and bonds look good too."

In this part . . .

Graphics are the basis of animation. Before you can make anything move, you need to create the graphics that form the building blocks of your animation. Chapter 3 describes all the types of graphics that you can use, from basic shapes created in Flash to sophisticated imported bitmap graphics. The Flash tools are quite capable, and you can create exciting effects with gradient fills, softened edges, the spray brush, the Deco tool, and transparency. The Flash editing features, as we describe in Chapter 4, offer more opportunities to create great-looking graphics — including skewing objects, using the Distort and Envelope options, and manipulating fills every which way.

In Chapter 5, you find ways to say great things with flexible text options and formatting. You can even break up text and animate it, letter by letter. To keep all the pieces of your animation from going completely out of control, in Chapter 6 you see how to use layers to organize your movie animation. You can use special layers to guide drawing tasks and hide objects behind a mask. (Peekaboo!)

Why do you improve your skills?

- Do you always try to improve?
- Did you receive some negative feedback?
- Were you told you needed to improve by your boss?
- Did you see someone who had great skill and become inspired to improve?

3

Getting Graphic

*I*n this chapter, you get down to the details of creating your own graphics in Flash. The Flash graphics tools (found on the Tools panel) offer you the capability to easily create interesting and professional-looking shapes. You can also import graphics created in other programs.

After you master all the techniques for drawing and editing, you can create some very cool graphics. If you're new to Flash, take the time to try out all the tools and techniques until you feel comfortable with them.

Sharpening Your Pencil

The Flash Pencil tool is designed to be used like a real pencil to create freehand shapes. Whenever you want to create a shape not available from other Flash tools (such as the Oval and the Rectangle tools), you can use the Pencil. But the Pencil tool goes beyond a regular pencil's capabilities by incorporating cool features that smooth or straighten what you draw. In addition to those features, the Pencil also includes the *shape-recognition* feature (perfect for those who are less artistic). Draw something that approximates a triangle, and Flash forgivingly perfects it for you. In this section, we explain exactly how to use this tool.

To start, click the Pencil tool on the Tools panel. To draw without changing the Pencil modifier, move the cursor onto the Stage, click, and draw. After you release the mouse button, Flash modifies the shape according to the active modifier setting, as we explain in the next section.

Setting the Pencil modifier

When you choose the Pencil tool, the Options area at the bottom of the Tools panel changes to display the drawing mode modifier for the Pencil tool. Choose the mode you want from the Pencil Mode drop-down list. The Pencil modifier has three drawing modes:

- **Straighten:** Straightens lines and converts sloppy squares, rectangles, circles, ellipses, and triangles to perfect ones.

- **Smooth:** Smoothes out curved lines, eliminating unsightly bumps and lumps. You can specify the amount of smoothing.

- **Ink:** Slightly smoothes and straightens your curves and lines but leaves them mostly the way you drew them.

In Figure 3-1, on the left, you see a sloppy jagged line, perhaps a bolt of lightning. See how the lightning looks after Flash modified it by using the Straighten drawing mode to create perfectly straight lines?

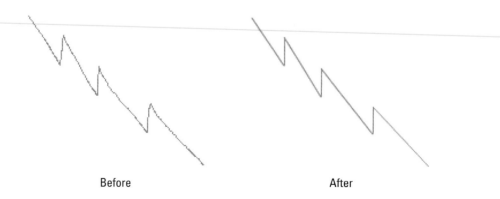

Before   After

Figure 3-1: Use the Straighten mode to draw straight lines.

How to set smoothing and shape-recognition preferences

You can tell Flash just how much you want it to smooth or straighten curved lines when you draw with the Pencil tool. Choose Edit➪Preferences (Windows) or Flash➪Preferences (Mac) and click the Drawing category. In the Smooth Curves drop-down list, select one of the following options:

- **Off:** Flash doesn't smooth or straighten at all.

- **Rough:** Flash smoothes or straightens only slightly, honoring your own work as much as possible.

- **Normal:** Flash smoothes or straightens a medium amount. Normal is the default setting.

- **Smooth:** Flash smoothes and straightens more so that you get fewer bumps and jolts.

In the same way, you can tell Flash how picky you want it to be in recognizing lines, circles, ovals, squares, rectangles, and arcs (90 degrees and 180 degrees). For lines, select Off, Strict, Normal, or Tolerant from the Recognize Lines drop-down list. Normal is the default. Use Tolerant if you're a klutz; use Strict (or even Off) if you don't want Flash fiddling too much (or at all) with your work. For other shapes and arcs, select an option from the Recognize Shapes drop-down list. You have the same Off, Strict, Normal, and Tolerant options.

Suppose that you want to animate some waves on your Web site. You start to draw the outline of the waves. Figure 3-2 shows how the waves look before and after Flash smoothes them out by using Smooth mode. For more complex shapes, Ink mode helps you look good without taking away too much of your own authorship.

Before   After

Figure 3-2: Smooth mode makes you look like a real smoothie when it comes to drawing curves.

Setting the stroke type

While drawing with the Pencil tool (and any of the other drawing tools), you can also control the type of *stroke* (line style), its *width* (also called *height* or *weight*), its *cap* (ending), and how it joins with other strokes. To modify stroke settings, follow these steps:

1. **Click the Pencil tool to make it active.**

2. **Open the Property inspector if it's not open by choosing Window⇨ Properties.**

The Property inspector appears, as shown in Figure 3-3. As we explain in Chapter 1, the Property inspector changes depending on which tool is active and which part of the Flash window you're using.

3. **To change the line width, type a new value in the Stroke text box and press Enter/Return, or drag the slider bar.**

The first available stroke width on the Style drop-down list is Hairline, which creates a hairline-width line. Flash measures *weights* (widths) of other line types in points. You can create a line up to 200 points wide. (One point equals ½ of an inch.)

4. **Click the Style drop-down list to display the available line styles and select a new line style.**

Figure 3-3: Control line type and width.

You can choose from seven line styles, including dashed and dotted.

5. **From the Scale drop-down list, select an option to control how lines scale.**

The Scale options specify how the thickness of strokes scale if you include them in a symbol and then scale the symbol. (We discuss symbols in Chapter 7.)

- *Normal:* Thickness scales both horizontally and vertically.

- *Horizontal:* Thickness scales horizontally only. This applies to vertical lines, so that they become thicker as you scale them.

- *Vertical:* Thickness scales vertically only. This applies to horizontal lines so that they become thicker as you scale them.

- *None:* Lines don't become thicker as you scale them.

6. **(Optional) Select the Hinting check box.**

   Stroke hinting makes slight adjustments to avoid blurry horizontal or vertical lines. If your lines don't look as clear as you'd like, try selecting this option.

7. **To control the endings of lines, click the Cap drop-down list and select one of the styles:**

   - *None:* The end is square with no added ending.

   - *Round:* A rounded cap is added to the end of the line. The length of the cap is half the line's width.

   - *Square:* A squared cap is added to the end of the line. The length of the cap is half the line's width. See Figure 3-4.

Figure 3-4: These lines were all drawn 88 pixels long, but the bottom two lines have caps, so they're longer.

8. **Click the Join drop-down list and select one of the styles (see Figure 3-5) to control how lines look when they meet:**

   - *Miter:* A pointed corner

   - *Round:* A rounded corner

   - *Bevel:* A squared-off (beveled) corner

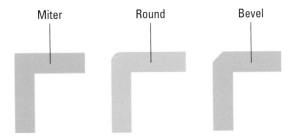

Figure 3-5: You can choose how lines meet. How romantic!

9. **(Optional) In the Miter box, you can drag to change the value or click and enter a value to help prevent beveling a miter join.**

   When you draw two lines that meet at a sharp angle with a *miter join* (a sharp point), you might get a bevel instead. If you chose a miter join, you can increase the value in the Miter text box to get a nice sharp point where the two lines meet.

You can create custom line styles, as well. In the Property inspector, click the Edit Stroke Style button to the right of the Style drop-down list. In the Stroke Style dialog box that opens, you can create your own designer line styles.

Setting the color

When using the Pencil tool, you can set the color of the stroke in the Property inspector or in the Colors section of the Tools panel. In either location, click the Stroke Color box to open the color palette and then select a color.

We explain more about using colors in the section "A Rainbow of Colors," later in this chapter.

Creating Shapely Shapes

In the preceding section, we explain that you can draw shapes by using the Pencil tool. You can also draw lines, rectangles, squares, ovals, and circles by using the shape tools. Use these tools when you want more control over your shapes — for example, when you want to draw perfect circles, perfect squares, and straight lines.

Line up

To draw a line, choose the Line tool in the Tools panel. Click the Stage at the desired starting point of the line and drag to the ending point. Then release the mouse button. To keep your lines at multiples of 45 degrees, press Shift while dragging. Flash creates the line at the 45-degree angle closest to your drag line.

When you use the Line tool, you can modify the line weight, style, and color in the same way as for the Pencil tool, as we discuss in the preceding section.

Be square

To draw a rectangle, choose the Rectangle tool in the Tools panel. Click the Stage at one corner of the rectangle and drag to the opposite corner. Then release the mouse button. To create a square, press Shift as you drag.

The Rectangle tool is on a flyout toolbar on the Tools panel. The flyout displays the last tool you used, so you may not see the Rectangle tool. Instead, you may see the Oval tool, the PolyStar tool, the Rectangle Primitive tool, or the Oval Primitive tool. Click (with a long click) any one of these to display the flyout, where you can find the Rectangle tool.

When you click the Rectangle tool, you can modify the line weight, style, and color of the rectangle in the same way that you can modify a line when you use the Pencil tool. You can't see the effect of caps when you create a rectangle because it's a closed shape; however, if you later cut out part of the rectangle, the remaining lines take on the cap you specified.

Unlike lines, rectangles contain *two* objects: the *fill* (the area inside the stroke) and the *stroke* (the outline of the rectangle).

Flash provides the following tools for adjusting the settings for rectangles:

- ✔ **Fill Color:** Determines the color that fills the inside of the rectangle. You can click the Fill Color box — either in the Property inspector or in the Colors section of the Tools panel — and select one of the colors in the palette that opens. You can also select from the gradients displayed at the bottom of the palette. (See the section "A Rainbow of Colors," later in this chapter, for details about customizing colors and gradients.)

- ✔ **Stroke Color:** Determines the color of the stroke (the outline) of the rectangle. Click the Stroke Color box — either in the Property inspector or in the Colors section of the Tools panel — and select a color from the palette.

- ✔ **Black and White:** Sets the stroke color to black and the fill color to white. Click the Black and White button in the Colors section of the Tools panel.

- ✔ **No Color:** Sets either the stroke color or the fill color (whichever tool is pressed) to no color. You have to click either the Stroke Color box or the Fill Color box to find the No Color box in the upper-right corner of the palette of colors.

- ✔ **Swap Colors:** Switches the stroke and fill colors.

- ✔ **Rectangle Corner Radius:** Creates a rectangle with rounded corners. (It's located in the Rectangle Options section of the Property inspector.) By default, the Lock Corner Radius icon allows you to set one radius for all four corners. However, you can click the icon to unlock the setting, enabling you to separately enter a different value for each of the rectangle's corners in the Rectangle Corner Radius text box. The rectangle that you draw has nicely rounded corners, as you specified. Use a value of 0 (zero) for a sharp corner. You can create cute cutout corners by using a negative number for the radius, as shown in Figure 3-6.

You can specify the dimensions of the rectangle in advance. Select the Rectangle tool, press Alt (Windows) or Option (Mac), and then click the Stage. The Rectangle Settings dialog box opens, with Width and Height text boxes that you can use to get exactly the size rectangle you want. You can also set a corner radius here. When you click OK, the rectangle appears immediately. You can then move it to the location you want.

The Rectangle Primitive tool also creates rectangles. For more information, see "Getting primitive" later in this chapter.

Be an egg

To draw an oval, choose the Oval tool in the Tools panel. Click the Stage at one corner of the oval and drag to the opposite corner. (Ovals don't really have corners, but you'll get the idea after you try one or two.) Then release the mouse button. To create a perfect circle, press and hold Shift while you drag.

Figure 3-6: Where did my corner go?

The Oval tool is on a flyout toolbar on the Tools panel. The flyout displays the last tool you used, so you may not see the Oval tool. Instead, you may see the Rectangle tool, the PolyStar tool, the Rectangle Primitive tool, or the Oval Primitive tool. Click (with a long click) any one of these to display the flyout, where you can find the Oval tool.

After you click the Oval tool, you can change the line color, type, and weight in the same way as we describe for the Pencil tool, in the "Setting the stroke type" section earlier in this chapter. You can set the colors as we describe in the preceding section on drawing rectangles.

You can specify the exact width and height of the oval. Select the Oval tool, press Alt (Windows) or Option (Mac), and then click the Stage. The Oval Settings dialog box opens. Use the Width and Height text boxes to specify the size you want, and then click OK to create the oval.

Go for the stars

The PolyStar tool is on the same flyout as the Rectangle and Oval tools. This tool creates stars and polygons. Follow these steps:

1. **Display the Property inspector.**

   Choose Window⇨Properties to display the inspector if it's not already open.

2. **In the Tools panel's Rectangle tool flyout, choose the PolyStar tool.**

3. **In the Property inspector, click the Options button to open the Tool Settings dialog box.**

4. **In the Style drop-down list, choose Polygon or Star.**

5. **In the Number of Sides text box, enter a number.**

   The maximum number is 32, which is probably plenty.

6. **In the Star Point Size text box, enter a value between 0 and 1 to indicate the depth of the points.**

   A lower value, such as 0.1, creates deeper points, making your star spiky looking. A higher value, such as 0.8, creates shorter points. See Figure 3-7. This setting is irrelevant for polygons.

7. **Drag on the screen to create the star or polygon.**

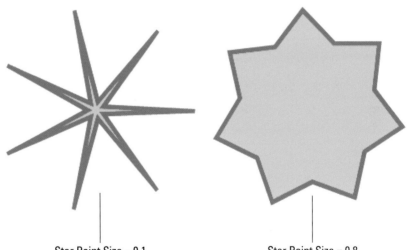

Star Point Size = 0.1   Star Point Size = 0.8

Figure 3-7: You can create a wide variety of stars.

Mixing and Matching Shapes

After you create shapes on the Stage, you need to understand what happens when two objects touch. It's a little weird, but you soon see how flexible the Flash drawing tools are. Two basic rules exist about objects that touch.

Cutting up shapes

The first rule is that when you use the Pencil or Line tool to draw a line that intersects any other shape or line, the line acts like a knife to cut the other shape or line. The line you draw is also cut into segments. You don't see the effect until you try to select or move one of the objects. Suppose that you want to draw a broken heart. You can draw the breaking line by using the Pencil tool. You now have several objects, and you can easily move apart the two halves of the heart. In the right-hand heart (see Figure 3-8), we erased the line and separated the halves of the heart.

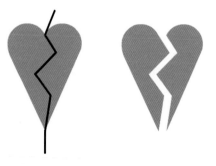

Figure 3-8: Intersect any shape with a line, and the line splits the shape and is itself segmented.

Placing objects on top of each other

The second rule about objects that touch is that when you place one shape on top of another, the top shape replaces whatever is beneath it. Again, you can see the results only when you try to select or move the shapes. But now it gets a little complicated:

- ✔ If the two shapes are the same color, they merge into one combined shape.
- ✔ If the two shapes are different colors, they remain separate.

Figure 3-9 shows a circle and a triangle on the left. They are the same color. On the right, you can see the result after moving the circle down over the triangle. Presto! It's a scoop of chocolate ice cream on a sugar cone. If you try to select the shape, it's now one object.

Figure 3-9: Build complex shapes by combining basic shapes of the same color.

When you combine shapes of different colors, you create cutouts. Rather than adding the shapes together, the top shape just replaces the area beneath it. Figure 3-10 shows how you can create a cutout. We display the grid on the Stage (find more about that in Chapter 4) so that you can see that the image on the right is a cutout.

Figure 3-10: A cutout. There's a hole in the bucket!

To create a cutout effect, follow these steps:

1. **Create two separate shapes of different colors.**

2. **Move one shape on top of another shape.**

3. **Deselect the shape that you moved by clicking anywhere off the shape.**

4. **Select the top shape again, and either drag it away from the bottom shape to create the cutout or delete it.**

See Chapter 4 for details on selecting and moving objects.

Keeping Objects Safe and Secure

What do you do if you want to put objects next to or on top of each other while maintaining their integrity? Two methods of drawing keep your objects safe from cutups, replacements, and cutouts. We discuss these in this section.

Using the object-drawing model

You can use the *object-drawing model* to keep your objects whole, no matter what else they touch. When you draw using this model, objects maintain their integrity — no dishonest objects here! Other objects on top of or beneath these objects do not cut up, cut out, or merge with them.

To draw any object with the object-drawing model, follow these steps:

1. **Choose any drawing tool in the Tools panel.**

 2. **Click the Object Drawing modifier in the Options section so that the button darkens.**

   You click the modifier again to turn off the Object Drawing modifier.

   You can also press the J key to toggle the object-drawing model.

3. Draw your object.

Your object now has a blue rectangular bounding box around it. This bounding box is similar to the one you see when you turn objects into a symbol (as we explain in Chapter 7) or group objects. (See Chapter 4 for more information.)

If you change your mind and don't want your object to stay separate from touching objects, select the object and choose Modify⇨Break Apart.

You can convert existing objects to object-drawing model shapes. Just select the shape, and choose Modify⇨Combine Objects⇨Union.

Getting primitive

A special type of shape, a *primitive,* does not merge with other objects. These objects act like objects that you draw using the object-drawing model. Two primitives are available: a rectangle and an oval. These primitives allow you to specify certain properties — *parameters* — that define their shape.

Creating a rectangle primitive

When you draw a rectangle primitive, you can create a rounded rectangle by specifying a radius for the corners. Use the Rectangle Corner Radius text box or slider bar in the Property inspector to specify a value. But you can do the same with the regular Rectangle tool, as we describe earlier in this chapter, so what's the point? The difference is how you can edit the radius of the corners, after you create the rectangle. When you select a rectangle primitive, you see markers at

Figure 3-11: Change the radius of a rectangle primitive's corners by dragging the corner markers.

the corners. You can drag these markers to change the corner radii, as shown in Figure 3-11, or you can use the Rectangle Options section of the Property inspector.

The other difference between a normal rectangle and a rectangle primitive is that the primitive acts like objects that you draw using the object-drawing model. You can't merge it or cut it out. Similarly, when you select it, you see a bounding box around the entire shape.

To draw a rectangle primitive, select the Rectangle Primitive tool in the Tools panel. Display the Property inspector (choose Window⇨Properties) and specify one or more corner radii in the Rectangle Options section, as explained in the discussion of the Rectangle tool earlier in this chapter.

Then click the Stage at one corner of the rectangle and drag to the opposite corner. The rectangle is selected, so you can immediately drag the corners to adjust them if you want. Whether you're changing the radius in the Property inspector or dragging the rectangle itself, click the Lock Corner Radius icon (to unlock the corners) in the Property inspector if you want to change just one corner.

The Rectangle Primitive tool is on a flyout toolbar on the Tools panel. The flyout displays the last tool you used, so you may not see the Rectangle Primitive tool. Instead, you may see the Rectangle tool, the Oval tool, the PolyStar tool, or the Oval Primitive tool. Click (with a long click) any one of these to display the flyout, where you can find the Rectangle Primitive tool.

Creating an oval primitive

To draw an Oval primitive, select the Oval Primitive tool in the Tools panel. Display the Property inspector (choose Window⇨Properties) and specify the Start Angle, End Angle, Inner Radius, and whether the path should be closed, as explained next. Then click the Stage at one corner of the oval and drag to the opposite corner.

The Oval Primitive tool is on a flyout toolbar on the Tools panel. The flyout displays the last tool you used, so you may not see the Oval Primitive tool. Instead, you may see the Rectangle tool, the PolyStar tool, the Oval tool, or the Rectangle Primitive tool. Click (with a long click) any one of these to display the flyout, where you can find the Oval Primitive tool.

When you draw an oval primitive, you can specify the following parameters in the Property inspector:

- **Start and End Angle:** By separately specifying a start angle and an end angle, you can create part of an oval (or circle), as shown in Figure 3-12. When specifying angles, note that 0 degrees is to the right and that degrees increase in a clockwise direction. In the Property inspector, enter values in the Start Angle and End Angle text boxes, or drag the sliders.

- **Inner Radius:** By specifying a value from 0 to 99, you can indicate the percentage of the oval's fill that you want to remove, thereby creating a donut (yum)! See Figure 3-12 for an example. Enter a value in the Inner Radius text box, or drag the slider.

- **Close Path:** Select this check box to include a fill as well as an outline around the entire shape. (The Close Path check box is selected by default.) Deselect the Close Path check box to omit the fill and draw an outline only. If you used the Start Angle and End Angle controls to create part of an oval or a circle, you get an unfilled shape when you deselect the Close Path check box, as shown in Figure 3-12.

Figure 3-12: I had a donut. A little creature came and ate a bite. Then it went on to eat the rest, leaving only the outline!

When you deselect the Close Path check box to create an open oval, you draw only the outline. What happens if you defined the oval without an outline? The entire object disappears! To get it back, choose Edit⇨Undo and add an outline. For detailed instructions, see the discussion of the Rectangle tool earlier in this chapter.

Figure 3-12 shows oval primitives with the following parameters from left to right: an inner radius; no inner radius, but start and end angles; a closed path with an inner radius and start and end angles; and finally, an open path with an inner radius and start and end angles. You can see that opening the path removes the fill.

When you select a closed Oval Primitive, you see two markers, one at the inner radius (or center, if the inner radius is 0) and one at the outer radius. You can drag the inner radius to change it. Drag the outer radius marker to change the start and end angles.

Creating Curves with the Pen

The Pen tool lets you draw *Bezier* curves, also called splines. Bezier curves are named after the French mathematician Pierre Bézier, who first described them. By using the Pen tool, you can create smooth curves that flow into each other. You can also create straight lines.

You can set preferences for the Pen tool by choosing Edit⇨Preferences (Windows) or Flash⇨Preferences (Mac) and clicking the Drawing category. We suggest enabling the Show Pen Preview option to display a preview of the line or curve while you draw. This setting helps you get a better idea of what the result will be. Click OK when you finish setting your preferences.

To create a line or curve, choose the Pen tool in the Tools panel. What you do next depends on whether you want to draw a straight line or a curve. The following sections show you how to draw both.

Drawing straight lines

To draw a straight line with the Pen tool, follow these steps:

1. **To create a line segment, click the start point and then click the end point.**

2. **Continue to add line segments by clicking additional points.**

3. **Double-click to complete the process.**

   Flash previews segments in a color that depends on the layer you're working on — see the color of the square next to the current layer as shown on the Timeline. (Chapter 6 explains layers in full.) When you choose another tool or press the Esc key, Flash displays Beziers in the current stroke color.

Close a figure by pointing near the start point. You see a small circle at the cursor. Click the start point, and Flash closes the figure.

Drawing curves

Drawing curves with the Pen tool involves a couple of steps, depending on the complexity of the curve that you want to create. The main principle to understand is that you define the curve by specifying the location of anchor points. Each *anchor point* controls a bend in the curve. To draw a curve with the Pen tool, follow these steps:

1. **Click where you want to start and drag the mouse in the desired direction. About one-half of the way to the next anchor point (the end of the curve), release the mouse button, as shown in Figure 3-13(a).**

   You see *tangent lines* that define both the direction and length of each part of the curve, as shown in Figure 3-13(b).

(a)   (b)   (c)

Figure 3-13: Drawing a curve with the Pen tool: 1, 2, 3, and you have a big nose!

2. **To create one curve, move the mouse cursor to the desired end of the curve; then double-click to end the curve, as shown in Figure 3-13(c).**

   If you set preferences to show a preview of the curve (as we explain earlier in the section "Creating Curves with the Pen"), you also see a stretchy line attached to your mouse cursor that previews the shape.

3. **To continue to draw curves, again click and drag in the desired direction, release the mouse button, and move the mouse cursor to wherever you want the end of the next curve to be. Double-click to end the curve.**

For both lines and curves, you can press and hold Shift to constrain the lines or curves (the tangent lines) to 45-degree angles. Drawing curves with the Pen tool takes practice, but you'll soon get the hang of it. Of course, you can easily modify your curves, as we explain in Chapter 4.

Getting Artistic with the Brush

The Brush tool lets you create artistic effects that look like painting. You can adjust the size and shape of the brush, and if you have a pressure-sensitive pen and tablet, you can adjust the width of the stroke by changing the pressure on the pen.

To paint with the Brush tool, select it on the Tools panel and then click and drag anywhere on the Stage. Press and hold Shift while you brush to keep your strokes either horizontal or vertical. The brush doesn't have a stroke (line) color. The brush creates only fills. Use the Fill Color swatch in the Property inspector or in the Colors section of the Tools panel to select a fill color.

REMEMBER

The Brush tool is on a flyout toolbar on the Tools panel. The flyout displays the last tool you used, so you may not see the Brush tool. Instead, you may see the Spray Brush tool. Click (with a long click) any one of these to display the flyout, where you can find the Brush tool.

When you choose the Brush tool, the Brush modifiers appear in the Options section of the Tools panel, as shown in Figure 3-14.

Figure 3-14: The Brush modifiers control how the brush functions.

Brush Mode modifier

The Brush Mode modifier determines how the brush relates to existing objects on the Stage. Here are your choices for Brush Mode. (Figure 3-15 shows some examples.)

✔ **Paint Normal:** You just paint away, oblivious to anything else. Use this setting when you don't need to worry about other objects.

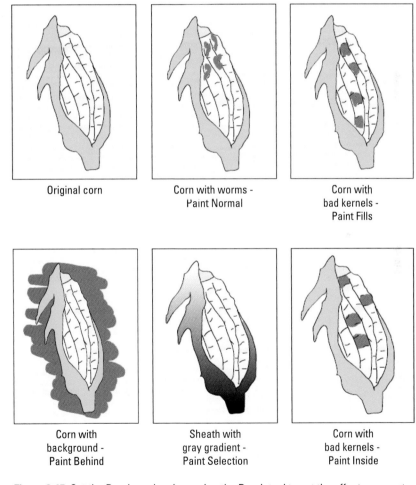

Original corn

Corn with worms -
Paint Normal

Corn with
bad kernels -
Paint Fills

Corn with
background -
Paint Behind

Sheath with
gray gradient -
Paint Selection

Corn with
bad kernels -
Paint Inside

Figure 3-15: Set the Brush mode when using the Brush tool to get the effect you want.

✔ **Paint Fills:** You paint fills and empty areas of the Stage. The paint doesn't cover lines. Note that your lines seem to be covered while you paint, but they reappear when you release the mouse button.

- ✔ **Paint Behind:** You paint behind and around existing objects, but only in blank areas of the Stage. While you paint, the brush seems to cover everything, but your existing objects reappear when you release the mouse button. You can messily paint over your objects, knowing that they won't be affected.

- ✔ **Paint Selection:** You paint only a filled-in area that you previously selected. While you paint, your existing objects are covered, but they reappear when you release the mouse button. You don't need to worry about painting within the lines because Flash fills only the selected area.

- ✔ **Paint Inside:** You paint inside lines. Only the fill where you start brushing is painted. Paint Inside also paints an empty area on the Stage if (and only if) that's where you start brushing. Again, at first, the paint seems to cover up everything, but when you release the mouse button, Flash keeps your paint nice and neat, inside the lines — like every little kid discovers in kindergarten.

Brush Size drop-down list

Click the Brush Size drop-down list and select a size in the list of circles. This list defines the width of the brush. If you use a Brush mode that helps you draw neatly, such as Paint Selection, you don't need to be too concerned with the size of the brush. On the other hand, if you're creating an artistic effect by using Paint Normal mode, the width of the brush is important.

Brush Shape drop-down list

Flash offers several brush shapes you can choose from. Click the Brush Shape drop-down list and select one of the shapes. Each shape produces a different effect, especially when you paint at an angle — you just need to try them out to see what works best. Figure 3-16 shows a honey jar drawn with various brush shapes.

Figure 3-16: Each brush shape creates a different effect — especially at the ends of the stroke.

Pressure and Tilt modifiers

If you have a pressure-sensitive pen and tablet, Flash also displays a Pressure modifier so that you can vary the width of your strokes according to the pressure you put on your pen while you draw. Click the Use Pressure tool (refer to Figure 3-14) to turn on this feature.

Flash fully supports pressure-sensitive pens and adds the ability to use the opposite end of the pen to erase — just like a real pencil. Figure 3-17 shows this type of pen and tablet.

A pressure-sensitive pen works together with a tablet to help you draw in Flash. The tablet tracks the movement and pressure of the pen while you draw. You can also use the pen as a mouse to choose menu and dialog box items. In other words, if you want, you can use the pen for all of your Flash work. Alternatively, you can use the pen and tablet just for drawing and use the mouse when you want to work with menus and dialog boxes.

Photo courtesy of Douglas Little of Wacom

Figure 3-17: This Wacom pen and tablet set is easier to draw with than a mouse and enables you to easily vary the brush width as you draw.

The Tilt modifier varies the angle of your brush stroke when you vary the angle of the stylus on the tablet. For example, holding the stylus straight up and down produces a different shape of brush stroke than the one you get if you hold the stylus at a 45-degree angle to the tablet.

Use the Tilt modifier for fine control over your brush strokes. Click the Use Tilt tool in the Options section of the Tools panel to turn on this feature. You see the effect most clearly with a large brush size and one of the narrow brush shapes. When you start to draw, change the angle of the stylus to the tablet. Watch the cursor shape turn, giving you a hint as to the shape of the brush stroke. Try brushing at a few angles to see how this works.

See the "A Rainbow of Colors" section, later in this chapter, for an explanation of the Lock Fill modifier, one of the brush tool's modifiers.

Brush smoothing

Smoothing brush strokes is similar to smoothing pencil strokes. You can finely adjust how much your brush strokes are smoothed after you finish drawing them. You can set smoothing anywhere from 0 to 100.

To set brush smoothing, follow these steps:

1. **Click the Brush tool.**

2. **Open the Property inspector if it's not open. (Choose Window⟳ Properties.)**

3. **In the Smoothing section, enter a new Smoothing value or drag upward or downward to set a new value.**

   The lower values change your strokes less. Therefore, if you set Smoothing to 0, the brush stroke is closest to what you actually drew. Lower values create more vectors, resulting in a larger file size for your movie. The higher values smooth and simplify your strokes more.

Creating Graffiti with the Spray Brush

You can create the effect of spray paint, or *stippling* (filling an area with dots), by using the Spray Brush tool.

The Spray Brush tool allows you to quickly fill up an area with polka dots of any color. You can substitute a graphic or movie clip symbol in the Library for the dots. (We discuss symbols in Chapter 7.) Figure 3-18 shows a flower that uses the Spray Brush tool in several places.

 To create a spray of dots using the default settings, click the Spray Brush tool on the Tools panel and drag anywhere on the Stage to place the dots. You specify the color of the dots by opening the Property inspector (choose Window⟳Properties), and clicking the color swatch in the Symbol section.

REMEMBER

The Spray Brush tool is on a flyout toolbar on the Tools panel. The flyout displays the last tool you used, so you may not see the Spray Brush tool. Instead, you may see the Brush tool. Click (with a long click) either of these to display the flyout, where you can find the Spray Brush tool.

Figure 3-18: The Spray Brush tool easily adds a fine level of decoration.

Setting symbol properties

You can specify your own symbol to use in place of the dots. Because you can't control the spacing between the dots, simple symbols work best. To use your own symbol, follow these steps:

1. **Create a symbol, or import one into the Library. (We explain all about symbols in Chapter 7.)**

2. **Click the Spray Brush tool in the Tools panel.**

3. **Open the Property inspector (Window⇨Properties) if it's not already open. In the Symbol section, click the Edit button.**

   The Select Symbol dialog box opens.

4. **Choose the symbol you want to use and then click OK.**

5. **If desired, enter new values for Scale Width and Scale Height in the Property inspector.**

   Scaling enables you to use large symbols in your spray. For example, you can scale the width and height to 15%. You can also scale upward by using values of more than 100%.

6. **To create a variety of sizes, select the Random Scaling check box.**

7. **To rotate the symbol around your cursor as you drag, select the Rotate Symbol check box.**

8. **To randomly rotate the symbol, select the Random Rotation check box.**

9. **Drag on the Screen to place the spray.**

   Figure 3-19 shows a raindrop symbol using random scaling.

Figure 3-19: It's raining, it's pouring.

The Spray Brush tool makes it easy to quickly add hundreds of dots or instances of your symbol to your movie. This can make the movie balloon in size quickly. Check your movie size before and after, and don't go overboard!

Setting brush properties

You have control over the width, height, and angle of the brush, whether you use the default dots or your own symbol. To set brush properties, follow these steps.

1. **Click the Spray Brush tool in the Tools panel.**

2. **Open the Property inspector (Window⇨Properties) if it is not already open.**

3. **In the Symbol section, click the Edit button to choose a symbol in the Library. (See Chapter 7 for more about symbols.)**

4. **Also in the Symbol section, you can select check boxes for random scaling, rotating a symbol, or adding random rotation.**

5. **In the Brush section, enter a value for the Width.**

   The width is the horizontal dimension. If you drag vertically when you place the spray, the resulting shape is the width that you specified.

6. **Enter a value for the Height.**

   The height is the vertical dimension. If you drag horizontally when you place the spray, the resulting shape is the height that you specified.

7. **To specify an angle, enter a Brush Angle value.**

8. **Drag on the Stage to place the spray.**

Working with Spray Brush dots

It could get very difficult to delete some of those dots if they were all individual objects! Luckily, when you create a spray, they're grouped as one object. (We discuss groups in Chapter 4.) With the Selection tool active, click inside a group of dots, and you'll see a blue border. You can press Del(ete) to delete them, or you can drag them to move them. If you really do want individual objects, select them and choose Modify⇨Break Apart. For more information on editing objects, see Chapter 4.

Pouring on the Paint

The Paint Bucket tool creates fills that fill shapes with color. You might want to fill an enclosed area that you created with the Line or Pencil tool. You can also fill enclosed shapes created with the Pen or Brush tool, which we discuss earlier in this chapter. The Paint Bucket tool is also handy for changing existing fills. You can change the color as well as fiddle around with gradient and bitmap fills. (See Chapter 4 for more on editing fills.)

 To use the Paint Bucket, choose it in the Tools panel. Set the color by clicking the Fill Color tool and selecting a color. Alternatively, you can use the Fill Color swatch in the Property inspector.

The Paint Bucket tool is on a flyout toolbar on the Tools panel. The flyout displays the last tool you used, so you may not see the Paint Bucket tool. Instead, you may see the Ink Bottle tool. Click (with a long click) either of these to display the flyout, where you can find the Paint Bucket tool.

Flash can fill areas that aren't completely closed. The Gap Size modifier (in the Options section of the Tools panel) determines how large of a gap Flash will overlook to fill in an almost enclosed area. Choices range from Don't Close Gaps to Close Large Gaps. Because *small* and *large* are relative terms, you might have to experiment to get the result you want. After you choose an option from the Gap Size modifier, click any enclosed or almost enclosed area to fill it, as shown in Figure 3-20.

Figure 3-20: Fill areas that aren't completely closed by using the Gap Size modifier.

After you use the Paint Bucket to fill a shape created with another tool, you can delete the outline of the shape and keep just the fill.

Strokes, Ink

You use the Ink Bottle tool to create an outline on an existing shape. You can use the Ink Bottle tool also to change an existing line, or *stroke*.

To use the Ink Bottle tool, click it on the Tools panel. Click the Stroke Color tool to select a color. Use the Property inspector, as we explain earlier in this chapter (in the discussion of the Pencil tool) to select a line thickness and line style. Then click anywhere on the shape. If the shape has no existing line, Flash adds the line. If the shape has a line, Flash changes its color, width, or style to the settings you specified in the Property inspector.

The Ink Bottle tool is on a flyout toolbar on the Tools panel. The flyout displays the last tool you used, so you may not see the Ink Bottle tool. Instead, you may see the Paint Bucket tool. Click (with a long click) to display the flyout, where you can find the Ink Bottle tool.

A Rainbow of Colors

Flash offers you lots of color options. By default, Flash uses a palette of colors that are "Web safe" but these days, when almost all computers can displays millions of colors, you can create your own colors. So, feel free to experiment!

Solid citizens

When you choose either the Stroke Color or Fill Color tool, Flash opens the *current color palette*, which is the active set of colors that Flash uses.

Creating new colors or editing existing colors

Flash provides two ways for you to specify your own colors:

- ✓ Choose the Stroke Color or Fill Color tool in the Tools panel and click the Colors Window button in the upper-right corner of the palette to open the Color dialog box.
- ✓ Choose Window⇨Color to open the Color panel.

These two methods duplicate each other; here, we explain how to use the Color panel, which is shown in Figure 3-21.

If you select an object before you use the Color panel, when you change the color in the panel, the object's color changes immediately to the new color.

To create a new color or edit an existing color in the Color panel, follow these steps:

1. **Click the Stroke Color or Fill Color icon to specify which color you want to change — stroke or fill.**

   Click the icon to the left of the Stroke Color or Fill Color box — not the box itself. (If you click the box, you open the color palette.)

2. **Type the color specs in the text boxes, use the sliders (click the current value) to drag to the desired color, or find a color in the color space that's close to the one that you want. Then click that color.**

   You can specify a color using any of three methods. RGB specifies a color according to red, green, and blue components; HSB specifies a color by hue, saturation, and brightness. You can also define a color by using *hexadecimal notation*, which is the color system used on the Web.

Fill color   Swap colors   Options menu

Stroke color   Fill style   Spec range slider

Black and White   Color space   Preview

No color   Alpha (transparency opaqueness value)

Hexadecimal color specs   RGB color specs

HSB color specs

Figure 3-21: Use the Color panel to create your own colors.

You can click any HSB or RGB specification and use the vertical slider to vary its value from zero to its highest possible value.

3. **Set the level of opacity/transparency (also called _alpha_) by using the Alpha (A) slider/text box.**

A setting of 0% is completely transparent, and 100% is opaque.

4. If you want to create a new color swatch, click the Options menu icon and choose Add Swatch.

Flash saves the new color to the color palette so that you can access it from the Stroke Color or Fill Color boxes on the Tools panel, the Property inspector, and the Swatches panel. If you like it, save it!

Managing colors

If you've added or changed colors, you can save this new palette. (A *palette* is a set of colors.) You can then save the palette for use in other Flash movies or import a color palette from another Flash movie (so that you don't have to bother creating the colors again). Color palettes are saved as .clr files and are called *Flash color set* files. To save a color palette, choose Save Colors from the Swatches option menu. (Choose Window⇨Swatches to open the Swatches panel and then click the Options menu icon in the upper-right corner of the panel to display the menu.) In the Export Color Swatch dialog box, choose a location for the file, name it, and click Save.

Adobe Fireworks and Photoshop use Color Table files (.act files), and Flash can save and import these as well. To save your color palette as an .act file, choose Color Table (*.act) from the Save as Type drop-down list in the Export Color Swatch dialog box.

To import a color palette that you've saved, use the Options menu of the Swatches panel. Choose Add Colors if you want to append this imported palette to an existing palette. Choose Replace Colors if you want the imported palette to replace an existing palette. You can use the same Swatches panel Options menu to manage your color palettes. Choose from the following options:

- **Duplicate Swatch:** Creates a duplicate of a swatch. Do this when you want to create your own color and use an existing color as a basis.
- **Delete Swatch:** Deletes a color.
- **Load Default Colors:** Replaces the active color palette with the Flash default palette.
- **Save as Default:** Saves the active color palette as the default palette for any new Flash movies that you create.
- **Clear Colors:** Clears all colors except black and white — for when you really want to start from scratch.
- **Web 216:** Loads the legacy Web-safe, 216-color palette.
- **Sort by Color:** Sorts the display of colors by luminosity.

Using color themes

If you would like some help gathering a palette of compatible colors for a project, *kuler* colors can come to the rescue. Kuler is an Adobe-supported online collection of color themes, available independently at http://kuler.adobe.com. Kuler is also a community, so you can upload your themes to share with others. From within Flash, choose Window⇨Extensions⇨Kuler to open the kuler panel. Figure 3-22 shows the Create tab. (You may have to register with an Adobe ID to access kuler.)

Use the Browse tab to find color themes that you like. From the Choose Which Themes You Wish to Display drop-down list, you can display themes by Highest Rated, Most Popular, Newest, Random, Saved (by you), and Custom (saved custom searches).

When you find a theme that you like, choose it and click the Add Selected Theme to Swatches button to add the colors to your Swatches panel. To edit a theme so that it's more to your liking, choose the theme and click the Edit Theme in Create Tab button. You can also find these options by clicking the arrow on the right side of any theme, after you choose the theme.

The Create tab is where you get creative, of course. Start by selecting one of the *harmony* rules. A harmony rule is a principle that governs how the colors in the theme relate to each other. For example, the Shades harmony rule results in colors that are all lighter and darker versions of the same color. If you want free rein, choose Custom.

You can double-click a theme on the Browse tab to open it on the Create tab.

To edit a color theme, choose a color swatch in the kuler panel to highlight that color's position in the color wheel. Then drag the position marker around to change the color, or inward/outward to make it lighter or darker. Alternatively, you can enter RGB values, use the RGB sliders, or enter a hexadecimal value in the Hexadecimal Code text box.

Click a color in the theme and click the Bull's-Eye button to make that color the base color. The base color is important when you choose a harmony rule other than Custom because all of the other colors relate to the base color according to the rule that you have chosen.

When you're done creating a beautiful color theme, don't forget to click the Save Theme button to name and save your theme. You can then find that theme by clicking the Browse tab and choosing Saved from the Choose Which Themes You Wish to Display drop-down list.

Color in Theme, including base color

RGB specifications

Brightness

Color wheel

Select Rule

KULER

About   Browse   Create

Select Rule: Triad

Base Color

R: 232

G: 44

B: 12

Hex: E82C0C

Save Theme

Set Fill Color

Upload Theme
to Kuler

Add a Color to the Theme

Set Stroke Color

Remove This Color from the Theme

Affect Colors According to Harmony Rule   Hexadecimal code

Add This Theme to Swatches

Figure 3-22: The kuler panel is the place to go for mixing and matching colors.

You can also quickly add the colors to the Swatches panel by clicking the Add This Theme to Swatches button. Finally, be a good community member and share with others — click the Share This Theme button to upload the theme to the kuler Web site so that others can use it.

Gradient colors

So you're bored with solid colors and want something more interesting. *Gradients* are combinations of two or more colors that gradually blend from one to another. Flash can create gradients of as many as 16 colors — quite a feat. The gradient can be linear or *radial* (concentric), as shown in Figure 3-23.

Flash offers a few standard gradients that you can find at the bottom of the color palette. But you often need a more customized look, and Flash has the tools to create just about any gradient you want.

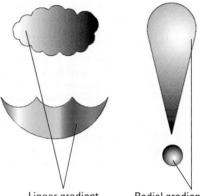

Linear gradient   Radial gradient

Figure 3-23: Linear and radial gradients make your graphics more interesting than plain solid colors.

Radial gradients look best on curved objects. A circle can suddenly look like a sphere when you fill it with a radial gradient. If you put white at the center of a radial gradient, it gives the impression of light highlights. Linear gradients look best on straight objects.

To create your own gradient, follow these steps:

1. **Choose Window⇨Color to open the Color panel. (Refer to Figure 3-21.) Then choose Linear Gradient or Radial Gradient from the Color Type drop-down list.**

   You see a gradient bar at the bottom of the panel with color pointers that specify the colors of the gradient and where the gradient changes from one color to the next.

   If you select a fill before you use the Color panel, the object's fill color changes immediately when you change the gradient in the Color panel.

2. **To use an existing gradient as a starting point, click the Fill Color box on the Tools panel and choose a gradient from the bottom of the color palette.**

   You can also choose Window⇨Swatches to open the Swatches panel and choose a gradient from the bottom of the color palette there.

3. **To specify the color for each color pointer, click and hold the pointer and then release the mouse button. (This is like a long mouse click.) When the color swatches appear, select a color.**

   You can click the Fill Color box and select an existing color from the color palette or specify a new color by using the methods we describe in the earlier section, "Creating new colors or editing existing colors."

   Note that when you click a pointer, its point turns black to indicate that it's the active pointer. The square beneath the point displays the color pointer's current color.

4. **To change the number of colors in the gradient, add or delete color pointers.**

   To add a color pointer, click where you want the pointer to appear, just below the gradient bar. To delete a color pointer, drag it off the gradient bar.

5. **To adjust where the color changes, drag a color pointer to the left or right.**

6. **To add control over how colors are applied to a selected shape beyond the gradient, click a Flow button to define one of the following overflow modes:**

   - *Extend Color:* Extends the last or outermost gradient color past the end of the gradient
   - *Reflect Color:* Fills the shape by mirroring the gradient pattern
   - *Repeat Color:* Repeats the gradient from beginning to end

   To use these effects, fill a shape with a gradient and then use the Gradient Transform tool to reduce the size of the gradient so that it no longer completely fills the shape. (We discuss the Gradient Transform tool in Chapter 4.) Then try out the three overflow modes to see the results.

   Select the Linear RGB check box to create a gradient that complies with Scalable Vector Graphics (SVG) standards. SVG is an XML language for describing 2D graphics.

7. **To save the gradient, click the Options menu icon in the upper-right corner of the Color panel and choose Add Swatch.**

The new gradient now appears in the color palette of the Fill Color box on the Tools panel and in the Swatches panel. Go ahead and use the Paint Bucket tool to fill something with it!

You can also move a gradient's center and focal points, change its width and height, rotate it, scale it, skew it, and tile it. See Chapter 4 for more on editing gradients.

Bitmap fills

You can create the coolest, weirdest fills by importing a bitmap graphic and using the bitmap to fill any shape. For a hypothetical Web site protesting genetically engineered foods, for example, we could find a bitmap of a bug (representing the Bt bacteria genetically engineered into corn) and use it to fill a graphic of corn. Figure 3-24 shows the result.

To use a bitmap graphic to fill a shape, follow these steps:

1. **Create the object or shape that you want to fill.**

2. **Select the fill.**

3. **If you haven't already imported the bitmap, choose File⇨Import⇨Import to Library, choose the bitmap you want, and then click Open/Import.**

   We explain more about importing graphics in the section "The Import Business — Using Outside Graphics," at the end of this chapter.

4. **From the Color panel, choose Bitmap Fill from the Color Type drop-down list and choose your bitmap from the swatches that appear at the bottom of the panel.**

   Flash applies the bitmap to the selected fill. You may need to scale the bitmap. See the section on transforming fills in Chapter 4 for details.

Figure 3-24: You can fill any shape with a bitmap, repeated over and over and over.

If the Fill swatch in the Property inspector or the Tools panel already shows the bitmap fill you want, you can use the Paint Bucket tool to fill any enclosed area with that fill. You can also choose the Brush tool and brush with the bitmap. Use a brush size that's thick enough to clearly show the bitmap.

Locking a fill

Flash has another trick up its sleeve for gradient or bitmap fills. A *locked fill* looks as though the fill is behind your objects and the objects are just uncovering the fill. As a result, if you use the same fill for several objects, Flash locks the position of the fill across the entire drawing surface instead of fixing the fill individually for each object. Figure 3-25 shows an example of a locked fill. In this figure, you see some windows and portholes filled with a locked bitmap of the sky. Doesn't it look as though the sky is really outside the windows?

Figure 3-25: When you lock a fill, the fill's pattern continues across the Stage but appears only where you use it.

 To lock a fill, choose the Brush tool or the Paint Bucket tool with a gradient or bitmap fill, as we explain in the two preceding sections. Then click the Lock Fill modifier in the Options section of the Tools panel. Start painting where you want to place the center of the fill and continue to other areas.

Pattern fills

If you like a decorative look, you can use the Deco tool to create a number of pattern effects.

 Flash CS5 adds 10 new effects for a total of 13 options.

Each type of pattern offers you lots of flexibility, so you can really let your creative juices flow!

 The Deco tool creates lots of objects! Sometimes, they're grouped so that you can click any one to select them all and then delete or move them. (We discuss groups in Chapter 4.) Other times, you end up with many individual objects, so be careful where you put them. They can quickly take over the world — and make your Flash file size huge!

 To use the Deco tool, click the Deco tool on the Tools panel. Then choose the pattern effect you want from the Drawing Effect section of the Property inspector. (Choose Window⇨Properties.) These effects are described in the following sections.

Vine fill

The Vine fill creates a vine of flowers and leaves. To create a vine, choose the Deco tool on the Tools panel and then choose Vine Fill from the Drawing

Effect drop-down list in the Property inspector. Click once anywhere on the Stage, or click inside a closed shape to fill that shape. Figure 3-26 shows the vine with pink flowers and green leaves.

Figure 3-26: One click covered the entire wall. If only putting up wallpaper were so easy!

In the Property inspector, you can vary the vine in the following ways:

- **Leaf:** Click the color swatch to choose another color or click the Edit button to choose a graphic or movie clip symbol from the Library to replace the leaf with another symbol. (We explain how to create symbols in Chapter 7.)

- **Flower:** Click the color swatch to choose another color or click the Edit button to choose a graphic or movie clip symbol from the Library to replace the flower with another symbol.

- **Branch Angle:** Specify a new angle to change the angle of the branches. This is like rotating the pattern.

- **Branch Color:** Click the color swatch to change the color of the branches

- **Pattern Scale:** Enter a value to scale the entire pattern. You can scale both up (more than 100%) for a less busy look and down (less than 100%).

- **Segment Length:** Enter a value to set the length between the leaf and flower nodes.

✓ **Animate Pattern:** Select the Animate Pattern check box to automatically animate the drawing of the vine so that each section goes to a new keyframe in the Timeline. Instant animation! (We explain animation in Chapter 9.)

✓ **Frame Step:** Enter a value to specify how many frames you want to include for each second of the animation.

Grid fill

The Grid fill creates a simple, rectangular array. By default, it uses a black square as the arrayed object. You can include as many as four tiles by checking them in the Property inspector (Window➪Properties). In the same location, you can vary the pattern:

✓ **Color or Symbol:** For each tile, click the Color swatch to change the color or click the Edit button to choose a graphic or movie clip symbol from the Library.

✓ **Pattern:** In the Advanced Options section, choose Tile Pattern (rows and columns), Brick Pattern (alternate rows shifted), or Floor Pattern (diagonal columns and rows). You can also select the Paint over Edge check box to spill outside a closed area and the Random Order check box to mix up the order of the tiles.

✓ **Horizontal Spacing:** Enter a value to set the horizontal spacing.

✓ **Vertical Spacing:** Enter a value to set the vertical spacing.

✓ **Pattern Scale:** Enter a percent to scale the object that you're arraying and, therefore, the entire pattern.

Figure 3-27 shows a grid pattern. We thought the black square was pretty boring, so we filled a big drop with little droplets and chose the Brick Pattern option.

Figure 3-27: Droplets within a drop.

Symmetry brush

The Symmetry brush creates four types of symmetrical designs. To choose one, click the Deco tool on the Tools panel and display the Property inspector (Window➪Properties). Use the default black square or click the color swatch to choose another color. Alternatively, click the Edit button to choose a graphic or movie clip symbol. (We explain symbols in Chapter 7.) Then choose one of the following from the Advanced Options drop-down list:

- **Reflect Across Line:** Displays a vertical green line with a rotation handle at one end and a moving handle at the other. Drag the rotation handle to rotate the line. Drag the moving handle to move the line. Click on one side of the line to place the specified object, and you automatically get a mirror image on the other side of the line.

- **Reflect Across Point:** Displays a green circle. Click on one side of the circle to place the specified object, and you automatically get a mirror image on the other side of the point.

- **Rotate Around:** Displays two green lines. One line is like the line for the Reflect Across Line symmetry; the other appears at an angle that determines the number of objects placed around the point. You can drag the end of the second line to change the angle. Click on one side of the vertical line, and you get a radial pattern around the central point. You can continue to place more objects, as shown in Figure 3-28.

- **Grid Translation:** Displays a horizontal and a vertical axis with handles near the axes' origin that let you change the distance and angle of the grid. Click to create a grid pattern.

Figure 3-28: With two clicks, we created this radial pattern of flowers.

3D Brush

The 3D Brush works like the Spray Brush tool; you drag to fill an area. The default shape is small squares, like the Grid fill. You can select up to four objects. In each case, you can use the default shape (and click the color swatch to choose a color), or click Edit and choose a symbol from the Library.

The 3D Brush places the objects so that some seem to be in front of others, resulting in a 3D effect. In the Advanced Options section, you can set the following.

- **Max. Objects:** Type a number or click and drag up or down. The maximum (and default) is 10,000!

- **Spray Area:** Click and type a number or drag up or down. This setting affects the width of the spray.

- **Perspective:** Select this check box to apply a perspective angle to the collection of objects.

- **Distance Scale:** Sets the *distance range,* meaning the intensity of the 3D effect.

- **Random Scale Range:** Creates random sizes of your objects. You control the range of sizes.

- **Random Rotation Range:** Creates random rotations of your objects. You control the range of rotation.

Building Brush

The Building Brush creates skyscrapers, and you can choose from four types. We get the best results when we drag upward with the brush; that's how you make your skyscraper rise to the sky. Use the Building Size text box/slider to specify the width of the skyscraper.

Decorated Brush

Amazingly, the Decorated Brush effect has 20 (count 'em, 20!) decorations. We don't need to list them for you because you can click the drop-down list in the Advanced Options section and see them for yourself. Figure 3-29 shows a sampling. Needless to say, we ran out of room! In the same section, you can choose the pattern color, size, and width.

Figure 3-29: The Decorated brush offers borders galore.

Fire animation

This Deco tool not only creates fire: It animates it. Don't let it burn a hole in your screen! We got the best results when we dragged horizontally while placing the fire. Also try simply clicking to place the flame. In the Advanced Options section, you can choose the following:

- **Fire Size:** Enter a value from 50% to 250%, or drag up or down to change the value.

- **Fire Speed:** Enter a speed from 50% to 200%, or drag up or down to change the value.

- **Fire Duration:** Enter the number of frames, from 10 to 200, that the animation will cover. For more information on animation and frames, see Chapter 9.

- **End Animation:** Select the End Animation check box to create an animation that totally consumes the flames, leaving nothing left.

- **Flame Color:** Click the color swatch to choose a new color.

- **Flame Core Color:** Click the color swatch to choose a new color.

- **Fire Spark:** Click and type a number or drag the slider to specify the amount of sparks that fly off the flame. The available range is from 0 to 10.

Try the Fire animation in a new Flash movie. Specify the settings, drag some flames on the Stage, and then press Enter to play the animation. Hot stuff!

Flame Brush

The Flame Brush creates flame-like images that we don't think look very much like flames. The only two settings are the Flame Size (from 2 to 20 pixels) and the Flame Color. Whichever color you choose, you'll also see other colors in your flames. Drag the brush on the Stage to place the flames.

Flower Brush

The Flower Brush creates amazingly lush flowers, leaves, and fruit. Optionally, you can add branches, which look vine-like. You can draw four types of flowers. In the Advanced Options section, specify the following settings:

- **Flower Type:** Choose Garden Flower, Rose, Poinsettia, or Berry from the drop-down list.

- **Flower Color:** Choose from the color swatch.

- **Flower Size:** Click and enter a value from 50% to 200% (for truly humongous flowers), or use the slider to drag up or down.

- **Leaf Color:** Choose from the color swatch.

- **Leaf Size:** Click and enter a value from 50% to 200%, or use the slider to drag up or down.

- **Fruit Color:** Choose from the color swatch.

Select the Branch check box to add a branch element and then choose its color from the color swatch.

Figure 3-30 shows a trellis covered with the four types of flowers.

Figure 3-30: It looks like summertime, but what are the poinsettias doing there?

Lightning Brush

The Lightning Brush creates awesome lightning, animated or still. Use this brush against a dark background to create a night sky effect. In the Advanced Options section, customize your lighting as follows:

- **Lightning Color:** Click the swatch to choose a color, such as white or yellow.
- **Lighting Scale:** Choose a size from 10% to 100%. You could use a lower percentage to show lightning that's far away.
- **Animation:** Select the check box to create a cool lightning animation.
- **Beam Width:** The beam is the main line of the lightning. Other lines extend from the beam, like branches from the trunk of a tree. Click and enter a width from 1px to 20 px, or drag the slider to adjust the value.
- **Complexity:** The complexity determines how many lines extend from the main beam. You can set a value from 0% (just the beam) to 100% (for a full light show).

Particle System

The Particle System effect creates a waterfall-like cascade of boxes (or any symbol that you choose) and animates them. On one hand, you can control many aspects of this effect; on the other hand, the effect looks out of control no matter what choices you make.

Select the Particle 1 check box so that you have at least one particle. The default shape is a little square. Click the color swatch to change the color. If you click the Edit button, you can choose a symbol from the Library. (See Chapter 7 for more on symbols.) Select the Particle 2 check box to add another square (you'll probably want to change the color) or symbol.

You can specify the following settings in the Advanced Options section:

- **Total Length:** Click and enter the number of frames to define the length of the animation. You can choose a number from 1 to 200.

- **Particle Generation:** Click and enter the number of frames to define how long you want new particles to appear. You can choose a number from 0 to 200, but if you choose 0, nothing happens!

- **Rate per Frame**: Click and enter the number of particles that you want to create per frame. Higher numbers create a more complex cascade.

- **Life Span:** After a while, the particles die. Click and enter the number of frames you want the particles to last.

- **Initial Speed:** The particles move! Click and enter an initial speed in pixels.

- **Initial Size:** Click and enter the initial size of the particles, from 10% to 200%.

- **Minimum Initial Direction:** Because the particles move, they also have a direction. You can create a smaller or larger range of direction. Click and enter the minimum initial direction, in degrees.

- **Maximum Initial Direction:** Click and enter the maximum initial direction, in degrees.

- **Gravity:** The particles fall, too. The higher the gravity (in pixels), the longer the cascading effect. You can choose a number from –20 to 20. If you use a negative number, the particles rise, rather than fall.

- **Rotation Rate:** You can rotate the particles. Click and enter a number in degrees, from –180 to +180.

Smoke Animation

The Smoke Animation effect doesn't look much like smoke; instead, it creates gray balls that change shape and rise slightly. Some of the balls fade out.

In the Advanced Options section, you can change the size, speed, duration, and color of the smoke. You can also set the background color. Select the End Animation check box to greatly multiply the length of the animation and make all the smoke balls disappear.

Tree Brush

The Tree Brush enables you to draw 20 kinds of trees, some of which aren't trees at all. Some of the trees you can draw are an apricot tree, a Christmas tree, a ginkgo tree, and a maple tree. Some of the non-trees are a vine, a garden plant, and grass. In the Advanced Options section, you can choose the type of plant, and set the tree scale, branch color, leaf color, and flower/fruit color. For trees that don't have flowers or fruit, the latter setting is meaningless. Getting your tree to look like a tree is somewhat difficult. In most cases, you should start from the bottom and drag upward to grow your tree. Try dragging at various speeds until you get the result that you want.

Drawing Precisely

If drawing in Flash seems too loosey-goosey to you, you need to know about a few features that can help you draw more precisely. Other programs do offer more precise tools, but Flash might have the tools you need.

The ruler rules

To help you get your bearings, you can choose View⇨Rulers to display the Flash ruler along the top and left side of the Stage, as shown in Figure 3-31.

To give yourself more room to work while you create drawing objects on the Stage, you can hide the Timeline by choosing Window⇨Timeline. Do the same to display the Timeline again when you need to work with layers or start animating your work.

By default, the ruler is measured in *pixels*. Computer screens are measured by how many pixels they display horizontally and vertically. Pixels are useful for Web site work because Web browsers work with only this unit. A pixel, however, is not a fixed physical size because it depends on the resolution capacity and settings of your screen. You might find it easier to think in inches or millimeters.

You can set the ruler to the unit of measurement that is most helpful to you. Choose Modify⇨Document to open the Document Settings dialog box. In the Ruler Units drop-down list, choose one of the units (pixels, inches, inches [decimal], points, centimeters, or millimeters) and then click OK.

Guides

Figure 3-31: Display the ruler to help you draw more precisely; for more control, drag guides onto the Stage.

When the ruler is displayed, lines appear on the top and side rulers whenever you drag an object — either while creating it or editing it. For example, when you drag to create a rectangle, you see a line on each ruler telling you where you started and where you ended up. If you're moving the rectangle, Flash displays two lines on each ruler indicating the outside dimensions of the rectangle. You can easily move the rectangle 1 inch — or 50 px — to the left by looking at the lines on the top ruler.

Using guides

Guides help you lay out the Stage more precisely. *Guides* (refer to Figure 3-31) are horizontal and vertical lines that you can use as drawing aids while you work. Don't worry — guides never appear in the published Flash Player file. To use the guides, you must display the rulers, as we describe in the preceding section.

To display the guides, you need to drag them from the rulers. Drag from the left ruler to create a vertical guide, and drag from the top ruler to create a horizontal guide. (If you still don't see the guides, choose View⇨Guides⇨Show Guides and make sure that there's a check next to the Show Guides menu item.)

To customize the guides, choose View➪Guides➪Edit Guides to open the Guides dialog box, where you can choose the guide color or clear all the guides. To force objects to *snap* (attach) to the guides, select the Snap to Guides check box in the Guides dialog box. You can use the Snap Accuracy drop-down list in the Guides dialog box to choose how precisely Flash snaps to the guides. To lock the guides so that they don't move while you work, choose View➪Guides➪Lock Guides. To remove an individual guide, drag it back to its vertical or horizontal ruler.

Working with the grid

You can display a grid on the Stage to help you draw more accurately and gauge distances. The grid exists only to guide you — it never appears when the movie is printed or published on a Web site. Simply displaying the grid doesn't constrain your objects to points on the grid. Use the grid by itself when you want a visual guide for drawing, sizing, moving, and laying out the Stage.

To display the grid, choose View➪Grid➪Show Grid. Use the same command to hide the grid again. You can set the size of the grid squares and change the color of the grid lines in the Grid dialog box. To open the dialog box, choose View➪Grid➪Edit Grid.

You can change the units of measurement used for the grid by choosing Modify➪Document. In the Modify Document dialog box, select the unit that you want in the Ruler Units drop-down list and then click OK.

Snapping turtle

When you want even more precision, you can turn on snapping. *Snapping* tells Flash to snap objects to the intersections on the grid or to other objects. Usually, you want the grid on when you use snapping so that you can see the snap points.

To turn on snapping, choose the Selection tool and click the Snap to Objects modifier in the Options section of the Tools panel or choose View➪ Snapping➪Snap to Objects. To snap to the grid, choose View➪Snapping➪ Snap to Grid. Use the same method to turn snapping off again.

Snapping pulls your cursor to the grid points and to existing objects while you work. You can take advantage of snapping both while drawing new objects and editing existing objects. When you have snapping on and select an object, Flash displays a small, black circle and snaps the circle to the grid points.

Setting snap-to-grid preferences

You can get downright picky about how Flash snaps to grid points. Do you want the end of a line (for example) to always snap, or should it snap only if it's close to a grid point or an existing object? To set your preferences, choose View➪Grid➪Edit Grid. In the Snap Accuracy drop-down list, select one of the options, which range from Must Be Close to Always Snap.

Setting snap-to-objects preferences

Because snapping applies to objects as well as grid points, you can separately set how Flash snaps to objects. Choose Edit➪Preferences (Windows) or Flash➪Preferences (Mac) and then click the Drawing category. From the Connect Lines drop-down list, select Must Be Close, Normal, or Can Be Distant. Although Flash calls this the Connect Lines setting, it affects rectangles and ovals as well as the lines you draw with the Line and Pencil tools.

This setting also affects how Flash recognizes horizontal and vertical lines and makes them perfectly horizontal or vertical. For example, the Can Be Distant setting adjusts a more angled line than the Must Be Close setting.

Pixel, pixel on the wall

If the grid isn't precise enough, you can snap to pixels. Choose View➪ Snapping➪Snap to Pixels to toggle snapping to pixels. If Snap to Pixels is on, Flash automatically displays the pixel grid when you zoom in to 400% or higher. With Snap to Pixels on, you can snap all objects that you create or move to the pixel grid.

When Snap to Pixels is on, you can press the C key to temporarily turn off pixel snapping. In the same situation, you can hold down the X key to temporarily hide the pixel grid (but not while you're in the process of drawing).

You can also precisely align existing objects. For more information, see Chapter 4.

The Import Business — Using Outside Graphics

So maybe you're the lazy type — or totally without artistic talent — and you really need help. Flash hasn't given up on you completely. Rather than create your own graphics, you can use the work of others. Although Flash creates vector-based graphics, it can import both bitmap and vector graphic files.

When using others' artwork, be careful about copyright issues. For example, some graphics available on the Web can be used for personal, but not commercial, purposes. Most Web sites that offer graphics for downloading offer a policy explaining how you can use their graphics.

Importing graphics

To import a graphic file, follow these steps:

1. **Choose File⇨Import⇨Import to Stage.**

   The Import dialog box opens.

2. **In the dialog box, locate and choose the file that you want.**

3. **Click Open/Import to open the file.**

   The file appears on the Stage. If the file is a bitmap, it also goes into the Library. To import a graphic file directly into the Library without displaying it on the Stage, choose File⇨Import⇨Import to Library.

A cool feature of Flash is its capability to recognize and import sequences of images. If the image file that you choose in the Import dialog box ends with a number — and other files in the same folder have the same name but end with consecutive numbers (for example, `animal1.png`, `animal2.png`, and so on) — Flash asks whether you want to import the entire sequence of files. Click Yes to import the sequence. Flash imports the images as successive frames on the active layer so that you can use them as the basis for animation. (Chapter 9 explains more about frames and animation.) Table 3-1 provides a list of the types of files you can import into Flash.

Table 3-1	Files That Flash Can Import	
File Type	*Windows*	*Mac*
Adobe Illustrator (`.ai`) through version CS5	X	X
AutoCAD DXF (`.dxf`); 2D only	X	X
Bitmap (`.bmp`)	X	X*
Enhanced Metafile (`.emf`)	X	
Flash Player 6/7 (`.swf`)	X	X
FutureSplash Player (`.spl`)	X	X
GIF/animated GIF (`.gif`)	X	X
JPEG (`.jpg`)	X	X

File Type	Windows	Mac
MacPaint (.pntg)*	X	X
Photoshop (.psd)	X	X
PICT (.pct, .pic)*		X
PNG (.png)	X	X
QuickTime image (.qtif)*	X	X
Silicon Graphics Image (.sgi)*	X	X
Targa (.tga)*	X	X
TIFF (.tif)*	X	X
Windows Metafile (.wmf)	X	

*Only if QuickTime 4 or later is installed

You can also simply copy and paste graphics. From the other application, copy the graphic to the Clipboard; then return to Flash and choose Edit⇨Paste. However, in some cases, you might lose transparency when using this method. See Chapter 13 for details on exporting objects.

Flash CS5 offers special controls for importing Photoshop and Illustrator files. For Photoshop files, you can import the layers intact. When you import the file, a dialog box opens where you can specify which layers you want to keep. You can convert layers to Flash layers or to keyframes. For each layer, you decide whether to import the layer with editable layer styles or as a flattened (simple) image. For Illustrator files, you can maintain the ability to edit text and paths in Flash. These and other controls give you a huge amount of power over the result of the import. Choose Edit⇨ Preferences and choose PSD File Importer or AI File Importer to set default settings when you import these files. You can change these settings whenever you import a file.

Using imported graphics

Vector graphics from any drawing program become a grouped object that you can use like any other Flash object. The .wmf format, which is a Windows vector graphics format, also imports in this way. These formats work especially well when imported into Flash. You can sometimes find .wmf graphics in clip art collections and on the Web.

You can import text from a text editor, and Flash turns it into a Flash text object so that you can edit and format it within Flash. See Chapter 5 for more on text.

When you import a bitmap graphic, you often need to take some steps before you can use the graphic in your Flash file. You can manipulate your graphics in several ways to make them more Flash friendly:

- **Delete the background.** Some files may include a rectangular background you don't want. To get rid of that background, deselect the imported object, select just the rectangular background, and press Delete. If that doesn't work, read on.

- **Ungroup the graphic.** Ungrouping separates grouped elements into individual elements. Ungrouping retains most of the features of your graphic. Select the graphic and choose Modify⇨Ungroup. If you find that you still can't work with your graphic properly, read the next item.

- **Break apart the graphic.** Break imported graphics to separate them into ungrouped, editable elements. Breaking apart is useful for reducing the file size of graphics that you import. Breaking apart converts bitmaps to fills, converts text to letters and outlines, and breaks the link between an OLE (Object Linking and Embedding) object and its source application. In other words, the Break Apart command is a powerful tool. Select the graphic and choose Modify⇨Break Apart. You may have to repeat the process to break the graphic completely apart.

- **Trace the bitmap.** Flash can work magic. If you want total control within Flash, convert a bitmap to a vector graphic.

To trace a bitmap, follow these steps:

1. **Import the bitmap — don't deselect it or perform any other action on it.**

2. **Choose Modify⇨Bitmap⇨Trace Bitmap.**

   The Trace Bitmap dialog box opens.

3. **In the Color Threshold text box, type a number to represent the threshold.**

   The higher the number, the fewer the colors you get in the final vector graphic. For close results, try a value of 10.

4. **In the Minimum Area box, type a number to represent the number of nearby pixels that Flash considers when assigning a color to a pixel.**

   For greatest fidelity, try a value of 1.

5. **From the Curve Fit drop-down list, select an option to represent how smoothly Flash draws the outlines.**

   For the most exact results, select Pixels.

6. **From the Corner Threshold drop-down list, select an option to represent how Flash reproduces sharp edges.**

   For sharpest results, choose Many Corners.

7. **Click OK to close the Trace Bitmap dialog box, and then deselect the graphic to see the result.**

Figure 3-32 shows the result on our hummingbird photograph.

Figure 3-32: You can convert complex bitmaps to vector drawings.

When you import a bitmap graphic, Flash places it in the current movie's Library. For best results, don't delete the original graphic from the Library, even if you have modified it. Flash continues to refer to the graphic after you have converted it to a symbol. (Chapter 2 explains all about the Library. See Chapter 7 for our total wisdom on symbols.)

Whether you created your graphics in Flash or imported them, you probably need to edit them in many ways. Chapter 4 explains the details of editing objects.

4

You Are the Object Editor

This chapter tells you all you need to know about editing objects. You can manipulate objects in a zillion ways to suit your artistic fancy. The Flash editing tools can give you precisely the results that you want. Sometimes you need to edit because you made a mistake (rarely, of course), but often, editing is just part of the creation process. You might also need to alter imported graphics so that they fit into the scheme of things.

Selecting Objects

Before you can edit any object on the Stage, you need to select it. Flash offers many ways to select objects. After you get the hang of using the Flash selection tools, you'll find them efficient and easy to use.

Selecting with the Selection tool

To select an object, click the Selection tool (the dark-colored arrow in the Tools panel) and click the object. That sounds pretty basic. But just when you thought it was safe to skip the rest of this section, we add some ifs and buts, so read on.

What defines an object? A shape that includes an outline (also called a *line* or a *stroke*) and a fill (such as a filled-in circle) has two objects — the outline and the fill.

Most of these selection guidelines don't work when you use the object-drawing model for creating objects. When you use the object-drawing model to draw an object (such as a rectangle), both the stroke and the fill are considered one object, so you can't select the stroke or the fill individually. (We explain the object-drawing model in Chapter 3.) The same holds true for symbols, which we cover in Chapter 7.

Here are some pointers for selecting objects:

- ✔ **If the object doesn't have an outline and is just a fill,** you're home free. Click the object with the Selection tool, and it's selected.

- ✔ **If the object has an outline and a fill,** clicking the fill selects only the fill. The outline remains deselected. To select both the fill and the outline, double-click the object.

- ✔ **To select the entire object,** you can use the Selection tool to create a selection box. Click at one corner and drag to an opposite corner, making sure that the bounding box completely encloses the object or objects that you want to select, as shown in Figure 4-1.

- ✔ **To select just an outline,** click the outline with the Selection tool. Still, you never know when an outline is really several objects, like the one in Figure 4-1, which is made up of several curves. To select the entire outline, double-click it.

- ✔ **To select several unconnected objects,** select one object, press and hold the Shift key, and select additional objects. When you press Shift, you can add to already selected objects and select as many objects as you want.

Figure 4-1: Create a bounding box with the Selection tool.

To deselect all selected objects, click any blank area. If you selected several objects and want to deselect one object, press Shift and click that object.

So you're happily drawing away, using the various drawing tools. Then you want to select one of the objects, but you forget to change to the Selection tool. Oops! You draw another object by accident. Immediately choose Edit➪Undo. Then use one of the Flash shortcuts:

- ✐ Press the V key to switch to the Selection tool.

- ✐ To temporarily switch to the Selection tool while you're using another tool, hold Ctrl (Windows) or ⌘ (Mac) while you select an object or objects.

Lassoing your objects

For you rodeo types, you can lasso your objects so that they can't escape. The Lasso tool creates a customized selection area and selects everything inside, as well as self-contained objects (such as object-drawing model objects, symbols, and text) that cross the lasso line. Use the Lasso tool when you want to select a number of objects that are near other objects that you want to remain free.

To lasso objects, click the Lasso tool on the Tools panel.

To lasso freehand, make sure that the Polygon Mode modifier (in the Options section of the Tools panel) is not selected. Click anywhere on the Stage and drag around the objects that you want to select. Flash creates a selection area while you drag. Release the mouse button close to where you started it to close the lasso's loop, as shown in Figure 4-2.

Figure 4-2: Lasso freehand to select only the objects you want.

You might find that freehand lassoing is hard to control. If you tend to inadvertently cut across objects rather than glide around them, use the Polygon Mode modifier to draw polygons instead — like a lasso with a very stiff rope.

To lasso by using straight lines, follow these steps:

1. **Click to choose the Lasso tool.**

2. **Click the Polygon Mode modifier in the Options section of the Tools panel.**

3. **Click where you want the first line of the polygon to start.**

4. **Click again where you want the first line to end.**

5. **Continue to click, creating line segments as you go.**

6. **Double-click when you finish lassoing the objects.**

Selecting everything in one fell swoop

Suppose that you want to select or deselect all objects at one time. Flash has some handy shortcuts to help you do that:

✔ **To select everything:** Press Ctrl+A (Windows) or ⌘+A (Mac). Or, choose Edit⇨Select All. The Select All command selects all objects on all layers except for objects on locked or hidden layers. (See Chapter 6 for an explanation of layers.)

✔ **To select everything on one layer:** Click the layer name.

✔ **To deselect everything:** The easiest method is to click off the Stage or on any blank area of the Stage. Alternatively, you can press Ctrl+Shift+A (Windows) or ⌘+Shift+A (Mac). Or, choose Edit⇨Deselect All. The Deselect All command deselects all objects on all layers.

To lock a group or symbol so that you can't select or edit it, select the group or symbol and choose Modify⇨Arrange⇨Lock. To unlock a group or symbol, choose Modify⇨Arrange⇨Unlock All. (See the section "Getting Grouped," later in this chapter, to find out about groups. Chapter 7 is all about symbols.)

Moving, Copying, Deleting, and Erasing

The most common changes that you make to objects are to move, copy, delete, and erase them. Usually, these are straightforward tasks — but Flash has a few tricks up its sleeve, so keep on truckin'.

Movin' on down the road

Before you can move an object, you have to select it. After you select your object or objects, place the mouse cursor over any selected object until your cursor displays the dreaded four-headed arrow. (Okay, most people don't dread it at all.) Then click and drag to wherever you're going. Press Shift while you drag to constrain the movement to a 45-degree angle. (Lines and strokes don't show the four-headed arrow until you drag them.)

Moving precisely with Snap Align

When you drag an object, you see vertical and horizontal dashed lines when your object approaches existing objects. This Snap Align feature displays temporary dashed lines when you move objects to show you when the edges of objects are aligned, both vertically and horizontally, with existing objects.

Snap alignment is great for quickly aligning two objects without using the Align panel. While you drag a selected object, the dashed lines appear when you move an object in alignment with an existing object, as shown in Figure 4-3. You also see the lines when you drag an object close to any edge of the Stage.

To turn on snap alignment (although it is on by default), choose View⇨Snapping⇨Snap Align. You see a check mark next to the Snap Align item. Repeat the process to turn off snap alignment.

Figure 4-3: The Snap Align feature displays alignment between objects while you move them.

You can customize your snap alignment settings. Choose View⇨Snapping⇨ Edit Snapping to open the Edit Snapping dialog box. Then click the Advanced button to expand the dialog box, as shown in Figure 4-4.

In the Edit Snapping dialog box, you can also turn on snap alignment for the centers of objects — for easy centering of objects — by selecting both check boxes in the Center Alignment section.

Flash assumes that a border exists around the edge of the Stage. To change the border width, type a different number in the Stage Border box. To change the precision for alignment between objects, type a number in the Horizontal and Vertical boxes in the Object Spacing section of the dialog box. Click OK when you're finished to close the dialog box.

Figure 4-4: Make your snap alignments snap to your orders.

You can also use the grid and turn on the snapping feature for moving and copying objects. (See Chapter 3 to find out about the grid and snapping.) For example, you can attach one object to another by moving your first object until it snaps to the second, using the small black circle at the cursor as a guide.

The Snap Align feature aligns objects by their edges. Object snapping aligns objects by their transformation point. See the "Changing the Transformation Point" section, later in this chapter, for more information.

You can also use the four arrow keys on your keyboard to move a selected object or objects. Each press of an arrow key moves the selection one screen pixel in the direction of the arrow. Press Shift plus an arrow key to move the selection by 10 screen pixels.

Moving with the Clipboard

You can move an object by cutting to the Clipboard and pasting if you want to move the object to another layer, scene, file, or application. After you select the object or objects, choose Edit➪Cut. Alternatively, press Ctrl+X (Windows) or ⌘+X (Mac). Choose another layer or scene or open another file and do one of the following:

- **To paste the selection in the center of the display:** Choose Edit➪Paste, or press Ctrl+V (Windows) or ⌘+V (Mac).

- **To paste the selection in the same position relative to the Stage:** Choose Edit➪Paste in Place, or press Ctrl+Shift+V (Windows) or ⌘+Shift+V (Mac).

Moving with the Property inspector

If you want to place objects precisely, use the Property inspector. After you select an object or objects, choose Window➪Properties, as shown in Figure 4-5.

Use the X and Y values to specify the location. The X setting specifies horizontal distance and the Y setting specifies vertical distance — and both are measured from the top-left corner of the Stage. To change a value, click it, type a new one, and then press Enter; or, drag the value up or down.

Figure 4-5: Use the Property inspector to place objects precisely.

Moving with the Info panel

You can also use the Info panel to specify the X and Y positions of objects. Choose Window➪Info to open the panel, as shown in Figure 4-6. You can use the grid next to the X and Y text boxes to specify whether you're measuring either from the upper-left corner or the center of the selection. Just click the grid to toggle between the two options. Flash uses the units you specify in the Document Settings dialog box. (See the section in Chapter 3 on drawing precisely for information on setting the units.) Then enter the desired X and Y location in the X and Y text boxes.

Remember that moving an object onto another existing object on the same layer may do one of the following:

Figure 4-6: The Info panel.

✔ Join it, if the objects are the same color

✔ Cut it out, if the objects are different colors — unless you drew the object in object-drawing mode or you used a primitive shape (oval or rectangle)

See the section in Chapter 3 on mixing and matching shapes for more information.

Aligning objects with the Align panel

The Snap Align feature, as we explain in the "Moving precisely with Snap Align" section, earlier in this chapter, is the quick way to align objects. However, for more options and precision, use the Align panel. The Align panel gives you the tools to line up two or more objects vertically or horizontally and also lets you put equal space between three or more objects. Align and space objects to make your Flash movie look professional, as opposed to something that you might create at 3 a.m. when your vision is too blurry for you to see straight.

To align objects, select the objects and choose Window➪Align to open the Align panel, as shown in Figure 4-7. In the panel, choose the option that you want for aligning or distributing objects. For example, you can align objects along their tops, their left sides, or any other direction. You can match the size of objects (resize them) by using the Match Size buttons, or you can make the spaces between objects the same with the Space buttons. Experiment with the options in this panel until you get the results that you want.

Figure 4-7: Use the Align panel to line up and evenly distribute objects.

To perfectly center one object on the Stage:

1. **Select it and open the Align panel.**

2. **Click the To Stage button.**

3. **Click both the Align Vertical Center and the Align Horizontal Center buttons.**

   Flash centers the object on the Stage.

A quicker way is to cut and paste the object because Flash automatically pastes objects at the center of the display (which is at the middle of the Stage if you haven't panned or scrolled the display).

If you use the To Stage button, be sure to deselect it when you're finished because it can cause unexpected results the next time you use it.

Copying objects

After you spend loads of time creating a cool graphic, you might want to copy it all over the place. The easiest way is to clone it directly by dragging. Just select the object and press Ctrl (Windows) or Option (Mac) while you drag. Flash makes a copy and moves it wherever you drag.

You can also copy objects to the Clipboard. Select an object or objects and then choose Edit➪Copy or press Ctrl+C (Windows) or ⌘+C (Mac). You can paste the selection on the same layer or move it to another layer, scene, or file by using one of these techniques:

- **To paste the selection in the center of the display:** Choose Edit➪Paste, or press Ctrl+V (Windows) or ⌘+V (Mac).

- **To paste the selection in the same position relative to the Stage:** Choose Edit➪Paste in Place. If you're on the same layer, scene, and file, you now have two copies, one on top of the other. The new object is selected, so you can immediately drag it to a new location.

Because Flash pastes objects from the Clipboard to the exact center of the display, cutting and pasting is a great technique for centering objects on top of each other. For example, if you want to create two concentric circles, one on top of the other, create the circles in separate locations. Cut and paste the larger circle first and the smaller circle second. You now have perfect concentric circles, as shown in Figure 4-8, and you can move them together to the desired location. This technique works only if the Stage is at the center of your display — that is, if you haven't scrolled the display.

Figure 4-8: Perfectly concentric circles create a bull's-eye!

When you paste a new object, be sure to move the new object right away if it covers an existing object on the same layer. If you deselect the new object, it either joins the existing object (if the objects are the same color) or cuts it out (if they're different colors). Of course, that might be your intention. See the section in Chapter 3 on mixing and matching shapes for more information, including how to avoid this joining and cutout behavior.

Makin' objects go away

Making objects go away is easy. Just select them and press Delete or Backspace (Clear on a Mac).

Erasing objects

Erasing objects is like using a blackboard eraser (remember those?) or pencil eraser. Flash erases, pixel by pixel, where you erase. Luckily, Flash offers some tools that help you control the process.

To erase objects, choose the Eraser tool on the Tools panel. Click and drag across any object to erase where you drag. The eraser erases objects drawn with or without object-drawing model on. However, it does not erase grouped objects, symbols, or text. (We cover grouping later in this chapter. We cover text in Chapter 5 and symbols in Chapter 6.)

To erase all the objects on the Stage — and even objects off the Stage — double-click the Eraser tool. All gone!

You can control how the eraser works. You can set the size and shape of the eraser. For example, if you need to get into a small spot, make the eraser smaller. To set the size, click the Eraser Shape button in the Options section of the Tools panel. In the drop-down list that appears, you can choose a circle or square shape, and both shapes come in several sizes.

You can specify several eraser modes to fine-tune your results. To set the Eraser Mode modifier, click the Eraser Mode button to display the following options:

- **Erase Normal:** Dragging erases strokes and fills wherever you drag.

- **Erase Fills:** You can erase only fills, so you can messily drag over strokes without harming them. The strokes look like they're erased as you drag, but they magically reappear when you release your mouse button.

- **Erase Lines:** You can erase only strokes, so you can messily drag over fills without harming them. The fills look like they're erased as you drag, but they magically reappear when you release your mouse button.

- **Erase Selected Fills:** Select fills before you start. Then, dragging erases only the fills you selected and nothing else.

- **Erase Inside:** If you start dragging on a fill, you erase only that fill. All other fills are immune. If you start dragging in an empty area, nothing happens at all. This mode does not affect strokes.

The Faucet modifier is like using the Delete key for fills and strokes. Choose the Eraser tool, click the Faucet modifier, and click any fill or stroke to instantly delete it. You don't even have to select the object first.

Making Shapes More Shapely

Suppose that you created an object and now you want to tweak it a bit. Flash has many techniques to help you perfect your artwork, and you can modify both lines and fills.

Reshaping shapes and outlines

The Selection tool can do more than select objects. It can also reshape them as long as you didn't create them by using the object-drawing model or a primitive shape. When you reshape with the Selection tool, you do *not* select the object.

To reshape an outline or a fill, choose the Selection tool and place the mouse cursor near the object or on the edge of the object:

- ✏ **If you see a corner next to the cursor,** you can move, lengthen, or shorten an end point, as shown on the left side of Figure 4-9.

- ✏ **If you see a curve next to the cursor,** you can reshape a curve, as shown on the right side of Figure 4-9.

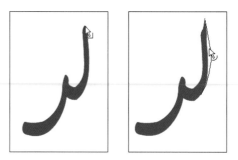

Figure 4-9: The Selection tool modifies end points and curves.

Click and drag in the desired direction. Flash temporarily displays a black drag line to show you what the result will look like when you release the mouse button. If you don't like the result, choose Edit➪Undo — or press Ctrl+Z (Windows) or ⌘+Z (Mac) — and try again.

Like with drawing, you might find it helpful to increase the zoom factor. Try editing at 200% or 400%.

Using the Subselection tool

You can use the Subselection tool to reshape individual strokes or fills created by using the Pen, Pencil, Brush, Line, Oval, or Rectangle tools. When you use the Subselection tool, you move *anchor points,* which are small circles that appear on the object. To use the Subselection tool, follow these steps:

1. Choose the Subselection tool (the light-colored arrow in the Tools panel).

2. Click the stroke (outline) or fill to display the anchor points.

3. Hover the cursor over an anchor point to see the anchor cursor, a small circle.

4. Click and drag the anchor point to modify the shape.

   Sometimes, you need to click an anchor point before dragging it to tell Flash that you want to move it.

5. To change the direction of a curve, click any anchor point to display tangent lines and drag the tangent line handles (the little dots at the ends of the tangent lines), as shown in Figure 4-10.

Figure 4-10: Subtle changes are easy with the Subselection tool.

The tangent lines indicate the direction of the curve. See the section in Chapter 3 on drawing curves with the Pen tool for information on anchor points and tangent lines.

If you use the Subselection tool to click a graphic and points aren't displayed on its edges, you might have grouped the graphic (as we describe later in this chapter), or you might have created it with the object-drawing model, or maybe you didn't create it with the Pen, Pencil, Brush, Line, Oval, or Rectangle tool. Try choosing Modify➪Ungroup or Modify➪Break Apart and then using the Subselection tool.

You can also delete anchor points. Flash reshapes the shape without that anchor point. Select the object with the Subselection tool, select an anchor point, and then press Backspace or Delete.

When you use the Subselection tool on an oval or rectangle primitive, you can change only its parametric properties. For example, you can change the corner radius of a primitive rectangle. To do so, you need to drag at one of the corners. For a primitive oval, you can change the inner radius, start angle, and end angle; you need to drag from the center or the right quadrant.

Adjusting curves with the Pen tool

You can make adjustments to objects that you drew with the Pen tool. Click the Pen tool and then click the object. You now see anchor points along the curves and lines. Here's what you can do:

- ✐ **Add an anchor point.** Hover the cursor over any place that doesn't already have one. You see a little plus sign. Just click wherever you want to add the point. Alternatively, click and hold the Pen tool to display the flyout and choose the Add Anchor Point tool.

- ✐ **Delete an anchor point.** Hover the cursor over any anchor point. You see a little minus sign. Click the anchor point. Alternatively, click and hold the Pen tool to display the flyout and choose the Delete Anchor Point tool.

- ✐ **Convert an anchor point.** Anchor points can be curve points or corner points. To convert from one to the other, click and hold the Pen tool to display the flyout and choose the Convert Anchor Point tool. Then click any object you created with the Pen tool and click an anchor point. If you're converting to a curve point, immediately drag to position the tangent line handles.

Freely transforming and distorting shapes

For way-cool distortions and reshapings, use the Free Transform tool, with its Distort & Envelope options. The Free Transform tool can work its magic on objects, groups, instances, or text blocks. In addition to its special ability to create distortions, it's flexible enough to move, rotate, scale, and skew objects. Flash has other tools that rotate, scale, and skew — we cover them later in this chapter.

Figure 4-11: We love the Free Transform tool!

To use the Free Transform tool, select an object, symbol instance, group, or text block. (See Chapter 7 for more about symbols. We discuss groups later in this chapter.) Click the Free Transform tool in the Tools panel. The object displays a bounding box with handles and a *transformation point,* shown as a circle at the center of the bounding box, as shown in Figure 4-11.

You can perform the following transformations on the selected object:

- ✐ **Move.** Place the cursor on the object itself; when you see the four-headed arrow, click and drag to move the selected object.

✏ **Set the center for rotation and scaling.** Place the cursor on the transformation point; when you see the small circle, you can drag the circle at the center of the bounding box to move the transformation point. The *transformation point* is the base point used for the current rotation or scaling operation.

✏ **Rotate.** Place the cursor just outside any corner handle; when you see the circular arrow, drag the object to rotate it around the transformation point.

Press Shift while you drag to constrain the rotation to 45-degree increments. Press Alt (Windows) or Option (Mac) while you drag to rotate around the diagonally opposite corner from your cursor.

✏ **Scale both dimensions.** Place the cursor on any corner handle; when you see the broken, two-headed arrow, drag inward or outward. Press Shift while you drag to ensure that the object is scaled proportionally without being distorted.

You can select as many objects as you want, and Flash scales them all. When you select more than one object, Flash places the handles around an imaginary bounding box that encompasses all the objects. Sometimes you might not get exactly the result you want with this method, so check carefully.

↕ ✏ **Scale one dimension.** Place the cursor on any side handle; when you see the two-headed arrow, drag inward or outward to scale in the direction that you're dragging.

⤨ ✏ **Skew.** Place the cursor anywhere on the bounding box except the handles; when you see the parallel lines, drag in any direction. (We cover skewing in more detail in the "Getting skewy" section, later in this chapter.)

In the following sections, you find out about the more exciting transformations that you can create with the Free Transform tool.

Tapering objects

You can turn a square into a trapezoid by tapering. When you *taper,* you use the Free Transform tool to drag a corner handle. While you drag, the adjoining corner moves an equal distance in the opposite direction, as shown in Figure 4-12. You can taper any shape except rectangle and oval primitives.

Figure 4-12: Tapering turns a square into a trapezoid.

To taper, press Ctrl+Shift (Windows) or ⌘+Shift (Mac) while you drag on a corner handle of the bounding box. You can also use the Distort option of the Free Transform tool: Click the Distort button in the Options section of the Tools panel and press Shift while you drag any corner handle. (This technique is ideal for people who have trouble pressing both Shift and Ctrl or ⌘ at the same time.)

Distorting objects

For even weirder effects, you can *distort* shapes (objects) — but not primitives, symbols, symbol instances, text, or groups. When you distort an object, you change the shape of the bounding box, and the shape is stretched in the same amount and direction as the bounding box, as shown in Figure 4-13.

Figure 4-13: Drag the bounding box into a new shape; the object follows suit.

To distort shapes with the Free Transform tool, press Ctrl (Windows) or ⌘ (Mac) and drag either a corner or a side handle on the bounding box. To use the menu, choose Modify➪Transform➪Distort.

Stretching the envelope

You can make even more refined changes in the shape of the bounding box by using the Envelope command. With this option, the bounding box takes on editing points like you see when you use the Pen tool. As you drag the points, tangent lines appear, as shown in Figure 4-14.

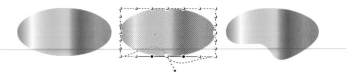

Figure 4-14: The oval is like taffy when you push the envelope.

To use the Envelope command, select an object — a shape — but not a symbol, instance, text, or group. Click the Free Transform button on the Tools palette and then click the Envelope button in the Options area. (To use the menu, choose Modify➪Transform➪Envelope.) Drag any of the points in or out and then drag the end of any of the tangent lines to change the direction of the curve.

To end a free transformation, click anywhere off the selected object.

Straightening lines and curving curves

Just like you can straighten and smooth strokes by using the Straighten and Smooth modifiers of the Pencil tool, respectively, you can straighten and smooth strokes and fills of existing objects. (See Chapter 3 for more about the Pencil tool.)

You can activate the Straighten and Smooth modifiers repeatedly and watch while Flash slightly reshapes your strokes or fills each time. Eventually, Flash reaches a point where it can't smooth or straighten anymore.

Choose Edit⇨Preferences and then choose the Drawing category to adjust how Flash calculates the straightening and smoothing. Change the Smooth Curves and Recognize Shapes settings.

To straighten a stroke, follow these steps:

1. **Select the object.**

   It's often useful to select several connected strokes.

2. **Choose Modify⇨Shape⇨Advanced Straighten.**

3. **In the Advanced Straighten dialog box that appears, select the Preview check box to see whether you like the result before closing the dialog box.**

4. **Click the value to the right of the Straighten Strength text box and then drag the slider upward. Release the mouse button to see the results.**

5. **Continue to try various strengths until you find the one that works for you.**

   Flash straightens out curves and recognizes shapes, if appropriate.

6. **Click OK to close the Advanced Straighten dialog box.**

A simpler way to straighten an object is to select it with the Selection tool active and repeatedly click the Straighten modifier button in the Options section of the Tools panel.

Smooth softens curves and reduces the number of segments that create a curve. To smooth a curve, follow these steps:

1. **Select the object.**

   It's often useful to select several connected strokes.

2. **Choose Modify⇨Shape⇨Advanced Smooth.**

   The Advanced Smooth dialog box appears, as shown in Figure 4-15.

3. **Select the Preview check box to see whether you like the result before closing the dialog box.**

4. **Click the value to the right of the Smoothing Strength text box and then drag the slider upward. Release the mouse button to see the results.**

Advanced Smooth

☑ Smooth angle below: 90

☑ Smooth angle above: 110

Smoothing strength: 60

☑ Preview

OK

Cancel

Figure 4-15: Use the Advanced Smooth dialog box to be a smooth operator.

5. **If you want, adjust the angles, above and below which the smoothing applies by entering angle values in the Smooth Angle Below and Smooth Angle Above text boxes.**

   You can clear one of the check boxes (but not both) to restrict smoothing to only below or only above a certain angle.

6. **Continue to try various strengths until you find the one that works for you.**

7. **Click OK to close the Advanced Smooth text box.**

A simpler way to smooth an object is to select it with the Selection tool active and repeatedly click the Smooth modifier button in the Options section of the Tools panel.

Modifying line endings

You can use *line caps* to customize the ends of lines that you draw. (See the section on setting the stroke type in Chapter 3 for details on caps.) You can change existing line caps. You can also choose a join style for the meeting point of two lines. Select a line and display the Property inspector. (Choose Window⇨Properties.) Select a new option in the Cap or Join drop-down list. You'll notice the effect more on wide lines.

Optimizing curves

Flash offers a technique for curves called optimizing. *Optimizing* reduces the number of individual elements in a curve, thus reducing the size of your file and resulting in faster download times on your Web site. You can optimize repeatedly, just as you can with smoothing and straightening. Optimizing works best for complex art created with many lines and curves. The visual result is somewhat like smoothing but might be subtler.

To optimize, select the object or objects and choose Modify⇨Shape⇨Optimize. Flash opens the Optimize Curves dialog box, as shown in Figure 4-16.

As you can see in the dialog box, you can specify an Optimization Strength to determine how much Flash optimizes curves. Select the Preview check box to see the result without dismissing the dialog box. If you mangle your work too much on the first try, undo it and try again with a different setting. You can select the Show Totals Message check box to see how many curves Flash cut out and the percentage of optimization that number represents. Click OK to close the dialog box.

Figure 4-16: Optimize to reduce the number of curves.

WARNING!

Be careful to check the results after optimizing. Flash sometimes eliminates small objects that you may want to retain. If you don't like the results of optimizing, choose Edit➪Undo.

Expanding and contracting fills

You can expand and contract shapes. Expanding and contracting works best on shapes with no stroke (outline) because Flash deletes the outline when executing the command. If you want to expand or contract a shape with a stroke, scale it. We explain scaling later in this chapter in the "Scaling, scaling . . ." section. The advantage of expanding and contracting is that you can specify a change in size in terms of pixels.

To expand or contract a shape, select it and choose Modify➪Shape➪Expand Fill. The Expand Fill dialog box appears, as shown in Figure 4-17. Type a number in the Distance box, using the units that you have set for the entire movie. By default, movies are measured in pixels. (See the section in Chapter 3 on drawing precisely for the details on setting movie units.)

Figure 4-17: The Expand Fill dialog box.

To expand a shape, select the Expand option. To contract a shape, select the Inset option. Then click OK.

Softening edges

Softening edges is another shape-modification tool. You can soften edges of a shape to get a graphic to look like you created it in a bitmap image editor, such as Adobe Photoshop. Figure 4-18 shows some text before and after its edges are softened. Note that adding softened edges can increase your file size.

Figure 4-18: Soften the edges of objects to create cool effects.

You can create this effect by breaking apart the text twice before softening the edges. We discuss breaking apart objects later in this chapter; Chapter 5 explains more specifically about breaking apart text into editable shapes.

To soften edges, select the object or objects and choose Modify⟹Shape⟹Soften Fill Edges. Flash opens the Soften Fill Edges dialog box, as shown in Figure 4-19.

To soften edges, follow these steps:

1. Set the distance, which is the width of the softened edge.

The distance is measured in pixels unless you have changed the document units. (See the section in Chapter 3 on drawing precisely for information on setting the units in the Document Properties dialog box.)

Figure 4-19: Soften up your boss . . . uh, graphics.

2. Select the number of steps, which means the number of curves that Flash uses to create the softened edge.

Try the Flash default first and change it if you don't like the result. You can increase the number to get a smoother effect.

3. Select the Expand option to create the softened edge outside the shape or the Inset option to create the softened edge within the shape.

4. Click OK to create the softened edge.

Your shape is still selected, so click anywhere outside it to see the result. If you don't like it, press Ctrl+Z (Windows) or ⌘+Z (Mac) and try again using different options.

You can also create soft edges by using gradients that blend into the Stage color or with partially transparent colors. Chapter 3 explains more about using colors. In addition, Flash has a blur filter that you can use on text, movie clip symbols, and buttons. Chapter 7 describes filters.

Converting lines to fills

Flash offers lots of great ways to fill a shape — for example, with gradients and bitmap images. But what about those boring strokes or outlines? You can convert lines to fills and make them fun, fun, fun. (See Chapter 3 for an explanation of fills, including gradients and bitmap images.)

Mind you, there's not much point in converting a line to a fill if it's so thin that no one would ever see a fill in it. Figure 4-20 shows some waves we created by using the Pencil tool and a 10 point–wide line. We converted the line to a fill and then used the Paint Bucket tool to fill the line with a gradient.

Figure 4-20: Change the line to a fill and use the Paint Bucket tool to change the fill.

To convert a line to a fill, select the line and choose Modify⇔Shape⇔Convert Lines to Fills. You don't see any visible difference when you deselect the line, but now you can change the fill to anything you want.

Transforming Fills

The Gradient Transform tool offers a unique way to edit gradient and bitmap fills. You can perform the following changes to a fill:

- Move its center point.
- Change its width or height.
- Rotate it.
- Scale it.
- Tile it.
- Change the radius of a radial gradient.
- Move the focus of a radial gradient.
- Skew (slant) it.

From this list, you can see that there's no point in fiddling with solid fills. They would look the same no matter what direction, size, or scale they were. (See the section in Chapter 3 on colors for colorful coverage of gradient and bitmap fills.)

To edit a fill, choose the Gradient Transform tool. This tool is well hidden; you'll find it by clicking (and holding) the Free Transform tool on the Tools panel to open the submenu. Click any gradient or bitmap fill. Flash places an editing boundary and editing handles around the fill. The editing boundary varies with the type of fill — bitmap, linear gradient, or radial gradient, as shown in Figure 4-21.

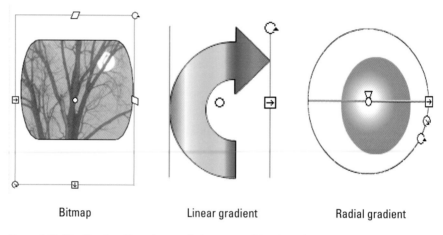

| Bitmap | Linear gradient | Radial gradient |

Figure 4-21: The Gradient Transform tool places an editing boundary around the fill.

After you have a fill with an editing boundary, you're ready to go ahead and fiddle with the fills. Here's how to make changes:

✔ **Move the center of a fill.** Drag the center point, marked by a small circle at the center of the fill. You can move a center fill to move the center of a radial gradient, move the stripes of a linear gradient, or place a bitmap off center.

✔ **Move the focal point of a fill.** Drag the focal point, marked by a triangle along the center line of a radial gradient. For example, moving the focal point makes the apparent direction of light move from side to side in a radial gradient with a lightly colored center.

✔ **Change the width of a fill.** Drag the square handle on one side of the editing boundary. To change the height of a fill, drag the handle on the bottom of the editing boundary. If a fill doesn't have one of these handles, you can't edit the fill that way. Changing the width of a linear fill that's perpendicular to the direction of its stripes is the same as scaling the fill — the stripes get wider (or narrower).

✔ **Rotate a fill.** Drag the rotation handle, which is a small circle just outside the corner of the editing boundary. On a radial gradient, use the bottom of the three handles on the circumference of the boundary.

✔ **Scale a fill.** To scale a bitmap fill, drag the circular handle at the lower-left corner of the editing boundary — inward to scale down and outward to scale up. To scale a radial gradient, drag the middle circular handle on the editing boundary. Figure 4-22 shows a bitmap gradient at its original size and scaled down. Flash tiles the bitmap if you scale down significantly.

Figure 4-22: Scale a bitmap fill to make it larger or smaller.

If you scale down a bitmap so that you see many tiles, the next time that you want to edit the bitmap, Flash places an editing boundary around each tile so that you have to edit each one individually. That could take a long time! If you want to edit a bitmap in several ways, save scaling down for last.

✔ **Skew (slant) a fill.** Drag one of the rhombus-shaped handles on the top or side of the editing boundary. You can skew only if the fill is a bitmap. Skewing is different from rotating because the bitmap is distorted. Figure 4-23 shows an example of a skewed bitmap.

Figure 4-23: Skew a bitmap fill for really weird results.

Later in this chapter, we explain how to rotate, scale, and skew entire objects.

Transferring Properties

You can use the Eyedropper tool to copy stroke and fill properties from one object to another. (See the section on bitmap fills in Chapter 3 for instructions on using the Eyedropper tool to create bitmap fills.)

To transfer properties, follow these steps:

 1. **Click the Eyedropper tool.**

2. **Click an outline or a fill.**

   If you click an outline, Flash activates the Ink Bottle tool. If you select a fill, Flash activates the Paint Bucket tool and turns on the Lock Fill modifier. (For more information on the Lock Fill modifier, see the section in Chapter 3 that discusses locking a fill.) If you don't want a locked fill, click the Lock Fill modifier in the Options section of the Tools panel to deselect it.

3. Click another outline or fill.

Flash transfers the properties of the original outline or fill to the new object.

Finding and Replacing Objects

One way to change an object is to change its properties. You can find graphics objects by color or bitmap and then replace the color or bitmap. For example, you can easily change every blue fill or stroke to red if your Web color scheme changes.

You can find and replace according to color, bitmap, text, and font (Chapter 5); sound; or video (Chapter 11). You can also find and replace symbols (Chapter 7).

To find and replace objects, choose Edit⇨Find and Replace to open the Find and Replace dialog box, as shown in Figure 4-24.

In the Search In drop-down list, choose to search in the entire Flash movie document or only in the current scene. (See Chapter 9 for a full explanation of scenes.)

Figure 4-24: The Find and Replace dialog box finds lost sheep and can change their color.

In the For drop-down list, select what you want to find: text, font, color, symbol, sound, video, or bitmap. The dialog box changes according to the choice you make. For example, to find and replace a color, follow these steps:

1. **Click Color from the For drop-down list.**

2. **Click the top Color button and select a color that exists in your document.**

3. **Click the Replace with Color button and select the replacement color that you want.**

4. **Mark one or more of the three check boxes — Fills, Strokes, and Text — to define what type of objects you want to find.**

5. **Click Find Next to find the next occurrence of the color or click Find All to find every object with that color.**

6. **Click Replace to replace the color of the currently selected object or click Replace All to replace the color of every object.**

7. **Click the Close button of the dialog box to return to your movie.**

Find and Replace is an efficient way to make mass changes of color, text, symbols, sound, video, or bitmaps.

Transforming Objects

Earlier in this chapter, in the "Freely transforming and distorting shapes" section, we explain how you can use the Free Transform tool to reshape objects. You can do many of the same tasks by using the Transform command.

To scale, rotate, and flip objects, choose Modify➪Transform and then choose one of the submenu commands. When you scale, rotate, or skew an object, Flash kindly remembers the object's qualities so that you can return the object to the state it was in before you fiddled around with it.

Scaling, scaling . . .

Most of the time, scaling by using the Free Transform tool (as we describe earlier in this chapter) is the easiest, fastest way to go. When you want more precision, however, scale the selected object in the Property inspector. Choose Window➪Properties. Change the value in the W (width) box, the H (height) box, or both.

To make sure that the proportions of the object stay the same, click the padlock next to the W and H values so that it looks locked. When you change either the W or the H value, the other box adjusts proportionally.

For yet more scaling options, select an object and choose Window⊅Transform to open the Transform panel, as shown in Figure 4-25.

The controls in the Transform panel work only if an object is selected. If you forgot to select an object, you don't need to close the panel; just select an object.

To scale the selected object or objects, click the Scale Width (left) value and type a scale value between 1 and 1000 and press Enter (Return), or drag the number up or down to change its value. Any value less than 100 reduces the size of the object, so a value of 10 creates a new object at 10 percent of the original object, and a value of 1000 multiplies the object's size by a factor of 10. By default, the Constrain icon is closed, meaning that changing the width also changes the height.

Duplicate Selection and Transform

Remove Transformation

Figure 4-25: Use the Transform panel to scale, rotate, and skew objects with great precision.

To make a copy of an object at a scaled size, click the Duplicate Selection and Transform button (the left button in the lower-right corner of the panel) before scaling. The copy appears on top of the original object but is selected so that you can move it immediately if you want. Figure 4-26 shows an example of how you can use scaling and copying together to create the impression of objects at varying distances. After you make the copy, just move it to a new location. When you're finished, click the Close button of the Transform panel to close it.

Figure 4-26: The brain creatures are attacking!

To return the object to its original properties before transformation, click the Remove Transform button at the lower-right corner of the Transform panel.

'Round and 'round and 'round we rotate

Most of the time, you can probably use the Free Transform tool to rotate objects, as we explain earlier in this chapter. If you want to rotate something by an exact number of degrees, such as 20 degrees, use the Transform panel. Select the object and choose Window⇨Transform to open the Transform panel. (Refer to Figure 4-25.)

To rotate the selected object or objects clockwise, type a value between 1 and 359, or drag the number up or down to change its value. To rotate counterclockwise, specify a value between −1 and −359. Then press Enter or Return.

If you don't like the results, click the Remove Transform button (in the lower-right corner of the panel) and try again.

To make a copy of an object at a different rotation, click Duplicate Selection and Transform (the left button in the lower-right corner of the panel) before specifying the rotation. The copy appears on top of the original object but is selected so that you can immediately move it.

If you want to rotate a section by 90 degrees by using the menu, do the following:

- ✔ **To rotate right (clockwise):** Choose Modify⇨Transform⇨Rotate 90° CW.
- ✔ **To rotate left (counterclockwise):** Choose Modify⇨Transform⇨Rotate 90° CCW.

When you rotate, Flash rotates the object around its center. To rotate around a different point on the object, you can convert the object to a group or symbol and change its *registration point,* the point on an object that Flash references when rotating. See the section later in this chapter on changing the transformation point, which also discusses registration points.

You can create groovy circular patterns by using the rotate and copy functions, as shown in Figure 4-27. Unless the object you're working with is completely symmetrical, you need to change the registration point.

Getting skewy

Skewing is a variation of rotating. Rather than rotate an entire object, you slant it horizontally, vertically, or both. Skewing a square creates a rhombus (diamond). In Figure 4-28, you see a simple arrow before and after skewing.

Figure 4-27: Rotate and copy an object at the same time to add flower power to your site.

Figure 4-28: A skewed arrow looks like it's in a hurry.

The easiest way to skew objects is by using the Free Transform tool. Just select an object, choose the Free Transform tool, and drag along one of the sides of the boundary.

Usually, you can eyeball the skewing process. If you want precision or to combine skewing with scaling, use the Transform panel. Select the object and choose Window⇨Transform to open the Transform panel. To skew the selected object or objects, click the Skew option.

Use the left box to skew horizontally. To skew clockwise, click the current value and then either type a value between 1 and 89 or drag up. To skew counterclockwise, click the current value and then either type a value between –1 and –89 or drag down. Then press Enter or Return.

To skew vertically, click the current value and then either type a value in the right box or drag up or down. Positive values skew clockwise, and negative values skew counterclockwise. If that sounds confusing, just try something and see whether you like it. If you don't, click Remove Transform (the button in the lower-right corner of the panel) and try again.

To make a copy of an object at a skewed angle, click the Duplicate Selection and Transform button (the left button in the lower-right corner of the panel) before starting the skewing operation. The copy appears on top of the original object but is selected so that you can move it immediately.

Flippety, floppety

Flipping reverses an object so that you have a mirror image of your original object. You can flip both horizontally (left to right or vice versa) and vertically (up to down or vice versa). Flash flips objects about their center so that they stay in their original position on the Stage.

Figure 4-29 shows a curlicue design in its original form, flipped horizontally and flipped vertically. If you flip an object horizontally and then vertically, you end up with an object that has been mirrored in both directions.

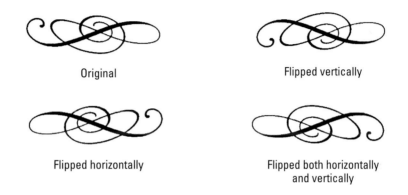

Original   Flipped vertically

Flipped horizontally   Flipped both horizontally
                                                        and vertically

Figure 4-29: You can flip objects vertically, horizontally, or both.

To flip an object, select it and choose Modify➪Transform➪Flip Vertical or Flip Horizontal. To flip an object in both directions, flip it in one direction and then in the other.

To create symmetrical objects, you need to change the object's registration point from the center to one side or corner. Later in this chapter, in the "Changing the Transformation Point" section, we explain how to use flipping to create symmetrical objects.

Combining Objects

You can combine objects in various ways to create new and more interesting shapes. You can perform the following actions:

- ✔ **Union:** Combines two objects into one object. The effect is similar to grouping objects, which we cover in the next section of this chapter. (In fact, you can use the Ungroup command to separate the objects again.) Combining two objects puts a boundary around them, like the boundary you see when you use the object-drawing model. To combine objects, select them and choose Modify➪Combine Objects➪Union.

See the section on keeping objects safe and secure in Chapter 3 for more information on how to use the object-drawing model.

✓ **Intersect:** Creates a shape that is the intersection of two overlapping shapes; the shape that remains is from the top object, as shown in Figure 4-30. However, this works only with objects that you create by using the object-drawing model. (We explain the object-drawing model in Chapter 3.) To intersect objects, select them and choose Modify➪Combine Objects➪Intersect.

Figure 4-30: A quarter-circle is all that's left after using the Intersect feature.

✓ **Punch:** Removes the object on top from an object beneath it. This operation requires two objects that you drew by using the object-drawing model. If you put a smaller circle on top of a larger circle, the Punch feature is like punching a hole in the larger circle (but it doesn't hurt). Select two overlapping objects and choose Modify➪Combine Objects➪Punch.

✓ **Crop:** Creates a shape that is the intersection of two partially overlapping shapes that you created by using the object-drawing model; removes any part of the bottom object that extends beyond the shape of the top object. Select two overlapping objects and choose Modify➪Combine Objects➪Crop.

Getting Grouped

When you know how to create objects, you can get carried away and create so many objects on the Stage that they're hard to manage. You might want to move a number of objects at once. Although you can select them all and move them, that technique might not be enough. For example, you might inadvertently leave behind one piece and discover that it's hard to move that piece in the same way that you moved the rest. That's why Flash provides *grouping*. You select multiple objects and group them once. From then on, you can select them with one click. If you move one of the grouped objects, the rest come along for the ride.

In Flash, grouping has an additional advantage: If you put objects on top of each other, they merge if they're the same color, or they create cutouts if they're different colors, unless you draw them using the object-drawing model or a primitive shape. One way that you can avoid such friendly behavior and keep the integrity of objects is to group them. (You can also put them on different layers, as we explain in Chapter 6, or you can turn them into symbols, as we explain in Chapter 7.)

Grouping objects is easy. Select them and choose Modify⇨Group. You shortcut types can press Ctrl+G (Windows) or ⌘+G (Mac). When you group objects and select them, all the objects are surrounded by one blue selection border.

After you group objects, you can ungroup them at any time. Select the group and choose Modify⇨Ungroup. You can also break apart a group. See the discussion later in this chapter on breaking apart objects.

If you want to edit an element of the group without ungrouping first, Flash lets you do so. To edit without ungrouping, follow these steps:

1. **Using the Selection tool, double-click any object in the group.**

   Flash dims other objects on the Stage and displays the Group symbol above the Stage.

2. **Edit any of the group components.**

   You'll probably have to deselect the objects that you don't want to edit.

3. **Return to regular editing mode.**

   Double-click any blank area with the Selection tool, click the current Scene symbol to the left of the Group symbol, or click the Back arrow to the left of the scene symbol.

Changing the Transformation Point

When Flash rotates or scales an object, it uses a *transformation point* as a reference. This point is generally the center of the object. For positioning and certain transformations of lines and shapes, Flash uses the upper-left corner. You might find that the point Flash uses isn't suitable for your needs. For example, you might want to rotate an object around its lower-left corner. For a single rotation or scaling of a simple graphic object, use the Free Transform tool and drag the transformation point — the little circle — to the desired location. If you deselect and reselect the object, you see that the circle has returned to its original central position.

Changing the transformation point is useful when you want to create symmetrical objects by flipping. To use flipping to create symmetrical objects, follow these steps:

1. **Select the object.**

2. **Click the Free Transform tool and drag the transformation point to one edge of the object, from where you want to mirror the object.**

3. **Choose Edit➪Copy to copy the object to the Clipboard.**

4. **Choose Edit➪Paste in Place to paste the copy on top of the original.**

5. **Choose Modify➪Transform➪Flip Vertical or Flip Horizontal.**

   You see your original and the copy. The copy has been flipped so that it's a mirror image of its original.

6. **(Optional) To create a four-way symmetrical object, group the original and mirrored objects (as we explain in the previous section) and change the transformation point to one side of the combined group. Then repeat Steps 3, 4, and 5, this time flipping in the other direction.**

Figure 4-31 shows a weird creature created by copying, changing the transformation point, and then flipping. The straight lines assist in placing the transformation point accurately.

Groups, symbol instances, text, and bitmaps have a *registration point,* which Flash uses to animate and transform these objects. When you use the Free Transform tool to move the circle on these objects, the circle keeps its position even after you deselect and reselect it. To move registration point, follow these steps:

Figure 4-31: Create scary, symmetrical creatures by manipulating the transformation point.

1. **Select a group, symbol instance, text object, or bitmap.**

2. **Click the Free Transform tool.**

   Flash displays a small circle at the transformation point.

3. **Drag the circle to the desired location.**

4. **Click anywhere else on the Stage to hide the registration point.**

To return the registration point to its original position, double-click it.

Breaking Apart Objects

With the Break Apart command, you can break apart text, groups, instances of symbols, and bitmaps into separate objects that you can edit individually. To break apart one of these types of objects, select it and choose Modify➪Break Apart.

What happens to your objects when you break them apart? Do they splatter all over the Stage? Here's what happens when you break apart the following objects:

- **Text:** Flash divides the words into individual letters, each one a separate object. If you use the Break Apart command a second time on one of the letters, the letter becomes a shape that you can modify like any other shape.

  Break apart blocks of text and then choose Modify➪Timelines➪ Distribute to Layers to animate individual letters. See Chapter 5 for more information about text and Chapter 6 for more on layers.

- **Shapes created in the object-drawing model:** The shape loses its object-drawing model status, as if you had drawn it without using the object-drawing model.

- **Groups:** Flash breaks up the group into its component parts. The result is the same as ungrouping.

- **Instances of symbols:** The symbol becomes a shape. (Symbols are covered fully in Chapter 7.)

- **Bitmaps:** Flash converts the bitmap to a fill. You can then erase parts of it.

Establishing Order on the Stage

Flash stacks objects in the order in which you create them. If you draw a circle and then an overlapping square, the square looks like it's on top of the circle because you created it more recently.

If you place an object on top of another object, the two objects become one if they're the same color. If they're different colors, the top object cuts out the underlying object.

One exception is if you use the object-drawing model to draw the objects. Oval and rectangle primitives are another exception. A different way to keep the integrity of objects is by grouping them or turning them into symbols. (Symbols are covered in Chapter 7.) Groups, object-drawing model shapes, primitives, and symbols are always stacked on top of regular objects. Therefore, to move objects above existing groups or symbols, you need to group them or convert them to a symbol. You might also need to turn some imported graphics into a symbol or group before you can move them in the stack.

If you draw an object and it immediately disappears beneath another object, it's often because you tried to draw the object on top of a group, primitive, or symbol. Group the object or change it to a symbol if it must be on top.

Another way to reorder objects is to put them on different layers. You can then reorder the objects by reordering their layers. (See Chapter 6 for the details.)

As long as you have objects that can maintain their integrity, you can change their stacking order. You can move them up or down in the stack or from the top or bottom of the stack — all within the same layer. To change the stacking order of an object, select the object and choose Modify⇨Arrange. Then choose one of these options:

- ✔ **Bring to Front:** Brings the selected object to the tippy-top of the stack.

- ✔ **Bring Forward:** Brings the selected object up one level.

- ✔ **Send Backward:** Moves the selected object down one level.

- ✔ **Send to Back:** Sends the selected object down, down, down to the bottom of the stack.

Figure 4-32 shows an example of two objects stacked in different ways: a big bitmap star and a small vector star.

Figure 4-32: The big, old-fashioned bitmap star and the small, up-and-coming vector star vying to be in front.

Undoing, Redoing, and Reusing

Sometimes you do something in Flash and decide that it's a mistake. Oops! For this situation, you can undo actions. You can even redo the actions that you undid. Finally, if you're environmentally conscious, you can reuse earlier actions to avoid wasting any more of your energy.

Undoing actions

To undo your last action, choose Edit⇨Undo or press Ctrl+Z (Windows) or ⌘+Z (Mac). You can continue this process for a very long time. This is the familiar — and default — type of undo, and Flash calls it *document-level undo*.

To set the number of undo steps that Flash remembers, follow these steps:

1. **Choose Edit⇨Preferences (Windows) or Flash⇨Preferences (Mac).**
2. **In the Preferences dialog box that appears, click the General category.**
3. **From the Undo drop-down list, select Document-Level Undo.**
4. **In the text box just below the Undo drop-down list, enter the number of undo actions you want Flash to track.**

    The default is 100, and the allowable range is from 2–300.

Later in this chapter, in the "Reusing actions with the History panel" section, we explain another way to undo actions.

Redoing actions

Maybe you were right the first time. After you undo an action, suppose that you want to redo it. You can do that, too. To redo actions, choose Edit⇨Redo or press Ctrl+Y (Windows) or ⌘+Y (Mac).

If you haven't undone anything, you can use the same command (and keyboard shortcut) to repeat your last action, in which case it's called the Repeat command.

Using object-level undo and redo

Generally, undos and redos apply to every action you take in Flash. But sometimes you might find object-level undo and redo more helpful.

Object-level undo applies only to editing symbols, which we cover in Chapter 7. When you use object-level undo and redo, Flash remembers actions by symbol. Therefore, when you're editing a symbol, using the Undo command applies only to changes that you made to that symbol, even though you have made other changes to your movie in the meantime. If you use a lot of symbols, object-level undo offers you more flexibility. Object-level redo works in the same way.

You can use only one type of undo and redo at a time. To use object-level undo and redo, choose Edit⇨Preferences (Windows) or Flash⇨Preferences (Mac). Select the General category. In the Undo drop-down list, select Object-level Undo. You see a message explaining that switching from one type of undo to another will delete your current undo history. Flash can keep track of only one stream at a time. Click OK to close the message and click OK again to close the Preferences dialog box.

Deleting your current history is not generally a problem. But if you are in the middle of a long, complicated experiment and might need to undo many steps, choose another time to switch.

Reusing actions with the History panel

If you make several changes to an object and would like to make the same changes to other objects, you can save time and increase accuracy by saving and reusing the steps for the operations that you perform. Flash tracks the steps in the History panel.

The History panel lists every command that you perform in Flash during one session. When you save and close the file, the history list isn't saved for the next time. Choose Window⇨Other Panels⇨History and the History panel appears, as shown in Figure 4-33. The shortcut is Ctrl+F10 (Windows) or ⌘+F10 (Mac).

You can use the History panel to troubleshoot recent steps, repeat steps, undo steps, or save steps as commands for future use.

Figure 4-33: The History panel keeps track of everything you do.

By default, Flash records up to 100 steps in the History panel. You can change the number of steps recorded by choosing Edit⇨Preferences (Windows) or Flash⇨Preferences (Mac) to open the Preferences dialog box. On the General tab, change the value for Undo levels. If you want to be able to go back and save earlier steps as commands, you probably need to record more than the default 100 steps.

Undoing steps

One of the simplest things that you can do in the History panel is to undo one or more operations. You can also undo operations by choosing Edit⇨Undo, but you can see more specific descriptions of the operation. For example, the Move operation appears in the History panel as Move {x.0, y.–103.0}. To view the specifics, right-click (Windows) or Control-click (Mac) any history item and choose View⇨Arguments in Panel. With these details, you can more easily predict the result of undoing an operation.

You undo steps by using the slider on the left side of the History panel:

- **Undo the last operation that you performed.** Drag the slider up one step.

- **Undo several steps.** Drag the slider to the step above the first step that you want to undo. For example, if you want to undo three steps, drag the slider up three steps — it's now next to the step previous to the one that you undid. This is the last step that has still been executed. You can also click to the left of a step, along the slider. The slider scrolls up to that step and undoes all the later steps.

When you undo a step, the step appears dimmed in the History panel.

Replaying a step

You can repeat any command from any time during a Flash session. For example, if you filled an object with a specific color, you can fill another object with the same color, even if you have performed other operations in the meantime.

To replay a step, click the step itself (not the left side of the step along the slider) in the History panel. Then click the Replay button. (You can't replay every step; such steps display a red X. If the Replay button is not active when you click a step, you can't replay that step.) If you want to replay the step on a different object, first select that object, and then click the Replay button.

Copying steps

 You might want to keep a list of certain steps or use them in a different movie. Select one or more steps in the History panel and click the Copy Selected Steps to the Clipboard button.

To use these steps in another Flash movie, open the movie and choose Edit⇨Paste in Center. To apply the steps to an object, select the object first.

Flash copies the step or steps as JavaScript code. Therefore, when you paste the step or steps into a word processor or text editor, you see the JavaScript code, which looks more complex than the step listed in the History panel. Usually, you can figure out what it means, even if you don't know JavaScript. For example, `Fill Color: '#0000ff'` appears as `fl.getDocumentDOM().setFillColor('#0000ff');`.

Saving commands

If you want to save a step or set of steps to use the next time that you open the movie, save a command. Saving a command is even useful if you want to re-execute some steps several times later in the same session because scrolling back to find the exact steps that you want to reuse can be time consuming.

To save a command, follow these steps:

1. **In the History panel, select the steps that you want to save.**

   You can drag along the step names (not along the left side, where the slider is). You can also use the usual methods of selecting multiple objects in a list. Click the first object, press Shift and click the last, or press and hold Ctrl (Windows) or ⌘ (Mac) and click each step that you want to select.

To see more details about the commands, click the Options menu button (in the upper-right corner of the panel), and choose View⇨Arguments in Panel.

2. Click the Save Selected Steps as a Command button.

This button is in the lower-right corner of the History panel. The Save as Command dialog box opens.

3. Enter a name for the command.

You can simply summarize the steps. For example, you might name a command `fill blue, rotate 90`.

4. Click OK to close the dialog box.

When you save a command, it appears on the Commands menu. The menu in Figure 4-34 shows the command `Fill blue #99ffff`, which fills any selected shape with blue. To use that command, you simply select a shape and then choose Commands⇨Fill blue #99ffff. Presto! It's all finished. As you can imagine, you can combine complex commands and save them to automate the authoring process of creating Flash movies.

Manage Saved Commands...
Get More Commands...
Run Command...
Copy Font Name for ActionScript
Copy Motion as XML
Export Motion XML
Fill blue #99ffff
Import Motion XML

Figure 4-34: Saved commands appear on the Commands menu.

Clearing the History panel

If you don't want the History panel to record everything that you do — perhaps it makes you feel as if you don't have any privacy left anymore — you can clear the history list. Clearing the history list doesn't undo any steps. To clear the History panel, click the Options menu button at the upper-right corner of the panel and choose Clear History. Then click Yes.

For good Commands menu housekeeping, choose Commands⇨Manage Saved Commands to open the Manage Saved Commands dialog box. In this dialog box, you can delete or rename a selected command. When you're finished, click OK to close the Manage Saved Commands dialog box.

What's Your Type?

W e assume that occasionally you want to say something on your Web site, so this chapter covers text in all its forms and formats. You can use Flash to create the text for your Web pages if you want (although you don't have to). But if you want flashy text effects, Flash is definitely the way to go.

Typography is the art or process of arranging text on a page, and basically that's what this chapter is all about. Many graphics programs call text *type*. We use the words interchangeably here — we don't care what you call it.

Presenting Your Text

The majority of text on most Web sites is formatted by using HyperText Markup Language (HTML) and Cascading Style Sheet (CSS) coding to set the font, size, and color of the text. Using HTML and CSS code is ideal for larger amounts of text because the code is fairly easy to create and loads quickly.

For smaller amounts of text that you want to have special formatting or effects, Flash offers more options than HTML. Of course, if you want to animate your text, you can use Flash. For example, an animated logo usually includes not only the graphic art but also the name of the organization, which is, of course, text.

Grapple with enigmas and master our mysteries!

Grow your brain with our brain teasers! Unravel baffling ·iddles, and cut your ·th on curious ·ndrums!

Here are some innovative things you can do with text:

- Rotate, scale, skew, or flip text without losing the ability to edit the text.

- Turn text into shapes and modify them any way you want. However, after you turn text into shapes, you can't edit the text characters by simply typing. Figure 5-1 shows some text that was modified this way.

- Create transparent type.

- Create hyperlinked text that sends the user's browser to another Web page when the user clicks the text.

Figure 5-1: You can turn text into a shape and modify it to your heart's content.

- Enable viewers to control some aspect of the movie by entering text in a text box.

- Load text, such as sports scores or current weather, dynamically from a server.

- Connect text in two text blocks so that the text flows automatically from one to the other.

Creating text

Creating text in Flash, using the default settings, is simple. Follow these steps:

1. **Click the Text tool on the Tools panel.**

2. **Specify the text starting point on the Stage.**

   - *To specify the width of the text,* click the Stage on the left edge where you want your text to start and then drag to the right to the width that you want. Flash places a square block handle in the upper-right corner of the text block.

   - *To create a text block that expands while you type,* just click the Stage at the desired starting point. Flash places a round block handle in the upper-right corner of the text block.

3. **Start typing.**

   To force a return to the left margin after you type one or more lines, press Enter or Return. Otherwise, if you specified a width, the text wraps to the next line when it fills up that width.

4. **After you finish typing, click anywhere off the Stage to deselect the text.**

   If you got long-winded, you might not see all of your text because the text block isn't high enough. Use the top or bottom handle to drag outward and increase the text block's height until you can see everything you typed.

Congratulations — you just said something! We hope it was worthwhile.

Editing text

After you type text, it never fails that you want to change it. Editing text is easy in Flash, but you first have to select the text. Here are the selection techniques:

- **To edit an entire text block:** Click the Selection tool and then click the text. Flash places a selection border around the text. You can move, rotate, and scale all the text in a text block this way, just like you would with any other object. For example, you can use the Free Transform tool to scale the text.

- **To edit the content of the text itself:** Double-click the text with the Selection tool active. (Or click the Text tool and then click the text.) Flash switches to the Text tool automatically and places the text cursor where you clicked or double-clicked the text, more or less.

- **To select a character or characters individually:** Click the Text tool and drag across one or more characters. Do this when you want to edit only those characters.

- **To select a word:** Click the Text tool and double-click any word to select it.

- **To select a string of words or block of text:** Click the Text tool, click at the beginning of the text you want to select, and then Shift-click at the end of the desired selection.

- **To select all the text in a text block:** Click the Text tool, click in a text block, and then press Ctrl+A (Windows) or ⌘+A (Mac).

To change the content of the text, select the characters or words that you want to change, as we explain in the preceding list. Type to replace the selected text. Other text-editing techniques are the same as in your word processor. For example, you can press the Delete key (Windows) to delete characters to the right of the text cursor or press the Backspace key (Windows) or Delete key (Mac) to delete characters to the left of the cursor.

Checking spelling

Spell checking works like the spell checker in your word processor, so you'll probably find it easy to use. This feature shows Adobe's commitment to reducing typos on the Web!

The first step is to set up the parameters for spell checking. Choose Text⇨ Spelling Setup to open the Spelling Setup dialog box, as shown in Figure 5-2. If the Check Spelling item isn't available on the Text menu, you need to open this dialog box and close it again.

The Spelling Setup dialog box has three sections:

- ✔ **Document Options:** Choose which parts of a movie that you want to check. For example, you may not want to spell check symbol and bitmap names.

- ✔ **Personal Dictionary:** You can change the location of the file that holds words that you add to the dictionary. Click the Edit Personal Dictionary button to add words directly. Otherwise, you add words when you are checking the spelling of specific text.

- ✔ **Checking Options:** Set options that define how spell checking works. For example, you can choose to ignore words in uppercase or with numbers.

You can also choose which language dictionaries you want to use in the Dictionaries list (in the upper-right corner of the Spelling Setup dialog box).

Figure 5-2: Use the Spelling Setup dialog box to specify how spell checking works.

When you're finished, click OK to return to your movie. You're now ready to check spelling.

To check spelling, you can select text if you want to check just that text, or leave all the text deselected to check the entire movie. Choose Text➪ Check Spelling to open the Check Spelling dialog box, as shown in Figure 5-3.

If you selected text, Flash checks that text first and then asks whether you want to check the rest of the document. Click Yes to continue or click No to end the spell check. For each misspelled word, you can do one of the following:

Figure 5-3: The Check Spelling dialog box.

✓ Choose one of the suggestions and then click Change to change that instance of the word.

✓ Choose one of the suggestions and then click Change All to change all instances of the word.

✓ Click Ignore to go to the next misspelled word.

✓ Click Ignore All to ignore all instances of that word and go to the next misspelled word.

✓ Click Delete to delete the word.

✓ Click Add to Personal to add the word to the Personal Dictionary so that it won't appear as misspelled in the future.

To finish spell checking, click Close. You may see a message (before or after you choose Check Spelling from the menu) asking whether you want to start from the beginning of the document. Click Yes to do so. When spell checking is complete, you see a Spelling Check Completed message. Click OK to return to your movie.

Finding and replacing text

If you need to change all instances of the word *big* to *large,* for example, you're in luck. The Find and Replace feature comes to the rescue. In Chapter 4, we discuss how to find and replace color. Here we explain the steps (which are similar) for finding and replacing text:

1. **Choose Edit⇨Find and Replace.**

   The Find and Replace dialog box appears.

2. **In the For drop-down list, choose Text.**

3. **In the Text box, enter the text that you want to find.**

4. **In the Replace with Text box, enter the replacement text.**

5. **(Optional) Enable one or more of the three check boxes on the left to define what type of text you want to find: Whole Word, Match Case, and Regular Expressions.**

   Regular expressions are formulas you use to locate specific text patterns in a text string. Regular expressions are beyond the scope of this book, but you can find a good tutorial at www.regular-expressions.info/tutorial.html.

6. **(Optional) Select one or more of the check boxes on the right to define where you want Flash to look for text.**

   • *Text Field Contents* searches text objects.

   • *Frames/Layers/Parameters* looks for frame labels and scene names (see Chapter 9), layer names (see Chapter 6), and component parameters (see Chapter 10).

- *Strings in ActionScript* looks for text in ActionScript.

- *ActionScript* looks for all ActionScript code.

7. To edit each object on the Stage, select the Live Edit check box.

Flash highlights the text on the Stage and you type the replacement text there.

8. Click the appropriate button as needed:

- Click *Find Next* to find the next occurrence of the text.

- Click *Find All* to find all occurrences of the text.

- Click *Replace* to replace the currently selected object.

- Click *Replace All* to replace all instances of that text.

When Flash finds the specified text, the box at the bottom of the Find and Replace dialog box displays its location and type along with the entire text so that you can see the context of the text you're replacing. You can resize the Find and Replace dialog box as well as the columns in the list of found items. When you're finished, click the Close button in the Find and Replace dialog box to return to your movie.

Setting text attributes

Of course, you don't always want to use the Flash default font and size for your Web site. Boring! You can set the attributes before you start typing or edit the attributes of existing text. To edit existing text, double-click the text block and then select the characters or words you want to format. To either set or edit attributes of text, display the Property inspector (Window➪Properties).

Text Layout Framework (TLF) text offers many cool features that you don't get with Classic text, the text that Flash used before TLF. For details, see the following discussion. We note where the settings differ for the two types of text.

Figure 5-4 shows the Property inspector when some TLF text is selected. The Property inspector changes slightly, depending upon which type of text you select.

Specifying the type of text

At the top of the Property inspector is the Instance Name text box. An *instance name* identifies the text object so that you can refer to the text in ActionScript. (See Chapter 10 for the scoop on ActionScript.) Instance names are handy because the contents of the text field can change while your Flash movie is playing. However, if you give your text field an instance name, you can always refer to it in your ActionScript even though you don't know the contents of the text field ahead of time.

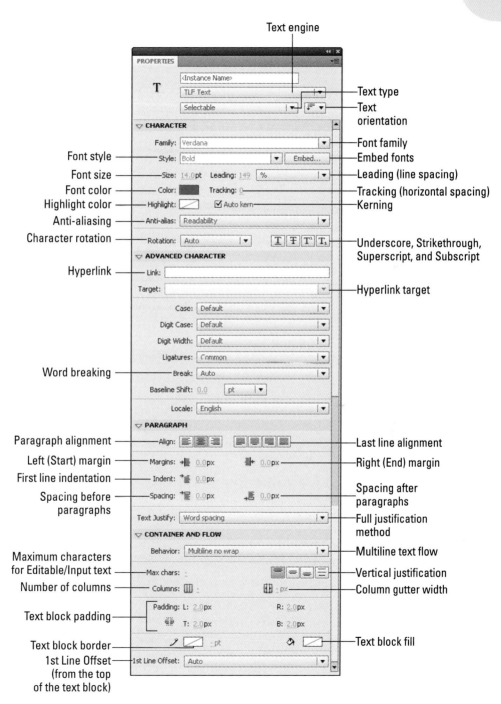

Figure 5-4: The Property inspector is the place to liven up your text.

The Instance Name text box disappears if you choose Classic Text from the Text Engine drop-down list just below (described next) and then choose Static Text.

The Text Engine drop-down list has two options, TLF Text and Classic Text. You get great extra features with TLF text, but you may want to use Classic text for a while to maintain compatibility with older versions of the Flash player. Only Flash Player 10 and later can display TLF text properly.

The next item is the Text Type drop-down list. (It's a good thing the Flash creators didn't call it the Type Type drop-down list.) This list offers different options for TLF and Classic text, but the results are similar:

- **TLF Text Type drop-down list:** Specify how the text will function on a Web site. You can create three types of TLF text:

  - *Read Only:* To disallow any interaction with the text, choose Read-Only. You would use this option when you simply want users to read the text, not to select and copy, or change it.

  - *Selectable:* If you want users of your Web site to be able to select text and copy it to the Clipboard, make the text selectable. If you're providing data from an external source (such as a Web server) or an internal source (such as ActionScript), you might want users to be able to select and copy the text to use elsewhere. Selectable text is often used for data such as sports scores, current weather, and stock prices.

  - *Editable:* You want users to be able to edit the text. Normally, you would add some ActionScript that would interact with the text that users type. For example, typing a color might change the color of an image.

- **Classic Text Type drop-down list:** You can create three types of Classic text:

  - *Static text:* Regular text that doesn't change or do anything although you can animate it. (This is like the Read Only option for TLF text.)

  - *Dynamic text:* Text that changes based on available data. (This is like the Selectable option for TLF text.)

  - *Input text:* Text that viewers can edit. You can use input text, for example, for forms and surveys or to interactively create values that affect the movie. (This is like the Editable option for TLF text.)

For Classic text, you can separately use the Selectable button at the bottom of the Character section of the Property inspector to make the text selectable.

The last item in the top section of the Property inspector is the Change Orientation of Text drop-down list, from which you can choose from Horizontal or Vertical (ideal for certain Asian languages), as shown in Figure 5-5.

Formatting text with good character

The Character section of the Properties inspector doesn't make sure that what you write reflects your good character, but it can make your characters look good. To choose a font for selected text, choose from the Family drop-down list, which helpfully provides a sample of the font. Some fonts also let you choose a style from the Style drop-down list: Regular, Italic, Bold, or Bold Italic.

NEW FEATURE CS5

Click the Embed button to open the Font Embedding dialog box. You embed fonts to make sure that they'll show up properly even on computers that don't have the fonts you use. Embedding fonts is not new, but this new dialog box makes it easier to embed the fonts you need for your entire movie.

D
o
w
n

w
e

g
o
!

Figure 5-5: Try vertical text for a change of direction.

On the left of the Font Embedding dialog box, click the Add button to add fonts, or click the Minus button to delete selected fonts from the list. On the right, you can give fonts easy-to-remember names and specify whether to include the entire font (all characters) for a selected font or only a subset (to reduce the size of your file). Click OK when you're done.

Also in the Character section of the Property inspector, you can change several important font settings:

- **Size:** Click, type a font size, and press Enter, or drag the slider to the desired value.

- **Leading:** *Leading* (rhymes with *head*-ing) is line spacing. To change the leading, click and enter a new value or drag the slider. To the right, you can use the drop-down list to specify leading by percent (%) or points (pt). The value you specify affects an entire line of text, even if you select only a word or character. (For Classic text, you'll find this setting in the Paragraph section, where it's called Line Spacing.) Figure 5-6 shows you the effects of different leading values.

The more text you write, the less likely that people will read all of it.

The more text you write, the less likely that people will read all of it.

Figure 5-6: You can make more text look like less with some leading magic.

You may choose to measure leading (line spacing) in points (pt, $\frac{1}{72}$ of an inch) because font size is measured in points. For example, if your text is 18 pt high and you want to double-space the lines, use a leading of 18 pt to create a space exactly one line high between lines of text.

✔ **Text color:** Click the Text (Fill) Color swatch to open the color palette, and select a color. (For more information on colors, see Chapter 3.) The first concern is that the text is legible against its background. Also consider that text is often unreadable in front of complex graphic images, no matter what the color.

✔ **Tracking:** *Tracking* is the horizontal spacing between all the letters. Perhaps you need the text to fit into a tight space, or you want to stretch it out without changing the font size. Figure 5-7 shows some text with various tracking settings. To change tracking, type a value in the Tracking item and press Enter or drag the slider bar to the desired value. For Classic text, this item is called Letter Spacing.

Split the scene and leave it clean

Split the scene and leave it clean

Split the scene and leave it clean

Split the scene and leave it clean

Figure 5-7: Stretched and condensed text.

✔ **Highlight:** You can highlight the background behind text with any color you want. Highlighted text looks like you drew over it with a semi-transparent highlighting marker. To highlight text, click the Highlight color swatch and choose a color from the color palette. You can also adjust the Alpha (opacity) or remove a highlight (choose the white box with a red diagonal line through it). Because selected text is already highlighted, you need to deselect the text (click off the Stage) to see the result. You can't highlight Classic text.

You can also select fonts, font sizes, and font styles directly from the Text menu. This menu is devoted entirely to helping you format your text.

✔ *Kerning* reduces the spacing between certain letters, such as *V* and *A*. Because of the diagonal line on the *A* and *V,* without kerning, the letters might look too far apart. Figure 5-8 shows an example of text with and without kerning. By default, Flash uses a font's kerning information, which is embedded in the font definition. With smaller font sizes, kerning can make text hard to read, so you can turn it off. To turn off kerning, select the characters that you want to adjust and clear the Auto Kern check box in the Property inspector.

VACATION
VACATION

Figure 5-8: The first line uses kerning; the second line doesn't.

✔ *Anti-aliasing* is a method of making text look smoother — reducing the jaggies that sometimes create stair-like lines on text. Anti-aliasing is especially helpful for smaller font sizes. You have three anti-aliasing options:

- **Readibility:** If you're worried about the jaggies, try choosing the Readability option from the Anti-Alias drop-down list. This option embeds the fonts.

- **Use Device Fonts:** If you're worried about file size, you can use *device fonts,* which are fonts that are always available on the user's computer. For more information on the Use Device Fonts option, see the sidebar, "Using device fonts."

- **Animation:** Use the Animation option to ignore alignment and kerning information and embed font outlines. The result is a smoother animation.

The way that your type looks on the Stage is only an approximation of how it will look when you publish or export your movie. To see a more accurate rendering of how your type will look when you publish or export it, view your movie by choosing Control➪Test Movie➪In Flash Professional.

You can rotate individual characters. We're not sure why you'd want to do this because it will probably give your viewers a pain in the neck from looking at the screen sideways. Actually, some of these settings are especially valuable when you're working with certain Asian languages that are written vertically. To rotate text, select it and choose 270° from the drop-down list. You can also choose 0° or Auto. You can't rotate individual characters of Classic text in the Property inspector.

The last settings in the Character section of the Property inspector offers four buttons to create underlined, struck through, superscript, and subscript text. For Classic text, you can select the Superscript or Subscript button, but you need to first deselect the Selectable button to the left.

Using device fonts

If you'd like a space-saving alternative to embedding your fonts, you can use Flash's three *device fonts* that the Flash Player always converts to the closest available font on the local computer:

✔ _sans: A sans serif font similar to Arial (Windows) and Helvetica (Mac).

✔ _serif: A serif font similar to Times New Roman (Windows) and Times (Mac).

✔ _typewriter: A font that looks like it has been typed on a typewriter. (Are you old enough to remember what that is?) It's similar to Courier New (Windows) and Courier (Mac).

When you use device fonts, your resulting published movies are smaller, so download time is shorter. With device fonts, your text also might be more legible in text sizes less than 10 pt. To use device fonts, specify one of the device fonts from the top of the Family drop-down list in the Property inspector, and then deselect the text. Then select Use Device Fonts from the Anti-Alias drop-down list in the Property inspector. (If you're using Classic text, this setting applies only to horizontal static text.) When you publish your movie, select the Device Font check box on the HTML tab (Windows only) of the Publish Settings dialog box. Chapter 13 tells you more about publishing settings.

For Classic text, at the end of the Character section, click the Selectable button to create text that users can select. The Render Text as HTML button preserves formatting, such as fonts and hyperlinks, with certain HTML tags. You need to create the formatting by using ActionScript.

Finally, if you're creating input Classic text, click the Show Border around Text button to display a black border and a white background for the text field. This border helps users know where to enter text in an input text block. Then use the Maximum Characters item in the Options section to specify the maximum allowable characters that users can input. For example, you could limit a ZIP code to five digits.

Setting advanced character properties

When you select TLF text, you see an Advanced Character section in the Property inspector. Most of the settings in this section aren't available for Classic text.

The first two boxes let you hyperlink text and set the target: how the hyperlink's address opens. Enter a URL (Web address) and then choose one of the targets; the most common are _self (same window or tab) and _blank (new window or tab). Flash underlines the text. For Classic text, you'll find these two text boxes in the Options section of the Property inspector.

You can then set the following advanced properties for TLF text:

- ✔ **Case:** Choose Upper Case, Lower Case, Caps to Small Caps, or Lower Case to Small Caps. The font needs to support small caps for the last two options to work.

- ✔ **Digit Case:** This setting affects numbers. Some fonts have options to display numbers either all the same height (the Lining option) or with ascenders that rise higher and descenders that drop lower (the Old Style option). The Default option keeps the numbers according to the default setting in the font.

- ✔ **Digit Width:** You can choose from Default, Proportional, or Tabular options.

- ✔ **Ligatures:** *Ligatures* are combinations of letters that sometimes have variations that help them fit together better. A common example is fi, in which the i's dot is omitted. To be able to see ligatures, the font you're using must contain them. Two examples are Bickham Script Pro and Hypatica Sans Pro. You can choose Minimum, Common (such as fi and fl), Uncommon, or Exotic (such as ct and st).

- ✔ **Break:** This option determines how words break when the text is too wide for the text block. Auto doesn't break up any words, All places each letter on its own line, Any breaks words as needed for a fairly straight right margin. The No Break option is to maintain compatibility with previous versions.

- ✔ **Baseline Shift:** You can move the text above or below the baseline. Click and enter a value or use the slider. From the drop-down list to the right, choose to specify the value in points (pt) or by percentage (%). You can also choose Superscript or Subscript. In Figure 5-9, we created a drop-cap for first letter (W) with a negative baseline shift.

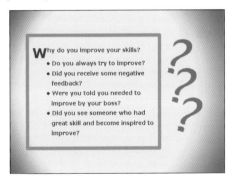

Figure 5-9: You can create a drop-cap effect by lowering the baseline for a letter. Margin and indent values align the bulleted text.

- ✔ **Locale:** You can choose from a huge selection of languages. The locale affects justification rules in a text block. If you're writing in Urdu, you probably want your justification rules to be appropriate for Urdu.

Flash usually stores outlines of the text in your movie when you publish or export it, so your audience will see your fonts in your movie even if those fonts are not installed on your audience's computer. However, not all fonts displayed in Flash can be stored as outlines when you publish or export your movie. To test whether Flash can export a font with a movie, choose View➪ Preview Mode➪Anti-Alias Text. If the text appears jagged, Flash cannot export the text with the movie. If you want to use type in a font that Flash can't export, you can break apart the type into shapes, as we describe at the end of this chapter. However, this option increases the size of your movie file and makes the text no longer editable.

Setting up paragraph formats

In the Paragraph section of the Property inspector, you can set paragraph attributes such as alignment, margins, indents, and paragraph spacing. Use these settings whenever you type more than one line of text. (You are getting long winded, aren't you!) Select the paragraph before making changes. You have the following options:

- **Align:** You can align text along the left margin or right margin of the text block. You can also center text. You can create an even edge along both margins, called *full justification* or *justified text*. By default, text is left aligned. Click the button that shows the alignment you want.

  Three new choices allow you to place the last line of the paragraph at the left, center, or right. The last line is usually less than the full width of the text block.

- **Margins:** The *margin* is the space between the text block border and your text. By default, the margin is 0 pixels. You can increase the margin to guarantee some space around the text. You can set only the left (Start) and right (End) margins (not the top or bottom ones). To set a margin, click either the Start or End Margin item. Enter a value in pixels and press Enter or click and drag in either direction.

- **Indent:** Indentation creates an indented first line. It's equivalent to placing a tab at the beginning of a paragraph. (Remember your sixth-grade teacher who told you to always start each paragraph with an indent?) To indent the first line, type a value for the First Line Indent item or click the value and drag up or down. Figure 5-9 uses a larger left margin and a negative indent value (to create an *outdent*) to align the bulleted text.

- **Spacing:** Use the Space before Paragraph item to add space before each paragraph. You use the Space after Paragraph item to add space after each paragraph. If you use both, the numbers are added together between paragraphs. Click, enter a value, and press Enter, or drag in either direction. (This setting isn't available for Classic text.)

✓ **Text Justify:** Fully justified text usually adds extra space between the words to fill out the lines of text. However, you may want to add extra space between the letters. Choose between the Word Spacing and Letter Spacing options.

If you're creating Classic text, you change the line spacing in the Paragraph section. Click the Line Spacing item, enter a value and press Enter, or drag in either direction. For TLF text, you use the Leading item in the Character section, as described in the previous section of this chapter.

Flash remembers paragraph properties from movie to movie. When you change paragraph properties for one movie, those properties rear their ugly heads in your next movie. If your text automatically indents at the beginning of paragraphs or has extra space between the paragraphs, check the Paragraph section of the Property inspector.

Going with the flow

TLF text (but not Classic text) lets you easily create columns, flow text from one text block to another, and more. Most of the features in this section are new. The Container and Flow section of the Property inspector enables you to use these features:

✓ **Behavior:** This item controls how words wrap to the next line. By default, if you have more text than can fit in the text block's width, the words wrap (the Multiline option). You can also choose Single Line (no wrapping), Multiline No Wrap (you must press Enter to get a new line), and Password (shows asterisks). (The Password option is available when you create editable text, as we describe earlier in this chapter.)

This setting also applies to your published movie. For example, if you create editable text, you might let users write a short novel in an input box. In that case, you certainly want the text to wrap, because who ever heard of a novel all on one line? The Password setting would be an obvious choice in a text box where you are requesting a password from your Web site's viewers.

✓ **Maximum Characters:** This setting applies only to Editable text (called Input text if you're using Classic text) and specifies the maximum allowable characters that users can type in a text box. For example, you could limit a ZIP code to five digits. For Classic text, this setting is in the Options section.

✓ **Vertical alignment:** You can control where your text sits vertically in the text block. Your options are Top, Center, Bottom, and Justify. Justified text spreads out to take up the entire text block, in effect changing the leading (line spacing). Classic text doesn't offer this setting.

✓ **Column gutters:** The *gutter* is the width between the columns. Click, enter a value in pixels, and press Enter, or drag the slider.

Figure 5-10: You can use your space in more ways when you have the option to create columns.

✓ **Columns:** Columns are new and available only for TLF text. Click, enter the number of columns you want, and press Enter, or drag the slider. Figure 5-10 shows some text in one column on the left and two columns on the right.

✓ **Padding:** *Padding* is the space between the text and the border of the text block. It's like a margin except that you can set it in all four directions. Padding isn't available for Classic text. Use the L (left), R (right), T (top), and B (bottom) items to enter the padding in pixels.

✓ **Container border color:** If you're using TLF text, you can give the text block (also called a *container*) a border, as you see in Figure 5-10. Click the Container Border Color swatch and choose a color or use the swatch with the red, diagonal line to remove the border. When you add a border, the padding (just discussed) becomes more important because a little white space between the border and the text helps legibility.

✓ **Container background color:** Your text block can have a background (fill) color, but be sure that the background doesn't interfere with your text. Click the Container Background Color swatch and choose a color or use the swatch with the red, diagonal line to remove the background.

✓ **1st Line Offset:** You can add space between the top of the text block and the text using the Padding feature (described earlier in this list), but the 1st Line Offset drop-down list offers a more flexible way to add space at the top. Choose Ascent to count to the top of the highest letter. Choose Line Height to include the normal spacing between the lines of text. The Auto option automatically generates a value that seems to be similar to Ascent. Then choose the pt item to display a value where you can click, enter an offset value in points, and press Enter, or drag the slider.

Specifying text block properties

Some text settings are available when you select the text block, as opposed to text within the text block. The distinction isn't always intuitive and to confuse matters, many settings appear in the Property inspector in both cases. In this section, we cover settings that you can specify only when you select the text block.

Setting position and size

The Position and Size section of the Property inspector is no different for a text block than for any other object that you might select. Here, you can specify the X (horizontal) and Y (vertical) position, measured from the upper-left corner of the Stage. You can change the size of the text block by adjusting the W (width) and H (height) values. Of course, you can just select the text block and drag, but these settings offer you much more precision. For each setting, click, type a value, and press Enter, or drag the slider.

Specifying 3D position and view

The 3D Position and View section determines how the text looks in 3D space. For example, by increasing the Z value, you can make the text look smaller, as if it is farther away. For more information, see "Changing 3D position and rotation" in Chapter 7.

You can apply color effects, such as transparency, brightness, and tints to text. You also add *blends,* which affect how overlapping text blends. Because these effects also apply to certain types of symbols, we cover them in Chapter 7. Finally, you can add cool effects, called *filters,* to text. For more on filters, see the end of this chapter.

Flowing text from one container to another

The main purpose for the new text container settings is to flow text from one text block to another. If you move or resize either text block, the text reflows, adjusting to the new situation. To link two text blocks, follow these steps:

1. **Choose the Text tool in the Tools panel. Drag from left to right to define the desired width.**

2. **Type your text.**

   Type enough text so that you can't see it all. You can resize the height by dragging on the top or bottom handles, but you want some text to be hidden so that it can flow to the second text block.

3. **Repeat Step 1 to create a second text block.**

   Don't type text in the second text block because the text will flow from the first text block.

4. **Click the Selection tool in the Tools panel and select the first text block.**

   You see two small boxes on the text block's border. The left box, called the *in port*, flows text into the text block; the right box, called the *out port*, flows text out of it.

5. **Click the out port on the text block's border.**

   You see a special cursor, as shown in Figure 5-11. As you move the cursor away from the box, it changes to look like a box with text inside.

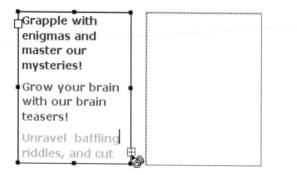

Figure 5-11: Flow text from one container to another.

6. **Click inside the second text block.**

   The text flows to the second text block, and you see a line connecting the outgoing box of the first text block and the incoming box of the second text block, as shown in Figure 5-12.

7. **To get the text just the way you want it, resize one or both of the text blocks by dragging the top or bottom square handles, as shown in Figure 5-13.**

Figure 5-12: After clicking inside the second text block, the text flows from the first text block.

Figure 5-13: The text now flows nicely and doesn't confuse the brain.

Creating Cool Text Effects

Flash wouldn't be worth its salt if you couldn't create some flashy effects with text. You can manipulate text in several ways:

- **Transform text just like other objects.** In other words, you can scale, rotate, skew, and flip text. Select the text block (not the text itself) first. (Chapter 4 explains the many ways that you can transform objects.) Figure 5-14 shows an example of skewed text.

- **Convert type to shapes by breaking it apart.** Select the text and choose Modify➪Break Apart. Flash creates separate shapes from each letter so that you can then edit the text in the same way that you edit shapes. However, you can no longer edit the text as text, so check your words before converting them! (Refer to Figure 5-1 for an example of text turned into shapes.)

If you're creating Classic text, the first time that you use the Break Apart command, words are broken up into individual letters. Use the command again, and letters are turned into shapes.

✔ **Apply special graphic effects (called *filters*) to text.** Select the text block for TLF text (but select the text itself for Classic text) and expand the Filters section of the Property inspector. Click the Add Filter button at the bottom and choose one (or more) of the following filters: Drop Shadow, Blur, Glow, Bevel, Gradient Glow, Gradient Bevel, or Adjust Color. Each filter has a number of settings that you can adjust to get just the right effect. Figure 5-15 shows these effects in the order listed here.

Figure 5-14: This text is skewed to match the angles of the skewed rectangles.

You can animate text to your heart's content. To animate text, you usually break it apart so that you can move letters individually. You can then use the Modify➪Timeline➪Distribute to Layers command to put each letter on a separate layer. After that, you can animate each letter. (See Chapter 9 for the details on animation.)

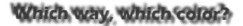

Am I seeing double?

Is my vision blurred?

I'm getting a weird, glowy feeling

IS IT COMING AT ME?

Is it coming or going?

Which way, which color?

Is it a picture?

Figure 5-15: Filters are shortcuts to cool looking (but not necessarily legible) text.

6

Layering It On

In This Chapter

▷ Creating layers

▷ Modifying layers

▷ Using guide layers

▷ Creating holes with mask layers

lash lets you organize objects on the Stage in layers. *Layers* keep objects separated from each other. Flash either combines or creates cutouts when two objects overlap if you don't use the object-drawing model (as we explain in Chapter 3). By placing the two objects on different layers, though, you avoid this behavior yet retain the appearance of overlapping objects. In addition, by rearranging your layers, you can easily rearrange the order of your objects — that is, which objects appear to be on top and which appear to be on the bottom.

Layers are also necessary for error-free animation. To move one object across the Stage in front of other objects, such as a background, you need to put the moving object on its own layer. If you want to animate several objects across the Stage, put each object on a separate layer.

You can hide layers. Flash doesn't display objects on hidden layers. Hidden layers are great for hiding some objects temporarily while you figure out what to do with all the rest of the stuff on the Stage.

Finally, you use layers as a storage place for sounds and ActionScript code. (See Chapter 10 to find out more about ActionScript.) For example, you can name a layer Music and put your music there. Then you can easily find the music if you want to change it. Layers provide a great way to keep the various components of your movie organized. In this chapter, you get all the information you need to use layers effectively.

Creating Layers

Flash lists layers at the left side of the Timeline. New movies start out with one layer, named Layer 1. You can, and should, change the name of this layer and new layers to something more descriptive, as shown in Figure 6-1.

Figure 6-1: Flash keeps you organized by listing all your layers.

If you're the organized type, think about your animation in advance and decide which layers you need. However, animations often don't work out the way you plan, and you might find yourself creating layers after you create objects. Either way, your method for creating layers is the same.

 To create a layer, click the New Layer button at the bottom of the layer list (or choose Insert➪Timeline➪Layer). Flash displays the new layer above the active layer and makes the new layer active, as shown in Figure 6-2. To name the layer, double-click its name, type something meaningful, and then press Enter (Windows) or Return (Mac).

Figure 6-2: A new layer.

Using layers

Any object that you create goes on the active layer. You can tell which layer is active because it's highlighted and has a pencil icon next to its name. (Refer to the Lines layer in Figure 6-1.) To change the active layer, just click any inactive layer's name. You can also click anywhere in the layer's row on the Timeline.

To help make your work easier, Flash automatically changes the active layer to match any object that you select. So, if you're working on a layer named Text and then select a shape on a layer named Shapes, Flash automatically activates the Shapes layer. Any new objects that you create are now on the Shapes layer. Of course, if that's not the layer you want, switch to any other layer at any time by clicking its name.

When you click a layer to make it active, Flash selects all the objects on that layer that exist in the current frame. (Even if a layer is already active, you can click its name to select all its objects.) This feature is helpful for working with all the objects on a layer and discovering which objects a layer contains. If you don't want the objects selected, click anywhere there's not an object.

Because in many cases, each animated object needs to be on its own layer, you often need to distribute objects to their own layers. Select the objects and choose Modify⇨Timeline⇨Distribute to Layers. This command saves lots of work!

Changing layer states

Besides being active or inactive, layers have three states that determine how objects on that layer function or look; you can

- ✔ Show or hide a layer.
- ✔ Lock or unlock it.
- ✔ Display objects on a layer as outlines.

Use these states to help you organize how you work. The more objects and more layers that you have, the more you need to use these layer states.

Above the layer list, on the right side, you see an eye, a lock, and a box. These aren't mystical symbols. The following sections explain what they are and how to use them.

Show/Hide

Use the Show/Hide icon (as shown at the left) to hide all objects on a layer (also called *hiding a layer),* reducing clutter while you work. To hide a layer, click below the Show/Hide icon on that layer's row. Flash places a red X under the eye icon. All the objects on that layer disappear. Click the X to get them back again. To hide (or show) all the objects on the Stage, click the Show/Hide icon itself.

Keep in mind, however, that you can't work on a hidden layer. And, don't forget hidden layers because by default, they do appear in your published movies. (For information about specifying whether hidden layers appear in published movies, see Chapter 13.)

To show or hide all layers *except* one, Alt-click (Windows) or Option-click (Mac) below the Show/Hide icon on that layer's row. You can also right-click (Windows) or Control-click (Mac) a layer and choose Hide Others from the contextual menu that appears.

Lock/Unlock

Use Lock/Unlock to prevent objects from being edited by locking their layers. Lock a layer when you want to avoid changing objects by mistake. To lock a layer, click below the lock icon on that layer's row. Flash places a lock in the layer's row. Click the lock to unlock the layer again. The lock disappears, and you can now edit objects on that layer. You can lock *all* layers by clicking the lock icon directly. Click the lock icon again to unlock all the layers.

To lock or unlock all layers *except* one layer, Alt-click (Windows) or Option-click (Mac) below the lock icon on that layer's row. You can also right-click (Windows) or Control-click (Mac) a layer and choose Lock Others in the contextual menu.

Outlines

Use Outlines to display objects as outlines of different colors. Outlines help you see which layer objects are on because each layer uses a different color, as shown in Figure 6-3. To display outlines, follow these steps:

1. **Click below the Outlines (box) icon on that layer's row.**

   Flash puts a colored box in the layer's row, and all objects on that layer are now shown as outlines in that color. (Text is still filled in, however.)

2. **Click the box to display objects on that layer normally.**

To display *all* layers as outlines, click the Outlines icon directly. Click it again to see your objects as normal. You can work on outlined layers, but all new objects appear as outlines, so telling how they appear when displayed normally is difficult.

To display all layers as outlines except for one layer, Alt-click (Windows) or Option-click (Mac) below the Outline icon on that layer's row.

Figure 6-3: All the objects on the Stage are shown as outlines except for text.

Getting Those Layers Right

Good layer housekeeping can help keep you sane. Delete layers that you no longer need. Rename layers when their content changes. Copy layers with their entire contents rather than re-create them from scratch. Here, we explain how to keep control over layers.

You can select more than one layer at a time. To select a contiguous group, click the first layer, hold down the Shift key, and then click the last layer in the group. To select more than one layer when they're not all together in a group, click the first layer, press and hold Ctrl (Windows) or ⌘ (Mac), and then click any additional layers that you want to select.

Deleting layers

When you work, you might find that a layer no longer has any objects. It's a layer without a purpose in life, so delete it. Select the layer and click the Trash can icon at the bottom of the layer list. You can also drag the layer to the Trash can (Delete) icon.

When you delete a layer, you delete everything on the layer. However, some objects on a layer might not be visible because you see only what exists on the Stage in the current frame. For example, if you introduce a circle in Frame 15 of a layer named Circle but you're in Frame 1, you don't see that circle. Deleting the Circle layer, however, deletes the circle although you can't see it. (We discuss frames in more detail in Chapter 9.)

To check for objects on a layer, right-click the layer and choose Hide Others from the contextual menu. Click the first frame on the Timeline and then press Enter (Windows) or Return (Mac) to run any existing animation. Objects on that layer appear during the animation, if they exist.

Copying layers

You can copy a layer, along with its entire contents, throughout all frames. If you create a great bouncing ball but now want two balls, copy the layer. You can then modify the position of the second ball throughout the Timeline without having to re-create the ball itself. Now you have two bouncing balls.

To copy and paste a layer, follow these steps:

1. **Click the layer name to select the layer.**
2. **Choose Edit➪Timeline➪Copy Frames.**

3. **Click the New Layer button to create a new layer.**
4. **Click the new layer to make its frames active.**
5. **Choose Edit➪Timeline➪Paste Frames.**

Renaming layers

Rename a layer whenever you want. By default, Flash names layers Layer 1, Layer 2, and so on. When you use a layer, rename it to reflect its contents. To rename a layer, double-click the layer name and type a new name. Then press Enter (Windows) or Return (Mac).

Reordering layers

In Chapter 4, we explain how to change the order of objects on the Stage when they're on the same layer. When objects are on different layers, though, a new rule applies: The order of the layers indicates the display order of objects on the Stage. Therefore, objects on the uppermost layer in the list are always on top, objects on the second layer appear one level down, and so on. Objects on the last layer in the list appear on the bottom level of the Stage, behind everything else.

In fact, a simple and effective way to control object stacking is to put objects on different layers and then move the layers higher or lower in the layer list. To move a layer, just click and drag it within the layer list to the desired position. Figure 6-4 shows an example before and after moving a layer. The ball and the oval are on different layers. The top image looks a little odd, but when you reorder the layers, their objects are reordered as well — you can then see a ball and its shadow.

Figure 6-4: Change layer order to change the object order on those layers.

Changing the layer order can help you more easily select and edit objects that are covered by other objects. Simply drag the layer to the top of the list, and the objects in that list then appear on top. When you finish editing the objects, drag the layer back to its original location.

Organizing layers

Sometimes layers can get out of hand. You might have several layers with sounds on them or several layers for each animation. Tame those layers by putting them into folders. Instant organization! For example, you could create a Sounds folder and folders for each animation group.

To create a folder, click the New Folder icon below the layer list. You see a new folder just above the active layer. Name the folder the same way you name a layer: Double-click it, type the name, and then press Enter (Windows) or Return (Mac). You can distinguish a folder from a layer by its folder icon.

After you have a folder, you fill it up with layers by dragging layers into it. Click and drag a layer just under the folder's name and then release the mouse button. At the same time, the layer's name becomes indented so that you can easily tell that it's in a folder, as shown in Figure 6-5.

Figure 6-5: Put your layers into folders to keep yourself organized.

You can even put folders in folders. Just drag one folder into another. A folder within a folder is a *nested* folder, and the folder that it's in is the *parent* folder.

Here are some other things that you can do with folders:

- **Remove a folder from a folder.** Drag the nested folder above its parent folder.

- **Remove a layer from a folder.** Drag the layer above the folder name or to another location where it doesn't darken a folder.

- **Collapse or expand individual folders.** Click the folder's arrow, at the left of its icon.

- **Expand or collapse all folders.** Right-click (Windows) or Control-click (Mac) and then choose Expand All Folders or Collapse All Folders from the contextual menu.

- **Hide or lock an entire folder and its layers.** You can hide or lock a folder just like you hide or lock a layer. (See the "Changing layer states" section, earlier in this chapter.) Click below the eye (Show/Hide) or lock (Lock/Unlock) icon on the folder's row.

- **Reorder folders.** You can change the order of folders, which automatically changes the order of the layers that they contain. Just drag any folder up or down. For more information, see the preceding section.

- **Copy the contents of a folder to another folder.** To make a quick shortcut for copying layers and their contents, you can copy folders. Collapse the folder and click the folder name. Choose Edit⇨Timeline⇨Copy Frames, and then create a new folder. With the new folder active, choose Edit⇨Timeline⇨Paste Frames.

- **Delete folders.** Delete folders the same way you delete layers. Select the folder and then click the Trash can icon.

Deleting a folder deletes all layers in the folder and everything on those layers. Luckily, Flash warns you before you take the plunge.

Modifying layer properties

You can use the Layer Properties dialog box, as shown in Figure 6-6, to change certain layer properties, such as the color used for the layer's outlines and the layer height. Most settings, however, are easily accessible from the layer list. Select a layer (or a folder) and choose Modify⇨Timeline⇨Layer Properties to open the Layer Properties dialog box.

Here's how to use this dialog box to get the most from your layers:

- **The Name text box displays the current name of the layer.** You can rename the layer here if you want.

- **Change the layer states by selecting (or deselecting) the appropriate check boxes.** Usually, you change these states directly in the layer list, as we explain earlier in this chapter, in the "Changing layer states" section.

✔ **You can change the type of layer (guide or mask) by choosing from the list of layer types.** We cover guide and mask layers later in this chapter.

✔ **You can change the color that Flash uses when the layer is displayed as outlines.** Click the Outline Color swatch and choose another color in the color palette.

✔ **Select the View Layer as Outlines check box to turn on outlines.** As we explain earlier in this section, you can accomplish this task easily from the layer listing.

Layer Properties

Name: Lines

☑ Show ☑ Lock

Type: ◉ Normal
○ Mask
○ Masked
○ Folder
○ Guide

Outline color: ▨

☐ View layer as outlines

Layer height: 100% ▾

OK

Cancel

Figure 6-6: Fine-tune layer settings here.

✔ **You can change the layer height to two or three times the normal height.** One reason to change the height of a layer is to more easily view sound waves on a layer that contains a sound. Open the Layer Height drop-down list and choose a value.

After you finish using the Layer Properties dialog box, click OK.

Another reason to display a larger layer height is to see larger previews of your keyframes in the Timeline. (Click the Options menu in the upper-right corner of the Timeline and choose Preview or Preview in Context from the pop-up menu.)

Working with Guide Layers

A *guide layer* is a layer that's invisible in the final, published animation. You can use guide layers for the following purposes:

✔ **Layout:** Although you can display onscreen guides to help you draw precisely (as we describe in Chapter 3), you can also place gridlines on guide layers to help you lay out the Stage, as shown in Figure 6-7. Graphic designers use these types of gridlines to figure out how to create a balanced, pleasing effect in their art.

✔ **Drawing:** You can import a bitmap graphic onto a guide layer and draw over the graphic on a regular layer by using the Flash drawing tools. This technique of drawing over a graphic can be a big help when creating your artwork.

In previous versions of Flash, guide layers also allowed you to guide an animated object along a path. You don't need guide layers for this purpose any more. However, you can still create the type of tween used in previous versions; it's called a Classic Tween. For more information on animation, see Chapter 9.

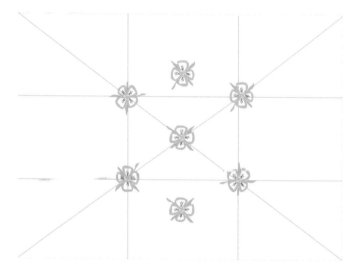

Figure 6-7: A grid on a guide layer helps you lay out your design.

Of course, you could use a regular layer and then erase whatever you don't want to appear in the final movie. But if you need to go back and make changes, you would have to create the guide layer again. Using a guide layer gives you the flexibility of keeping the layer in the movie file, knowing that it will never appear in the published animation.

Hidden layers appear in the published SWF file, but guide layers don't appear.

To create a guide layer, create a new layer. Then right-click (Windows) or Control-click (Mac) and choose Guide from the contextual menu. The layer is now a guide layer. Use the same procedure to convert a guide layer back to a regular layer.

Opening Windows with Mask Layers

A *mask layer* hides every object on its related layers except those inside a filled shape or text object. You can use mask layers to create peepholes or spotlight effects. Figure 6-8 shows a keyhole shape on a mask layer that hides the entire scene except for the part within the keyhole. The Indian bazaar scene is a rectangle much larger than the section displayed through the keyhole.

Creating a mask effect

Follow these steps to create a mask layer, the object on the mask layer, and the objects behind the mask layer:

Figure 6-8: You can use a mask layer to create a hole through which you can see the layer or layers below.

1. **Create the objects that you want to show through the hole in the mask layer.**

    These objects can be on one or more layers. Place all the layers that you want to be masked next to each other and at the top of the layer list.

2. **Select the topmost layer in the layer list and then click the New Layer button to create a new layer at the top of the list.**

    This layer will become the mask layer.

3. **Create, insert, or import one filled shape, text, or an instance of a symbol on the new layer.**

    See Chapter 7 for more about symbols.

    The filled part of the shape, text, or instance will become the hole. In other words, it will be transparent. For an example, see the keyhole shape in Figure 6-8. Unfilled portions of the object will become opaque, so everything will become the opposite of its current state.

4. **Right-click (Windows) or Control-click (Mac) the layer's name and then choose Mask from the contextual menu.**

    Flash turns the layer into a mask layer and locks the mask layer as well as the layer just below it in the layer list. The masked layer is indented in the layer list. You see the mask effect displayed. (To link more than one layer to the mask layer, see the next section, "Editing mask layers.")

Editing mask layers

Because Flash locks both the mask layer and the layer or layers that are masked, you cannot edit them until you unlock them. Click the lock icon above the layer list to unlock all the layers, or unlock the mask and masked layers only. Flash removes the mask effect. After you finish editing the layers, lock them again to redisplay the mask effect.

When you create a mask layer, Flash links only the layer directly below it to the mask layer. A layer linked to a mask layer is masked. If you place objects that you want to be masked on several layers, you need to change the property of all those layers from normal to masked.

All the layers that you want to be masked must be directly under the mask layer.

Here's how to link a layer to a mask layer:

- ✓ Drag a normal layer directly below a mask layer, and Flash links it to the mask layer in addition to existing masked layers. Then lock the layer.

- ✓ Right-click (Windows) or Control-click (Mac) the layer and choose Properties. Then select the Mask option in the Layer Properties dialog box. Then lock the layer.

Similarly, you can unlink a layer from its mask layer by using one of these methods:

- ✓ Drag the linked layer above the mask layer.

- ✓ Right-click (Windows) or Control-click (Mac) the layer and choose Properties. Then select the Normal option in the Layer Properties dialog box.

Mask layers are more fun when you animate them. You can move them, change their sizes, and change their shapes. If you create a keyhole like the one shown in Figure 6-8, you can move the keyhole past the masked layers, revealing what lies beneath while the keyhole moves. You can use the same technique to create an effect of a spotlight moving around a stage, revealing whatever it lights up. (Chapter 9 covers animation.)

Part III
Getting Symbolic

The 5th Wave — By Rich Tennant

"Well, shoot—I know the animation's moving a mite too fast, but <u>dang</u> if I can find a 'mosey' function in the toolbox!"

In this part . . .

Symbols can represent the deeper levels of life, and Flash symbols let you get down deep into the mechanics of animation. In this part, you discover three kinds of symbols — graphic symbols, button symbols, and movie clip symbols — and how to use them.

Manipulating symbols is a critical feature of Flash. Symbols enable you to easily place duplicate graphics in your movie without significantly increasing the movie's size, and symbols are necessary when you start to animate. This part of the book also gives you the lowdown on buttons, which are central to the Web lifestyle in the 21st century. Flash lets you create buttons that change when you pass the mouse cursor over them and again when you click them. You can even make animated buttons. Part III provides you with the basis for creating great animations.

Heavy Symbolism

Flash offers a way to simplify your work, using symbols. A *symbol* can be any object or combination of objects, animation, or a button. When you create a symbol, the objects (or animation or button) become one object. Sounds like grouping, yes? (If you've already read Chapter 4, you know what we mean.) The difference is that Flash stores the definition of the symbol in the Library. (To open the Library, choose Window⬄Library.) From the Library, you can now effortlessly insert multiple copies of the symbol into your movie. Each copy is called an *instance*.

Besides making your life easier when you want to use a set of objects more than once, the use of symbols significantly reduces the size of your files. Instead of storing each instance that you use, Flash stores one definition for the symbol and refers to that definition each time you display an instance of the symbol. You can place symbols inside other symbols, which is called *nesting*. Used this way, symbols are the building blocks for complex graphics and animation. Motion-tweened animation requires symbols, groups, or text, so you often create symbols when preparing to animate. (Chapter 9 explains tweened animation.)

So, symbols are all-around good guys, and you should use them as much as possible.

Understanding Symbol Types

Flash offers three types of symbols: graphic, movie clip, and button. Each type is made up of one or more objects or animation, but each type has a different purpose. Understanding these types is important to understanding symbols and Flash animation in general.

Using graphic symbols

Graphic symbols are the simplest and most obvious type of symbol. When you create a Flash movie, you create objects on the Stage. Some objects may remain still, such as backgrounds. Other objects are animated — after all, what would Flash be without animation? Use graphic symbols for collections of static objects or for simple animation. Figure 7-1 shows a graphic symbol created from several curves and circles.

You create graphic symbols to reduce the size of your file and to make it easier to add multiple copies of a graphic to your movie. Symbols are stored in the Library and are available to not only the movie in which you create them but also to any other movie. You don't have to re-create the wheel.

Flash ignores sounds and ActionScript inside graphic symbols. ActionScript code (which we explain in detail in Chapter 10) is the key to creating interactive movies. For that reason, don't use graphic symbols if you want to use ActionScript to directly control them — use movie clip symbols instead.

Figure 7-1: A graphic symbol, created from several objects, has a single selection border.

Using movie clip symbols

A *movie clip* is like a movie within your movie that you can manipulate by using interactive controls (which you can read about in Chapter 10). Movie clips are crucial for complex animation and especially for interactive animation. A movie clip has its own Timeline independent of the movie's main Timeline. For example, you can go to a movie clip at any point in the movie, play it, and then return to where you left off on the Timeline. You can also attach movie clips to buttons. We explain how to create movie clips in this chapter; Chapter 8 discusses using movie clips with buttons. Chapter 9 covers using movie clips in animation, and Chapter 10 explains how to use and control movie clips by using interactive controls.

Flash comes with a library of *components,* which are special movie clips that allow you to add user-interface elements — such as radio buttons, check boxes, and scroll bars — to your movies. Choose Window➪Components, expand the User Interface item, and drag one of your choices to the Stage. Then use the Component Parameters section of the Property inspector (choose Window➪Properties if you need to open the Property inspector) to set the parameters of the component. For example, you can choose the CheckBox item and then specify its label and other properties. For more information on components, see Chapter 12.

Using button symbols

Button symbols create *buttons* — those little graphics that you click on Web pages to take you to other pages on the site or the Internet. In Flash, you can use buttons for this type of navigation, but you can also use buttons to interact with your site. For example, you can let viewers decide whether they want to see a movie — when they click the button, the movie starts. You can also use advanced scripting to create buttons that control interactive games and other viewer activities. However you want to use buttons, button symbols are the way to start. You can add movie clips and interactive controls to buttons. Find out about buttons in Chapter 8.

Creating Symbols

For graphic symbols and button symbols, usually you create the objects that you need and then turn them into a symbol. The same is true of movie clips if they are static and you use ActionScript to control them. However, when you use a movie clip as a type of animation, you can use one of two approaches:

- Create an animation on the Stage and then convert it to a movie clip symbol.
- Create the movie clip symbol, create the initial objects, and then create the animation.

In the next few sections, we explain the various ways of creating symbols, for whichever purpose you want to use them.

Each type of symbol has its own icon that's used in the Library. The following table shows what type of symbol each icon represents:

Symbol	What It Represents
	Movie clip
	Button
Graphic icon	Graphic

Creating symbols from existing objects

To create a symbol from unanimated objects you've already created, follow these steps:

1. **On the Stage, select the objects that you want to convert to a symbol.**

2. **Choose Modify⇨Convert to Symbol, or press F8.**

   The Convert to Symbol dialog box opens, as shown in Figure 7-2.

3. **In the Name text box, type a name for the symbol.**

   A common convention is to name the symbol in a way that's unique and also indicates the symbol type. For example, btn_ help could be the name for a button symbol that will become a Help button on a Web site.

   Convert to Symbol

   Name: Symbol 1

   Type: Movie Clip ▼ Registration: ●○○

   Folder: Library root

   Advanced ▶

   OK

   Cancel

   Figure 7-2: The Convert to Symbol dialog box.

4. **In the Type list, select the type of symbol you want to create: graphic, button, or movie clip.**

5. **Click the Folder link to specify where to store the symbol in the Library.**

   The default option puts the symbol in the Library root. When you click the Folder link, the Move to Folder dialog box opens. You can choose the Existing Folder option and choose a folder that you created in the Library. (We explain how to create folders in the Library in Chapter 2.) You can even use the New Folder option and create a new folder on the spot. Click Select to close the dialog box.

6. **Choose the desired registration point in the Registration grid.**

The *registration point* determines how Flash applies certain transformations, such as rotation, to the symbol. (See Chapter 4 for a discussion of registration points.) The default registration point is at the upper-left corner of the symbol.

7. Click OK to create the symbol and close the dialog box.

The objects that you selected become one object, indicated by a single selection border around all the objects. Flash also stores the symbol in the Library. (Chapter 2 explains how to use the Library.)

Creating empty symbols

Rather than create a symbol from existing objects, you can create an empty symbol and then create the objects for the symbol. If you know in advance that you want to create a symbol, you can use this method.

To create an empty symbol, follow these steps:

1. With no objects selected, choose Insert⇨New Symbol, or press Ctrl+F8 (Windows) or ⌘+F8 (Mac).

The Create New Symbol dialog box opens.

2. In the Name text box, type a name for the symbol.

3. In the Type list, select the type of symbol you want to create — graphic, button, or movie clip — and then click OK.

Flash switches to symbol-editing mode, which we describe in the section "Editing symbols," later in this chapter.

4. Create the objects or animation for the symbol in the same way you do in regular movie-editing mode.

5. Choose Edit⇨Edit Document to leave symbol-editing mode and return to your movie.

Your new symbol disappears! Don't worry — Flash saved the symbol in the Library. To find out how to insert an instance of the symbol on the Stage, see the "Inserting instances" section.

Converting an animation to a movie clip symbol

You can create a movie clip symbol by converting regular animation to a movie clip. Use this method when you already have the animation created on the Timeline. To convert an animation on the Stage to a movie clip symbol, follow these steps:

1. On the layer listing, select all layers containing the animation by clicking the first layer and pressing Shift while you click the last layer in the group.

Alternatively, you can press Ctrl (Windows) or ⌘ (Mac) and click additional layers.

2. **On the Timeline, right-click (Windows) or Control-click (Mac) and choose Copy Frames to copy all the frames of the animation to the Clipboard.**

   Alternatively, you can choose Edit⇨Timeline⇨Copy Frames.

3. **With no objects selected (click somewhere off the Stage to be sure that no objects are selected), choose Insert⇨New Symbol.**

   The Create New Symbol dialog box opens.

4. **In the Name text box, type a name for the movie clip.**

5. **In the Type list, select Movie Clip as the type of symbol. Then click OK.**

   Flash switches to symbol-editing mode so that you can edit the symbol.

6. **Click the first frame of the Timeline to set the start of the movie clip symbol.**

7. **Choose Edit⇨Timeline⇨Paste Frames to paste the animation into the Timeline and create the symbol.**

   You now see the animation on your screen in symbol editing mode, as shown in Figure 7-3. We discuss editing symbols later in this chapter.

Figure 7-3: If you want lots of fruit trucks, turn the animation into a movie clip symbol.

8. **To return to the main movie and Timeline, choose Edit⇨Edit Document.**

9. **To delete the animation from the main movie (now that you've saved it in a movie clip), select all layers as you did in Step 1 and choose Edit⇨Timeline⇨Remove Frames.**

   You can delete the animation from the main movie because your Library now has a movie clip that contains that animation. When you choose the movie clip in the Library panel, you can click the small Play button in the upper-right corner of the Library panel's window to play the animation.

Creating a symbol by duplicating a symbol

One more way to create a graphic, button, or movie symbol is to duplicate an existing symbol. To duplicate a symbol, follow these steps:

1. **Open the Library. (Choose Window⇨Library.)**

2. **Select the symbol that you want to duplicate.**

3. **Click the Options menu in the upper-right corner of the Library window and choose Duplicate.**

   Flash opens the Duplicate Symbol dialog box.

4. **In the Name text box, type a name for the duplicate. Select the type of symbol that you want to create if you want a different kind from the original.**

5. **Click OK to close the dialog box and create the duplicate symbol.**

Modifying Symbols

Flash is a master of flexibility, and sometimes you need to make changes. Of course, you can change symbols after you create them. Here we explain the procedures you need to know.

Changing the properties of a symbol

You might need to change a symbol's properties. For example, you might create a graphic symbol and then realize that you need it to be a movie clip. No problem!

To change the properties of a symbol, follow these steps:

1. **Choose Window⇨Library to open the Library.**

2. **Right-click (Windows) or Control-click (Mac) the symbol's icon (not its name) and choose Properties.**

The Symbol Properties dialog box opens.

3. **If the symbol is a graphic, button, or movie clip, select the type of symbol that you want in the Type list and then click OK.**

   Note that this change doesn't affect symbols that you've already inserted on the Stage.

Editing symbols

An *instance* is a copy of a symbol that you insert into your movie. Part of the power of symbols lies in their control over instances. If you edit a symbol, Flash updates all instances of that symbol in the movie. You can change a symbol once and save yourself the time of creating the same change for every instance of that symbol. For that reason, it's worthwhile to make a symbol whenever you want to use a certain shape or group of shapes more than once.

You can edit a symbol in three modes:

- **Edit in symbol-editing mode.** Switches you to symbol-editing mode. You see only the symbol. Right-click (Windows) or Control-click (Mac) a selected symbol and choose Edit.

- **Edit in place.** Lets you edit a symbol while still viewing other objects on the Stage. Other objects are dimmed while you edit the symbol. Right-click (Windows) or Control-click (Mac) a selected symbol and choose Edit in Place.

- **Edit in a new window.** Opens a new window where you can edit your symbol. You see only the symbol. Right-click (Windows) or Control-click (Mac) a selected symbol and choose Edit in New Window.

The value of editing in place is that you can see how your change works with the rest of the objects that you have on the Stage. For example, if you want to make your symbol bigger, you may need to make sure that it doesn't obscure some nearby text. However, if you have lots of stuff on the Stage, editing in symbol-editing mode or in a new window can help you focus more easily on the symbol itself.

To edit a symbol, follow these steps:

1. **Select any instance of the symbol on the Stage.**

2. **Right-click (Windows) or Control-click (Mac) the instance and choose Edit, Edit in Place, or Edit in New Window.**

   Choosing Edit puts you into symbol-editing mode. Flash displays the symbol name at the top of the screen. If you choose Edit in Place, other objects are dimmed, as shown in Figure 7-4.

This kaleidoscope animation is on the companion Web site at www. dummies.com/go/flashcs5fd.

3. **Edit the symbol in any way you want.**

4. **After you finish editing, do the following:**

   • *If you chose Edit or Edit in Place,* click the scene name to the left of the symbol name or choose Edit⇨Edit Document.

   • *If you chose Edit in New Window,* click the Close button.

You are now back in your main movie.

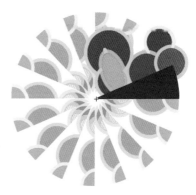

Figure 7-4: One symbol, which includes a wedge and some circles, is being edited.

Using Symbols from Other Movies

After you create a symbol and store it in the Library, you can use that Library in any other movie. You can also open the Library from any other movie and use its symbols in your current movie.

If the other movie is open and its Library is open, you can access that movie's Library from within your current movie. Libraries of any open movie are available from any other open movie. Just choose that other movie in the drop-down list at the top of the Library panel. (Choose Window⇨Library to open the Library.)

To use a symbol from the Library of another movie that is closed, follow these steps:

1. **Choose File⇨Import⇨Open External Library.**

   The Open as Library dialog box opens.

2. **Select the movie file.**

3. **Click Open.**

   Flash displays the Library of the other movie in a new Library window.

The new Library might hide your current movie's Library. Just drag the new Library by its title bar so that it rests under the current Library until it docks there. In the new Library, many Options menu items and icons are disabled to prevent you from making changes in the other movie's file.

To use a symbol from the other Library, drag the symbol onto the Stage. When you do this, Flash places a copy of the symbol in the current movie's Library. (See Chapter 2 for more information about the Library.)

You can also update or replace any graphic, button, or movie clip symbol in your movie's Library with the content of a symbol from any other Library on your hard drive or network. Accessing a symbol in this way is called *author-time sharing* of symbols or assets.

When you share a symbol while you're creating a movie (during *authoring*), the symbol in your current movie keeps its original name, but the contents take on the properties of the symbol you're sharing. If you have already replaced a symbol and the outside symbol changes (because it has been edited), use author-time sharing to update the symbol in your current drawing.

To update or replace a graphic, button, or movie clip symbol in your movie with the properties of another symbol, follow these steps:

1. **Open the Library (choose Window⇨Library) and select the symbol you want to update or replace.**

2. **From the Library Options menu, choose Properties.**

   The Symbol Properties dialog box opens.

3. **Click Advanced, if necessary, to see the expanded dialog box. In the Source section, click Browse.**

   The Locate FLA File dialog box opens.

4. **Navigate to the movie (`.fla`) file that contains the symbol you want to use. Select it and click Open.**

   The Select Symbol dialog box opens; see Figure 7-5. You see a list of the symbols in the movie that you selected.

5. **Choose a symbol and click OK.**

   When you choose a symbol, you see a preview in the preview box, so you can easily find the symbol you want, as shown in Figure 7-5. When you click OK, you're back in the Symbol Properties dialog box.

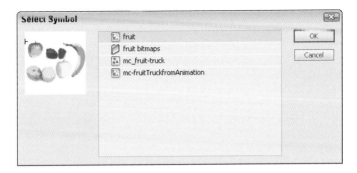

Figure 7-5: Choose another symbol to take on its properties.

6. **In the Source section of the Symbol Properties dialog box, select the Always Update Before Publish check box if you want to automatically update the symbol if the original has changed.**

   Enable this check box to create a link between the source symbol and the symbol in your current movie.

7. **Click OK.**

You now have a symbol in your Library that has its original name but looks like the symbol you chose from the other movie.

Using the Flash Library

Flash comes with three common libraries you can use. To access these libraries, choose Window➪Common Libraries and then select the one you want. Flash includes buttons, sounds, and classes (building blocks for developing ActionScript applications). These libraries are also a good place to pick up ideas and see what you can create in Flash.

Using the Flash For Dummies Library

The Flash Libraries contain some good examples, but they miss many basic shapes and simple objects, some of which are hard to draw in Flash. We decided to fill in the gaps! We created a Library of art, geometric shapes, and fun shapes that you can use in your movies. You'll find 79 items in all! The *Flash For Dummies* Library is named `Flash CS5 For Dummies Library. fla`. You can find it at `www.dummies.com/go/flashcs5fd`.

To use this Library, go to `www.dummies.com/go/flashcs5fd` and download `Flash For Dummies Library.fla`. In Windows, download it to the `Program Files\Adobe\Adobe Flash CS5\en_US\Configuration\Libraries` folder on your hard drive. (The en_US folder indicates an English version of Flash.) On the Mac, download it to the `Applications/Adobe Flash CS4/Configuration/Libraries` folder on your hard drive.

After that, you can open this Library the same way you open other common Libraries: Choose Window⇨Common Libraries⇨Flash CS5 For Dummies Library.fla. We hope you enjoy it!

Working with Instances, for Instance

After you create a symbol, you can use it in many ways. You can insert it in your movie, inside other symbols, or even in other movies. Each copy of the symbol is called an *instance.* You can change the properties of an instance so that it differs from its parent symbol. For example, you can change the color of an instance — the original symbol remains unchanged.

Inserting instances

To insert an instance of a symbol, follow these steps:

1. **Choose Window⇨Library (Ctrl+L or F11 for Windows or ⌘+L or F11 for the Mac) to open the Library, as shown in Figure 7-6.**

2. **In the layer list, choose the layer where you want the instance to be placed.**

   See Chapter 6 for the full story on layers.

3. **Click a keyframe on the Timeline where you want the instance to be placed.**

   Flash places instances only in *keyframes* (frames that define a change in your animation). If you don't select a keyframe, Flash puts the instance in the first keyframe to the left of the current frame. (See Chapter 9 for more about keyframes.)

4. **Drag the symbol from the Library to the Stage.**

   You can drag from the list of items or directly from the preview at the top of the Library.

When you insert a graphic instance, you need to consider how it fits in your entire animation. For example, the instance might be the starting point for some animation, or it might be part of the background that remains static throughout the animation. Perhaps you want the instance to suddenly appear at some point in the animation. If the instance contains animation, you need to insert it at its proper starting point. (Chapter 9 explains how to copy graphics across any number of frames to create a static background and covers the entire topic of animation in detail.) A movie clip instance, however, takes up only one frame on the Timeline. It plays and loops automatically unless you create ActionScript code to control it. (Chapter 10 talks about ActionScript.)

Editing instances

A symbol's children don't have to be carbon copies of their parents, thank goodness. Instances of a symbol can differ from their parent symbol by color, type, and play mode. You can also rotate, scale, or skew an instance, leaving the parent symbol unchanged.

Figure 7-6: Insert an instance of a symbol by dragging it from the Library.

When you edit an instance, Flash remembers the changes. If you later edit the symbol, Flash doesn't forget the changes you made to the instance. Suppose that you create a red circle graphic symbol, and then you create several instances of it and change one instance to pink. Then you edit the (still red!) circle symbol to change it to an oval. All the instances are now ovals, but the one you turned pink is still pink. The instance's shape has been updated, but the pink color remains.

In the Property inspector (choose Window➪Properties) you can change an instance's color (or tint), brightness, or transparency, giving you some useful control over the appearance of your instances. To change an instance's color, brightness, or transparency, follow these steps:

1. **Select the instance.**

2. **Choose Window➪Properties to open the Property inspector.**

3. **Expand the Color Effect section and select one of these options in the Style drop-down list:**

   - *None:* Adds no color effect.
   - *Brightness:* Changes the lightness or darkness of the instance.
   - *Tint:* Changes the color of the instance.
   - *Advanced:* Changes both the color and the alpha.
   - *Alpha:* Changes the opacity/transparency of the instance.

4. **Make the desired changes, as we explain in the next few sections.**

   You see the changes that you make in the Property inspector immediately in your selected instance.

Changing brightness

When you choose Brightness in the Style drop-down list, a text box and a slider appear. Type a brightness percentage or drag the slider and see the result in the symbol instance. High brightness makes the image light, and 100% brightness makes the instance white. (It disappears if you have a white background!) Low brightness makes the image dark; 0% percent brightness turns the instance black.

Changing tint

When you choose Tint from the Style drop-down list, you can choose the color and then the amount of the color (the tint), by percentage, that you want to apply. Figure 7-7 shows the controls for this option. You can select a color by clicking the Tint Color swatch and choosing from the color swatches, by dragging the sliders, or by typing red, green, and blue values (if you know them).

Specify the percentage of the color you want to apply by typing a value in the Tint Amount text box or by dragging the slider to choose a percentage. When the percentage is set to 100%, the instance changes to the color you specified. If the percentage is set to 0%, Flash leaves the instance unchanged.

The Flash method of specifying a color gives you great flexibility and precision. You can choose a color and use the tint control to create a meld of the current color and your chosen color.

Changing color and transparency at the same time

Select Advanced from the Style drop-down menu to change the red, green, and blue color values and the transparency at the same time. Figure 7-8 shows the controls, which are complex.

Use the controls on the left to specify the color or transparency as a specific percentage of the current value. Use the controls on the right to change the color or transparency to a specific, absolute amount. Flash calculates the new color value by multiplying the current value by the percentage you specified and then adding the value from the right side. As you can see, this method provides lots of control — but it might make you crazy first.

To simply change both the color and the transparency of an instance, choose Tint from the Style drop-down list to change the color and then choose Advanced, changing only the left Alpha setting.

Changing transparency

Choose Alpha from the Style drop-down menu to change the transparency of an instance. (*Alpha* enables levels of transparency, and you can think of the term as somewhat synonymous to *opacity*.) Use the slider or type a value in the text box. A value of 0 means that your instance becomes completely transparent: In that case, when you return to the Stage, all you see is the selection border and the small plus sign that marks the symbol's registration point. When you deselect the instance, you see absolutely nothing! (Chapter 4 explains more about a symbol's registration point, including how to move it. See the section on groups.)

Figure 7-7: Changing the tint used on a symbol instance.

Figure 7-8: The Advanced controls for instances.

Partial transparency lets your background show through. A partially transparent instance blends in with your background, creating a softer effect. However, transparency is a complex feature and can slow down the loading and playing of a movie.

Adding filters and blends

You can apply special graphic effects called *filters* to text, buttons, and movie clips — but not to graphic symbols. Select the item and expand the Filters section of the Property inspector, if necessary. Click the Add Filter button and choose one (or more) of the following filters: Drop Shadow, Blur, Glow, Bevel, Gradient Glow, Gradient Bevel, or Adjust Color. The Filters section then displays further controls so that you can specify how you want the filter to look. You can get some cool effects this way. You can even add multiple filters to an object.

The Adjust Color filter is a way to change a symbol's brightness and tint in one place. Instead of choosing the color from a color swatch, as described previously in the "Changing tint" section, you adjust contrast, saturation, and hue values.

To apply filter settings from one object to another, you can copy and paste one or more filters.

To copy and paste filters, follow these steps:

1. **Select the object that has the filter (or filters) that you want.**

2. **In the Filters section of the Property inspector, select the filter that you want to copy.**

3. **Click the Clipboard button. From the pop-up menu, choose Copy Selected or Copy All.**

4. **Select the object that you want to have the filters.**

5. **Click the Clipboard button. From the pop-up menu, choose Paste.**

You can also apply blending modes to movie clips. *Blending modes* determine how movie clips that overlap blend with each other at the point of overlap. To apply a blend, select a movie clip instance (one that overlaps another instance) and adjust the color and transparency as we explain in the previous sections. Then choose a blend mode from the Blending drop-down list of the Property inspector's Display section. The results depend a lot on the colors and alpha of the overlapping symbols. You can choose from the following blending modes:

🖙 **Normal:** The default; applies colors with no change.

🖙 **Layer:** Enables you to stack symbols on top of each other with no change in their color.

🖙 **Darken:** Replaces areas lighter than the blend color, leaving the darker colors unchanged.

🖙 **Multiply:** Multiplies the color of the selected symbol and the overlap color mix (the blend color), resulting in a darker color.

🖙 **Lighten:** Replaces darker areas, leaving the lighter color.

🖙 **Screen:** Multiplies the inverse of the blend color and the symbol's color, giving a bleaching effect.

🖙 **Overlay:** Blends the two layers by multiplying or screening the colors.

🖙 **Hard Light:** Creates a spotlight effect.

🖙 **Add:** Creates a lightening dissolve effect.

🖙 **Subtract:** Creates a darkening dissolve effect.

🖙 **Difference:** Subtracts the colors, with a negative-like effect.

🖙 **Invert:** Inverts the color of the selected symbol.

🖙 **Alpha:** Applies an alpha mask, making the symbol transparent.

🖙 **Erase:** Removes all color, effectively making the selected symbol disappear!

Changing an instance's type

The instance type — graphic, movie clip, or button — comes from the symbol type, but you might want to change it. For example, if you created some animation and saved it as a graphic symbol, you might want to use it as a movie clip. Rather than change the symbol type, you can change only the type of the instance that you have inserted.

To change the instance type, follow these steps:

1. **Select the instance.**

2. **Choose Window⇨Properties to open the Property inspector.**

3. **From the Instance Behavior drop-down list, in the top section of the Property inspector, select one of the following types:**

   • *Graphic:* If the graphic contains animation, select Graphic from the Instance Behavior drop-down list. Then determine how the animation will run by expanding the Looping section of the

Property inspector. From the Options drop-down list, choose one of the following:

Loop plays the animation contained in the instance over and over during the frames occupied by the instance.

Play Once plays the animation one time from the frame you specify.

Single Frame displays any one frame of the animation. In other words, the animation doesn't play; you specify which frame the movie displays.

- *Button:* To create a button, select Button from the Instance Behavior drop-down list. Then specify how the button will function in the Tracking section of the Property inspector. From the Options drop-down list, select Track as Button if you're creating single buttons. Select Track as Menu if you're creating pop-up menus. You can specify an Instance Name in the Instance Name text box at the top of the Property inspector.

- *Movie Clip:* To create a movie clip, select Movie Clip from the Instance Behavior drop-down list. Then specify an Instance name in the Instance Name text box at the top of the Property inspector. You use this name with certain ActionScript controls so that you can refer to and control the instance. (For more information about ActionScript, see Chapter 10.)

If you select a movie clip or button instance, you can select the Cache as Bitmap check box in the Property inspector. *Runtime bitmap caching* optimizes playback of a Flash movie in a browser. Use bitmap caching only when you have a complex background that remains the same throughout the movie. By storing the background as a bitmap, the Flash player can play the animation faster and more smoothly because it doesn't have to redraw the image throughout the movie.

Replacing an instance

Suppose that you create a complex animation with bouncing bunnies all over the Stage. Suddenly your boss decides that some of the bouncing bunnies should be bouncing squirrels instead. Meanwhile, you had already edited all the bunnies to make them different sizes and colors. You need a way to replace some of the bunnies with squirrels without losing their sizes and colors.

To replace an instance, follow these steps:

1. **Create the squirrel symbol (or whichever new symbol you need).**

   Flash stores the new symbol in the Library.

2. **Select an instance of the bunny — that is, your original instance — on the Stage.**

3. Choose Window⇨Properties to open the Property inspector.

4. Click the Swap Symbol button to open the Swap Symbol dialog box, as shown in Figure 7-9.

Figure 7-9: The Swap Symbol dialog box makes life easy when you change your mind.

5. In the dialog box, select the squirrel or any other symbol.

6. Click OK to swap the symbols and close the Swap Symbol dialog box.

Flash retains your color effects and size changes but changes the symbol.

Unfortunately, you must repeat this process for all the bunnies you want to change on the Stage, but it's better than reinserting all your instances and re-creating the instance changes.

If your boss actually wants you to change all the bunnies to squirrels, your job is much simpler. Just edit the bunny symbol (as we describe in the "Editing symbols" section, earlier in this chapter) to replace the bunny image with a squirrel. Then all the instances of that symbol instantly change to squirrels yet retain the color effects and size changes that you gave them while they were still bunnies.

Duplicate a symbol when you want to use one symbol as a springboard for creating a new symbol. Follow the instructions in the "Creating Symbols" section, earlier in this chapter. Make any changes that you want to the new symbol and place instances on the Stage.

Breaking apart an instance

You can break apart an instance into its component objects. The original symbol remains in the movie's Library. You might want to use the instance as a starting point for creating a completely new symbol, or you might want to animate the components of the symbol so that they move separately. Other instances remain unchanged.

To break apart an instance, select it and choose Modify↪Break Apart. If an instance contains symbols or grouped objects within it, you can use the Break Apart command again to break apart those internal objects as well.

Changing 3D position and rotation

You can move and rotate movie clip instances in 3D space. (Other symbols aren't invited to this 3D party!) When you change a movie clip instance in this way, it's considered a 3D object. This feature let's you create the appearance of depth and adds to the realism of your movies.

When you use Flash's 3D features, you must publish your movie using the Flash Player 10 (or later) and ActionScript 3.0 settings. Earlier versions of the Flash Player and ActionScript don't support these 3D features. For more information on publish settings, see Chapter 13.

Moving movie clip instances

You can move movie clip instances in all three directions (called *translation),* using the 3D Translation tool. Of course, moving an object in the X (horizontal) and Y (vertical) directions doesn't require a special tool; however, you often want to move a movie clip instance in all three directions at once, so the 3D Translation tool is very handy. Figure 7-10 shows an instance of a movie clip before using the 3D Translation tool (on the left) and after moving it toward the viewer (on the right).

The 3D Translation tool has two modes:

✔ **Global mode:** Moves the movie clip relative to the Stage. The 3D Translation tool defaults to Global mode.

✔ **Local mode:** Moves a nested movie clip relative to its parent movie clip.

y-axis (vertical)
x-axis (horizontal)
z-axis

Figure 7-10: The 3D Translation tool moves movie clips in all three directions.

Here's how to move a movie clip instance:

1. **Choose the 3D Translation tool from the Tools panel.**

   The 3D Translation tool is part of a flyout that also contains the 3D Rotation tool. If necessary, click and hold the 3D Rotation tool (discussed next) and then choose the 3D Translation tool from the flyout.

2. **Click an instance of a movie clip symbol on the Stage.**

   The 3D axis appears on the movie clip.

3. **Set the mode, global or local, using the Global Transform button in the Options section of the Tools panel.**

   Select the Global Transform button to use global mode. Deselect the button to use local mode.

4. **To move the movie clip, do one of the following:**

   • To move the movie clip horizontally, drag the red x-axis arrow to the left or right. (The cursor shows a small "x" while you drag.)

   • To move the movie clip vertically, drag the green y-axis arrow up or down. (The cursor shows a small "y" as you drag.)

   • To move the movie clip in the z direction (toward or away from the viewer), drag the black dot at the center of the axes up (away from the viewer) or down (toward the viewer). (The cursor shows a small "z" as you drag.) If you move the movie clip toward you, it appears larger; if you move it away from you, it appears smaller.

Note that if you rotate the movie clip instance so that you're not looking directly down at it, as we explain in the next section, you see a z axis, rather than just a dot.

For greater control over 3D position, you can use the Property inspector. Display the Property inspector (Window➪Properties) and select a movie clip instance. Expand the 3D Position and View section to display the controls. To change one of these controls, click the current value and type a new value or drag up or down on the value. You can set the following controls:

✔ **X:** The horizontal position on the Stage of the movie clip instance.

✔ **Y:** The vertical position on the Stage of the movie clip instance.

✔ **Z:** The z axis position of the movie clip instance. Values less than 0 are closer to the viewer; the instance looks larger. Values higher than 0 are farther away and look smaller.

The W value is the perspective width. It shows how wide the object looks. The H value is the perspective height and shows how high the object looks. These values are for information only; you can't change them.

✔ **Perspective Angle:** The apparent angle of view. This value works like a camera lens' angle of view. The default value is 55°, which is a normal camera lens. Values can range from 1° to 179°. A higher value makes the object appear closer; a lower value makes the object appear farther away. Try adjusting the value. With certain types of rotation, the results can be positively weird!

✔ **Vanishing Point X Position:** The horizontal position of the z axis.

✔ **Vanishing Point Y Position:** The vertical position of the z axis.

The location of the vanishing point controls how an object moves along the z axis. The vanishing point affects all movie clips on the Stage that have a 3D transformation or rotation. By default, the vanishing point is at the center of the Stage.

Rotating movie clip instances

You can rotate the position of a movie clip instance in all three directions using the 3D Rotation tool. Like with translation, described just previously, you can rotate globally or locally. Figure 7-11 shows a movie clip instance in its initial state (on top) and rotated in all three directions (on the bottom).

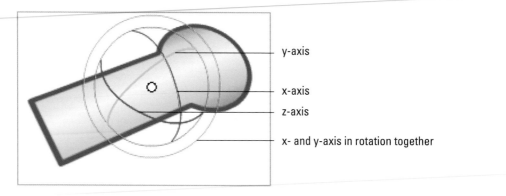

Figure 7-11: The 3D Rotation tool lets you drag your movie clips any which way.

Follow these steps to rotate your movie clip instance:

1. Choose the 3D Rotation tool from the Tools panel.

The 3D Rotation tool is part of a flyout that also contains the 3D Translation tool. If necessary, click and hold the 3D Translation tool (just discussed) and then choose the 3D Rotation tool from the flyout.

2. Click an instance of a movie clip on the Stage.

The 3D Rotation control appears on the movie clip instance. If the control appears in a different location, double-click the control's center point to move it back to the selected instance.

3. Set the mode, global or local, using the Global Transform button in the Options section of the Tools panel.

Select the Global Transform button to use global mode. Deselect the button to use local mode.

4. To rotate the movie clip instance, do one of the following:

- To rotate the movie clip around the red x axis, drag the x-axis control.

- To rotate the movie clip around the green y axis, drag the y-axis control

- To rotate the movie clip around the blue z axis, drag the z-axis control. This movement is like a 2D rotation.

- To rotate the movie clip around the x and y axes simultaneously, drag the orange circle on the outer edge of the control. This control allows you to freely rotate the movie clip in 3D space.

The small circle in the 3D Rotation control is the center point of the rotation; you can drag it to control the rotation's center. Double-click it to return it to the center of the object.

Pushing Buttons

*W*hen you view a Web page, you click buttons to move to other pages or sites. As you probably know, these buttons are graphical images, but they're hyperlinks as well. If you start to pay attention to these buttons, you see that some of them change when you pass your mouse cursor over them. They change again when you click them. Occasionally, they make a sound when you click them.

Flash can create these types of buttons and more. You can animate Flash buttons so that they move or rotate when viewers pass their cursors over them or click them. You can add interactive controls (actions) to buttons so that passing over or clicking them starts other movies or creates other effects.

In this chapter, you find out how to create buttons that look the way you want. You also discover how to make more complex buttons that include sounds, movie clips, and simple ActionScript. To discover more about ActionScript and interactivity, see Chapter 10.

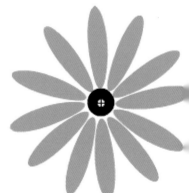

Creating Simple Buttons

Before you create a button, stop and think about what you want the button to accomplish on a Web page and how you want it to look. When designing a Web site's navigation, designers often create a series of similar buttons that lead to pages within a site. This similarity provides a coherent style for the site. Buttons usually include some text to identify the button's purpose.

A *button* is a symbol that responds to a mouse. (See Chapter 7 for the low-down on how to create and edit symbols.) In this section, we cover buttons basics.

Understanding button states

A button has four states that define characteristics of the button. Figure 8-1 shows a button in its four states.

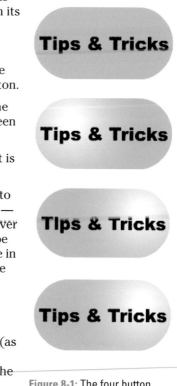

- ✔ **Up:** What the button looks like when the mouse pointer is not over the button. The viewer initially sees the Up state of a button.

- ✔ **Over:** What the button looks like when the pointer is over the button but it hasn't been clicked.

- ✔ **Down:** What the button looks like when it is clicked.

- ✔ **Hit:** The area of the button that responds to the mouse. The user doesn't see this area — it's invisible. When you pass the pointer over the hit area, the pointer is considered to be over the button. When you click anywhere in the hit area, the button works. Because the user doesn't see the Hit state, you can't animate it.

A typical, simple button might show a lit-up effect for the Over state and an indented look (as though the button is pressed in) for the Down state. In this example, the Down state moves the highlight to the right, giving the impression of movement when the user clicks the button.

Figure 8-1: The four button states.

Radial gradients are useful for creating a lit-up or pushed-in look. Use a light color or white to create the appearance of a highlight. Use a dark color or black to create an indented look. Just changing the color of the fill (often to a lighter color) is enough to make it seem lit up.

The button shown in Figure 8-1 is on the companion Web site at www.dummies.com/go/flashcs5fd. Look for capsule.fla. To try out the buttons in this movie, choose Control➪Test Movie➪In Flash Professional.

Making a basic button

To create a simple button, follow these steps:

1. **Choose Insert➪New Symbol to open the Create New Symbol dialog box.**

2. **In the Name text box, type a name for the button.**

   When you have many symbols in a movie, it helps to name them according to their type and purpose. For example, if a button will be labeled Submit a Resource, you might name it btnSubmitResource.

3. **From the Type drop-down list, select the Button option.**

4. **Click OK.**

   You're now in symbol-editing mode. Flash displays the special Timeline for buttons, with four frames: Up, Over, Down, and Hit, as shown in Figure 8-2. Note the dot in the Up frame, indicating that the frame is a keyframe. (For more information about keyframes, see Chapter 9.) The word *Up* is highlighted, indicating that the Up frame is active.

5. **Create the graphic for the Up state.**

   You can use the Flash drawing tools, an imported graphic, or an instance of a graphic or movie clip symbol. You can create as many layers as you want for the button. For an animated button, use a movie clip symbol. We explain how to create an animated button in the "Adding a movie clip to a button" section, later in this chapter.

Figure 8-2: The Flash symbol-editing mode for buttons displays a Timeline with four frames.

   If you want the button image for the four states to be in the same place, place the graphic in the center of the display and build the other states in the center as well. To do this, cut and paste the graphic. (See Chapter 4 for more about centering objects on the display.) If the button images aren't in the same place, the button shifts when the viewer passes the cursor over or clicks the button.

6. **Right-click (Windows) or Control-click (Mac) the Over frame and choose Insert Keyframe from the contextual menu.**

   Flash inserts a keyframe in the Over frame of the button. You can also choose Insert➪Timeline➪Keyframe or press F6. If you have more than one layer, place a keyframe on each layer. The graphic for the Up state remains on the Stage.

7. Create the graphic for the Over state.

You can use the graphic for the Up state as a starting point and change it. (Or leave it the same if you don't want the button to change when the mouse pointer passes over the button.) You can also delete the graphic and put a new one in its place.

8. Right-click (Windows) or Control-click (Mac) the Down frame and then choose Insert Keyframe.

Be sure to add a keyframe for each layer on your Timeline.

9. Create the graphic for the Down frame.

Repeat as in Step 7. Note that if the button functions as navigation to another page, your viewer will see this state for only a split second.

10. Right-click (Windows) or Control-click (Mac) the Hit frame and choose Insert Keyframe.

11. If necessary, create the shape that defines the active area of the button.

This shape should completely cover all the graphics of the other state. Usually, a rectangle or circle is effective. If you ignore the Hit frame, Flash uses the boundary of the objects in the Up frame, which might be what you want. Figure 8-3 shows the Timeline when a button is completed.

If you use text for the button, viewers have to click the letters precisely unless you create a rectangular hit area around the text. To cover an area of text, create a filled-in shape on a new layer. (We explain how to create shapes in Chapter 3.)

Figure 8-3: When you complete a button, all four frames are keyframes.

12. Click the scene name at the upper left of the screen (or the Back arrow to the left of the scene name) to return to the regular Timeline and leave symbol-editing mode.

13. If the Library isn't open, choose Window➪Library. Drag the button symbol that you just created to wherever you want it on the Stage.

You created a button!

A button is a symbol, but when you want to place a button on the Stage, you must drag the button from the Library to create an instance of the symbol. See Chapter 7 for a full explanation of symbols and instances.

Putting Buttons to the Test

After you create a button, you need to test it. You can choose from several methods. The fastest way to test a button is to enable it on the Stage. An enabled button responds to your mouse as you would expect — it changes as you specified when you pass the mouse over it or click it. To enable the buttons on the Stage, choose Control⇨Enable Simple Buttons. All the buttons on the Stage are now enabled. Have fun with your button! Pass the mouse over it, click it, and watch it change.

After you test your button, suppose that you want to select the button to move it. You try to click it to select it, and it only glows at you, according to the Down frame's definition. Choose Control⇨Enable Simple Buttons again to disable the buttons. Now you can select a button as you do any other object. In general, you enable buttons only to test them.

However, if you really want to select an enabled button, you can do so with the Selection tool by dragging a selection box around it. You can use the arrow keys to move the button. If you want to edit the button further, choose Window⇨Properties to open the Property inspector and edit the button's properties, as we explain in Chapter 7.

If you have other animations on the Stage, you can play an animation with the buttons enabled. Choose Control⇨Play or press Enter (Windows) or Return (Mac). By playing the animation, you can see how the buttons fit in with the rest of your movie.

Another way to test a button is to test the entire movie. Choose Control⇨ Test Movie⇨In Flash Professional. Flash creates an SWF file based on default publishing settings, just as it would if you were publishing the movie. Any animation plays, and you can test your buttons as well. When you're finished, click the Close box of the window. If your button contains movie clips, you must use this method of testing the button because the animation doesn't play on the Stage.

Creating Complex Buttons

Buttons can do more than just change color or shape. You can enhance a button in three ways:

✔ **Add a sound.** For example, you can add a clicking sound to the Down frame of a button so that users hear that sound when they click the button.

✔ **Add a movie clip.** To animate a button, you add a movie clip to it. You can animate the Up, Over, and Down frames, if you want.

✔ **Add an action (interactive control).** To make a button do something, you need to add an action to it by using ActionScript. Actions are covered in Chapter 10, but we discuss some of the basic concepts here.

Adding a sound to a button

For fun, you can add a sound to a button. Usually, sounds are added to the Over or Down frame — or both, if you want. Chapter 11 explains lots more about sound, but in this section, we explain how to add a simple sound to a button.

On the companion Web site at `www.dummies.com/go/flashcs5fd`, look for `click.wav`. You can add this sound to the Down frame of a button.

To add a sound to a button, follow these steps:

1. **Create the button symbol.**

2. **Choose File⇨Import⇨Import to Library to open the Import dialog box.**

3. **Select the sound file (in `.wav`, `.aiff`, or `.mp3` format) and click Open.**

   Flash stores the file in the Library.

4. **Choose Window⇨Library to open the Library.**

5. **If you aren't in symbol-editing mode, double-click the button's icon in the Library to enter symbol-editing mode.**

6. **Click the New Layer button at the bottom of the layer list to add a new layer.**

   See Chapter 6 for a full explanation of layers.

7. **Name the new layer *Sound* or *Click* or something similar.**

8. **In the new layer, right-click (Windows) or Control-click (Mac) the frame where you want to place the sound — for example, the Down frame — and choose Insert Keyframe.**

9. **Display the Property inspector.**

   Choose Window⇨Properties to open the Property inspector if it's not already open.

10. **In the Sound section, in the Name drop-down list, select the sound file that you want.**

Flash lists all the sounds you've imported into the Library. When you select the sound file, you see the sound wave indicator on the sound's layer in the frame where you inserted the sound, as shown in Figure 8-4.

Figure 8-4: When you add a sound to a button, the sound wave appears in the Timeline.

11. **With the new keyframe still selected, click the Sync drop-down list in the Property inspector and choose Event.**

The Event setting synchronizes the sound to the occurrence of an event: in this case, the clicking of the button. Event is the default setting.

12. **Click the scene name in the upper-left area of the layer list or the back arrow to the left of the scene name.**

Flash returns you to the regular Timeline and leaves symbol-editing mode.

You're finished! Now test the button as we explain in the earlier section, "Putting Buttons to the Test."

Be sure to look in Chapter 11 for more information on adding sounds to buttons and movies.

If you already added the sound to another movie, choose File➪Import➪Open External Library and choose the other movie. Click the desired keyframe and drag the sound from the Library to anywhere on the Stage. Flash places the sound in the selected keyframe.

Adding a movie clip to a button

If you think that simple buttons are b-o-r-i-n-g, you can animate them. To animate a button, you must create a movie clip symbol and then insert the movie clip into one of the frames. Generally, button animation is localized in the area of the button. If you want to make an elaborate button, you can animate all three frames — Up, Over, and Down.

To add a movie clip to a button, first create the movie clip. Chapter 7 explains how to create a movie clip symbol, and Chapter 9 explains how to create the animation to put in the movie clip.

For the following steps, you can use the movie clip that we provide on the companion Web site at www.dummies.com/go/flashcs5. Open flower power.fla. It's a blank movie with a Library that contains the symbols necessary to create a button with a movie clip.

If you've never created a button, review the steps in the "Making a basic button" section, earlier in this chapter. Then to create a button with a movie clip, follow these steps:

1. **If you're using the movie file included on the Web site, open** `flower power.fla`**; otherwise, open any new movie file.**

2. **Choose Insert⇨New Symbol to open the Create New Symbol dialog box.**

3. **In the Name text box, type a name for the button.**

4. **In the Type list, select the Button option. Then click OK.**

5. **Create the graphic for the Up state.**

   If you're using the movie from the Web site, choose Window⇨Library and drag the graphic symbol named Flower to the Stage. Press the arrow buttons on the keyboard (left, right, up, and down, as necessary) to center the flower symbol's registration point (shown by a little plus sign) exactly over the registration point (also a plus sign) on the Stage. (See upcoming Figure 8-5.) You can also cut and paste the symbol to center it. The flower graphic symbol is static, not animated.

6. **Right-click (Windows) or Control-click (Mac) the Over frame and choose Insert Keyframe from the contextual menu.**

   Flash inserts a keyframe.

7. **Create the graphic for the Over state.**

   For this example, delete the graphic on the Stage (it's still there from the Up frame) and drag the movie clip called Flower Rotating to the center of the Stage. Click the Stage and use the arrow keys to perfectly center the flower. The Flower Rotating movie clip animates the flower by rotating it.

8. **Right-click (Windows) or Control-click (Mac) the Down frame and choose Insert Keyframe.**

9. **Create the graphic for the Down state.**

   In this example, delete the graphic on the Stage and drag the Flower Light graphic symbol to the exact center of the Stage.

10. **Right-click (Windows) or Control-click (Mac) the Hit frame and choose Insert Keyframe.**

11. **Use the Rectangle tool and drag a square to cover the entire area of the symbol. Use the Selection tool to select and delete the fill, leaving only the square.**

If you don't perform this step, viewers must place the mouse cursor exactly over one of the petals to see the animation. By defining the Hit frame as a square, placing the cursor anywhere within that square activates the button. Your screen should look like Figure 8-5, shown with the Up frame active.

Figure 8-5: You can use the Flower Power library to create an animated button.

12. **Click the scene name (Scene 1) above the layer list to return to the regular Timeline.**

13. **Drag the button symbol that you just created from the Library to wherever you want the button placed on the Stage.**

    Congratulations! You just created a button with a movie clip.

To test the button that you just created, choose Control➪Test Movie➪In Flash Professional. Place the cursor over the button, click the button, and watch the animation. If you used the Flower Power movie from the Web site, first save the file on your computer by choosing File➪Save As and choosing a location on your hard drive. When you test this movie, the flower rotates and lightens when you pass the cursor over it. When you click the flower, it seems to freeze. When you're finished, click the Close box of the window.

If you want to see the final result of the preceding steps, check out `flower power-final.fla` on the companion Web site at `www.dummies.com/go/flashcs5fd`.

Adding an action for a button

A button doesn't do anything except look pretty until you give it the proper instructions. For example, a button can link you to another Web page or start a movie. See Figure 8-6 for an example of a navigation button. You find out about ActionScript in Chapter 10, which includes some button examples. In this section, though, we explain the basic principle of adding an action to a button — in this case, an action that links the user to another Web page.

Courtesy Macquarium Inc.

Figure 8-6: This movie sports beautiful bubble buttons.

As we explain in Chapter 10, by default, Flash CS5 uses ActionScript 3.0 as its programming language. After you have the ActionScript code for a button, you can use it as a template to create your own buttons.

You add an action for a button by placing the action on the Timeline, usually in the first frame. To create ActionScript for a button, follow these steps:

1. **If you haven't already done so, drag an instance of the button onto the Stage. If the button isn't selected, select it.**

2. **Open the Property inspector (choose Window⇨Properties). In the Instance Name text box at the top, enter a name for this instance of the button symbol, as shown in Figure 8-7.**

   The name can't include spaces. You can use an underscore or hyphen for readability, though.

   Each instance of a button symbol should have a different instance name.

Figure 8-7: Enter an instance name for your button.

3. **Click anywhere off the Stage to deselect the button.**

4. **Create a new layer and name it Actions.**

   Chapter 6 explains how to create layers.

5. **Select the button on the Stage.**

6. **Open the Code Snippets panel, shown in Figure 8-8. (Choose Window⇨Code Snippets.)**

   The Code Snippets panel contains a collection of often-used ActionScript snippets with which you can easily add ActionScript to your movie.

7. **Double-click the Actions item to expand it. Then double-click Click to Go to Web Page.**

   The Actions - Frame panel opens with the ActionScript code highlighted. Click anywhere to deselect the code so that you can read it. If you look

Figure 8-8: The Code Snippets panel is your handy shortcut to ActionScript code.

carefully, you'll also see a small "a" in the `actions` layer's keyframe in the Timeline; this indicates that the frame contains ActionScript.

8. **Follow the instructions in the Actions - Frame panel, substituting a URL for `http://www.adobe.com`.**

   We used `"http://www.peaceloveandhappiness.org"`, for Gurdy Leete's blog on Free Software for Art, Music and Personal Creativity, as shown in Figure 8-9.

9. **Close the Actions Frame panel and the Code Snippets panel, and then save your movie.**

   If the Compiler Errors panel opens when you close the Action panel or test your button (Control⇨Test Movie⇨In Flash Professional), it means that you made a mistake in your typing. Check your code, correct any errors, and try again.

You can add your button to an existing Web page. In such a case, the button might be the only Flash element on the page. You can also include buttons as part of an environment created completely in Flash. Either way, buttons are a valuable piece of the Flash arsenal.

Figure 8-9: You can easily customize a code snippet for your own URL.

Testing your button's URL navigation

To properly test a button, you need to publish your movie, upload it to your Web page, go online, and try it out. However, you can test the button on your hard drive first so that you can be fairly sure that it will work when you put it on your Web page.

To test your button without publishing it, choose Control➪Test Movie➪In Flash Professional and click the button. If you used an *absolute* (complete) URL, you should have no problem. Your browser should open and display the appropriate Web page. However, a relative (local) URL might not be available. For example, if your URL is `tips.html`, the button won't work unless you have a file named `tips.html` in the same folder as the Flash movie.

You can still test a relative URL on your hard drive. Continuing with the example of a link to `tips.html`, assume that on your Web server, `tips.html` is in the same folder as the Web page containing your Flash button so that you can use this simple local URL.

To test your button's ActionScript, follow these steps:

1. **After creating the button and its ActionScript containing a URL of `tips. html` (or whatever's appropriate in your situation), choose File➪Save to save the movie file.**

2. **Choose File➪Publish.**

   Flash publishes the file, creating an HTML file and an SWF file in the same folder as your FLA file. (These are default settings. See Chapter 13 for more information on publishing movies.)

3. **You need a file on your hard drive with the same URL that you used for your button. Create a file named `tips.html` (or whatever URL you used) on your hard drive in the same folder as your movie.**

   You can use either of two methods:

   ✔ **Make a copy** of the existing `tips.html` (if you have it on your hard drive) and move it to the folder containing your movie.

   ✔ **Create a new HTML document** and save it as `tips.html` in the same folder as your movie. This document can be a dummy document — you can put any text you want in it. For example, you can type **This is a test**

   HTML document. If you create this document in a word processor, be sure to save it as an HTML document. Otherwise, use the software that you normally use to create HTML documents.

4. **Open your browser, choose File⇨Open or Open File (depending on your browser), and open the HTML file for your Flash movie. (It has the same name as your movie.)**

5. **Click your button.**

   You should see `tips.html` displayed. If you don't, go back and check your ActionScript.

Part IV
Total Flash-o-Rama

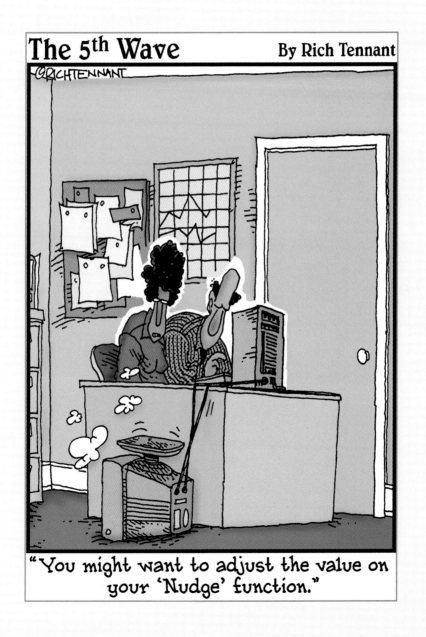

The 5th Wave — By Rich Tennant

"You might want to adjust the value on your 'Nudge' function."

In this part . . .

Moving imagery is the heart and soul of Flash. In this part, you make your Flash creations come to life through the power of animation and video. You find out about moving objects, changing their shapes, and how to let Flash create animation for you.

After you create your movie, you can make it interactive so that the viewer's Web experience is more meaningful and engaging. Flash ActionScript provides you with infinite interactive potential, so let your imagination soar. We also show you how you can use Flash's new Code Snippets to script your entire movie with ease.

Video and audio are an increasingly pervasive dimension of the Web, and your Flash movies can be part of that. Find out how to add sounds and music to your movies — from the simplest sound of a button click to the majestic tones of a full-fledged symphony — and to integrate video into your dynamic Flash extravaganzas.

9

Getting Animated

*I*n this chapter, we explain animation and making your graphics move. Are you ready to plunge into a world where you can make almost anything seem to happen? Hold on to your hat!

We start by explaining the basics of animation, including how to prepare for animation and how to work with the Timeline. Then we go into the specific techniques — frame-by-frame animation, tweening, and bones — that you can use to create great, animated effects in Flash. We cover motion tweening, shape tweening, inverse kinematics, and adding Springs. Plus, we give you the details of editing your animations.

Choosing Your Animation Technique

The secret of animation in Flash, like in animated movies, is that nothing ever really moves. A Flash movie creates the illusion of movement by quickly displaying a sequence of still images. Each still image is slightly different. Your brain fills in the gaps to give you the impression of movement.

One of the great things about Flash is that you can easily create complicated, spectacular extravaganzas of animation. And Flash stores lots of information in the super-compact vector format. Because the files can be small, they can be transmitted over the Web quickly. That's good for your Web site viewers.

Just like in a movie on film, each still image is contained in a frame. Each *frame* represents a unit of time. You create the animation by placing images in the frames, as shown in Figure 9-1. A frame can contain one object or none or many, depending on how crowded of a scene you want to create.

Figure 9-1: Movies are simply still images in sequence.

Time is your ally in Flash because you have complete control over it. You can look at each individual image in time and tweak it to your heart's content. Then you can step on the gas, play everything back at full speed, and watch everything appear to move.

In Flash, you create animation in three ways:

- **Frame by frame:** You move or modify objects one frame at a time. Frame-by-frame animation, although time consuming, is sometimes the only way to create complex animated effects. This method can certainly satisfy your appetite for total control.

- **Tweening:** You specify starting frames and ending frames and let Flash figure out where everything goes in the in-between frames — which is why it's called *tweening*. Tweening is much more fun and much easier than frame-by-frame animation. If you can create the animation you want by tweening, it's definitely the way to go. Flash offers three types of tweening: motion tweening, shape tweening, and classic tweening, all of which we describe later in this chapter, in the section "The Animation Tween."

- **Inverse Kinematics (IK):** You use the Bone tool to draw a chain of bones (an *armature*) that connects your objects. Then, when you move one of the bones, the whole chain of objects is pulled along with it. Just like when you shake someone's hand, her wrist, forearm, elbow, and upper arm move, too. This cool feature of Flash takes the automatic creation of animation to a whole new level.

Now with Flash Professional CS5, you can add Springs to your Bones, to make your animations even more life-like

Mastering the Timeline

The Flash Timeline is a powerful and flexible tool for creating amazing animations. Using the Timeline, you can motion tween objects, morph shapes, and add bones and Springs. You can also customize your Timeline many ways and use the controls in your Timeline to play the animation on the Stage. In a later chapter, we explore adding audio and video to your Timeline as well.

Touring the Timeline

The *Timeline* is the map of your animation sequence. If the Timeline isn't visible, choose Window⇨Timeline. Each layer has its own Timeline row. The Timeline has its own color coding to help you understand the structure of your animation, as shown in Figure 9-2.

Figure 9-2: Use the Flash Timeline to control your animations.

To customize your workspace, you can choose Window➪Workspace and choose from any of the workspace types. You can also undock the Timeline from the main Flash window. Just click the tab labeled Timeline (at the top of the Timeline) and drag the Timeline where you want it. Then you can resize it as an independent window. (Drag its left, right, or bottom edge.) If you get lost with the new arrangement, you can always dock the Timeline again by dragging it back to where it was.

Half the power of the Timeline is that it divides motion into *frames* — bits of time that you can isolate and work with — one at a time. The other half of the Timeline's power is that you can organize different components of your animation into different layers.

Click any frame to make it active. Remember to click in the row of the layer containing the graphics you want to animate. By clicking a frame, you can view your animation frozen at that moment of time.

As you read through the examples and steps in this chapter, you'll quickly get the hang of working with the Timeline.

Hide the layers that you're not interested in (click below the eye icon) to help you visualize the animation. Don't forget, though, to check the animation with all the layers displayed to see how everything looks together. You should also lock layers when you're finished with them to avoid unwanted changes. See Chapter 6 for further instructions on hiding and locking layers.

Playing your animations

Flash offers two ways of playing back your animations: on the Stage or in a new window. As your animations get more complicated, it's important to choose the correct method because only simple animations can be viewed on the Stage. Animations that are created or manipulated with code won't appear when you view your animation on the Stage. Also, animations in movie clips don't appear when tested on the Stage. (For more information on defining your animation as a movie clip, see Chapter 7.)

Here are the basic ways to test your movie:

- ✔ **In a new window:** This is the most powerful way to test your animation. Choose Control➪Test Movie➪In Flash Professional to view your animation in a new window — as it appears when published, showing all movie clip animations and all coded animations, and not showing motion paths, onion skins, and more.

- ✔ **On the Stage:** This method is generally the fastest way to test your animation because you don't need to wait for a new window to appear. However, it doesn't show animations in movie clips or coded animations. You can use the following methods to test your movie on the Stage:

- *Press Enter (Windows) or Return (Mac).* This plays your animation on the Stage, starting from Frame 1 (if the playhead is at the last frame of your animation or already at Frame 1). If the playhead is on a frame in the middle of your animation, click Frame 1 and then press Enter (Windows) or Return (Mac). Using this method does not reveal animations within movie clips.

- *Choose Control⇨Play.* This behaves just like pressing Return/Enter, as just described.

- *Drag the playhead.* This is sometimes the simplest method, but it tests your animation at the speed of your dragging, which is most likely not its correct speed. Also, it does not show any animations within movie clips.

- *Use the Controller.* The Controller toolbar can be handy. To view the Controller, choose Window⇨Toolbars⇨Controller. Use the Controller, as shown in Figure 9-3, to play, rewind, fast-forward, and stop your animation. You can also dock the Controller above the Timeline for greater convenience.

Figure 9-3: The Controller.

Turtle or hare?

All you need to do to make animation work is to view your sequence of still images over time at high speed. Unless you have a remarkable attention span, one image per second is way too slow. Silent movies typically ran at 16 or 18 frames per second (fps). With the arrival of talkies, the speed got bumped up to 24 fps for better quality sound. On your television, the speed is roughly 30 images per second.

The smoothness of the playback of your animation depends not only on the frame rate that you specify but also on the complexity of the animation and the speed of the computer that's playing it. Generally, 24 fps is a good choice for Web animation, and that's the default rate in Flash.

To change the frame rate for your animation, click the Frame Rate value (which displays a number and the letters fps) at the bottom of the Timeline, type a new number (in frames per second) and then press Enter (Windows) or Return (Mac).

Because you can set only one frame rate for all the animation in your current Flash file, you should set the frame rate before you start animating.

A Flash movie's frame rate represents the maximum speed at which the movie runs. Flash animation has no guaranteed minimum speed. If your animation is lagging or bogging down, increasing the frame rate doesn't help at all; in fact, it might make things worse.

Setting your frame view

You can change the display of the appearance of frames. You do this on the Timeline by choosing from the Frame View pop-up menu in the upper-right corner of the Timeline, shown in Figure 9-4. With this menu, you can

- **Set the width of frame cells to Tiny, Small, Normal, Medium, or Large.**

- **Choose to include a preview image of the contents of each frame in the Timeline display.**

  This is an awesome feature, like unspooling a reel of film. If you choose Preview, as shown in Figure 9-4, the preview image is scaled to fit the Timeline frame; if you choose Preview in Context, the preview image also includes any empty space in the frame.

- **Decrease the height of frame cells by choosing Short.**

- **Toggle tinting of frame sequences.**

- **Turn off the sound when scrubbing by deselecting Scrub Audio.**

Scrubbing is moving the Playhead back and forth to see or hear what's in a section of the Timeline.

Figure 9-4: Choosing the Preview Frame View.

Animating with Keyframes

Keyframes are the frames that are, well, key to your animation. You might insert a keyframe when you want to replace one object with another object, or you may just want to change a property of an object, such as its position, color, or size. Keyframes that designate changes in properties of an object are known as *property keyframes*, and are represented by a dot, as shown in Figure 9-2.

In animation, keyframes and property keyframes can be used as key moments in time that the software uses to calculate the in-between frames. You specify the state of each object only at a few keyframes or property keyframes, and the computer does all the work of calculating and rendering the changing state of each object in all the in-between frames — which is called *tweening.*

Motion tweening uses property keyframes to designate how an object moves or changes properties. In contrast, shape tweening gradually changes one shape to another and uses keyframes to specify an object's shape at specific times. Tweening not only means less work for you but also creates smaller files (which download faster) because you're describing your animations more concisely.

Frame after Frame after Frame

If your animation isn't a simple motion in an easily definable direction or a change of shape or color — and isn't a sequence you'd create by inserting and animating bones in your objects — you probably need to use frame-by-frame animation.

If you must, you must. Some complex animations just have to be created frame by frame. For example, the mouths in Figure 9-4 are frame-by-frame animation. Also, Figure 9-5 shows frames of an animation as the word *New!* is created from a few specks on the page.

The basic procedure is simple:

1. **Select a frame in the row of the layer that you want to use.**

   The animation starts in that frame.

2. **Right-click (Windows) or Control-click (Mac) the frame and then choose Insert Keyframe.**

   The first frame on a movie's Timeline is automatically a keyframe, so you don't have to create it.

3. **Create the graphic for the first frame.**

   You can import a graphic, paste a graphic from the Clipboard, or use the Flash drawing tools. (See Chapter 3 for help with creating or importing a graphic.)

4. **Right-click (Windows) or Control-click (Mac) the next frame and then choose Insert Keyframe again.**

   The next frame on the Timeline now has the same graphic as the preceding one.

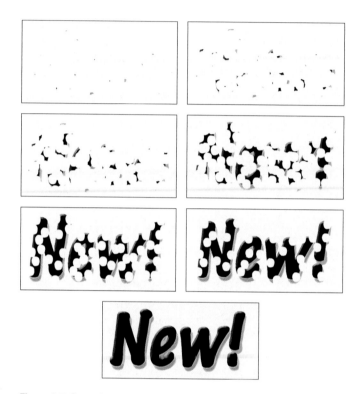

Figure 9-5: Sometimes a complex animation must be created frame by frame.

5. **Modify the graphic to create the second frame of the animation.**

6. **Repeat Steps 4 and 5 until you create all the frames that you need for your animation.**

While you work, you can continually check your cool animation by pressing Enter (Windows) or Return (Mac) to play it back.

The Animation Tween

You can save yourself lots of work (and reduce your file size, too) by using Flash to automatically calculate the frames in-between the keyframes you set up. You create a few keyframes, and Flash figures out what should go in between. In animation technobabble, that's *tweening* — a quick, fun way to create great animations.

You can do a lot with Flash's tweening capabilities, including

✔ **Motion tweening:** This is the type of tweening you're likely to use most of the time. With motion tweening, you can move your objects in a straight line from here to there. You can use motion tweening also to animate an object along any path that you create, even one with lots of curves.

You can also animate your movie clip's 3D position on the *z axis* (that is, its position in front of or behind other objects, which we describe later in this chapter).

✔ **Shape tweening:** This type of tweening gradually changes any shape to another shape, as shown in Figure 9-6. You create the first and last shapes. It's known as *morphing*. The results may be quite unpredictable and require a lot of computer processing but are usually interesting. You can add shape hints to try to tell Flash exactly how you want your shape to morph.

Figure 9-6: Shape tweening automatically morphs your shapes.

✔ **Classic tweening:** This is how motion tweening was accomplished in earlier versions of Flash. Classic tweening functions similarly to motion tweening, but its ending state is defined as a keyframe instead of a property keyframe, as shown in Figure 9-2. In almost every case, using Flash CS5 motion tweening is simpler, easier, and more powerful, so we explore Flash CS5 motion tweening rather than classic tweening.

With motion tweening and shape tweening, you can also

✔ **Animate an object's size.** For example, to make their movements more expressive, you can make objects appear to squash and stretch, as shown in Figure 9-7.

✔ **Rotate an object.** You specify the amount of the rotation. Flash combines the motion or shape tweening with the rotation so that you get both effects at one time.

✔ **Animate color or transparency.** Flash creates a gradual change in color based on your starting and ending colors.

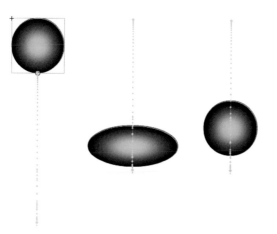

Figure 9-7: Squash and stretch makes objects more expressive.

Animating your graphic's transparency is a particularly cool effect because it lets you fade objects in and out, making them magically appear and disappear at just the right moment. And with motion tweens you can animate all filter properties, which can also produce really cool effects. For example, you can specify how much a glow or drop shadow changes during the tween. (See Chapter 7 to read about filters.)

Of course, you can create several animations, one after another, to mix and match effects. You can also combine frame-by-frame animation with tweened animation. Let your imagination soar!

From here to there — motion tweening

In motion tweening, you move an object from one place to another. The movement can be a straight line or any path that you can draw with the Pencil tool. Figure 9-8 shows a few frames from a motion tween that uses a looped path. While the animation progresses, the skateboarder image also scales down to 50% of its original size so that it appears to be moving away from you. In this example, the path is visible so that you can see how the animation works. When you play the finished animation the path is invisible.

Figure 9-8: You can draw any path and animate an object along the path.

Making a motion tween

When you motion tween your objects, you can move them and also tween their size, rotation, skew, transparency, and even their position in three-dimensional space.

For info on skewing an object, check out Chapter 4.

To create a simple motion tween animation, follow these steps:

1. **Create a new layer by choosing Insert⇨Timeline⇨Layer.**

2. **Right-click (Windows) or Control-click (Mac) an empty frame in the new layer where you want the animation to start. From the contextual menu that appears, choose Insert Keyframe.**

3. **Put a symbol instance, text field, or shape on the Stage.**

   You can create one there, or paste it there, or drag it onto the Stage from the Library. (See Chapter 2 for info on the Library.)

4. **Right-click (Windows) or Control-click (Mac) the keyframe you created and then choose Create Motion Tween from the menu that appears.**

5. **If your object is a shape, a dialog box appears asking whether you want to convert it to a symbol so that Flash can create a tween. In this case, click OK.**

   Flash adds a motion tween starting in the frame you choose.

6. **To increase the number of frames in which the image appears in your animation, click the keyframe and then drag the mouse on the Timeline to the right for the desired number of frames.**

   Flash duplicates your image throughout all intermediate frames.

7. **Click a frame in the tween other than the first frame of the tween.**

8. **Move the object to a new position.**

   A property keyframe appears in the current frame, and a *motion path* appears on the Stage (as shown in Figure 9-9), showing the path of the object from the previous frame to the current frame.

9. **If you want to change the object's size, rotation, color, or position in 3D space (as we explain in the sections that follow), make the adjustments at this point.**

   Figure 9-9: The motion path shows the path your animation takes.

   See the next three sections of this chapter for details.

   You're done! Press Enter (Windows) or Return (Mac) to play it.

When tweening, always animate each object on a separate layer that has no other objects on it. Otherwise, your animated objects might erase, connect to, or segment other objects — with messy results. And your animation probably won't work. Read Chapter 6 for more information on layers. If you're animating using bones, however, you want to put all the objects for one set of bones on a single layer. Otherwise, Flash doesn't let you connect your objects with the bones.

REMEMBER

If you plan to use motion tweening or bones, turn your objects into instances of symbols.

You can also use the preceding steps to create an image that remains still over a number of frames. Follow the steps, but stop before Step 7. This simply copies an object over a number of frames. You might want to do this for several reasons. Sometimes, you want a still image to sit unmoving for a while on a layer of your animation — as a background image, for example — while your animation moves in front. A background gives context to your animated objects. Even animated objects often need to remain on the Stage after they've finished moving about. A key element of animation is timing, and an animated character is often still for a few moments (even in elaborately animated Disney cartoons) before taking its next action.

Scaling and rotating an animated object

Okay, so you're creative and ambitious and want to do more. Changing other properties of your graphic while you're moving it is easy. In Step 9 of the procedure in the preceding section, you can scale and rotate (including skewing) your object, as shown in Figure 9-10.

Figure 9-10: Use the Free Transform tool to create animated changes in scale.

Use the Free Transform tool, located on the Tools panel, or any other method of changing size or rotation. (See Chapter 4 for instructions on scaling and rotating objects.)

Symbols have transformation points that are usually at the center of the graphic. When you tween along a path, you might want another point to follow the path. In the section on groups in Chapter 4, you find out how to change the transformation point to get the results you want.

Tweening color or transparency

To change a motion tweened object's color, transparency, or brightness, follow these steps:

1. **Click the frame in the motion tween span on the Timeline where you want to change its color.**

   A *tween span* is the group of frames in the Timeline in which a motion tween occurs. The tween span appears as a group of frames in the Timeline with a blue background, as shown in Figure 9-11.

   Figure 9-11: The tween span is the group of frames in your motion tween.

2. **Be sure the Selection tool is selected and then click the object.**

3. **Choose Window⇨Properties to open the Property inspector (if it's not already open). In the Property inspector (if necessary), click the disclosure triangle to the left of the Color Effect section to reveal the contents of that section.**

4. **Select one of the options (such as Tint or Alpha) from the Style drop-down list and make the desired adjustments.**

   When using Tint, don't forget to change the percentage of tint to apply it. Chapter 7 provides more detail about using the options from the Color Effect drop-down list.

5. **Check out your new tween by pressing Enter (Windows) or Return (Mac).**

You can mix and match motion animation with scaling, rotation, and color or transparency changes to create exciting effects. Animating semitransparent objects in front of each other creates interesting mixtures of color and gives a semblance of texture and depth in the 2D world of the Web. Decreasing Alpha (opacity) during a tween makes the object appear to fade as it becomes more transparent. Try out some possibilities and come up with ideas of your own.

Color fades are less work for the computer than alpha fades. If you need an object to fade in or out, your movie loads faster on older computers if you tween to or from the background color rather than tween to or from transparency.

Animating your movie clip's position in 3D space

Objects that you create in Flash are two-dimensional vector graphics, but you can easily animate the position of your 2D movie clips in 3D space to make your animations even more dazzling. (For more information on 3D changes to movie clips, see Chapter 7.) In Step 9 in the earlier section "Making a motion tween," you can make your changes to the 3D space of the object by changing the value of the z axis in the 3D Position and View section of the Property inspector. You can also select the object and use the 3D Rotation tool on the Toolbar to change its rotation in 3D space.

The Z value specifies your movie clip's position forward or backward along the z axis. Negative numbers move the movie clip closer to the viewer; positive numbers move the movie clip farther away from the viewer.

When you play the movie (choose Control⇨Test Movie⇨In Flash Professional), your movie clip appears to start in one position in 3D space and move to the second position you specify, as shown in Figure 9-12.

Figure 9-12: You can animate 2D Flash graphics in 3D space.

Drawing your own motion path

When you motion-tween an object and make it move, Flash draws a motion path on the Stage that shows the path the object takes during the animation.

You can change the motion path simply by moving the playhead on the Timeline to the time where you want the motion path to change, and then clicking the object and dragging it.

You can create animation that doesn't move in a straight line by editing the motion path that Flash creates, changing it from a straight line to any curves that you desire. You can even replace the motion path that Flash creates with a path that you draw and paste in its place. Suppose that you want to get the skateboarder shown in Figure 9-13 to do some tricks. To replace a motion path with a path that you draw, follow these steps.

1. **Create an object and motion-tween it, as described in the steps in the earlier section, "Making a motion tween."**

   The object's motion path appears on the Stage.

2. **Create a new layer, and then select the first frame in that layer.**

3. **Use the Pencil tool or the Pen tool, on the Stage, to draw a stroke that you would like to be the new motion path.**

   To read all about the Pencil tool and the Pen tool, see Chapter 3.

4. **Choose the Selection tool from the Tools panel, and then click the stroke to select it.**

5. **Right-click (Windows) or Control-click (Mac) the stroke; from the contextual menu that appears, choose Copy.**

6. **If the object with the motion path isn't visible in Frame 1 of the Timeline, click a frame in the Timeline where the object is visible. Select the motion path and right-click (Windows) or Control-click (Mac); from the contextual menu that appears, choose Paste.**

   Flash replaces the motion path with the stroke that you drew in Step 3.

7. **To view the change, choose Control⇨Test Movie⇨In Flash Professional.**

   The object animates along the new motion path, as shown in Figure 9-13.

   Figure 9-13: You make an object follow a motion path that you draw.

And now you can edit your new motion path in more ways.

Editing your motion path

You may want to revise your motion path without adding a new one. You can do so by moving it or changing its shape. To edit a motion path, follow these steps:

1. **Create an object and motion-tween it from one location to another as described in the steps in the earlier section, "Making a motion tween."**

   The object's motion path appears on the Stage.

2. **Choose the Selection tool in the Tools panel. (If the Tools panel isn't visible, choose Window⇨Tools.)**

3. **To move the entire motion path, click the motion path and drag.**

   The entire motion path moves, and the object moves along with it.

4. **To change the shape of the motion path, click the motion path where you want it to change and then drag.**

   The shape of the motion path changes at the point where you click and drag.

5. **To edit the curvature of the motion path, choose the Subselection tool from the Tools panel. Click an anchor point on the motion path; then click and drag one of the direction points that appears.**

   The curvature of the motion path changes as you drag the direction point, as shown in Figure 9-14.

6. **If you want to skew, rotate, or scale the motion path, you can choose the Free Transform tool from the Tools panel, and click and drag the handles.**

7. **To see the object animate with the revised motion path, choose Control⇨Test Movie⇨ In Flash Professional.**

   Figure 9-14: You can freely edit your motion path.

   The object moves along the new version of the motion path that you created.

In Figure 9-14, we made the skateboarder in *Poser,* which is a cool program for generating 3D people. You can find out more about Poser at http:// my.smithmicro.com.

Rotating the object on the motion path

You can easily add a rotation to a tweened object as it moves on a path. To add a rotation to a tweened object, do the following steps:

1. **Choose the Selection tool from the Tools panel. On the Stage, click the motion path of the tweened object.**

   The motion path is highlighted, showing that it's the current selection.

2. **You can add a rotation to the object in one of two ways:**

   • *In the Rotation section of the Property inspector,* click the Rotate value and then type a number for degrees or choose the number of times that you want the object to rotate (or both). From the Direction drop-down list, choose CW (for clockwise) or CCW (for counterclockwise).

   The object rotates clockwise or counterclockwise as it moves along the path, as shown in Figure 9-15.

Figure 9-15: You can add a rotation to an object on your motion path.

• *Select the Orient to Path check box.*

If you select Orient to Path — say, you're animating a skateboarder — the object rotates so that the nose of the skateboard follows the curvature of the path, as shown in Figure 9-16.

3. **To view your changes, drag the playhead on the Timeline, or choose Control⇨Test Movie⇨ In Flash Professional.**

The object rotates along the motion path in the way you specify.

Figure 9-16: You can orient your object so that it rotates according to the curvature of your motion path.

Using Motion Presets

A fast, cool way to learn about Flash's motion-tween capabilities is to use *Motion Presets,* which are prebuilt motion tweens that you can apply to any symbol instance to instantly create a complete motion tween. Flash CS5 comes with dozens of Motion Presets. You can apply a Motion Preset to an object to instantly make it bounce, squash, and stretch; fly on the Stage in a blur; throb and pulse; and more. To apply a Motion Preset, do the following steps:

1. **Put a symbol instance, text field, or shape on the Stage.**

   You can create one there, or drag it onto the Stage from the Library.

2. **Choose the Selection tool from the Tools panel, and then select the object that you put on the Stage.**

3. **If the Motion Presets panel isn't open, choose Window⇨Motion Presets. If necessary, click the disclosure triangle to the left of each folder in the Motion Presets to make the contents of the folders visible.**

4. **In the Motion Presets panel, click the Motion Preset that you want, and then click the Apply button at the bottom of the Motion Presets panel.**

5. **If the object on the Stage is a shape, a dialog box appears asking whether you want to convert it to a symbol so that Flash can create a tween. In this case, click OK.**

   Flash creates a motion tween with all the animation from the Motion Preset you choose, as shown in Figure 9-17.

Figure 9-17: You can use Motion Presets to instantly animate an object.

6. **To view your new animation, click and drag the playhead in the Timeline, or choose Control➪Test Movie➪In Flash Professional.**

One fantastic feature of Motion Presets is that you can create your own. In this way, you can build up a library of cool animations that you can instantly apply to any symbol instance, any text field, or any shape that you want. To create a custom Motion Preset, follow these steps:

1. **Choose the Selection tool from the Tools panel, and then right-click (Windows) or Control-click (Mac) one of the following:**

   • A tween span on the Timeline

   • A motion-tweened object on the Stage

   • A motion path on the Stage

2. **From the contextual menu that appears, choose Save as Motion Preset.**

3. **In the Save Preset As dialog box that appears, type a name in the Preset Name text field and then click OK.**

   The name of your new Motion Preset appears in the list of presets in the Custom Presets folder in the Motion Presets panel.

Using the Motion Editor

For even more control of your motion tweens, you can use the Motion Editor, which makes it easy for you to view every property keyframe in your animation and tweak each transformation with precision and in great detail. To use the Motion Editor, select a tween span on the Timeline, or select a tweened object or a motion tween path on the Stage. Then click the Motion Editor tab (if it's docked somewhere; probably next to the Timeline) or choose Window➪ Motion Editor (if the Motion Editor isn't visible).

As shown in Figure 9-18, the Motion Editor shows the values of each property of the selected tween in a graph. The value of the property is represented vertically, and the time on the Timeline is represented horizontally. Thus, when the value of a property (Alpha, for example) increases or decreases, the graph line goes up or down; and as time moves forward, the graph line moves forward. Then if, for example, you want to change how the transparency of an object is animated, you can add or delete keyframes; and you can move keyframes up, down, or sideways on the graph. This really makes you the master of Flash space and time!

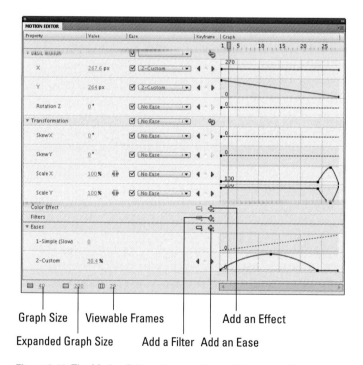

Figure 9-18: The Motion Editor gives you tremendous control over every property keyframe.

You can even adjust the curvature of the graphs by clicking a keyframe. (For the X, Y, and Z position properties, you can't adjust the curvature of the graph, but you can add and remove keyframes in the graph.

You can control the number of frames you see in the Motion Editor by clicking the Viewable Frames value near the bottom left of the Motion Editor, typing a new number, and then pressing Enter (Windows) or Return (Mac). If the number of Viewable Frames is set to 1, you might want to increase that number.

You can add a new color effect or filter to a tween by choosing the new item that you want from the Add drop-down menu (the plus sign) in the Color Effect or Filters row in the Motion Editor. A graph for the new item then appears in the Motion Editor.

Tweening shapes

In shape tweening, you change an object's shape at one or more points in the animation, and the computer creates the in-between shapes for you. You can get some great animation effects by using shape tweening. This process is often called *morphing*. You can see an example in Figure 9-19.

When shape tweening, you can combine changes in shape with changes in position as well as changes in size, color, and transparency. You should work with one shape per layer to avoid problems.

You can shape tween objects that you have created by using the Flash drawing tools.

You can't shape tween a symbol instance, text (type), or a group unless you break them apart into shapes by selecting them and choosing Modify⇨Break Apart. And you have to break apart text blocks twice — once to break the text block into individual letters and again to break the letters into shapes. You can also try to shape tween a bitmap image after breaking it apart, but the results are sure to be unpredictable.

Figure 9-19: A circle becomes a star!

If you break apart a symbol instance, text block, bitmap image, or group by using Modify➪Break Apart, you might have a number of shapes to animate. Be sure to put each animated object on a separate layer. You can do this easily by selecting the objects and choosing Modify➪Timeline➪Distribute to Layers, which we explain in Chapter 6.

To create a simple shape tween, follow these steps:

1. **If you want to start the animation on the first frame in the Timeline, by default, the first frame has a keyframe already so skip this step and go to Step 2. Otherwise, right-click (Windows) or Control-click (Mac) an empty frame where you want the animation to start and then choose Insert Keyframe.**

2. **Use the drawing tools to create the beginning shape.**

   You can create complex objects by merging objects of the same color or creating cutouts with objects of differing colors. (See Chapter 3 for details.)

   Lines and shapes can have disastrous results when used together in shape tweens. Try to stick to one or the other. Shapes seem to work the best.

3. **Create a keyframe after your first keyframe wherever you want it on the same layer of the Timeline by right-clicking (Windows) or Control-clicking (Mac) and then choosing Insert Keyframe.**

4. **Create the ending shape.**

   Delete the old shape and draw a new one, or you can use the first shape, still on the Stage, and modify it. You can also move the shape and change its color or transparency or both. You can quickly change the color by using the Color modifiers in the Tools panel. Use the Color panel to change opacity (Alpha). See Chapter 3 for more information on colors and transparency.

5. **Click anywhere in the tween before the last keyframe.**

6. **Choose Insert➪Shape Tween.**

   An arrow signifying a shape tween appears in the Timeline (as shown in Figure 9-20).

   Figure 9-20: The arrow in the Timeline signifies a shape tween.

7. **Choose Window➪Properties to open the Property inspector (if it's not already open).**

8. **In the Tweening section of the Property inspector, from the Blend drop-down menu, select an Angular Blend or a Distributive Blend.**

   • *Angular Blend:* Select the Angular Blend type for blending shapes with sharp corners and straight lines. It preserves corners and straight lines in the in-between shapes of your animation.

Using the Angular Blend on irregular shapes might cause the animation to vanish!

- *Distributive Blend:* If your shapes don't have sharp corners, use the Distributive Blend type (the default) for smoother in-between shapes.

9. **You're finished! Click the first frame and press Enter (Windows) or Return (Mac) to play the animation.**

Getting Flash to take a hint — using shape hints

Does the transformation of your shape animation look strange? Flash tries to figure out the simplest and most probable way to change one of your shapes into another, but this solution might not turn out the way you expect or want.

You can use the Flash shape hints feature to attempt to correct this problem. A *shape hint* is a marker you attach to a point on a shape at the beginning and end of a shape change. The shape hints signal to Flash exactly how you want this point and the area around it to move from the start to the end of the shape-tweening process.

You can use up to 26 shape hints per layer. Shape hints are displayed on the Stage as small, colored circles with a letter (a–z) inside. On the starting keyframe, the shape hint is yellow; and on the ending keyframe, it's green. When you first insert a shape hint — before you move it onto your shape — it's red. Figure 9-21 shows an example of beginning and ending shapes with shape hints.

Figure 9-21: Shape hints guide Flash as it tweens your shape.

From this book's companion Web site, at www.dummies.com/go/flashcs5fd you can download the Flash movie file shown in Figure 9-21. It's the 4to5 pt star w_shape hint.fla file.

To use shape hints, follow these steps:

1. **If you haven't already done so, create a shape animation by using shape tweening.**

   Refer to the set of steps in the preceding section for help with this task.

2. **Click the first frame of the shape tween.**

3. **Choose Modify⇨Shape⇨Add Shape Hint or press Ctrl+Shift+H (Windows) or ⌘+Shift+H (Mac).**

Your beginning shape hint appears as the letter *a* in a small, red circle somewhere on the Stage, as shown in Figure 9-22.

4. **Click the small, red circle and drag it to the part of your graphic that you want to mark.**

5. **Click the keyframe at the end of the shape animation.**

   The ending shape hint appears somewhere on the Stage, again as the letter *a* in a small, red circle.

Figure 9-22: Shape hints are red until you position them.

6. **Click the small, red circle and drag it to the point on your shape where you want your beginning point to move.**

   The ending shape hint turns green. (However, sometimes a bug in Flash CS5 causes them to remain red. They still work the same, even if they remain red.) If you go back to the first frame of the animation, the beginning shape hint should turn yellow, as shown in Figure 9-23.

7. **Press Enter (Windows) or Return (Mac) to play your movie.**

To remove a shape hint, click the first frame of the shape tween and right-click (Windows) or Control-click (Mac) a shape hint and then choose Remove Hint — or choose Remove All Hints to nuke them all. You can also choose Modify➪Shape➪Remove All Hints, but the layer with shape hints must be selected. (Your animation then reverts to its original tween.) Choose View➪Show Shape Hints to see all the shape hints in your current layer and keyframe. Choose it again to hide them. Again, the layer and keyframe with shape hints should be selected.

Figure 9-23: The beginning shape hint is yellow, and the ending shape hint is green.

Adjusting shape hints

To tweak your animation, click the keyframe at the start or end of your shape animation and move your shape hint. Then play your animation again to see the new result. The more complicated your shape animation, the more shape hints you need to use. For more complicated shape animations, you can also add more keyframes between your original starting and ending keyframe. This creates intermediate shapes at the new keyframes that you can then tween (using plenty of shape hints, of course). In other words, you can create two or more shape tweens, one immediately following the other.

If you aren't getting the results you want, make sure that you have placed your shape hints logically. If you have a curve with shape hints *a, b,* and *c* (in that order), don't have them tween to a curve with the shape hints in *c, b, a* order unless you want some unusual effects. Flash does a better job with shape hints when you arrange them in counterclockwise order, starting from the upper-left corner of your object.

Editing Animation

You might find that you usually don't get your animation to move perfectly the first time, but fortunately, Flash is quite forgiving. You can edit keyframes in assorted ways. For example, you can edit motion-tweened frames directly by Ctrl-clicking (Windows) or ⌘-clicking (Mac) a frame and then changing the position or other properties of the object on Stage.

You can't edit shape-tweened frames directly: You can view them, but you can edit your objects only in the keyframes, not in the in-between frames. You can overcome this restriction and edit your shape-tweened frames by inserting a new keyframe between your beginning and ending keyframe and then editing the new keyframe. You do this by clicking a frame in the Timeline and then choosing Insert⇨Timeline⇨Keyframe. *Note:* Don't choose Insert⇨Timeline⇨Blank Keyframe unless you want to nuke your existing shape-tween animation. Of course, you can always edit shape-tweened frames by simply changing the starting or ending keyframe that defines them.

When you edit a keyframe of a tweened animation, Flash automatically recalculates the entire tween.

The following sections explain some useful techniques for editing and managing your animations.

Adding labels and comments

Animation can get complicated after a while. You might find it helpful to add comments to the Timeline to explain what each part of the Timeline is doing. Also, when you start adding interactivity to your movies, you can add labels to shape tween frames and then refer to them in your ActionScript. (You can find out more about ActionScript in Chapter 10.)

To add a label or a comment to a frame, follow these steps:

1. **Select a frame.**

   See the next section for information on selecting a frame.

2. **Choose Window⇨Properties to open the Property inspector (if it's not already open).**

3. In the Name text box in the Label section, type the text for the label or comment and then press Enter (Windows) or Return (Mac).

To make the text function as a comment, choose Comment from the Type drop-down list, below the Label Name text box. (Frame label names can be used within ActionScript for navigation purposes, whereas frame label comments are simply comments.) Examples of comments are shown in Figure 9-24.

Figure 9-24: Adding comments as Frame Labels can help you keep track of what is going on in your Timeline.

Adding frame labels can be a nice way to lay out the timing of a movie — by typing what you want to happen where on your Timeline — for a kind of brief verbal storyboard. This can be particularly helpful when you're working with others on a project.

Selecting frames

Flash offers two styles of making selections on the Timeline:

- **Frame-based selection:** This is the default method for shape animations. In this method, if you click a frame or a keyframe, it's selected. To select a range of frames, you can click and drag over the frames that you want to select. Or, you can click the first frame, press Shift, and then click the last frame in the range.

- **Span-based selection:** In this method, if you click a frame, it selects the entire sequence containing that frame, from one keyframe to the next. Clicking and dragging moves the entire sequence (between the keyframes) along the Timeline in either direction. To select an individual frame, press Ctrl (Windows) or ⌘ (Mac).

Motion tweens and armature animations (inverse kinematics) use this method. Shape tweens can also use this method, but it's not the default for shape tweens. You can change the style of selection for shape tweens by first choosing Edit➪Preferences (Windows) or Flash➪Preferences (Mac). Then in the General category in the Preferences dialog box, select or deselect the Span Based Selection option in the Timeline section.

Copying and pasting frames

You can copy frames of motion tweens and shape tweens that contain content you want. Then you can paste the frames in another location.

To copy and paste frames, follow these steps:

1. **Select one or more frames, as shown in Figure 9-25.**

Figure 9-25: You can select the frames of one tween and paste them to another.

2. **To copy the frames to the Clipboard, choose Edit⇨Timeline⇨ Copy Frames.**

3. **Select the first frame of your destination or select a sequence of frames that you want to replace.**

4. **To paste the frames into their new location, choose Edit⇨Timeline⇨ Paste Frames.**

You can also copy frames by pressing and holding Alt (Windows) or Option (Mac) while you drag the keyframe or range of frames to a new location.

Copying and pasting motion

You can copy motion-tween information in Flash from one object to another. If you've created some nice animation for one character, for example, you can easily copy that same animation to other characters in your scene — or in another scene or movie.

To copy and paste motion from one symbol instance to another, follow these steps:

1. **In the Timeline, select the frames that contain the motion tween that you want to copy.**

   To get this to work properly, be sure to copy all the frames.

2. **To copy the motion information to the Clipboard, choose Edit⇨ Timeline⇨Copy Motion.**

3. **Select the symbol instance that you want to copy the motion information to.**

   The symbol instance should only be one frame long at this point; Flash will add the needed frames.

4. **To copy the motion information to the symbol instance you selected, choose Edit⇨Timeline⇨Paste Motion.**

The pasted motion tween appears, starting in the frame of the Timeline that contains the destination symbol instance.

This copies all the motion tween information from one symbol instance to another, including the information about the symbol's changes in position, changes in scale, changes in rotation and skew, changes in color (including tint, brightness, or alpha), changes in filter values, and changes in blend modes. (See Chapter 7 for information on filters and blend modes.)

Moving frames

You can easily move frames and their contents. Just select the layer, place the cursor over a frame or range of frames, and then drag them to their new home, as shown in Figure 9-26.

Figure 9-26: Move frames by selecting and dragging them.

Reversing your animation

You can make your animation play backward by selecting the relevant frames in one or more layers and choosing Modify⇨Timeline⇨Reverse Frames, or right-clicking (Windows) or Control-clicking (Mac) and choosing Reverse Frames. (This is an amazing and useful feature.) **Hint:** For shape tweens, your selection must start and end with keyframes.

To reverse a motion tween by itself, without other layers included, select the tween and right-click (Windows) or Control-click (Mac) and choose Reverse Keyframes.

Changing speed

After you set up your animation, play your movie to check the speed. If one part of your tweened animation is too fast or too slow, you can slide keyframes around on the Timeline to shorten or lengthen the time between keyframes. You can shorten or lengthen a tween as follows:

✓ **Shape tween:** Click a keyframe to select it and then drag it to another point on the Timeline.

✓ **Motion tween:** Place the cursor near the end keyframe so that a double arrow appears, and then click and drag in either direction.

These techniques give you lots of control over the timing of your animation.

Figure 9-27 shows two possible versions of the Timeline for the shape tween shown in Figure 9-19. The black dots on the Timeline are the keyframes. To create the version on the bottom, we dragged the last keyframe to the right, thereby lengthening the tween. Because the same change in shape now occurs over a longer period, the tween appears slower.

Figure 9-27: You can change the length of a tween.

The effect is even more noticeable when an object is moving across the stage during a tween. For example, if a symbol (or shape) moves from the left of the Stage to the right and you shorten the tween, the symbol (or shape) appears to move across the Stage more quickly because it must get from the left to the right in fewer frames.

Using onion skins

To help you visualize the flow of your animation, you can turn on the onion skinning feature. *Onion skinning* lets you see a "ghost image" of some or all of the frames in your animation. (Normally, you see only the current frame on the Stage.) Figure 9-28 shows an example of both regular and outlined onion skinning. Onion skinning displays frames as transparent layers, like the transparent layers of an onion skin.

Figure 9-28: Onion skinning helps you see where your animation is going.

 To display onion skinning, click the Onion Skin button at the bottom of the Timeline and adjust the Onion Skin markers at the top of the Timeline, as shown in Figure 9-29, to indicate the number of frames in which you want the onion skins to appear before and after the playhead.

 To display onion skinning with outlines, click the Onion Skin Outlines button, and adjust the Onion Skin markers at the top of the Timeline. Sometimes using Onion Skin Outlines makes it easier to see how your objects are animating.

 To edit any of the frames on the Timeline no matter where your current frame pointer is, click the Edit Multiple Frames button. If you also have onion skinning turned on, you can then edit any frame while viewing all the other onion-skinned frames.

 Click Modify Onion Markers to display a menu to help you adjust the way your onion markers work:

  ✔ **Always Show Markers:** Shows onion skin markers even when you turn off onion skinning.

  ✔ **Anchor Onion:** Locks the onion skin markers in their current position and prevents them from moving along with the current frame pointer, as they normally do.

✔ **Onion 2:** Applies onion skinning to the two frames before and the two frames after the *playhead* (the current frame pointer).

✔ **Onion 5:** Applies onion skinning to the five frames before and the five frames after the playhead.

✔ **Onion All:** Applies onion skinning to all the frames on your Timeline.

Figure 9-29: When you display onion skinning, markers are placed on the Timeline.

 Hidden or locked layers never show as onion skinned. Hide or lock layers to isolate them from the layers you really want to change and to keep your onion skinning from getting out of control. Chapter 6 explains how to hide and lock layers.

Moving everything around the Stage at once

If you move a complete animation on the Stage without moving the graphics in all frames and all layers at one time, you might quickly go nuts when you discover that every little thing must be realigned. Instead, retain your sanity and move everything at one time.

To move a complete animation, follow these steps:

1. **Unlock and unhide all layers that contain the animation you want to move and then lock or hide any layers that you don't want to move.**

   To lock (or unlock) a layer, click below the lock icon on that layer's row. To hide (or unhide) a layer, click below the eye icon on that layer's row. See Chapter 6 for more information on working with layers.

2. Click the Edit Multiple Frames button at the bottom of the Timeline.

If you ever need to resize a project, this button is your new best friend.

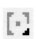

3. Drag the onion skin markers to the beginning and ending frames of your animation.

Alternatively, if you want to select all frames, click the Modify Onion Markers button at the bottom of the Timeline and then choose Onion All.

4. Choose Edit➪Select All.

5. Drag your animation to its new place on the Stage.

If you run into difficulties making this work:

- *In Step 3,* click the Modify Onion Markers button at the bottom of the Timeline and choose Onion All.

- *In Step 5,* use the keyboard arrows to move your animation to its new place on the Stage.

Connecting the Hip Bone to the Thigh Bone

With Flash's Inverse Kinematics (IK) tools, you can draw a chain of bones (an *armature*) to connect a set of objects and then animate all the objects automatically, simply by animating the position of one of the bones in the chain. Flash simulates the physics of your objects moving as if they were all connected by the chain. You can also draw a chain of bones inside a single shape so that when you move a bone, the part of the shape near the bone flexes. The bones are visible when you're creating your movie yet are invisible when you play the movie. Thus, your audience sees only the effect of the bones — not the bones themselves.

These tools can make it much easier, for example, to create animated characters and to animate their arms and legs (as shown in Figure 9-30, for example) as well as facial expressions.

To use inverse kinematics in your Flash movies, you must specify ActionScript 3.0 on the Flash tab of the Publish Settings dialog box. (See Chapter 13 for all the info about the Publish Settings dialog box.)

In the study of mechanics, when objects are connected in a dangling chain and caused to move by changing the position of the objects at the top, that's a *kinematic chain.* If the motion is created by moving the position of the objects at the bottom (for example, when you shake someone's hand, and that motion moves their forearm, elbow, and upper arm), that's *inverse kinematics.*

Figure 9-30: Use inverse kinematics to quickly create a "walk cycle."

Putting bones into your symbols

You can quickly and easily set up an armature of bones in your animation. The armature can contain a linear chain of bones. Or, the bones can be in a branched structure, like the branches of a tree; or the torso, legs, and arms of a human. The armature can connect movie clips, graphic symbols, or buttons. Or, as you can see in the next section of this chapter, the armature can be inside a shape, which bends and flexes when the armature is animated.

As usual, any movie clips and buttons you use can contain other movie clips for nested animations, if you like. (See Chapter 7 for more info on movie clips and graphic symbols, and see Chapter 8 for the lowdown on buttons.)

To create an armature that connects a set of symbol instances, follow these steps:

1. **Create movie clips, graphic symbols, or buttons; and then place instances of them on the Stage approximately how you want them to appear, all in one frame on one layer in the Timeline.**

   See Chapter 7 for more about symbols and instances.

2. Select the Bone tool from the Tools panel.

The Bone tool is part of a flyout that also contains the Bind tool. If necessary, click and hold the Bind tool (discussed next), and then choose the Bone tool from the flyout.

3. Click and drag from one symbol instance to another.

This creates a bone that connects the two symbol instances, as shown in Figure 9-31. The bone and the symbol instances appear in a new layer labeled Armature. The new layer is a *pose layer.* The bone has a head (which is rounded) and a tail (which is pointed).

For this step to work, you must click in an area of the symbol instance that isn't empty and drag to a nonempty area in the other symbol instance.

4. Repeat Step 3 for each of the symbol instances that you want to connect.

- *To make a chain of bones:* Click and drag from the tail of the bone in the last symbol instance to a new symbol instance.

  Another bone appears, connecting the previous symbol instance and a new one, as shown in Figure 9-32. The original bone is the *parent,* and the new bone is the *child.*

  Repeat this step for as many symbol instances as desired.

- *To make a branch:* Click a symbol instance that has a bone connected to the tail of its bone, and then drag to a new symbol instance that doesn't yet contain a bone.

  Another bone appears, connecting the previous symbol instance and a new one, as shown in Figure 9-33.

  Repeat this step for as many symbol instances as desired.

From our companion Web site (www.dummies.com/go/flashcs5fd), download the person-with-bones.fla file for a simple example of a person with animated bones that you can work with.

Figure 9-31: Connect your symbol instances with a bone.

Figure 9-32: You can build armatures as chains.

To join two armatures, select the Bone tool from the Tools panel, click a bone in one armature, and then drag to a bone in the second armature. This connects the second armature to the first one, in a single new armature in a single pose layer, as shown in Figure 9-34.

Unlike layers that contain a shape tween or a motion tween, which contain only one animated object per layer, an Armature layer contains multiple objects — a set of connected bones — animating on a single layer.

Figure 9-33: You can also build armatures as branches.

Adding bones to shapes

You can also use the Bone tool to build an armature (a set of bones) inside a single filled shape. For example, if you put the bones inside the shape of an arm, as shown in Figure 9-35, Flash bends the forearm and elbow part of the arm shape automatically when you move the bone in the forearm.

To build an armature inside a filled shape, follow these steps:

1. **Create a new layer by choosing Insert⇨Timeline⇨Layer.**

2. **Right-click (Windows) or Control-click (Mac) an empty frame in the new layer where you want your animation to start. From the contextual menu that appears, choose Insert Keyframe.**

3. **Draw a shape, or paste one onto the Stage.**

Figure 9-34: Join two armatures by clicking a bone in one and dragging it to the other.

Figure 9-35: You can put a set of bones inside a shape.

The shape can be as simple or complex as you like, but it must be a single, filled shape. (Check out Chapter 3 for all the info on creating fills.)

4. **Select the Bone tool from the Tools panel.**

5. **Click and drag inside the shape.**

   A bone appears inside the shape.

6. **Click the tail of a bone and then drag to create a new bone inside the shape.**

   A new bone appears, connected to the previous bone.

7. **Repeat Step 6 as desired.**

To see how the shape flexes, choose the Selection tool from the Tools panel, click the tail of a bone, and then drag. The shape should bend and bulge as the tail moves.

Adjusting how shapes flex with the Bind tool

To change how the shape flexes when you move a bone, you can use the Bind tool. With the Bind tool, you can control which points on the shape's stroke are bound to which bones, which allows you to make the shape flex how you want. These points are called *control points*. To adjust which points on the shape's stroke connect to which bones, follow these steps:

1. **Select the Bind tool from the Tools panel.**

    If the Bind tool isn't visible, press and hold the Bone tool in the Tools panel. From the pop-up menu that appears, choose the Bind tool.

2. Click the shape containing the bones.

The control points on the selected shape appear. (These may be difficult to see if the stroke is thick.)

Then you can do any of the following:

✓ **Click any bone to see which control points in the Stroke of the shape are connected to the bone.**

The control points that are connected to the bone appear highlighted in yellow, as shown in Figure 9-36. You can press Shift and then click to select multiple bones.

✓ **To connect a control point to a bone, click the bone (if it's not already selected), and then Shift-click a control point not highlighted in yellow.**

Figure 9-36: Click a bone to see the control points connected to it.

The control point becomes highlighted in yellow, showing that it's now connected to the selected bone.

You can Shift-drag to connect multiple control points.

✓ **To disconnect a control point from a bone, click the bone (if it's not already selected), and then Ctrl-click (Windows) or ⌘-Option-click (Mac) a control point highlighted in yellow.**

The control point is no longer highlighted in yellow, showing that it's no longer connected to the selected bone.

You can Shift+Ctrl-drag (Windows) or Shift+⌘+Option-drag (Mac) to disconnect multiple controls.

✓ **If a control point is connected to more than one bone, Flash highlights the control point with a yellow triangle. If you select that triangle, Flash highlights the bones it connects to.**

✓ **Click any control point to see which bone or bones are connected to it.**

The bone or bones that are connected to the control point appear highlighted in yellow. You can press Shift and click to select multiple bones.

✓ **To connect a bone to a control point, click the control point (if it's not already selected), and then Shift-click a bone.**

The bone becomes highlighted in yellow, showing that it's now connected to the selected control point.

✔ **To disconnect a bone from a control point, click the control point (if it isn't already selected), and then Ctrl-click (Windows) or ⌘+Option-click (Mac) a bone highlighted in yellow.**

The bone is no longer highlighted in yellow, showing that it's no longer connected to the selected control point.

To see the results of your adjustments, choose the Selection tool from the Tools panel, click the tail of a bone and drag, and watch how your shape flexes differently.

Adding constraints and Springs, using the Bind tool

If you click the tail of any bone and drag, by default, you can move the bone up and down and rotate it 360 degrees around the bone connected to its head. To make it easier to create realistic animations, you can constrain each bone's freedom of motion. That way, for example, if you put bones in a character's thigh and shin, the knee doesn't bend in the wrong direction.

You can also add Springs to your bones. *Springs* add a bouncy motion to your animated bones, which can add lifelike detail and interest — and all with almost no extra work for you. You simply select a bone and specify the strength of the Spring in the Property Inspector. You can also set a value for *Damping*, which is the speed at which the Spring loses energy. This is a truly fun feature that can easily add lots of expression to your animations.

To change a bone's freedom of motion or add Springs, follow these steps:

1. **Choose the Selection tool from the Tools panel, and then click an armature on the Stage.**

   The bones in the armature appear, as shown in Figure 9-37.

2. **Click a bone to select it.**

   The selected bone is highlighted in a different color.

   To set the constraint properties for several bones at once, Shift-click additional bones to select several bones.

Figure 9-37: These bones are all selected.

3. **Choose Window⇨Properties to open the Property inspector (if it's not already open). In the Property inspector (if necessary), click the disclosure triangle to the left of each section in the Property inspector to reveal the contents of that section.**

Then do any of the following:

✏ **To enable or disable the bone's freedom of rotation around the joint at its head:** Select or deselect (respectively) the Enable check box in the Joint:Rotation section of the Property inspector.

   If you deselect the Enable check box, the bone is connected rigidly to its parent, and only its children can move.

✏ **To constrain the bone's freedom of rotation around the joint at its head:** Select the Enable check box and the Constrain check box in the Joint:Rotation section of the Property inspector. To limit the amount of counterclockwise rotation, choose a Min value between 0 and –359. To limit the amount of clockwise rotation, choose a Max value between 0 and 359.

✏ **To enable or disable the bone's freedom of motion left and right:** Select or deselect the Enable check box in the Joint:X Translation section of the Property inspector.

   If you select the Enable check box, the bone can move freely left and right, stretching the length of its parent to accommodate the motion. If you deselect the Enable check box (the default setting), you can move the bone left to right, but the length of the parent bone won't stretch.

✏ **To constrain the bone's freedom of motion right and left:** Select the Enable check box and also the Constrain check box in the Joint:X Translation section of the Property inspector. To limit the amount of the bone's motion to the left, choose a Min value. To limit the amount of the bone's motion to the right, choose a Max value, and then press Enter (Windows) or Return (Mac).

   The numbers you choose specify the maximum number of pixels that the bone can move right or left.

✏ **To enable or disable the bone's freedom of motion up and down:** Select or deselect (respectively) the Enable check box in the Joint:Y Translation section of the Property inspector. To limit the amount of motion upward, choose a Min value. To limit the amount of motion downward, choose a Max value. (These directions are relative to the direction of the bone.)

   The numbers you choose specify the maximum number of pixels that the bone can move up or down.

✔ **To add Springs:** Choose a Strength value in the Spring section from 0 to 100. You can choose a value for Damper from 0 to 100 as well. The higher the Damper value, the more that the oscillations of the Spring are constrained.

To test your springs and other changes you make in your bones' constraints, choose the Selection tool from the Tools panel, click the tail of a bone, and drag to see how the armature moves and bounces.

Animating your bones and Springs

After you build your armatures, animating them is easy. You can animate them with or without adding the bouncy motion of Springs, which are new to Flash Professional CS5. To animate the bones and Springs (optional) in an armature, follow these steps:

1. **To make room for your animation, add frames in the pose layer (your Armature layer) by dragging the end of the last (or only) frame.**

   A double arrow appears as you move the mouse over the last frame. While you click and drag, the frames of the pose layer are highlighted from the frame containing the first pose to the last frame.

   A layer that contains an *armature* (a set of bones) is called a *pose layer.*

2. **To add a new pose to the pose layer (Armature layer), click in a frame, and choose the Selection tool from the Tools panel. On the Stage, reposition the bones in your armature as desired, by clicking the head or tail of a bone (or clicking a symbol connected to the bone) and dragging, as shown in Figure 9-38.**

   A keyframe marker appears in the current frame on the Armature layer.

3. **To see the armature animate, click the first frame and press Enter (Windows) or Return (Mac).**

Figure 9-38: Adding new poses to your armature animation is easy.

If you want to move an armature to another location on the stage, choose the Selection tool from the Tools panel and click the armature to select it. Then you can Ctrl-drag (Windows) or Option-drag (Mac). Or in the Position and Size section of the Property inspector, choose a new value for X or Y.

If you decide that a bone isn't the right length in a particular pose, you can change its length by choosing the Subselection tool and clicking and dragging the bone to the new length that you desire.

To delete a bone, select the bone and press Delete.

You can make your armature animations more compelling and realistic by controlling the acceleration and deceleration of motion near pose frames in your animations — *easing.* To add easing to an animation of an armature, do the following steps:

1. **In your pose layer on the Timeline, click a frame between two pose frames.**

2. **In the Ease section of the Property inspector, from the Type drop-down menu (shown in Figure 9-39), choose the type of easing that you want.**

   - *Simple:* This slows down the motion in the frames prior to the next pose frame.

   - *Stop/Start:* This slows down the motion in the frames after the first pose frame, then accelerates the motion, and then slows down the motion in the frames before the next pose frame.

Figure 9-39: Add an ease with ease.

3. **In the Ease section of the Property inspector, click the Strength value, type a number from –100 to 100, and then press Enter (Windows) or Return (Mac).**

This specifies the strength of the easing. Zero (0) is equivalent to no easing at all. A negative value increases the speed of the motion tween as the playhead nears the ending frame of the tween, and a positive value slows the speed as it nears the ending frame.

4. **To view your changes, move the playhead in the Timeline to the first frame of your animation and press Enter (Windows) or Return (Mac), or choose Control⇨Test Movie⇨In Flash Professional.**

If you want to add motion tween effects to your armature animation, convert it to a movie clip or graphic symbol. To convert your armature animation to a movie clip or graphic symbol in a motion tween, follow these steps:

1. **Choose the Selection tool from the Tools panel.**

2. **Double-click the armature.**

   The armature and all its associated objects are selected.

3. **Right-click (Windows) or Control-click (Mac) the selection. From the contextual menu that appears, choose Convert to Symbol.**

4. **In the Convert to Symbol dialog box that appears, type a name, choose Movie Clip or Graphic from the Type drop-down menu, and then click OK.**

   Your animation will no longer run by moving the playhead, but it's still there. You can see the animation within your new symbol by choosing Control⇨Test Movie⇨In Flash Professional.

5. **To add a motion tween to your symbol, right-click (Windows) or Control-click (Mac) the new symbol instance. From the contextual menu that appears, choose Create Motion Tween.**

   Now you can add motion tween effects to the symbol, including scaling, rotation, color effects, and 3D positioning, as described previously in this chapter.

6. **To view the motion tween plus the animation within the symbol, choose Control⇨Test Movie⇨In Flash Professional.**

Creating Animations with the Code Snippets Panel

The Code Snippets panel, which is new to Flash Professional CS5, allows you to create animations and add interactivity using prepackaged ActionScript 3.0 code. With a few clicks, you can add code for the following animations. These code snippets are found in the Animation folder of the Code Snippets panel, as shown in Figure 9-40:

✓ **Animate linear movement.** Animate Horizontally or Animate Vertically. Using these together can give you linear animations for any angle or direction.

✓ **Animate rotation.** Rotate Continuously,

✓ **Fade.** Fade in a Movie Clip or Fade Out a Movie Clip. Fading in and out via the Timeline can be labor intensive when dealing with many movie clips. However, these Code Snippets allow you to do it quickly and easily.

✓ **Move with Keyboard Arrows.** Allows the user to move objects using keyboard arrows.

✓ **Move an object once.** Move Horizontally or Move Vertically. The object simply jumps to a new location when the playhead reaches the frame containing the code snippet.

✓ **Rotate Once.** The object jumps to a new rotation when the playhead reaches the frame containing the code snippet.

Figure 9-40: Adding animation using the Code Snippets panel.

The Code Snippets panel contains code for much more than just animations, such as applying hyperlinks as described in Chapter 8, and we continue to explore the capabilities of this panel in Chapter 10 as well.

To add Code Snippets to animate objects, follow these steps:

1. **Select the object to which you want to apply the animation.**

2. **Open the Code Snippets panel (if it's not already open) by choosing Window⇨Code Snippets.**

3. **Open the Animation folder to reveal your animation choices, as shown in Figure 9-40.**

4. **Double-click the animation that you want to apply:**

- Move with Keyboard Arrows
- Animate Horizontally/Animate Vertically
- Fade In a Movie Clip/Fade Out a Movie Clip
- Rotate Continuously/Rotate Once
- Move Horizontally/Move Vertically

If the object that you select in Step 1 isn't an instance of a movie clip symbol or doesn't have an instance name, a dialog box appears requesting that you allow Flash to name and possibly create a movie clip instance. Otherwise, an Actions layer appears on the Timeline with an "a" in the current frame, indicating that it contains ActionScript code.

5. **If the dialog box appears, click OK.**

An Actions layer appears on the Timeline with an "a" in the current frame, indicating that it contains ActionScript code.

6. **Open the Actions panel (if it's not already open) by choosing Window⇨Actions, or clicking its tab.**

7. **If the ActionScript code for your animation doesn't appear in the Actions panel, select the frame from the Actions layer of the Timeline containing the ActionScript code.**

The ActionScript code appears in the Actions panel.

8. **Read the comments regarding the animation code in the Actions panel and make any modifications to the code that are allowed by the comments.**

For example, to change the speed of a Fade In animation, you can change the value in the code from .01 to .05 or any value from 0 to 1.

9. **If your Timeline contains layers with frames extending beyond Frame 1, add frames to the layer containing your animated object by right-clicking (Windows) or Control-clicking (Mac) a frame later in the Timeline and choosing Insert Frame.**

This adds frames to the layer containing your animated object. You may need to do this so that your animation doesn't disappear when the play-head moves beyond Frame 1.

10. **Test your animation by choosing Control⇨Test Movie⇨In Flash Professional.**

If you delete an object that you added a code snippet to, you also need to delete any code in the Actions window pertaining to that object. Otherwise, errors appear in the Compiler Errors window when you test your movie.

Making the Scene

Animations can get complicated fast, and one way to manage that complexity is by organizing them in layers and layer folders. (Hop to Chapter 6 for the lowdown on layers and layer folders.) Another way to manage the complexity of your animations is to break them into chunks of time — into scenes. You can then use scenes as the modular building blocks of your movies, which you can then rearrange any way you want.

Breaking your movie into scenes

When you create a new Flash movie file (for example, by choosing File⇨New and selecting ActionScript 3.0 on the General tab), by default, the file contains one empty scene, cleverly titled Scene 1. Any animations that you create then become part of Scene 1.

If you want to add a scene, choose Insert⇨Scene. The Stage clears, and the new scene name, such as Scene 2, appears above the upper-left corner of the Stage.

Manipulating that scene

To keep track of your scenes, open the Scene panel by choosing Window⇨Other Panels⇨ Scene. The Scene panel (as shown in Figure 9-41) lists all the scenes in your movie. When you choose Control⇨Test Movie⇨In Flash Professional, the scenes play in order, from the top of the list down.

Figure 9-41: The Scene panel lets you make a big scene.

Here's how to use the Scene panel to control your scenes:

- ✒ **To change the order in which scenes play:** Drag a scene's name on the Scene panel to a new place in the list.

- ✒ **To add a scene:** Click the Add Scene button in the lower left corner of the Scene panel.

- ✒ **To rename a scene:** Double-click the scene's name in the Scene panel, type the new name, and then press Enter (Windows) or Return (Mac).

- ✒ **To delete a scene:** Select that scene and then click the Delete Scene button at the bottom of the Scene panel.

- ✒ **To duplicate a scene:** Click the Duplicate Scene button at the bottom of the Scene panel.

- ✒ **To view a particular scene:** Click its name on the Scene panel. Or choose View⇨Go To and choose the name of the scene that you want from the submenu.

10

Getting Interactive

*S*ome of the real fun with Flash begins when you start to make your art and animations interactive. *Interactivity* means that a computer user's input triggers immediate changes on the computer screen, which the user can then respond to further, as if a conversation were taking place between the user and the computer. Examples can be as simple as clicking a button to go to another Web page, or as complex as a video jukebox.

Flash uses the ActionScript computer language to specify how the interactivity works. *ActionScript statements* are short instructions that tell Flash what to do next. By combining them, you can produce complex sets of instructions to create amazing animated graphics, giving your Flash movies sophisticated interactive capabilities. ActionScript provides you with tremendous flexibility in designing animations and interactivity, and only your imagination limits what you can do. In this book, we describe ActionScript 3.0. For more information about ActionScript 3.0, see the nearby sidebar.

About ActionScript 3.0

The most recent version of ActionScript is 3.0, which was thoroughly redesigned to better support big, complex applications that have lots of data. For those just starting out with Flash, one advantage of ActionScript 3.0 is that Flash movies powered by ActionScript 3.0 can perform up to ten times faster than those using earlier versions of ActionScript.

Flash Professional CS5 supports earlier versions of ActionScript, too. To use some of the latest features in Flash CS5, though, you need to use ActionScript 3.0. In this book, all our code is written in ActionScript 3.0 because that's the wave of the future.

To run Flash movies written with ActionScript 3.0, your users need Flash Player 9 or later. At this writing, more than 96% of the computer users in the world have Flash Player 9 or later, and that percentage is rising.

ActionScript is based on the same language specification as JavaScript, the popular computer language used extensively in Web page design. ActionScript is basically a powerful version of JavaScript with extensions for controlling Flash animations. If you know JavaScript, you can use much of that knowledge when working with ActionScript, and vice versa.

Flash Professional CS5 brings ActionScript coding to a whole new level of ease with its Code Snippets panel. With a single click, you can add bundles of code to navigate your timeline; hide, show, and drag objects; play movie clips; and more. Adding ActionScript code has never been easier. In this chapter, we describe the Code Snippets panel in detail, as well as traditional ActionScript coding techniques.

Coding with Snippets

Flash Professional CS5 offers the new Code Snippets feature, which greatly reduces the time it takes to add ActionScript to your Flash movies. The Code Snippets panel contains six folders:

- ✔ **Actions:** These are common actions for buttons, such as hiding, showing, or repositioning an object when a button is clicked. These are described later in this chapter. (We describe the code snippet for Click and Go to Web Page in "Adding an action for a button" in Chapter 8.)

- ✔ **Timeline Navigation:** You can use these snippets, for example, to create a Web site where each frame is a different Web page and you have buttons to navigate between the frames.

- ✔ **Animation:** These snippets include moving, rotating, and fading in and out objects. We describe these in Chapter 9.

✔ **Load and Unload:** To control the size of your Flash movie, you might not want to load all your images into the movie all at once. Also, it might be more efficient to refer to external text files or images in your movie rather than loading the files into your movie. So, if you want to make changes, you can just change the contents of image files or text files instead of changing your Flash file.

✔ **Audio and Video:** These contain ActionScript code for creating your own MP3 or video player.

✔ **Event Handlers:** You can use code snippets for event handlers to easily add your own code to respond to button clicks and other events, such as the pressing of a key or when the playhead enters a specific frame.

Buttons versus frames versus movie clips

You can quickly create ActionScript code from the Code Snippets panel or with the Actions panel described in the next section of this chapter. All the code that you create from the Code Snippets panel or the Actions panel is stored in frames on a Timeline. If a frame contains code, Flash denotes that with a small "a" in the frame. Some code that you add might execute when the playhead reaches it, whereas other code might not. The reason is that some code snippets execute when a button is clicked or a movie clip symbol is dragged, and so on, and other code executes when the playhead enters the frame that the code resides in.

Some Code Snippets require that you select an object before applying the snippet, and others require only that you position the playhead over the frame to which you want to add the code. For instance, you need to have a button selected to add the Code Snippets that begin `Click To`. You apply other Code Snippets to frames or movie clips.

Adding code to frames

One common piece of code that you might want to add to a frame is a *stop instruction,* which stops the movie at that frame. Other code snippets that you might want to assign in specific frames are Play a Movie Clip, Stop a Movie Clip, Move Horizontally/Move Vertically, and Rotate Once. (We describe Move Horizontally/Move Vertically and Rotate Once in Chapter 9.)

Adding a stop to a frame

Take a look at a simple example of using ActionScript in a frame: placing a `Stop` method at the beginning of the movie. You might want to do this, for example, if you're creating a Web site where each frame in your Flash movie is a separate page of your Web site. The movie loads, but the first thing that it encounters is a command to stop. Nothing happens until someone clicks a button to navigate to another frame of the Timeline. To add the `Stop` method to your Timeline, follow these steps:

1. **Choose Window⇨Actions to open the Actions panel (if it isn't open already).**

   If necessary, expand the Actions panel by clicking the Actions panel's icon or clicking the Actions panel's tab.

2. **Click the Code Snippets button on the right side of the Actions panel to show the Code Snippets panel (if it's not already visible).**

   You can dock the Code Snippets panel above the Actions panel for convenience.

3. **Drag the playhead to the frame where you want to stop.**

4. **In the Code Snippets panel, open the Timeline Navigation folder and double-click Stop at This Frame.**

   The code appears in the Script pane of the Actions panel, as shown in Figure 10-1. (You can click it to deselect it.) It also creates a new layer called Actions and places the code in a keyframe in that layer where the playhead resides.

Figure 10-1: The Actions panel contains the ActionScript code that you applied using the Code Snippets panel.

The information between /* and */ are comments. The next line contains the instruction to stop:

```
stop();
```

Each instruction in ActionScript is a *statement,* and statements are followed by a semicolon.

5. Choose Control⇨Test Movie⇨In Flash Professional.

stop(); halts your movie at the frame where it resides.

To get an idea of the scope of ActionScript, take a peek at the many categories and subcategories that you can choose in the left pane of the Actions panel. (Click the small triangle to open it.) For starters, you might browse briefly through the flash.display category and its subcategories. We discuss how to use this code later in this chapter.

Playing or stopping a movie clip

The Play a Movie Clip code snippet allows you to play an animation inside a movie clip symbol when the playhead reaches the frame with the code on the main Timeline. This, of course, is useful only if that animation is already stopped. The Stop a Movie Clip code snippet will stop the movie clip's animation. To play and stop a movie clip, do the following:

1. **In a new document, create a movie clip by choosing Insert⇨New Symbol. In the dialog box that appears, choose Movie Clip, and type in a name for the Movie Clip.**

2. **Add some artwork and create an animation on the symbol's Timeline.**

3. **Choose Edit⇨Edit Document to exit Symbol-editing mode.**

4. **Drag the movie clip symbol from the Library onto the Stage and type in an Instance name in the Property Inspector.**

   Frame 1 of Layer 1 now contains an instance of the movie clip.

5. **Choose Control⇨Test Movie⇨In Flash Professional to view your movie clip's animation.**

6. **Select the movie clip on the Stage. In the Actions folder of the Code Snippets panel, double-click Stop a Movie Clip.**

   An Actions layer appears with a single keyframe in Frame 1, containing the code for the code snippet in the Actions panel. You can choose Control⇨Test Movie⇨In Flash Animation to verify that the animation does not occur. It has been stopped.

7. **Right-click in a later frame in Layer 1, such as Frame 50, and choose Insert Frame.**

   The frames fill from 1–50.

8. **Move the playhead to Frame 25 (or approximately around there), select the movie clip, and then double-click Play a Movie Clip in the Code Snippets panel.**

   A keyframe appears on the Actions layer, and the code for the Play a Movie Clip appears in the Actions panel.

9. **Choose Control⇨Test Movie⇨In Flash Professional to view your movie clip's animation.**

   Test your movie. You should see the animation starting and stopping at the times you specified on the Timeline.

Clicking buttons

A common way to add interactivity is to create a button. The viewer clicks the button, and something happens (or stops happening). Usually, you add text near or on the button so that your viewers know what the button is for.

In Chapter 8, we describe how to add hyperlinks to your buttons. In this section, we describe how you can use buttons for so many other useful tasks — to start or stop animation, jump to different parts of a Timeline, hide and position objects, and more.

Navigating your Timeline with buttons

Here's an example of how to add ActionScript that enables a button to cause your movie to jump to a specific frame or new scene. You might want to do this, for example, if you have different parts of your Web page in different frames or scenes. You could use the button to change the look of your Web page by navigating to new frames. To allow a button to jump to a frame of your choice, follow these steps:

1. **Create the button and place an instance of the button on the Stage.**

   Chapter 8 shows you how to create buttons.

2. **Open the Property inspector if it isn't already open. (Choose Window⇨Properties.)**

   If necessary, expand the Property inspector to its full size.

3. **In the Instance Name text box near the top of the Property inspector, type a unique instance name for the button, such as myButton.**

   If you want to skip this step, Flash will automatically assign an instance name although we recommended that you name your instances yourself to more thoroughly describe them.

4. **Choose Window➪Actions to open the Actions panel (if it's not already open).**

   To expand the Actions panel, click the Actions panel's icon or click the Actions panel's tab.

5. **If the Code Snippets panel isn't open, click the Code Snippets button in the Actions panel.**

6. **Move the playhead to Frame 1 or the first frame that the button appears and select the button on the Stage.**

7. **Open the Timeline Navigation folder in the Code Snippets panel and double-click any of the following:**

   - *Click to Go to Frame and Stop:* This instruction stops at a frame that you specify.

   - *Click to Go to Frame and Play:* This instruction plays the frame that you specify in the Actions panel, rather than stopping at it. It plays until it reaches another stop instruction.

   - *Click to Go to Next Frame and Stop.*

   - *Click to Go to Previous Frame and Stop.*

   - *Click to Go to Next Scene and Play:* You can organize different parts of your movie or Web pages according to scenes. Be sure to use the Scene panel (Windows➪Other Panels➪Scene) to help you create, rename, and organize your scenes.

   - *Click to Go to Previous Scene and Play.*

   - *Click to Go to Scene and Play:* This code allows you to type in the name of any scene that you want to go to.

   The code that you choose appears in the Actions Panel, and a new Actions layer appears on the Timeline (if it doesn't already exist), and an "a" appears in a keyframe on that layer, in the frame on the Timeline where the playhead is.

8. **If you chose one of the Click to Go to Frame . . . options, in the Actions panel, delete 5 and type a new frame number. (Or type a frame label enclosed in quotes.) If you chose Click to Go to Scene and Play, then type in a new scene name.**

   These instructions are also explained in the comment sections at the top of the code in the Actions panel.

9. **Test your movie.**

   In our example shown in Figure 10-2, when the user clicks myButton, Flash goes to the frame labeled `Products`.

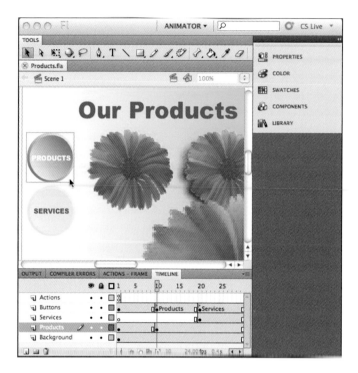

Figure 10-2: When the user clicks myButton, Flash goes to the frame labeled `Products`.

Hiding objects with buttons

Another thing you may wish to do with a button is to hide objects when a button is clicked. For example, you could click a button that causes objects to disappear from view. This may be useful when designing a game. Also, you could use this code snippet to create a button that hides itself when clicked. For example, say you create a card game where you click the back of a card that "hides" itself, revealing the playing card underneath, as shown in Figure 10-3. The back of the card is a button that hides itself when clicked. To use this code snippet, follow these steps:

1. **Choose Insert⇨New Symbol. In the dialog box that appears, choose Button and type in a name for the button.**

2. **Create the art for your button.**

   See Chapter 8 for information about buttons.

3. **Choose Edit⇨Edit Document to exit Symbol-editing mode, and then drag your button from the Library onto the Stage.**

Figure 10-3: You can hide an object when a button is clicked.

4. **In the Property inspector, type in a name for the instance, such as myButton.**

5. **Select the button and double-click Click to Hide an Object in the Actions folder of the Code Snippets panel.**

   The Actions layer appears on the Timeline, and the following code appears in the Actions panel after the comments:

   ```
   myButton.addEventListener(MouseEvent.CLICK, fl_ClickToHide);

   function fl_ClickToHide(event:MouseEvent):void
   {
   myButton.visible = false;
   }
   ```

6. **Choose Control⇨Test Movie⇨In Flash Professional to verify that when you click the button, it disappears.**

7. **To make another object disappear rather than the button, drag the other object from the Library and position it on the Stage.**

8. **While the object is still selected, give it an Instance name in the Properties panel, such as myDisappearingCircle.**

9. **Click the frame in the Actions layer containing the code and in the Actions panel change the following**

   ```
   myButton.visible = false;
   ```

   to

   ```
   myDisappearingCircle.visible = false;
   ```

10. **Choose Control⇨Test Movie⇨In Flash Professional to verify that when you click the button, myDisappearingCircle disappears.**

Changing your clicks to MouseOvers and more

The code snippets that begin with Click To activate when you click a button. You may want them to work differently, though: for example, when you move your mouse over a button rather than clicking it, or when a user presses the button rather than releasing it.

Table 10-1 lists the different events that you can assign to a button. Also see the upcoming section, "Adding Event Handlers" for how to create a variety of event handlers.

If you want to change a click to another mouse event, use the following steps. Instead of clicking the mouse to hide an object, as described in the preceding steps, you can cause the object to hide when the mouse moves over the object.

1. **Click the frame in the Actions layer containing the ActionScript code with the click event that you wish to modify.**

2. **In the Actions panel, locate the code**

   ```
   MouseEvent.CLICK
   ```

   and replace CLICK with another parameter, such as

   ```
   MouseEvent.MOUSE_OVER
   ```

   If the new mouse event that you type turns blue, you know that you typed it correctly. If the new event is black, check your spelling and capitalization.

3. **Choose Control⇨Test Movie⇨In Flash Professional.**

   When you move the cursor over your button, your object disappears.

Table 10-1	Mouse Events
Event	*When the Action Occurs*
CLICK	The user clicks the button.
MOUSE_DOWN	The cursor is over the object (or the button's hit area), and the user is pressing the mouse.
MOUSE_UP	The cursor is over the object (or the button's hit area), and the user releases the mouse.
MOUSE_OVER	The cursor moves over the object (or the button's hit area) without clicking.
MOUSE_OUT	The cursor moves out of the object (or the button's hit area) without clicking.
MOUSE_WHEEL	A mouse wheel is spun over the object.

Using Code Snippets to Manipulate Movie Clips

You can use the ActionScript in the Code Snippets panel with movie clips to do many things. You can start or stop a movie clip (as we describe earlier in this chapter), or create a custom cursor, or drag objects in a checkers game (which we describe in this section), and more.

You can use ActionScript with a movie clip in much the same way that you use it with a button; both the movie clip and the button are instances of objects that you can control with ActionScript. However, because movie clips have their own Timelines, you can also add Code Snippets (or your own ActionScript) to a movie clip instead of the main Timeline. We describe an example of this in a bit.

Dragging movie clips

With Flash, you can easily create objects that your audience can drag around the screen. Draggable movie clips can be both fun and useful. You can create draggable movie clips to use for games, drag-and-drop interfaces, and other purposes. In Figure 10-4, we show a checkers game with drag-and-drop checkers. (To change this to chess, just change the look of the pieces.)

In the following example, we add the code snippets into the Actions layer of the movie clips' Timelines instead of into the main Timeline. This way, we need to add Code Snippets only four times (2 checkers and 2 kings, instead of 24 checkers and multiple kings).

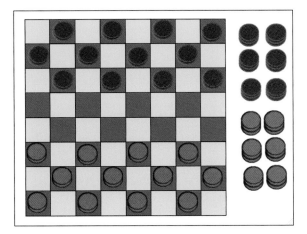

Figure 10-4: Create a checkers game with draggable checkers and kings.

To create draggable checker pieces that you can use in a checkers game, follow these steps:

1. **Choose Insert⇨New Symbol. Name it Red Checker and choose Movie Clip.**

   Create the artwork for your checker. (See Chapter 7 for more information about creating symbols.)

2. **While still in Symbol-editing mode, select the artwork, choose Window⇨Code Snippets to open the Code Snippets panel (if it's not already open), and double-click Drag and Drop in the Actions folder.**

   A dialog box appears asking you for permission to convert the artwork to a movie clip and create an instance name.

3. **Click OK in the dialog box.**

   An Actions layer appears in the movie clip's Timeline with Frame 1 containing the code snippet.

4. **Choose Edit⇨Edit Document to exit Symbol-editing mode.**

5. **Repeat Steps 1–4 for the Black Checker, Red King, and Black King.**

6. **If anything exists on the Stage, delete it, as well as anything in the Timeline — except a single layer with a single empty frame. Then create your artwork for the checkerboard.**

   For info about aligning objects, see Chapter 4.

7. **Lock the layer with the checkerboard and choose Insert⇨ Timeline⇨Layer to add a new layer.**

8. **Drag 12 Red Checkers from the Library onto the Stage, as well as 12 Black Checkers and as many Red Kings and Black Kings as you want, and arrange them.**

   If the checkers are too large or too small, double-click a checker or king and adjust its size in Symbol-editing mode. (Adjusting the size of a symbol changes the size for all of its instances.)

   Choose Edit⇨Edit Document to exit Symbol-editing mode.

9. **Test your game: Choose Control⇨Test Movie⇨In Flash Professional.**

   Your game appears in a new window with all pieces draggable.

   The FLA file of this checkers game (`checkers.fla`) can be found at `www.dummies.com/go/flashcs5fd`.

Creating custom cursors

Flash allows you to think outside the box while creating your interactive Web pages. Why settle for the same common cursor that everyone has when you can have something unique? And it's so easy to create your own cursor. You can even add animation to it, to give it more flair. For example, Figure 10-5 shows a kite created as a cursor, which could be used, perhaps, in a Web site for children. The kite's tail could be animated or not animated.

Figure 10-5: Use a kite for a cursor and animate its tail.

Creating a simple custom cursor

The Code Snippet's custom cursor works correctly when a movie is stopped and does not loop. (Otherwise, it creates itself again and again, which is probably not what you want.) To create a simple custom cursor, do the following:

1. **Move the playhead to the Frame where you want the custom cursor to appear.**

   Skip this step if your movie has only a single frame.

2. **On the Stage, draw or place the artwork that you want to use as your custom cursor.**

3. **Select the artwork and choose Modify⇨Convert to Symbol. In the dialog box that appears, give it a name, choose Movie Clip as the symbol type, and then click OK.**

4. **In the Property inspector, type an Instance name in the text box.**

5. **Open the Actions folder of the Code Snippets panel, and double-click Custom Mouse Cursor.**

   An Actions layer appears which contains your code.

6. **In the Actions layer, click the frame where the playhead is positioned. (Remember that you positioned the playhead in Step 1.) In the Timeline Navigation folder of the Code Snippets panel, double-click Stop at this Frame.**

7. **Test your new cursor by choosing File⇨Publish Preview⇨HTML.**

   Your artwork appears as your cursor in a new browser window.

Creating an animated custom cursor

Animated custom cursors are definitely fun. If you want to add a feeling of festivity to your Web page or Web site, this is definitely for you. We find that the easiest way to create the animated custom cursor is to create the animation in the movie clip symbol itself. Then you simply follow the steps in the preceding section to assign the symbol as the cursor.

To create an animated custom cursor, follow these steps:

1. **Open the Library if it's not open (choose Window➪Library). In the Library panel, double-click the movie clip symbol that we show you how to create in the previous section.**

   The movie clip symbol appears on the Stage for you to edit.

2. **Create the animation you desire.**

   See Chapter 9 to find out all about creating animations.

3. **Choose Edit➪Edit Document to exit Symbol-editing mode.**

4. **Test your new animated cursor by choosing File➪Publish Preview➪ HTML.**

Understanding ActionScript

Code Snippets are just a small snapshot of the enormous capabilities of ActionScript. ActionScript has numerous software building blocks that are ready for you to use, which are found in the left pane of the Actions panel (refer to Figure 10-1). These building blocks are organized into *classes* that share similar properties and capabilities. (The capabilities are *methods*.) You create instances of a class in ActionScript to use them in your Flash movies. These instances are *objects*. Buttons, for example, are one kind of object in ActionScript, and sounds are another.

Objects such as buttons, text, movie clips, and sounds have properties and methods built into them in ActionScript, and this makes it easy to use ActionScript to control them.

In this section, we give an overview of how to add code without using the Code Snippets panel.

The scope of ActionScript is huge. Flash Builder CS5 is a software product from Adobe that has ActionScript editing capabilities built in, which make programming ActionScript easier than composing it in the Actions panel. If you plan to do complex ActionScript programming, Flash Builder is a good tool for that.

Method acting

You can make an object work for you by calling on one of its built-in methods. You specify the object by name, followed by the dot (.) operator, followed by the method and the parameters that you want to pass to it.

For example, if you have a movie clip with an instance named owl, you can create a variable (using the definition keyword var) named my_color that can use ActionScript's built-in ColorTransform class and its transform and colorTransform properties to transform the color of the instance:

```
var my_color:ColorTransform = owl.transform.colorTransform;
```

You can set my_color by specifying it by name, followed by the dot (.) operator, followed by the color property (which describes its red, green, and blue intensity), and then setting all that equal to a hexadecimal number for the color you want, like this:

```
my_color.color = 0x990099;
```

In ActionScript, you specify a color by using hexadecimal format preceded by 0x. Then you can apply the change to owl by specifying the name of the instance you want to change (owl), followed by the dot (.) operator, the transform property, another dot operator, and the colorTransform property, and then setting all that equal to my_color variable:

```
owl.transform.colorTransform = my_color;
```

You can see the result of setting the colorTransform property in Figure 10-6. By setting the colorTransform property equal to the color 990099, the owl turns purple (99 red mixed with 00 green and 99 blue).

Figure 10-6: Specify a color in hexadecimal format.

Using an event handler

Event handlers are methods that execute after an event, such as when a button or movie clip is clicked or a frame is entered. You can use Code Snippets to quickly create your own event handlers. The Code Snippets panel offers the following event handlers:

- **Mouse Click Event:** The code that you add is executed when a mouse is clicked while over the button or movie clip.

- **Mouse Over Event:** The code that you add is executed when a mouse hovers over the button or movie clip.

- **Mouse Out Event:** The code that you add is executed when a mouse stops hovering over the button or movie clip.

- **Key Pressed Event:** The code that you add is executed when any key is pressed.

- **Enter Frame Event:** The code that you add is executed when the playhead moves from one frame to another frame anywhere on the Timeline.

You can use an event handler, for example, to change colors with a button or movie clip. In Figure 10-6, we show an owl movie clip that changes color when clicked. In the following steps, we describe how to create a movie clip, like the owl, or whatever you want, that can change colors when a button is clicked. To create this, follow these steps:

1. **Create a movie clip symbol, such as a circle.**

   See Chapter 3 to learn how to create symbols.

2. **Drag an instance of the symbol from the Library onto the Stage (if it's not already there). In the Properties panel, give it an instance name, such as myCircle.**

3. **Create a button and drag the button onto the Stage from the Library (if it's not already on the Stage). In the Property inspector panel, give it an instance name, such as myButton.**

   Check out Chapter 8 for details on creating buttons.

4. **Right-click Layer 1 and choose Insert Layer.**

5. **Rename the new layer** `Actions` **and select the first frame on that layer on the Timeline.**

6. **Select the button. In the Events Handler folder of the Code Snippets panel, double-click Mouse Click Event.**

The following code appears in the Actions panel with some comments above it. (Comments on a single line are preceded with / /. Comments on more than one line start with / * and end with * /).

```
myButton.addEventListener(MouseEvent.CLICK, fl_MouseClickHandler);

function fl_MouseClickHandler(event:MouseEvent):void
{
// Start your custom code
// This example code displays the words "Mouse clicked" in the
//          // Output panel.
trace("Mouse clicked");
// End your custom code
}
```

7. **In the Actions panel, change the code to the following:**

```
myButton.addEventListener(MouseEvent.CLICK, fl_MouseClickHandler);

function fl_MouseClickHandler(event:MouseEvent):void
{
var my_color:ColorTransform = myCircle.transform.colorTransform;
my_color.color = 0x990099;
myCircle.transform.colorTransform = my_color;
}
```

8. **To test your new button, choose Control⇨Test Movie⇨In Flash Professional. In the window that appears, click the button.**

The circle changes to purple.

You can download the FLA file for this example, called changingcolors. fla, at www.dummies.com/go/flashcs5fd.

Exploring ActionScript Further

Flash contains approximately one zillion more ActionScript methods and properties than the ones that we cover in this chapter. For more information, choose Help⇨Flash Help. In the Help window that appears, browse through the ActionScript 3.0 Language and Components Reference. In the following sections, we briefly explain a few more aspects of ActionScript programming to give you an idea of some of the possibilities.

If you're doing extensive programming, we recommend you consider using Flash Builder to create your code.

External scripting

Regardless of whether you use Code Snippets, Flash allows ActionScript 3.0 in only two places:

- **A keyframe on the Timeline:** This is the most common place for your code when you're starting out with Flash, and what we describe throughout this book, and in more detail in this chapter. Frames with ActionScript have a small "a" denoting that on the Timeline.

- **A separate ActionScript text file:** You can keep your ActionScript in separate text files that your Flash movie can load when needed. This makes it easier to reuse your beautiful ActionScript code in multiple movies. You can create your ActionScript files with any text editor that you like.

To create a separate new ActionScript file within Flash, choose File⇨New and then choose ActionScript File from the General tab of the New Document dialog box. You can type your ActionScript code in this file and save it.

You can also create ActionScript files by using Dreamweaver or a separate text editor, such as Notepad (Windows) or TextEdit (Mac). Be sure to save the file with the .as suffix, which stands for ActionScript, of course.

To create ActionScript files in TextEdit on a Mac, first choose TextEdit⇨ Preferences. In the Preferences window that appears (see Figure 10-7), on the New Document tab, select Plain Text rather than Rich Text in the Format section. On the Open and Save tab of the Preferences window, deselect Add ".txt" Extension to Plain Text Files in the section labeled When Saving a File (as shown in Figure 10-8).

To include the code from a separate ActionScript file in any part of your movie, simply add this ActionScript into a frame:

Figure 10-7: Select Plain Text rather than Rich Text.

```
include "your-filename-goes-here.as"
```

Your filename, ending with the extension .as, goes inside the quotes. This specifies an ActionScript file in the same directory as your FLA or SWF files.

Discovering more about ActionScript

ActionScript gives you tremendous power over your Flash movies. If you enjoy using ActionScript, you might want to check out some of the great resources we list in Chapter 17. Also check out Flash Builder. It has a great editor that helps you to find just the right methods and properties for your code.

Figure 10-8: Deselect adding a .txt extension to plain text files.

Extravagant Audio, High-Velocity Video

Silent movies have been gone for a long time now. Why should your Flash movies be silent? You can create music and sound effects that play continuously or are controlled by your animation Timeline. You can also add sounds to buttons to liven things up a little. You can edit sounds and control when they start and stop. But be aware that sound adds overhead to a movie, which slows down loading on a Web site, and some audiences might not be in the mood to hear any sound. If you're careful about how you use sounds, however, you can get great results.

You can also include video clips in your Flash animations. You can import video clips in a variety of file formats and then scale them, rotate them, tween them, stack them in layers, animate their transparency levels, and do all the other creative things that you're used to doing in Flash, just as though the video clips were regular Flash animations. And you can stream your video clips in Flash so that your audience may view the clips while they're downloading.

Acquiring Amazing Audio

To add some great sound to your Flash movie, you must first import the sound. You can import AIFF, WAV, Adobe Soundbooth, and MP3 sounds. Flash places these sounds in your Library. (See Chapter 2 for more about the Library.)

Sounds vary in sample rate, bit rate, and channels. These statistics are important because they affect the quality and size of the sound file. Of course, the length of the sound also affects its size. Here's what you need to know:

- **Sample rate:** The number of times the recorder samples an audio signal when it's recorded in digital form; measured in kilohertz (kHz). Try not to use more than 22 kHz unless you want CD-quality music.

- **Bit rate:** The number of bits used for each audio sample; sometimes called *bit resolution*. A 16-bit sound file is clearer with less background noise, but use 8-bit sound if you need to reduce file size.

- **Channels:** Typically one channel of sound *(monophonic)* or two channels *(stereophonic)*. In most cases, mono is fine for Flash files and uses half the amount of data that stereo uses.

Often, you need to take a sound as you find it unless you have software that can manipulate sounds. Luckily, you can set the specs of sounds when you publish your movie to an SWF file. You generally get the best results by starting with high-quality sounds and compressing during publishing. (Turn to Chapter 13 for details on settings for publishing Flash files.)

Audacity, shown in Figure 11-1, is an excellent program for recording and manipulating sound for your Flash movies — and it's free. Download it from http://audacity.source forge.net.

You can check a sound's stats after you import the sound into Flash. The next section explains how to import a sound.

Figure 11-1: Use Audacity to record and edit sound for your Flash movies.

Importing sounds

Importing a sound is easy. To import a sound, follow these steps:

1. **Choose File➪Import➪Import to Library to open the Import dialog box.**

2. **Locate the sound that you want to import.**

3. **Click Open (Windows) or Import to Library (Mac).**

Nothing seems to happen, but Flash places your sound in the Library. Choose Window➪Library to check it out (if the Library window isn't already open). To see the sound's stats, click the name of the sound in the Library window. Then click the Properties button (with the little *i* symbol) at the bottom of the Library window.

Placing sounds into a movie

After you import a sound into your movie's Library, you need to place it and set its parameters. To place sounds in a movie, follow these steps:

1. **Create and name a new layer for the sound.**

   Click the New Layer icon in the lower-left corner of the layer list to add a new layer. Each sound should have its own layer. Sounds are combined (mixed) when the movie is played.

2. **Choose Window➪Properties to open the Property inspector, if it isn't already open.**

   If necessary, expand the Property inspector to its full size.

3. **Select the keyframe in the new layer where you want the sound to start playing.**

   If you want to add the sound in a keyframe other than Frame 1, simply create the new keyframe where you want the sound to begin.

4. **In the Sound section of the Property inspector, from the Name drop-down list, select the sound that you want to place in your movie.**

   The Name drop-down list shows all sounds that you've imported. Below the name of the sound, at the bottom of the Property inspector, the sound's stats are listed (sample rate, channels, bit rate, duration, and file size), as shown in Figure 11-2.

   Flash places the sound on the active layer. The image of the sound waves appears on the Timeline between the keyframe you select in Step 3 and the next keyframe. If there isn't a next keyframe, you can add one to see the sound, or you can add frames until the sound wave line stops. (You can add frames by repeatedly pressing F5, which is equivalent to repeatedly choosing Insert⇨Timeline⇨Frame.)

5. **If desired, select an effect from the Effect drop-down list.**

These effects are self explanatory. For example, Left Channel plays the sound from only the left speaker. Fade In starts the sound softly and gradually brings it up to full volume. The default setting is None.

6. **From the Sync drop-down list, select one of the following synchronization options:**

Figure 11-2: Set sound parameters in the Property inspector.

- *Event:* Plays the sound when its first keyframe plays and continues to play the sound until it's finished, even if the movie stops. If Flash plays the keyframe again before the sound is finished, Flash starts the sound again. Use this setting for button sounds when you want the sound to play each time that the button is passed over or clicked. (Check out Chapter 8 for more information on adding sounds to buttons.) This setting is the default.

- *Start:* Plays the sound when its first keyframe plays and continues to play the sound until it's finished, even if the movie stops. If the keyframe is played again before the sound is finished, Flash doesn't start the sound again.

- *Stop:* Stops the sound.

- *Stream:* Synchronizes the sound to the Timeline. Flash skips animation frames if it can't draw them fast enough to keep up with the sound. The sound stops when Flash plays the last frame containing the sound wave. Use this option when you want to match the sound with a portion of the animation in your movie. You can insert an ending keyframe before placing the sound to control when the sound ends.

If your sound is set to Event, it will play to its finish even if not all the sound is visible on the Timeline. If your sound is set to Stream, it will play only for the frames on the Timeline where the image of the sound waves is visible.

You may want to edit the sound (as described in the next section, "Editing Sounds") to add a fade out so the sound doesn't end abruptly.

7. **Choose Repeat or Loop from the Repeat/Loop drop-down menu. If you choose Repeat, type the number of times you want to repeat the sound.**

 If you set a Stream sound to Repeat, your Flash Player movie's file size is increased by the number of times that the sound is repeated. Adobe recommends that you do not set stream sounds to Repeat.

 • *Loop:* The sound will repeat continuously.

 • *Repeat:* You can calculate the number of times that you need to play a sound throughout an animation by knowing the length (in seconds) of the sound, the number of frames your animation contains, and the frame rate. If your animation is 48 frames and the rate is 24 frames per second (24 fps; the default), your animation is 2 seconds. If your sound is 1 second long, loop it twice to play it throughout your animation. If you don't want to do the math, use a high number of loops, just to make sure.

After you place the sound, press Enter (Windows) or Return (Mac) or use the Controller to play your movie and hear the results.

Editing Sounds

After you place a sound, you can edit the sound to fine-tune its settings. You should delete unused or unwanted portions of a sound to reduce file size. You can also change the volume while the sound plays.

To edit a sound, follow these steps:

1. **Click a frame that contains a sound (or import a sound, as we describe in the preceding section, "Placing sounds into a movie").**

2. **Choose Window⇨Properties to open the Property inspector, if it isn't already open.**

 If necessary, expand the Property inspector to its full size.

3. **Click the Edit Sound Envelope button to open the Edit Envelope dialog box. (See Figure 11-3.)**

 The Edit Sound Envelope button, located next to the Effect drop-down list, is the button with an icon of a pencil on it.

Envelope line, left channel

Play Sound Envelope line,   Zoom Out
            right channel
Stop Sound   Zoom In

Seconds
Frames

Figure 11-3: Use the Edit Envelope dialog box to edit your sounds.

To see a specific section of a sound in more detail, click the Zoom In button. Zoom in when you want to edit small details of a sound.

To see more of a sound's time frame, click the Zoom Out button. Zoom out to edit the sound as a whole.

You can display sounds in terms of seconds or frames. Click the Seconds button (far left) to show sounds in seconds. Click the Frames button to display sounds by frames.

Deleting parts of a sound

Between the left (top) and right (bottom) channel display is a narrow strip that controls the starting and ending points of a sound. By deleting the beginning and end of a sound, you can eliminate unused portions of the sound. Along this strip are two vertical bars: one at the beginning of the sound and another at the end. These bars control when the sound starts and ends. Use them to edit the sound as follows:

- **Time In control:** This bar, on the left edge of the sound, specifies the start of the sound. Drag the bar to the right to delete the beginning of the sound.

- **Time Out control:** This bar, on the right edge of the sound, specifies the end of the sound. Drag the bar to the left to delete the end of the sound.

Changing the volume

On both the left and right channel displays, Flash shows an envelope line (refer to Figure 11-3) to indicate the approximate direction of the sound's volume. Where the volume changes, Flash places small squares, called *envelope handles.* To change the sound's volume, drag an envelope handle up (to increase the volume) or down (to decrease the volume). This is how you create sound fade ins and fade outs.

You can click an envelope line to add a new envelope handle. This new handle enables you to create a new direction for the sound's volume at the handle's location. To remove an envelope handle, click it and drag it out of the Edit Envelope window.

When you finish editing a sound, click OK to close the Edit Envelope dialog box.

Managing Sound

Sound can increase the size of your movie by such a great extent that you need to pay attention to how you use it. You should make every effort to compress the sound. You can also lower the sampling rate; however, your sound's quality is then reduced. Nevertheless, you should try out all the possibilities until you get the best results.

The *sampling rate* is the rate at which the computer measures sound and converts it into numerical data. The computer makes these sample measurements many thousands of times per second. A higher sampling rate provides more information about the sound — and, therefore, better audio quality — but all those extra measurements make for a much bigger data file.

Flash offers two ways to control the properties of a sound:

- **Use the Publish Settings dialog box to specify properties for all the sounds in a movie.** If you have only one sound or a few similar sounds, specifying settings this way is easy.

- **Use the Sound Properties dialog box to specify properties of specific sounds.** As long as you don't specifically override these properties when you publish, these settings stick. Use the Sound Properties dialog box when you want to specify different properties for each sound.

Because you specify the publish settings when you publish a movie, we discuss those settings in Chapter 13. In this section, we explain how to fine-tune sound properties in the Sound Properties dialog box.

To open the Sound Properties dialog box, open the Library (choose Window⇨Library) and double-click the icon of the sound that you want to work with. Figure 11-4 shows the Sound Properties dialog box.

Figure 11-4. Set individual sounds' properties here.

At the top of the dialog box, Flash displays statistics for the sound — its location, date, sample rate, channels, bit rate, duration, and file size. Use the Compression drop-down list to specify how you want to export the file. For each compression type, Flash displays the settings available for that type in the drop-down list. When you choose settings, look at the bottom of the dialog box, where Flash displays the new file size in kilobytes and in percentage of original size. The file size reduction can be pretty amazing. Here are the options available from the Compression drop-down list:

- **Default:** This option uses the compression settings specified on the Flash tab of the Publish Settings dialog box when you publish your SWF file. (Chapter 13 gives you more information on publishing to SWF files.)

- **ADPCM:** You can convert stereo to mono to cut down file size. Available sampling rates are 5, 11, 22, and 44 kHz. You can choose from 2, 3, 4, or 5 bit. Choose 5 bit for the best sound; the default is 4 bits. ADPCM is short for Adaptive Differential Pulse Code Modulation, and this compression method produces files that take up less storage space than CD-quality audio and is useful for short audio clips, such as button clicks. In case you're wondering what the heck this compression is, it's used to store music on Sony MiniDiscs.

- **MP3:** MP3 is a popular and efficient compression method. (To change the settings of an imported MP3 file, be sure to deselect the Use

Imported MP3 Quality check box.) You can convert stereo to mono and choose a bit rate measured in kilobits per second. You can choose from 8 Kbps (poor quality) to 160 Kbps (near–CD quality). Generally, you want something between these two extremes. Try a bit rate between 20 and 84 Kbps for a good balance of file size and quality. You can also choose the quality — Fast, Medium, or Best. The Fast option optimizes the sound for faster download from your Web site but with some quality compromise. For music, MP3 provides the best compression, letting you keep your quality as high as possible.

✒ **Raw:** This option exports the sound with no sound compression. You can convert stereo to mono and select the same sampling rates as for ADPCM.

✒ **Speech:** This option exports the sound with compression techniques specially designed for speech. You can select the same sampling rates as for ADPCM. A good choice for speech is 11 kHz.

After you specify a group of settings, click the Test button. This handy button lets you hear how your sound file sounds with each setting.

The Sound Properties dialog box also lets you update the original sound after you modify it with sound-editing software — just click the Update button. You can also click Import to import a sound file. The Stop button stops playing a sound that you're previewing.

When you're finished, click OK to finalize your settings and close the dialog box.

Video Magic

The Flash Player has achieved more universal adoption than any other Web video technology, so Flash can be a great way to deliver video over the Web. Flash Player version 6 and later can play video, and (as of this writing) Adobe claims that enormously more Web surfers have Flash Player 9 or higher, compared to Java, Apple's QuickTime Player, or RealOne Player. The Adobe Web site provides more details — you can check it out at

```
www.adobe.com/products/player_census/flashplayer
```

Flash can import FLV and F4V files. FLV is the file format developed years ago by the Flash team. This format is the only format that can be embedded within a SWF file itself. F4V is a newer format that uses MPEG4 video encoding and MP3 audio. The Flash developers recommend that you use this format whenever possible. It delivers better audio and video for the file size. (Even though F4V files work only with Flash Player 9 or higher, the number of people still using version 8 in the United States is quite miniscule.)

However, the Flash development team recognizes that many other video formats exist, and that many Flash Professional users will want to make use of them. For this reason, Adobe includes the Adobe Media Encoder CS5 application when you purchase Flash Professional CS5. You can use the Adobe Media Encoder to convert a wide variety of video formats. We describe how to convert your videos later in this chapter.

Four ways to use video in Flash

You may include video in your Flash movie in various ways, as follows:

- **Embed your FLV file in your SWF file** and play it in a Timeline — either a Movie Clip timeline, or the main Timeline. This lets you play your video from within your SWF file. This can work well for short video clips (perhaps ten seconds or less), but longer video clips might make your Flash file take a loooooooong time to download, and these clips might have problems with audio/video synchronization. For more information, see the section "Embedding a video" later in this chapter.

- **Stream video from your Web server.** You can connect to an FLV file or F4V file from within your SWF file and play the video while it down-loads from a plain-old Web server. This is a cool feature and definitely a good idea if you have a video longer than around ten seconds. Your audience can start to watch the video while it's still downloading, and the audio and video won't get out of sync. For more information, see the "Streaming a video" section later in this chapter.

- **Stream video from a Flash video streaming service.** You can play your video from a Web hosting service provider that specializes in Flash video. This can give you good performance if you want to do fancy things like host video-on-demand applications, Web cam chats, live-event broadcasts, and real-time collaboration applications. But it's definitely not cheap, so if you're a new Flash user, you probably don't need to think about this option for now.

- **Stream video from a Flash Media Server.** You can play your video from a Flash Media Server that you host. This can give you good performance for heavy-duty deployment of multiple Web video streams, as if you were your own Flash video streaming service. However, the Flash Media Server software is complex — and it's not cheap, with prices ranging from free for a developer version to $4,500 for the most powerful version. So unless your boss is investing zillions in a Flash video Web site, you again probably don't need to worry about this option.

Converting your video with Adobe Media Encoder

Whether you want to embed your video or stream it, you might need to convert it with Adobe Media Encoder. If your video is already in the FLV format for embedding, or FLV or F4V for streaming, you can skip this section. Otherwise, read on.

The Adobe Media Encoder is a stand-alone application that comes free with Flash Professional CS5. It's installed when you install Flash. Easy to use, Adobe Media Encoder converts many types of video formats so that they can be used by the Flash player.

To convert video files into F4V or FLV files, follow these steps:

1. **For Windows, choose Start⇨Adobe Media Encoder CS5. For Macintosh, find the Adobe Media Encoder CS5 folder in your Applications folder and double-click it to open it; then double-click the icon for Adobe Media Encoder CS5.**

   The Adobe Media Encoder window and menu appear.

2. **Click the Add button or choose File⇨Add.**

   An Open dialog box appears.

3. **Browse through your files, select the video file that you want to convert, and then click Open.**

   The name of the file appears in the window.

4. **Click the Settings button.**

   An Export Settings window opens, as shown in Figure 11-5.

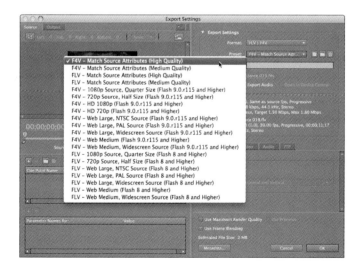

Figure 11-5: Use the Adobe Media Encoder Export Settings to edit or resize your video or adjust the sound quality.

5. **Do any of the following:**

- *Select a portion of the video, instead of the entire video:* Choose Custom as the Source Range and then move the small triangles to the new starting and ending points on the Timeline.

- *Choose a Preset or create a Custom preset.* Choose a preset from the Preset list, as shown in Figure 11-5. Or for a custom preset, choose the Video tab and type the new size and Audio quality.

- *Blur your video.* Choose the Filters tab and click Gaussian Blur.

6. **Click OK if you made any changes; otherwise, click Cancel.**

7. **To start the conversion, click Start Queue, or choose File⇨Start Queue.**

The conversion begins, as shown in Figure 11-6. When the conversion is complete, a new file exists in the same directory as the original file, and has an `.f4v` (or `.flv`) extension — ready for use in Flash.

Figure 11-6: The Adobe Media Encoder encodes a video.

Preparing to embed FLV video into Flash

If you have an FLV file that you want to embed into your Flash file, you first need to find out the frame rate of your video and make sure that your Flash document has the same frame rate. This helps avoid erratic playback.

It is not recommended that you embed videos longer than 10 seconds, especially if they contain audio. Otherwise, the audio may become out of sync with the video.

To find out the frame rate of a video in preparation for embedding the video, follow these steps:

1. **Open Adobe Media Encoder CS5 by double-clicking it in the Applications folder (Mac) or choosing it from the Programs list (Windows).**

2. **Click Add and choose the FLV file that you want to embed into Flash and click Open.**

   Your video appears in the queue and the timer starts. You now have two minutes to do Step 3, which will stop the timer.

3. **Click Settings.**

   The Export Settings window appears, as shown in Figure 11-7. And the timer stops.

4. **Make a note of the video's frame rate in the Export Settings pane.**

   You might also want to note the normal size of the video. (A typical size is 720 x 480 pixels.)

Figure 11-7: The Export Settings window of the Adobe Media Encoder displays the frames per second.

5. **Click Cancel and close the Adobe Media Encoder.**

   The Adobe Media windows close.

6. **In Flash, open or create a Flash document if one isn't open, and choose Modify⇨Document.**

   The Document Settings dialog box appears, showing the document's dimensions, frame rate, and other properties.

7. **To avoid unstable video playback, change the number in the Frame Rate text box to match your video's frame rate.**

Embedding a video

You can import an FLV file directly into your Flash animations. If your video is in a different file format, see the earlier section in this chapter to convert it into FLV. After your video is in FLV format, the Flash Import Video wizard makes it easy for you to embed it into your Flash document.

Embedding video in your Flash document is convenient if your video is short — perhaps 10 seconds or less. If the video is longer, downloading your video while the Flash movie plays is a better approach.

Before you embed video into Flash, first make sure that the frame rate of your FLV file and your Flash movie match, which we show you how to do in the preceding section. After that, you can make video clips part of your Flash movie by following these steps:

1. **On a separate layer, click a keyframe where you want to put your video (or create a keyframe by clicking a frame and choosing Insert⇨Timeline⇨Keyframe).**

2. **Choose File⇨Import⇨Import Video.**

   The Import Video Wizard appears.

3. **Select the On Your Computer option to import a video from your computer.**

4. **Click Browse (Mac) or Open (Windows).**

   The Open dialog box appears.

5. **In the Open dialog box, find and choose an FLV file and then click Open.**

   The Import Video Wizard now lists the name of the file you chose.

6. **In the Import Video dialog box, select the Embed FLV in SWF and Play in Timeline option (as shown in Figure 11-8), and then click Next (Windows) or Continue (Mac).**

Figure 11-8: Choose the video that you want to import.

7. **You probably want to select Movie Clip from the Symbol Type drop-down list, and you probably want to mark the check boxes for Place Instance on Stage, Expand Timeline If Needed, and Include Audio.**

   The Import Video Wizard gives you a choice of symbol type for your embedded video. Embedding your video as a movie clip symbol and with the audio track integrated are usually good choices. When you embed your video in a movie clip symbol, the video's Timeline is within the movie clip and plays independently of the main Timeline. This gives you a lot of flexibility and lets you move your video around easily within your Flash movie. However, if your Flash movie is mostly just going to play back the video on the main Timeline without doing much else, Embedded Video in the Symbol Type drop-down menu is an appropriate choice.

8. **Click Next (Windows) or Continue (Mac).**

   The Finish Video Import pane appears in the Import Video Wizard, summarizing your choices.

9. **If you want to change any of your choices, click Go Back (Mac) or Back (Windows). Otherwise, click Finish.**

The Flash Video Encoding Progress window appears. Encoding your video may take quite a while. When Flash finishes encoding your video, the window disappears, and the movie clip or clips (or embedded video symbol or symbols) containing your video appear on your Stage and in your library (which you can view by choosing Window➪Library, if it isn't visible).

Now your video segments are inside movie clips (if you choose that in Step 7), and as with any other movie clips, you can drag them around on the Timeline, rearrange them, rotate them, motion-tween them, paint on top of them in other layers, and tween their brightness and transparency — you can mangle them, destroy them, and bring them to life in all the usual Flash ways. This is pretty amazing. (See Chapter 9 for lots more animation ideas.)

Streaming a video

You can set up your Flash document to stream a video while the video appears inside your Flash movie. That means that viewers can see the video play fairly smoothly even while it's still downloading from the Web — without having to wait until the entire video has downloaded. This is a fantastic feature. You'll certainly want to do this rather than embed your video in Flash if your video is more than a few seconds long.

These streaming video files are in the .flv or .f4v Flash video formats. According to Adobe, "80% of online videos are viewed worldwide using Adobe Flash technology." Many of these online videos are at www.youtube.com and http://video.google.com.

To prepare to stream an FLV or F4V video file, follow these steps:

1. **Click a keyframe (or create one by clicking a frame and choosing Insert➪Timeline➪Keyframe).**

Your video will start on this keyframe.

2. **Choose File➪Import➪Import Video.**

The Video Import Wizard appears.

You're about to import a video file into your Flash movie. Ultimately, you will put the file on a Web server, but first, you need to create and publish the FLV file.

3. **Select the On Your Computer option if you want to import a video from your computer. If you want to import an FLV or F4V video file from the Web, select the Already Deployed to a Web Server, Flash Video Streaming Service, or Flash Media Server option, type the Web address of the video file into the URL text box, and skip to Step 7.**

4. **Click the Open (Windows) or Browse (Mac) button.**

5. **In the Open dialog box, find and choose a FLV or F4V file and then click Open.**

6. **In the Import Video dialog box, select the radio button for Load External Video with Playback Component.**

7. **Click the Next (Windows) or Continue (Mac) button.**

   The Skinning pane of the Import Video dialog box appears, as shown in Figure 11-9.

Figure 11-9: Choose the style and color of play controls you want for your video.

8. **From the Skin drop-down list, select the style and color of play controls you want for your video.**

   The *skin* is the graphic design of the video play controls. You can intuit the characteristics of some skins from their names. For example, the skin named `SkinOverPlaySeekMute.swf` has the play controls placed over the video and include Play, Seek, and Mute buttons. You're probably going to love fooling around choosing your skin — it's so easy. The skin you select from the drop-down list appears as a preview in the pane above the drop-down list.

9. **Click Next (Windows) or Continue (Mac).**

The Finish Video Import pane appears in the Import Video dialog box, summarizing what happens next. You might want to make notes on that because unfortunately, this information disappears when you click Finish in Step 10. Among other things, this pane tells you where your new FLV or F4V file will be located relative to your SWF file.

10. **If you want to change any of your choices, click Go Back (Mac) or Back (Windows). Otherwise, click Finish.**

When Flash finishes encoding your video, the encoded video and the player controls appear on the Stage. You may find it interesting to compare the file size of your new FLV or F4V file to the original video file size. (You can find the new FLV or F4V file in the location shown in Step 9.)

11. **Open the Property inspector (if it's not already open; choose Window⇨Property). In the Component Parameters section of the Property inspector, click the disclosure triangle to reveal the contents of the Component Parameters section (if they're not already showing).**

12. **In the Component Parameters section of the Property inspector, click the Value field of the "source" Property.**

The Content Path dialog box appears with the URL or path of the video.

13. **Enter the Web address of the final location for your FLV or F4V file on your Web server or Flash Media Server, as shown in Figure 11-10, and click OK.**

For example, you might type

```
http://www.helpexamples.com/flash/video/clouds.flv
```

14. **Upload your new FLV or F4V file to your Web server, your Flash Media Server, or your Flash Video Streaming Service to the Web address you enter in Step 13.**

15. **Choose Control⇨Test Movie⇨In Flash Professional.**

A new window appears showing your Flash movie, and, as shown in Figure 11-11, your video appears with the play controls in the style of the skin you chose in Step 8.

Figure 11-10: Enter the Web address of the FLV file.

Figure 11-11: An imported video appears with the play
controls in the skin style you choose.

16. Use the play controls to play your streaming video.

Your video FLV file plays from within your Flash movie while it downloads from your Web server, your Flash Media Server, or your Flash
Video Streaming Service. It probably looks great. This is pretty amazing.

17. **Add more elements to your Flash movie if you like.**

18. **Choose File⇨Publish Settings to choose the settings for your HTML file and SWF file in the Publish Settings dialog box, click Publish, and then click OK.**

    Flash creates an HTML file and an SWF file that contains your Flash movie. (See Chapter 13 to find out how to set your publish settings and publish your files.)

19. **Upload your HTML file and your SWF file to a Web server.**

    For others to see your video, you must upload four elements to the Web: the HTML file and the SWF file that you upload in this step, plus the FLV or F4V file that you uploaded in Step 14, and the skin file that you upload in the next step. The FLV or F4V file doesn't need to be hosted at the same site as the other elements, as long as you entered the Web address of the FLV or F4V file in Step 13.

20. **Upload the video skin you chose in Step 8. You can find a copy of it on your computer in the same folder as your FLA file.**

    This skin will need to be uploaded into the same folder as the HTML file that calls your SWF file.

    For instance, if you choose SkinOverPlaySeekMute in Step 8, you see a file there called `SkinOverPlaySeekMute.swf`, which you need to upload to your Web server in the same directory as your HTML file. (If you don't upload the skin, the video will still play, but it will have no video playback controls.)

Part V
The Movie and the Web

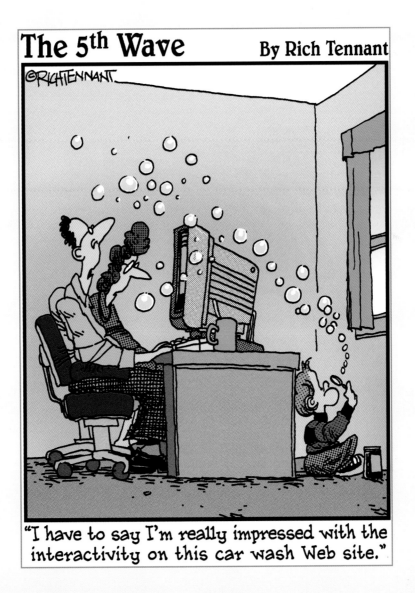

The 5th Wave   By Rich Tennant

"I have to say I'm really impressed with the interactivity on this car wash Web site."

LOADING...

In this part . . .

The not-so-secret desire of every Flash movie animation is to appear in bright lights on the Web. In this part, we show you how to make that happen. We explain how to put all the pieces together to create a way-cool Flash-only site. You see how to build a Web site that contains a complete navigational system so that viewers can quickly get the information they need.

We also discuss the nitty-gritty details of publishing your Flash movie so a Web browser can display it. Besides the Flash Player file, Flash can create the HTML code you need and the alternative images you might want to use in case a viewer doesn't have the Flash Player. Flash makes it easy: Just specify your settings and click Publish.

#FFFFCC

Putting It All Together

In This Chapter

▶ Building user interfaces with components

▶ Offering your viewers a preloader

▶ Putting together an entire Web site with Flash

▶ Checking out your viewers' Flash Player version

▶ Analyzing your movies with the Movie Explorer

▶ Making your site accessible to people with disabilities

*W*hen creating your Flash animation, you need to consider how you will integrate it with your entire Web site. Are you creating a small animation to insert into an existing HyperText Markup Language (HTML) site, or do you want your entire site to be *Flashed?* In this chapter, we cover techniques for creating entire presentations, Web pages, and sites using Flash.

If you plan to create Web pages, entire Web sites, or presentations using Flash, you might want to check out Flash Catalyst in Chapters 14 and 15. Flash Catalyst allows you to create your artwork in Adobe Photoshop or Adobe Illustrator, import the artwork directly into Flash Catalyst with all layers intact, and then create simple, elegant, interactive Web pages without writing code. For Web sites with more advanced functionality, Flash Catalyst is designed to be used with Flash Builder, a new product from Adobe that is a powerful tool for writing computer code. However, if you want to go beyond the limits of Flash Catalyst, building your Web site with Flash Professional and some of the techniques we describe in this chapter is probably easier than using Flash Catalyst with Flash Builder.

The FLA files for the examples in this chapter can be found at www.dummies/com/go/flashcs5fd.

Adding the Power of Components

Components in Flash are built-in, precoded wonders that simplify the creation of interactive Flash movies. Components can be used to add interaction and navigation elements to your Flash movies, allowing you to create surveys, forms, interactive art galleries, or even complete graphical user interfaces (GUIs) for your Flash movies. Among other things, you can also use components (with the help of some fairly sophisticated ActionScript) to access and manipulate data from the Web and other sources.

Flash CS5 ships with more than two dozen ActionScript 2.0 components and more than two dozen ActionScript 3.0 components. You can download more components built by Flash community members by choosing Help➪Flash Exchange.

When you create a Flash document or open an existing one, Flash displays either ActionScript 2.0 components or version 3.0 components in the Components window depending on the document's ActionScript version. (Choose Window➪ Components if it's not already open.) In this book, we focus on ActionScript 3.0 because of its performance improvements and features.

Some of the components that ship with Flash CS5 are

Figure 12-1: The Components panel.

- ✐ **RadioButton:** Make one choice from several buttons.

- ✐ **CheckBox:** Mark or clear each CheckBox.

- ✐ **Button:** Click to make something happen in your movie. (Button components have more features than button symbols.)

- ✐ **ComboBox:** These are drop-down lists.

- ✐ **List:** These are scrolling lists of choices.

- ✐ **Video playback controllers:** Your audience can start, stop, and adjust the volume of video and audio in your Flash documents.

To add a component to your Flash movie, drag it from the Components panel (see Figure 12-1) onto the Stage.

Components can add significantly to the size of your Flash Player movie, so consider the benefits of including them versus their cost in download time. For example, adding a check box to the checkers game in Chapter 10, changes the size of the SWF file from 4K to 20K. (However, adding many components does not increase its size over 20K.) You can find the SWF file in the same folder as your FLA file.

In the following sections, we look at how to use several types of components. We skip Button components because button symbols that you make yourself (as described in Chapter 8) are easier to use and usually do everything you need.

Using RadioButtons in a Flash movie

RadioButtons, shown in Figure 12-2, are groups of buttons that permit you to choose one (and only one) item from the group. The following example describes how to create RadioButtons and place them on the Stage. The next section describes how to add code to make them work.

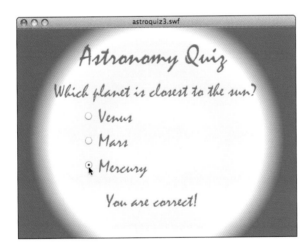

Figure 12-2: Use RadioButtons to allow the user to choose only one item.

Adding RadioButtons to the Stage

To use a set of RadioButtons in your Flash movie, follow these steps as we walk you through building a simple astronomy quiz. In essence, you add radio buttons to the Stage and give each radio button an instance name and a common group name:

1. **Choose Window⇨Components to open the Components panel, if it is not already open, and drag two or more RadioButtons from the User Interface folder of the Components panel onto the Stage, as shown in Figure 12-3.**

   The RadioButton component and a folder called Component Assets are added to the Library. (Instead of dragging, you could double-click the RadioButton to add it to the Stage, if you prefer.)

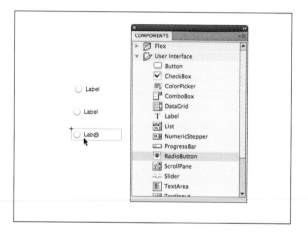

Figure 12-3: Adding RadioButtons by dragging them from the Components panel to the Stage.

2. **Open the Property inspector.**

   If the Property inspector isn't already visible (either as a separate window or as a tab in a tabbed window), choose Window⇨Properties.

3. **Select one of the RadioButtons and type a name in the Instance Name field at the top of the Property inspector.**

   This is the name which is used in the code to refer to the RadioButton. We used the names venus, mars and mercury for the three RadioButtons.

4. **In the Component Parameters pane of the Property inspector, select Enabled if it is not already selected, and type a name in the group-Name text box.**

   In Figure 12-4, we use Q1 for the group name. All three RadioButtons in this question of the quiz must have the same group name, so that only one RadioButton can be selected at a time. (Flash assigns a default groupName, which you can use if all your RadioButtons on the Stage belong to a single group.)

Figure 12-4: Set properties for your RadioButtons in the Component Parameters pane of the Property Inspector.

5. **In the Component Parameters pane of the Property inspector, do any of the following:**

- *Change the RadioButton's label.* Type a new label in the Label field, such as Venus, as shown in Figure 12-4. (The default label is Label, which you undoubtedly want to change, although it is not required for the RadioButtons to work.)

- *To make the RadioButton selected by default,* mark the Selected check box. (You would probably never do this for a quiz — that's like giving away the correct answer! However, if you were creating a shopping cart and you want a customer to choose between the shipping options: UPS or FedEx, you might want UPS to be already selected, because it is more likely they would choose that.)

- *To change the placement of the label,* choose a different placement from the labelPlacement drop-down list.

- *To associate additional information with the RadioButton,* enter the information in the Value field, such as the number of points that you add to your test score for choosing that answer. This information can be accessed with ActionScript code and used, for example, to compute a grade.

- *To hide your RadioButton,* deselect the Visible check box. Hidden RadioButtons do not function at all while they are hidden. You may want to hide your RadioButtons if you plan to use code to make them visible under some conditions specified in your code. However, this feature hides the RadioButton on the Stage as well as when your movie runs. This makes it difficult to select and unhide the RadioButton, unless you use the Movie Explorer, which we describe later in this chapter.

6. **Repeat Steps 3–5 for each RadioButton.**

7. **Choose Control➪Test Movie➪In Flash Professional to test that when you select one RadioButton, the others are deselected.**

   If your RadioButtons buttons don't work, check that they all have the same groupName in the Property inspector.

To change the look of the RadioButton labels, you can delete the Label in the Property inspector for each RadioButton, and then add text on the Stage using the Text tool, which is what we did in Figure 12-2. The RadioButton operates without a Label, but the text is positioned to appear as a label.

Adding code to make your RadioButtons operational

You can do approximately a zillion things using RadioButtons. In this section, we describe how to apply RadioButtons to our astronomy quiz. The quiz contains two text boxes: *You are correct!* and *Sorry, try again.* We make these text boxes invisible using code and then reveal one or the other depending on which RadioButton is clicked. This is an example of how to make RadioButtons work for you. Here are the steps:

1. **Add the title of the quiz (such as *Astronomy Quiz*, for example) and the question on the Stage using the Text tool. And, if you want, you can select each RadioButton and delete its label in the Property inspector, then on the Stage use the Text tool to type each potential answer (such as Venus, Mars or Mercury) beside its RadioButton.**

   Deleting the label and adding text offers you more variety of fonts. This can improve the look of the quiz. (For more information on adding text, see Chapter 5.)

2. **Choose Insert➪Timeline➪Layer to create a new layer and drag it below the existing layer. Then using the tools in the Toolbar, create some graphics for a background for your quiz.**

   We named the layer, *Background.* For more information on creating graphics, see Chapter 3.

3. **Click the Background layer to select it and choose Insert➪Timeline➪ Layer to create a new layer above it. Double-click the name of the layer on the Timeline and give it a new name.**

   We named our layer *You are correct/Try again.*

4. **Select the Text tool in the toolbar and draw a text box near the bottom of the Stage. Type "You are correct!" into the text box. In the Property inspector, choose TLF Text and Selectable and type an Instance name.**

   We called ours *youAreCorrect.*

   You can use a different name if you want, and then you need to replace *youAreCorrect* in the ActionScript code in the following steps with the new name.

5. **Repeat Step 4 to create the TLF text box containing the text, "Sorry, try again."**

   Call it *tryAgain*.

   Because neither of these text boxes (youAreCorrect and tryAgain) are visible at the same time, they can occupy the same space, one on top of each other, as shown in Figure 12-5.

Figure 12-5: Two text boxes can occupy the same space, because only one will be visible at a time.

6. **Choose Window⇨Code Snippets to open the Code Snippets panel, if it's not already open. Choose Window⇨Actions to open the Actions panel, if it's not already open.**

7. **Select a RadioButton on the Stage and in the Event Handlers folder in the Code Snippets panel, double-click Mouse Click Event.**

   This is one of the RadioButtons that you placed on the Stage in the preceding section. An Actions layer appears the first time you add the code snippet, and the Mouse Click Event code appears in the Actions panel.

8. **Repeat Step 7 for each RadioButton.**

9. **In the event handler created in Step 7 for the RadioButton that is the correct answer, delete `trace("Mouse clicked");` and add the following:**

   ```
   youAreCorrect.visible = true;
   tryAgain.visible = false;
   ```

10. **For the other two event handlers that are the incorrect answers, delete `trace("Mouse clicked");` and add the following:**

```
youAreCorrect.visible = false;
tryAgain.visible = true;
```

11. **In the Timeline, select the frame with the *a* in it in the Actions layer, and in the Actions panel, add the following code after the last line of code:**

```
youAreCorrect.visible = false;
tryAgain.visible = false;
```

This makes the text invisible initially, so it doesn't show until it's needed. The Actions panel is shown in Figure 12-6 with all the blank lines and comments deleted to save space.

Figure 12-6: The Timeline and the Actions panel displaying the code.

If you delete any instances that you already applied ActionScript to, be sure to also delete the ActionScript in the Actions panel that pertains to those instances.

12. **Test your movie by choosing Control➪Test Movie➪In Flash Professional.**

When the correct answer is chosen, *You are correct!* appears. Refer to Figure 12-2.

Using CheckBoxes in a Flash movie

CheckBoxes are square boxes that you can check or uncheck to indicate that an option is selected or deselected. Unlike RadioButtons, more than one CheckBox can be selected at a time.

The following steps describe an example of using CheckBoxes that display a movie clip for each checked box:

1. **Decide which elements of your Flash movie will change when a CheckBox is selected; then add those elements to the Flash movie if you haven't already done so.**

   For example, perhaps you made movie clips of a cat, a tree, and a field, and you want to use CheckBoxes so that users can choose as many or as few as they like. And let's say that you named the instances *cat, tree,* and *field* and the CheckBoxes `catBox`, `treeBox`, and `fieldBox`.

2. **Open the Property inspector.**

   If the Property inspector isn't already visible (either as a separate window or as a tab in a tabbed window), choose Window⇨Properties.

3. **Open the Components panel, if it is not already open by choosing Window⇨Components.**

4. **Drag a CheckBox from the Components panel onto the Stage.**

5. **Select a CheckBox. In the Property inspector, do the following:**

   - *Type an instance name.* For instance, you can enter **myCheckBox** (or **treeBox** or **catBox** or **fieldBox**).

   - *Change the CheckBox's label to something more explicit than its default, which is "Label".* Type a new label in the Label field. (Or you can blank it out, if you want, and use text instead.)

   - *To make the CheckBox selected by default,* mark the Selected check box. For example, if you're creating a shopping cart and you want everyone checking out to join your mailing list, you might have a selected checkbox with the label, *Join our mailing list.*

   - *To change the placement of the label,* choose a different placement from the labelPlacement drop-down list, as shown in Figure 12-7.

Figure 12-7: Changing the CheckBox's label placement.

6. **Repeat Steps 4 and 5 for each CheckBox that you want to add.**

7. **Choose Window⇨Actions to open the Actions panel if it isn't open already.**

8. **Choose Insert⇨Timeline⇨Layer and double-click the new layer's name in the Timeline and rename it *Actions*.**

9. **Select Frame 1 of your Actions layer in the Timeline and enter the following code in the Actions panel:**

```
tree.visible = false;
cat.visible = false;
field.visible = false;
treeBox.addEventListener(MouseEvent.CLICK, seeTree);
catBox.addEventListener(MouseEvent.CLICK, seeCat);
fieldBox.addEventListener(MouseEvent.CLICK, seeField);
function seeTree(event:MouseEvent):void {
    tree.visible = event.target.selected;
    }
function seeCat(event:MouseEvent):void {
    cat.visible = event.target.selected;
    }
function seeField(event:MouseEvent):void {
    field.visible = event.target.selected;
    }
```

You can replace seeTree, seeCat, and seeField with any names you like. In this example tree, cat, and field are the instance names of the movie clips, and treeBox, catBox, and fieldBox are the instance names of the CheckBoxes. (For information on how to create instances of movie clips, see Chapter 7.)

Statements 1, 2, and 3 make the CheckBoxes for the tree, cat, and field invisible. Statements 4, 5, and 6 add an event listener to each of the three CheckBoxes so that when you select one of the CheckBoxes, Flash executes the corresponding function seeTree, seeCat, or seeField These three functions are defined in the last lines of the code. As a result, when the user checks the tree CheckBox, for example, the Tree movie clip appears.

An *event listener* is a little bit of code that checks for events that may be connected to a particular object in your Flash movie (such as our CheckBoxes here) and performs a specified function when they occur. Picture an event listener as a tiny dedicated spy or ear always waiting to hear one particular click.

Using ComboBoxes in a Flash movie

A *ComboBox* is a text box that shows the current selection, combined with a drop-down list of alternate selections. The following example describes how to create a ComboBox that displays the item chosen from a list in a

Selectable TLF text box, as shown in Figure 12-8. In this example, the ComboBox contains a list of different dances to choose from. When a dance is chosen, the name of the dance appears in the text box below it. Of course, you could add code to perform any action when the name is chosen, such as show a movie clip of the dance. Feel free to modify these steps and improvise!

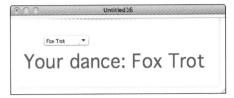

Figure 12-8: Displaying the user's choice from a ComboBox in a text box.

1. **Decide what elements of your Flash movie will change when a menu item in the ComboBox is selected. Add those elements to the Flash movie if you haven't already done so.**

   Specifically, for our dance example, you need to add a Selectable TLF text box, by drawing it with the Text tool and choosing TLF and Selectable in the Property inspector. Type an instance name in the Property inspector, such as *myInfo2*, which is what we use to reference the text box in the code.

   See Chapter 5 to discover how to create TLF text. In the text box on the Stage, you may want to type the initial message that you want to display.

2. **Drag a ComboBox from the Components panel onto the Stage.**

   You can use the Free Transform tool on the toolbar to resize your ComboBox. For example, you may want it to be longer in order to fit more text, or simply to look better.

3. **In the instance name box at the top of the Property inspector, type a name.**

   For example, we used myComboBox. If you use anything else, you need to change the code in the following steps.

4. **To control whether the user can edit the items in the ComboBox's menu list, mark or unmark the Editable check box in the Component Parameters section of the Property inspector, as shown in Figure 12-9.**

   Marking the check box allows the user to add their own answers into a ComboBox, instead of needing to choose from the list.

5. **To add a label onto the ComboBox, such as *Select dance* as shown in Figure 12-9, type it in the Prompt box in the Property inspector.**

6. **To restrict the characters that the user can type into the ComboBox, type the characters that you allow into the Restrict box in the Property inspector.**

   For example, if you want the user to be able to type numbers only, then add 0-9 into the Restrict box.

Figure 12-9: Setting the ComboBox's properties in the Property inspector.

7. **To create items in the menu list**

   a. Double-click the [] beside dataProvider in the Property inspector.

   A dialog box appears, as shown in Figure 12-10.

Figure 12-10: To add items in a ComboBox's menu list, click the plus sign in the Values dialog box.

   b. In the dialog box, click the plus sign to add a menu item or click the minus sign to delete a menu item.

   When you add a menu item to the list, it is excitingly named *label0, label1, label2,* and so on.

     c. To set the order of your ComboBox list items, click the upward-pointing triangle to move an item up the list and click the downward-pointing triangle to move a menu item down on the list.

8. **To change a menu item's name from *label0* (or *label1* or *label2* and so on) to something more interesting and meaningful, click in the Value column and type a more useful name there.**

   For example, you might change the name of each menu item to the name of a different kind of dance maneuver, such as Charleston, Fox Trot, Twist, or Mashed Potato.

9. **To add data to a menu item, click in the Value column beside *data,* and type in the text box that appears.**

   Data can be used in conjunction with code in many ways. For instance, if you have a ComboBox full of items for sale, the data could be the price of the each item.

10. **Click OK.**

    The dialog box closes.

11. **To change the number of items that can be displayed in the ComboBox without a scroll bar, change the rowCount in the Component Parameters section of the Property inspector.**

    The default number is 5.

12. **Create a new layer and label it Actions. Then choose Window➪Actions to open the Actions panel if it isn't open already.**

13. **Select Frame 1 of your Actions layer in the Timeline and enter the following code in the Script pane of the Actions panel:**

    ```
    myComboBox.addEventListener(Event.CHANGE, danceChosen);
    function danceChosen(e:Event):void {
      myInfo2.text = "Your dance: ";
      myInfo2.appendText(myComboBox.selectedItem.label);
          }
    ```

    You can replace *danceChosen* in the preceding code with any name you like. `myComboBox` in this example is the instance name of your ComboBox that we mention in Step 3, and `myInfo2` is the name of the TLF text box described in Step 1.

In the preceding code, in the definition of the function `danceChosen`, the two statements that change the text in `myInfo2` make the label of the ComboBox appear in the text box.

You could replace these statements with different statements in this function for a different result. For example, you might instead use some ActionScript code that sets the Flash playhead to move to different frame labels in different sections of the Flash movie that correspond to the selected label in the ComboBox.

The first statement adds an event listener to myComboBox so that when you select a menu item in myComboBox, the statements in the function danceChosen set the text of the TLF text box to the label of the ComboBox menu item that the viewer selects. (For another example of event listeners, see the previous section "Using CheckBoxes in a Flash Movie.")

When the user chooses a dance from the list, that dance appears in the TLF text box. Because the function inserts *Your dance:* before the text, the result might be *Your dance: Mashed Potato.*

The dance appears in the text box only if, in Step 4, Editable is not selected in the Property inspector, so that the user can't rename each item on the menu list. Otherwise, the code gets more complicated, which is a bit beyond the scope of this chapter.

TIP

If things aren't working when you test your ComboBox, be sure that your text box is large enough to contain the text. Also, check the ActionScript code that you typed for typos or other errors. Flash often reports these errors in the Compiler Errors panel when you choose Control⇨Test Movie⇨In Flash Professional. The error messages in the Compiler Errors window may seem obscure, but they can give you an idea of where your problem may be.

Using Lists in a Flash movie

A *List* component in Flash is a scrollable list of selectable items that displays more than one item at a time, and offers both horizontal and vertical scroll bars to access other items not shown. These scroll bars can be set to appear automatically if the List is sized too small to reveal all its content in either direction. A List is different from a ComboBox because it remains open and does not collapse into a single bar like the ComboBox.

Items in a List may have data associated with them, just like items in a ComboBox can have data. In the following steps, we show you how to create a list and add items to it, and then display the data value in a text box when the user selects an item, as shown in Figure 12-11. In our example, the data is the price of a selected guitar.

iAXE
Switch Stealth
Fender Telecaster

This guitar is priced at: $199

To use list components in your Flash movie, follow these steps:

Figure 12-11: The three items in this list were created by the three ActionScript statements that call the addItem method.

1. **Decide which elements of your Flash movie will change when a viewer selects a menu item in the list. Add those elements to the Flash movie if you haven't already done so.**

   In our example, you need to create a Selectable TLF text box to hold the guitar prices and give it the instance name, such as *myInfo3*.

   If your instance name is not myInfo3, then you need to change the code in the following steps to the new name. (Also, see Chapter 5 for information about creating TLF text.)

2. **Drag a List from the Components panel onto the Stage.**

3. **In the instance name text field at the top of the Property inspector, type a name, such as *myList*.**

   If you use a different name, then you need to change the following code.

4. **In the selection width field (labeled W) in the Position and Size section of the Property inspector, type a number to change the List box's width, if desired.**

   The width should be wide enough to show the desired text. For example, you might want a width of 300 pixels.

5. **Choose Window⇨Actions to open the Actions panel if it isn't open already.**

6. **If you do not already have an Actions layer in your Timeline, then choose Insert⇨Timeline⇨Layer to create a new layer and double-click the name of the new layer and rename it *Actions*. Select Frame 1 of your Actions layer in the Timeline and enter this code in the Actions panel:**

```
myList.addItem({label:"iAXE", data:99});
myList.addItem({label:"Switch Stealth", data: 199});
myList.addItem({label:"Fender Telecaster", data:399});
myList.addEventListener(Event.CHANGE, showPrice);
function showPrice(event:Event) {
    myInfo3.text = "This guitar is priced at: $" + event.
        target.selectedItem.data;
}
```

The labels and data in the `myList.addItem` statements are inside curly brackets that are inside parentheses.

You can replace `showPrice` with any name you like. `myList` in this example is the instance name of your list, described in Step 3, and `myInfo3` is the name of the TLF text field that we mention in Step 1.

In this example, we use ActionScript to create three list items (as shown in Figure 12-11). However, if you prefer, you can instead manually create the list items in the Property inspector. In that case, you don't need to type the first, second, and third statements in the preceding code. To manually create the list items, fill out the list in the way described in Steps 7–10 in the preceding section "Using ComboBoxes in a Flash movie."

In the first three statements in the preceding code, we use ActionScript to add three guitars to the list. The next statement adds an event listener to myList that "listens" for a viewer selecting a menu item in myList. When the viewer selects one of the menu items, the event listener performs the showPrice function, which is defined in the next lines of code. showPrice sets the text of the Selectable TLF text field to This guitar is priced at: $, with whatever dollar value is stored in the data field of the list menu item that the viewer selects. You can replace the statement in the showPrice function with other ActionScript code to do other things with the selected values.

Creating a Preloader

If you're ambitious and create a huge Flash file, downloading it to a viewer's browser might take a long time. Your audience won't wait forever. To solve this problem, you can create a *preloader,* which is a tiny movie that loads quickly and tells your viewers to wait.

Flash CS5 offers a sample preloader that you can modify and use as your own. This is nice because it already contains many lines of fancy ActionScript code that you don't have to bother to write yourself. The preloader plays a movie clip, which is called a *loading clip.* You can easily change the loading clip. This movie clip can be anything you want. For example, we changed the loading clip into kalaidoscopic text with letters growing and shrinking in a wave, as shown in Figure 12-12. You can virtually make your preloader appear however you want. Although, remember to keep it simple! (You don't want to have to build a preloader for your preloader.)

The sample preloader is designed so that it resides in Frame 1 and you place your movie starting in Frame 2. When the rest of the movie is loaded, the preloader continues to Frame 2. So that you don't have to move everything in an existing movie to start in Frame 2, we describe in the steps how you can create a new scene to contain your preloader.

You can modify the sample pre-loader and thus create your own pre-loader, by following these steps:

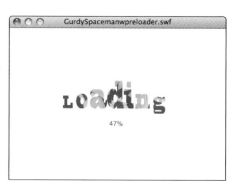

Figure 12-12: A preloader animation is useful for inspiring your audience to stick around, by informing them that the movie is loading.

1. **Choose File⊃New. In the dialog box that appears, choose ActionScript 3 and click the Templates tab.**

   The Templates tab appears, as shown in Figure 12-13.

2. **Choose Preloader for SWF and click OK.**

   This creates a new document containing a preloader in Frame 1, and you can move the rest of your Flash movie starting in Frame 2. However, these steps describe how to move the preloader to your own Flash document. But first, you want to modify the preloader.

Figure 12-13: Flash offers a sample preloader for your large Flash movie that you can use and modify.

3. **To modify the preloader, do any of the following:**

   - *To change the background,* unlock the Background layer, click the layer name in the Timeline to select it, and then press Backspace (Windows) or Delete (Mac) to remove the little squares on the layer. If you want to change the color of the Stage, select the Stage, and choose a new color in the Properties pane of the Property inspector. (If you want to add anything else to the background, you can do that now.)

   - *To modify the loading clip,* first double-click the loading clip in the Library. You can now make any changes to the symbol. Notice that the Timeline now contains the movie clip's animation, as shown in Figure 12-14. To see the movie clip's animation, you can press Enter (Windows) or Return (Mac). To add your new preloader animation, first insert a new layer in the Timeline and then delete Layer 1. Now you can add any artwork and animation that you want for your preloader. Choose Edit⊃Edit Document when finished.

- *To modify the font, color, size, and placement of the text that displays the percentage,* choose Window⇨Movie Explorer to open the Movie Explorer if it's not already open, and click the Select Text button to display the text in the movie. Then click percent_txt to select the dynamic text box that displays the percentage. In the Property inspector, you can change its color, text size, font and more. You can also move the text box, using the Selection tool in the toolbar.

4. **On the main Timeline, be sure all your layers are unlocked. Then select Frames 1 and 2 for the three layers in the timeline and choose Edit⇨Timeline⇨Copy Frames.**

Figure 12-14: You can edit the movie clip in the preloader in any way you want.

5. **Open the document that you want to add your preloader to.**

6. **Open the Scene panel by choosing Window⇨Other Panels⇨Scene. In the Scene panel, click the Add Scene icon at the bottom left of the Scene panel to add a scene. Drag it above the scene of your main movie, and give it a name, such as *preloader*.**

   See Chapter 9 for the lowdown on creating and changing the order of scenes.

7. **In the first scene (the preloader), select Frame 1 in Layer 1 and choose Edit⇨Timeline⇨Paste Frames.**

   These are the frames you copied in Step 4. You now have the preloader in your document.

8. **Select Frame 1 of the Actions layer and open the Actions panel. In Line 14 change the following:**

   ```
   gotoAndStop(2);
   ```

   to

   ```
   gotoAndPlay(2);
   ```

9. **Choose Control⇨Test Movie⇨In Flash Professional to view your movie.**

   Flash loops the movie clip in your preloader scene so that it plays over and over until your main movie is loaded.

When you test your preloader, your main movie might load so quickly that you don't even see the preloader. Choose View⇨Simulate Download in the Flash Player window to see how your preloader works while your main movie loads. You may need to resize the window to view the preloader. If it still loads too fast, choose View⇨Download Settings to choose a slower download speed. (See Chapter 13 for more information on testing a movie and analyzing its download performance.) You can also upload your file to a test page on your Web site to see how the preloader works.

Creating an Entire Web Site with Flash

You can use Flash to create your site's complete user interface, along with all the graphics and text. Some Web sites are almost 100% Flash (for example, www.madeinmtl.com, a beautiful Web site for tourists and other explorers of Montreal). However, most Web sites with Flash (including www.adobe.com) are a hybrid of Flash and HTML. So, a Flash Web site may have the following structure:

- ✔ **An HTML home page** that contains the following:

   • A *user interface* (and perhaps other graphics) built in Flash.

   • *Tests* that detect the Flash Player and Player version. (This is provided by default when you publish your Flash movie — see the "Testing for the Flash Player" section later in this chapter.)

   • *Alternate HTML content* for viewers who don't have Flash, and a button that viewers can use to get the Flash Player if they want, as described in the upcoming section, "Creating alternative sites."

- ✔ **Additional HTML** pages that, like the home page, utilize a user interface (and other graphics) built into Flash, for all the remaining pages in the Web site. You probably want each of these pages to also test for Flash, in case your viewers don't enter the site through your home page.

- ✔ **HTML pages that contain a non-Flash version** of the Web site if you want the site to be available to those who don't have and don't want to install the required version of Flash.

If you create your entire Web site from one big Flash file, your users can't use their browsers' Back buttons to navigate your Flash movie. An advantage of creating multiple HTML pages with Flash on each page is that the browser's Back button still works.

Your opening HTML page is usually the first thing your viewers see and may be the most important page on your site, so be sure to think carefully about your goals for this page. You may want to put lots of useful information or other important material on your home page so that your viewers quickly see that your site is worth exploring.

To match the color of a Flash movie in a Web page to the rest of the page, match the background colors of the movie (by choosing Modify⇨ Document) and the HTML page, as shown in Figure 12-15. (This technique doesn't work if your Web page uses an image for a background.)

Figure 12-15: Matching the background color of the movie to the rest of the Web page.

Your site probably contains buttons that people can use to navigate through your site, get more information, or contact you. You can create the navigation structure in many ways. Here are three:

- ✔ Use Code Snippets to trigger the display of movie clips or Flash Player movies (.swf files) or Hide or Show objects, and more. See Chapter 10 for an example of a button that hides/shows an object.

- ✔ Use buttons to assign the Click to Go to a Webpage Code Snippet, to link to other HTML pages on your site. You can, of course, create the HTML pages with Flash. (See Chapter 8 for more about navigating to URLs.)

- ✔ Use buttons to display information or graphics located on other parts of your Timeline by using the gotoAndPlay or gotoAndStop function. We discuss this option in the following section, "Using the Timeline to store Web content."

You can use combinations of these techniques, as well.

Using the Timeline to store Web content

In most cases, you use the Timeline to display frames in sequence — in other words, animation — but the Timeline can also store static frames. You can create anything on the Stage in those frames, and you can display what is in those frames whenever you want. You can use ActionScript to jump to a frame based on a user interaction and stop there until the next user interaction. Thus, different frames on the Timeline can become the equivalent of separate Web pages.

Suppose that you have several buttons on the left side of your page. You want viewers to see different graphics and animation on the right side of the page when they roll the mouse over each button. Perhaps rolling over one button displays a product description, and rolling over another button displays a description of a second product.

To create a set of buttons that move the playhead to different sections of the Timeline, follow these steps:

Figure 12-16: Each button will move the playhead to a different frame of the Timeline.

1. **In Frame 1, place instances of your buttons on one side of the Stage (for example, the left side, as shown in Figure 12-16), and label the layer,** *Buttons.*

2. **Open the Property inspector if it isn't already open. (Choose Window⇨Properties.)**

3. **Create a new layer and give it a name, such as** *Product Views.*

4. **Click the next frame in the Products Views layer, and choose Insert⇨ Timeline⇨Keyframe.**

5. **On the Stage, create the graphics and words for the product description or whatever you want displayed when a user rolls the mouse over the first button.**

   If you want to display animation when a user rolls over the first button, drag a movie clip from the Library. (Check out Chapter 7 for the scoop on creating movie clips.)

   Place the graphics so that they don't cover the buttons when the graphics appear.

6. **Repeat Steps 4 and 5 to create a product description on the Product Views layer for each button.**

   At each new keyframe, delete the previous content on the Product Views layer, and then add what you want to display for the new product description.

7. **Move the playhead to Frame 1 and select a button.**

8. **In the instance name text box at the top of the Property inspector, type a unique instance name for the button.**

   In this example, name the buttons *myButton1, myButton2,* and so on.

9. **Repeat Steps 8 and 9 for each button.**

10. **On the** *Buttons* **layer, add a frame at the same time on the Timeline as the keyframe for the last product description.**

    Now your buttons will stay visible when each product description is displayed.

11. **Move the playhead to Frame 1. Open the Code Snippets panel and in the Timeline Navigation folder, double-click Stop at This Frame.**

    An Actions layer appears. The code in the Actions panel consists of several lines of comments and then

    ```
    stop();
    ```

    If you don't do this, your movie simply plays through all the frames, displaying your product descriptions one after another. But you want viewers to see a particular product description only when they roll over a particular button.

12. **Select a button, open the Event Handlers folder in the Code Snippets panel, and click Mouse Over Event.**

    The following code is added to the Actions panel:

    ```
    myButton1.addEventListener(MouseEvent.MOUSE_OVER,fl_
            MouseOverHandler);

    function fl_MouseOverHandler (event:MouseEvent):void
    {
        trace("Moused over");
    }
    ```

13. **In the Actions panel, change the line `trace("Moused over");` to `gotoAndStop(2);` where 2 is the frame number containing the Product View.**

    You can also create labels for your frames and type in the frame label instead of the frame number into the code. Be sure to place quotes around the frame label in the code.

14. **Repeat Steps 12 and 13 for each button, replacing the 2 with the frame number for that button's product view.**

15. **Choose Control⇨Test Movie⇨In Flash Professional to try it out.**

    When you roll over a button, the graphics, text, and movie clip animation on the appropriate frame appears.

Figure 12-17 shows a Timeline with frames that are displayed when the mouse cursor passes over buttons. If you use Mouse Click Event rather than Mouse Over Event in Step 12, you can display different information when the mouse clicks each button.

You can build on this further by, for example, sending the user back to the first frame when the mouse rolls off the button — like this:

```
function menuChoice1A(event:MouseEvent):void
{
    this.gotoAndStop(1);
}
myButton1.addEventListener(MouseEvent.ROLL_OUT,
        menuChoice1A);
```

Figure 12-17: When the user moves the mouse over each button, the movie will jump to a different Frame on the Timeline.

You can place this code at the end of all your other code in the Frame 1 of the Actions layer in the timeline. Select Frame 1 in the Actions layer (which has an *a* in it). Then open the Actions panel by choosing Window➪Actions and add the code at the end of the existing code in the Actions panel. (Or you could add it to the top, if you prefer.) Notice that the new function is named menuChoice1A. You can choose any name, as long as it is unique, and as long as you replace the name in both places that it is used.

Testing for the Flash Player

Although more than 98% of the world's Web surfing population reportedly has the Flash Player installed, that's still not everyone, and some have fairly old versions of the Flash Player. For viewers who don't have the Flash Player, it often downloads automatically (as a result of the code that Flash places in the HTML file when you publish your SWF and HTML files, as we describe in Chapter 13). If Flash doesn't download automatically, those users might not be able to view your site.

You can test for the presence of the Flash Player and, perhaps more important, you can test to see which version of the Flash Player they have. If you're using features that exist only in Flash CS5, make sure that viewers have Flash Player 10, because many people might still have Flash Player 9 (or an even earlier version) installed.

Detecting the Flash Player version

You may detect a particular Flash Player version by simply selecting the Detect Flash Version check box in the HTML tab in Flash's Publish Settings before you publish your movie. (See Chapter 13 for specifying Publish Settings.) This does a great job of detecting a particular Flash Player version.

Then when your Web page comes up in a Web browser, if the Flash Player of the specified version can't be found or if the Web browser doesn't have scripting enabled, the resulting HTML code displays the sentence `Alternate HTML content should be placed here` on your Web page. You can edit the HTML to replace that sentence with whatever alternative content you want to display.

Creating alternative sites

Alternative HTML content could consist of HTML code for a page in a series of HTML-only, non-Flash pages, if you feel that your audience needs it. Some Flash sites include a complete set of non-Flash (HTML) pages for viewers who don't have the Flash Player and don't want to download it.

If you use features unique to Flash Player 10, you can also create, for example, a Flash 9 site that uses only features available in Flash 9. The overwhelming majority of Web surfers have Flash Player 9 or later. But don't forget how much time you spend updating your Web site now. Imagine updating two or three sites! Make sure you think carefully about who your audience is and the consequences of having so many alternatives.

For detailed information on how many computer users have which versions of the Flash player, check out the latest statistics at `www.adobe.com/products/player_census/flashplayer/version_penetration.html`. You may be surprised by the statistics.

Using Movie Explorer

Movie Explorer is a great tool for analyzing an entire movie. When you start creating complex relationships among several Timelines, you might have trouble remembering what you've done. Movie Explorer lays out the entire structure of your movie for you to see, and is also a great tool for troubleshooting problems. By visually displaying your movie's components, you can more easily find where the trouble lies.

Another use for Movie Explorer is to analyze other people's FLA files. When you open someone else's Flash file, you might wonder where all the action is. It might all be hidden in movie clips and ActionScript that calls other movies and movie clips. Movie Explorer can help you ferret out the magic behind the animation.

To open Movie Explorer, choose Window➪Movie Explorer. The Movie Explorer is shown in Figure 12-18.

You usually know what you're looking for when you open Movie Explorer: say, ActionScript or movie clips. Use the buttons at the top of Movie Explorer to specify which movie elements are shown in the main window:

A ➤ **Show Text:** Displays all text objects in the movie.

➤ **Show Movie Clips, Buttons, and Graphics:** Displays a list of those objects.

➤ **Show Action Scripts:** Lists all ActionScript in the movie.

➤ **Show Video, Sounds, and Bitmaps:** Lists those objects.

➤ **Show Frames and Layers:** Shows each frame and each layer that contains objects.

Figure 12-18: Explore with the Movie Explorer.

➤ **Customize Which Items to Show:** Opens the Movie Explorer Settings dialog box, where you can indicate which items you want to display by selecting or deselecting them in a list of check boxes. You can also choose to display Movie Elements (showing the elements of your movie organized by scene), Symbol Definitions (a separate listing by symbol), or both. Click OK to close this dialog box.

Movie elements are shown in a hierarchical manner in Movie Explorer. For example, if a frame has an action attached to it, you see a plus sign (Windows) or a disclosure triangle (Mac) next to the button. Click any plus sign or right-pointing triangle to expand the display — in this case, to reveal the ActionScript attached to that frame. Click any minus sign (Windows) or downward-pointing triangle (Mac) to collapse the display.

In the Find text box, you can type any expression to search the entire movie. Suppose that you want to know whether a movie contains the navigate ToURL action. Just type **navigateToURL** in the Find text box, and Movie Explorer displays every instance containing that word.

The Find feature is not case sensitive, which is handy if you can't remember how things are capitalized. But the Find feature is sensitive to spaces, so if the movie contains *navigateToURL* and you type **navigate To URL**, you don't get any results.

You can use Movie Explorer to select objects on the Stage or frames. Just click the item in Movie Explorer, and Flash selects the object or frame. (If you select a frame, Flash also includes the frames up to the next keyframe.) If you select a scene, Flash selects the first frame of the scene.

Movie Explorer contains an extensive menu that you can access by clicking in the upper-right corner of the Movie Explorer panel, or you can right-click (Windows) or Control-click (Mac) inside the Movie Explorer panel.

Some of the more useful features of this menu follow:

- **Show in Library:** Opens the Library (if it isn't already open) and highlights the object that you previously selected in the Movie Explorer.

- **Rename:** Lets you rename the selected object, such as a button instance.

- **Copy All Text to Clipboard:** Copies all the text in the Movie Explorer to the Clipboard so you can paste it into another application.

- **Print:** Prints the entire contents of the Movie Explorer. All items, whether collapsed or expanded, are printed.

If you have difficulty understanding one of the more advanced Flash files from the resource Web sites that we recommend in Chapter 17, try opening Movie Explorer. Look for actions and movie clips. You might be surprised at what you can discover by using this tool.

Making Your Site More Accessible

Flash includes capabilities that make it possible for you to make Flash more accessible to people with disabilities. Most of the components in Flash CS5 are designed to be accessible to the visually impaired through the use of *screen readers,* which generate spoken descriptions of the contents of your Flash screens. Screen reader software is widely available from a variety of companies.

Users can also navigate most of Flash's components by using the keyboard rather than the mouse — this is automatically built into the components. And ActionScript has features that can enhance the accessibility of Flash documents.

One of the easiest ways to make your Flash movie more accessible to people with disabilities is to use the Accessibility panel. When you add buttons, movie clips, text fields, input text fields, or components to your movie, you can use the Accessibility panel to make them accessible to screen readers. (Not all components can be made accessible, but most can.) To make a button, movie clip, dynamic text field, input text field, TLF text, or component accessible, follow these steps:

Figure 12-19: Use the Accessibility panel to make elements of your movie accessible to people with disabilities.

1. **Open the Accessibility panel. (Choose Window⇨Other Panels⇨Accessibility.)**

2. **Select the button, movie clip, dynamic text field, input text field, TLF text, or component on the Stage.**

3. **From the Accessibility panel, select the Make Object Accessible check box, as shown in Figure 12-19.**

4. **If you selected a movie clip in Step 2 and you want objects embedded in the movie clip to also be accessible, select the Make Child Objects Accessible check box.**

   For example, select the Make Child Objects Accessible check box if you want to allow text objects in the movie clip to be read by the screen reader software.

5. **In the Name box, type a name for the symbol or component.**

   The screen reader can read this name aloud.

6. **In the Description box, type a description of the symbol or component.**

   The screen reader can read this description aloud.

7. **In the Shortcut box, type a keyboard shortcut that viewers can use to select the object, if appropriate.**

   For instance, if the object is a RadioButton that needs to be selected to receive input, follow this step.

   The screen reader can then use this information to read aloud something like, "The shortcut for this text field is Ctrl+K." (Not all screen readers support this feature.) Typing information in the Shortcut box doesn't actually implement keyboard shortcut functionality. You need to use ActionScript to detect and respond to any shortcut key presses.

8. **In the Tab Index box, you may enter the number corresponding to the object's tab index value, if appropriate.**

   The *tab index* determines how users can use the Tab key to navigate and select the buttons, check boxes, and other controls in your movie. For example, suppose that you have three buttons with a tab index of 1, 2, and 3, respectively. When the movie starts, if the user presses the Tab key three times, the button with the tab index of 3 would be selected for input.

If you have the Accessibility panel open when nothing in your movie is selected, the panel offers you the option to Make Movie Accessible, which is selected by default. This allows screen readers to read the different objects in the Flash movie. You definitely want this option selected if you want to make your movie accessible to screen readers and other hardware and software for people with disabilities. Of course, you also have to use the Accessibility panel to name each object, as we describe in the preceding steps, for this to be useful.

13

Publishing for the Flash Player

In This Chapter

▷ Reducing your movie's size for fast download

▷ Testing your Flash movies

▷ Publishing Flash movies to SWF, HTML, and other formats

▷ Using Publish Profiles

▷ Posting your movie to your Web site

▷ Exporting movie and image files

▷ Creating movies that viewers can print

*W*hen your Flash movie is completed, you need to publish it in its final form — most likely an SWF (pronounced *swiff*) file that you can post on your Web site. In this chapter, we explain how to prepare a Flash movie for publishing as an SWF file and help you determine the ideal publish settings for your needs. We also discuss how to publish to other graphic file formats, such as PNG, in case you want to create a non-Flash site or use your material in another program. We cover all the bases so that you can get your animation up and running on the Web.

The filenames of Flash-published movies end with the .swf suffix. *SWF* originally stood for *Shockwave Flash,* but nobody uses that term for Flash movies anymore even though the abbreviation remains the same. So, we refer to SWF files as *Flash Player files,* not Shockwave Flash files.

Flash converts your movie data into a highly compact and efficient form in an SWF file; the SWF file contains only the information needed for playback of your movies. In contrast, when you save your movies by choosing File⇨Save (or File⇨Save As), they are saved with the .fla suffix. They are saved in a format that can be read by the Flash CS5 application, but not the Flash Player. The FLA file contains lots of information about layers, Library items, your video source files, and so on, which you need when you are creating your movies — and which the Flash Player doesn't need.

Optimizing Movies for Fast Download

Throughout this book, we offer suggestions for designing a Flash movie with speedy downloading in mind. In this section, we put the suggestions together so that you can review your movie as a whole before you publish it.

Simplifying artwork

By simplifying the artwork in your movie, you can greatly reduce the size of a Flash movie, thereby increasing its speed. Here are the most important techniques:

- ✔ **Use symbols for every object that appears more than once.** You can turn any object or group of objects into a symbol. *Nest* your symbols: For example, turn an object into a symbol and then use it in a movie clip or button. Remember that you can change the color of symbol instances — you don't need to create a new symbol. (Chapter 7 covers symbols in detail.)

- ✔ **Group objects whenever possible.** Groups are almost as efficient as symbols. (Chapter 4 explains how to create groups.)

- ✔ **Use vector graphics rather than bitmaps when you can.** If you do use bitmaps, don't animate them unless you need to. Bitmaps and bitmap animation can increase your Flash Player file size and thus the download time. However, with the rising adoption of faster broadband Internet access, bitmaps are an increasingly important part of Flash projects, including the sites referred to in this book. (Chapter 3 explains how to import a bitmap.)

- ✔ **Reduce bitmap size when possible.** You can reduce the size of the bitmap and thus reduce its quality in Publish Settings. Often you can reduce the size and quality of an image with almost no noticeable effect. We describe how to do this later in this chapter.

- ✔ **Optimize curves.** (Choose Modify⇨Shape⇨Optimize.) You can optimize curves to reduce the number of lines used to create a shape. This can be tiresome on a large project, but if you really need to reduce the size of your Flash movie, this may help. (Check out Chapter 4 for further explanation.)

- ✔ **Use solid lines rather than dashed, dotted, and other line types when possible.** Try to avoid custom line widths. (We explain line types in Chapter 3.)

✒ **Use the Pencil tool rather than the Brush tool when possible.** The Pencil tool uses fewer bytes in your movie.

✒ **Avoid using transparency when you don't need it.** Using transparency doesn't make your Flash file bigger, but it can slow down playback because of the extra calculation required. On the other hand, sometimes transparency effects make your movie look really great. (See Chapter 7 to find out about changing the transparency of the elements in your movie.)

✒ **Use solid fills rather than gradients.** Gradients are more complex and make the Flash Player file bigger. However, gradients are also key to the Flash look that is so popular. They help to make vector graphics look less flat.

Optimizing text

Text can consume lots of bytes. Here's what you can do to reduce the byte bite:

✒ **Reduce the number of fonts and font styles (bold, italic) as much as possible.** Use simpler sans serif fonts if you can. You get the best results file-size-wise with the device fonts (sans, serif, and typewriter) although you might find these device fonts boring. Flash doesn't need to store the outlines of device fonts in the SWF file, so these take up fewer bytes. And usually your Flash projects will look better if you don't use too many fonts — a useful rule in the graphic design world is to avoid using more than two or three fonts in a design, as suggested in Figure 13-1. (See Chapter 5 for more information on fonts.)

Figure 13-1: If you use more than two or three fonts, people may start to think that you're designing a ransom note.

✔ **If you create input text fields or dynamic text fields, limit the text and specify any restrictions that you can in the Font Embedding dialog box (shown in Figure 13-2).** Select a text box. Then, in the Character pane of the Property inspector, click the Embed button. See Chapter 5 for more info on character and font embedding. For example, exclude unnecessary character outlines, such as numbers.

Figure 13-2: Select the character sets you want to embed in your Flash movie.

Compressing sound

You can compress sounds to reduce the file size. When you compress individual sounds in the Sound Properties dialog box, as shown in Figure 13-3, you can fine-tune settings for each individual sound in your movie. (To see the Sound Properties dialog box, double-click the sound icon in the Library.) Later in this chapter, we review how to compress sound when you publish a Flash movie. Use the MP3 format whenever possible because it compresses well. If you need more information on compressing sounds, check out Chapter 11.

Here are some other ways that you can reduce the size of your sound files:

✔ Adjust the sound's Time In and Time Out points to prevent silent areas from being stored in your SWF file.

✔ Reuse sounds by using different In and Out points and by looping different parts of the same sound.

✔ Don't loop streaming sound.

See Chapter 11 for more information on editing, looping, and streaming sound.

Sound Properties

calliope.mp3

/Users/professorgurdyleete/Documents/
Techniques/Ch07/calliope.mp3

Sunday, June 9, 2002 12:02 PM

44 kHz Stereo 16 Bit 48.5 s 581.9 kB

Compression: MP3

☐ Use imported MP3 quality

Preprocessing: ☑ Convert stereo to mono

Bit rate: 48 kbps

Quality: Fast

48 kbps Mono 290.9 kB, 50.0% of original

Device sound:

OK
Cancel
Update
Import...
Test
Stop
Advanced

Figure 13-3: Fine-tune the compression settings for each sound in your movie here.

Animating efficiently

One of the most effective ways to reduce file size is to use tweens. (See Chapter 9 for details on this animation technique.) Frame-by-frame animation creates larger files. Keeping animation localized in one area also helps. Small animations (animations where the objects don't move much) produce smaller file sizes than wide-area animations.

Testing Movies

Before publishing your movie, you should test it. The first step is to simply play your animation, as we explain in Chapter 9. However, playing the animation on the Stage doesn't provide you with enough information to determine problems caused by file size. To find those kinds of bugs, you have to use the Test Movie command or test your movie in a browser. The following sections tell you how to test both ways.

Flash CS5 is optimized for the tasks that you perform when creating a Flash movie (such as drawing, adding keyframes, showing and hiding layers, and typing ActionScript code). It's not optimized for playing back your animation — the Flash Player is optimized for that. Your FLA file contains lots of information that you need when you're creating your movies — but that the Flash Player doesn't need. The Flash Player plays only SWF files, which you can create when you choose File➪Publish.

Using the Test Movie command

After creating your animation, choose Control⇨Test Movie⇨In Flash Professional to view your animation. Then you can use the Bandwidth Profiler (and other tools described in the following steps) to provide estimates of downloading speed so you can find bottlenecks that pause your animation. You can also see the results of movie clips and all ActionScript code.

If you're using movie clips, they won't play when you choose Control⇨Play. To see them play, you must choose Control⇨Test Movie⇨In Flash Professional or Control⇨Test Scene.

To test a movie or scene, follow these steps:

1. **Choose Control⇨Test Movie⇨In Flash Professional (or Control⇨Test Scene if you just want to test the scene that you are working on).**

   Flash publishes your movie to an SWF file by using the current settings in the Publish Settings dialog box (see the section "Publishing Flash Movies" later in this chapter) and opens a new window. You see your animation run. You can change the settings in the Publish Settings dialog box (choose File⇨Publish Settings) before using this command.

2. **The new window that appears (with your movie playing in it) has a main menu. On this main menu, choose View⇨Download Settings and choose a downloading speed between that of a 14.4 modem (1.2 Kbps) to a T1 line (131.2 Kbps).**

   If you repeatedly change the download settings, you get a better sense of their effect. To specify your own settings, choose Customize, and in the Custom Modem Settings dialog box, enter the menu text that you want to appear on the menu and the bit rate in bytes per second. Click OK. Then open the Download Settings menu again and choose your customized setting, which now appears on the menu.

3. **Choose View⇨Bandwidth Profiler to see the graph that shows the downloading performance.**

   The Bandwidth Profiler (as shown in Figure 13-4) displays the byte size of each individual frame. Frames with bars that rise above the lower red horizontal line cause loading delays.

4. **To see settings for any one frame, stop the movie by clicking the frame's bar.**

   To the left of the bandwidth profiler, Flash displays the movie's statistics: dimensions, frame rate, file size, movie duration, and the amount of animation to preload in frames and seconds. You also see the size of each individual frame.

5. **Choose View⇨Streaming Graph to see how the Flash movie streams into a browser.**

Figure 13-4: When you test a movie, Flash helps you analyze the downloading performance of your movie.

6. **Choose View⇨Frame by Frame Graph (shown in Figure 13-5) to see which frames contribute to delays.**

A frame whose bar extends above the red line may cause a bottleneck when the movie downloads at the connection speed you choose in Step 2. Playback may stop at any frame where the bar extends above the red line, until the whole frame has downloaded.

By default, Flash opens the SWF window in Streaming Graph mode.

Figure 13-5: In the Frame by Frame Graph, you can see the size of the download for each frame.

7. **Choose View➪Simulate Download if you want to see the Flash movie play as if loading at the speed you choose in Download Settings in Step 2.**

8. **To close the SWF window, click its Close button.**

After you analyze your movie, you can go back and optimize it to eliminate delays. A short delay in the first frame is usually acceptable, but significant delays during the movie result in jerky animation or pauses.

If you have a long movie divided into scenes, you can save time by using the Test Scene command instead of the Test Movie command.

Testing a movie in a Web browser

The final steps of testing a movie are publishing it and viewing it in a Web browser. For a quick view, you can use the Publish Preview command. Flash publishes your movie to an SWF file, creates the appropriate HTML file, and opens the HTML file in your default browser. Viewing your Flash Player file in a browser reveals how the browser will display the movie when you upload it to a Web site.

Flash uses the current settings in the Publish Settings dialog box to create the preview, including the types of file formats that you have selected.

To preview your movie in a browser, follow these steps:

1. **Choose File➪Publish Settings to open the Publish Settings dialog box. Choose the desired file formats and publish settings, and then click OK.**

   See the "Publishing Flash Movies" section, later in this chapter, for more information on the Publish Settings dialog box.

2. **Choose File➪Publish Preview and choose the desired format from the submenu.**

   Flash opens your browser and runs your movie.

3. **Close your browser to end the preview.**

As with any Web page material, you need to consider the following when testing a Flash Player file:

✔ **The browser that your audience is using:** Preview your Flash Player file in the current version of Internet Explorer (IE), Mozilla Firefox, Google Chrome, and Safari. You should probably try at least one earlier version of IE, too. And maybe the current Opera browser, too. Okay, so you probably won't do all this, but don't say that we didn't tell you.

✓ **The resolution of viewers' screens:** Test at least the following common settings: 800 x 600 and 1024 x 768. Remember that the amount of material that appears on the screen changes with the resolution. If you preview at 800 x 600, you can be sure that people with higher resolutions can see your entire movie, but then again, a Flash movie that fits in a 800 x 600 screen may look pretty humble on a 1280 x 1024 screen.

Professional Web site developers take this testing phase seriously. No matter how good an animation looks on your screen, it's not a good animation if it doesn't translate well to your target number of viewers' screens.

Saving Your Work in Flash CS4 Format

If you're collaborating on a Flash project with a group of friends or coworkers and they're still using Flash CS4 (the predecessor of Flash CS5), there is still hope for them. You can save your work in Flash CS4 format.

To save your work in Flash CS4 format, follow these steps:

1. **Choose File⇨Save As.**

   The Save As dialog box appears.

2. **Choose where you want to save your file and then type the filename you want to use.**

3. **Click the Save as Type (Windows) or Format (Mac) drop-down list and select Flash CS4 Document.**

4. **Click Save As.**

If you're using features new to Flash CS5, a window appears (as shown in Figure 13-6), listing the new features that won't be saved in the Flash CS4 file and asking whether you want to continue. Click the Save as Flash CS4 button if you want to continue. If you do so, some of the data in your file won't be available in this saved version. So be sure to save a CS5 version as well to keep all of your data intact.

Figure 13-6: Pay attention to this warning message.

Publishing Flash Movies

So you're finally ready to publish your Flash masterpiece. It's time to choose File⇨Publish Settings. This brings you to the Publish Settings dialog box. Don't be overwhelmed by all the options. Typically, you use only a few of them. Start by specifying the settings. Then publish the movie to create the SWF file viewed on a Web page.

After you specify the settings, you can click OK rather than Publish if you want to go back to your Flash movie file and choose Control⇨Test Movie⇨In Flash Professional to see the results of your settings. You can try various settings until you're satisfied. Then click Publish to create the final SWF (Flash Player) file. Published files are in the same folder as your FLA movie file by default; you can specify another location if you want. Of course, you can also move the files afterward.

The Publish Settings dialog box lets you easily specify all your settings in one place. Then you click the Publish button, and Flash creates the SWF (Flash Player) file according to your settings. Choose File⇨Publish Settings to open the Publish Settings dialog box with the Formats tab on top, as shown in Figure 13-7.

Flash automatically names the files that it creates for you, using the Flash movie's name and adding the appropriate file extension, such as .html and .swf. You can see the names in the Formats tab of the Publish Settings dialog box. To specify your own name for a file, click the File text box and type the new name. To revert to the default filenames, click the Use Default Names button.

Figure 13-7: Your one-stop place for starting to publish your Flash movie.

Most of the time, you need only the Flash (.swf) and HTML formats. But if you want other formats, select them on the Formats tab. When you mark an additional format, the dialog box adds a new tab for that format (except for the projector formats, which don't need one).

After you mark the formats you want, click each tab to specify the settings for that format. The next few sections of this chapter explain each format, why you might want to use it, and how to specify the settings.

After you finish specifying all your settings, click the Publish button. Flash does your bidding, creating the files that you need to put your great creation on the Web.

Publishing to SWF

The second tab in the Publish Settings dialog box (choose File➪Publish Settings) is the Flash tab, which creates the Flash Player file, also called an SWF file. On this tab, shown in Figure 13-8, you specify settings that affect the SWF file.

Flash gives you options in four categories:

✔ Flash Player and ActionScript version

✔ Settings for images and sounds

✔ SWF settings

✔ Advanced settings

Figure 13-8: Specify how Flash creates the SWF (Flash Player) file.

Flash Player and ActionScript version

In this category, you specify the version of Flash Player that you want to require and the version of ActionScript that you want to use.

✔ **Player:** Allows you to save in the following ways:

- *Flash Player 10:* This is the most recent Flash Player and has complete compatibility with Flash CS5. As of January 2010, in the United States and Canada 94.2% of Web-surfing computers had Flash Player 10 installed.

  Up-to-date information regarding the popularity of the different Flash Players can be found at

  www.adobe.com/products/player_census/flashplayer/version_penetration.html

- *Flash Player 5–9:* These are previous version formats for backward compatibility. If you use new features but choose an old Flash Player version, Flash warns you of potential problems when you publish your movie. You might want to choose Flash Player 9 to see whether you're warned of any problems. If not, you can publish for that player and reach a slightly larger audience. Or you can do the same for Flash Player 8.

- *Flash Lite 1.0–4.0:* Use this for playing Flash movies on some mobile phones.

- *Adobe AIR 2:* Use this for creating rich Internet applications that can be deployed as desktop applications — but that's a subject for another book.

✓ **ActionScript version:** Choose from the following:

- *ActionScript 3.0:* This is the newest, most powerful, and up-to-date version. Introduced in Flash CS3, ActionScript 3.0 introduced fundamental changes in the underpinnings of ActionScript, making it possible for ActionScript 3.0 code to execute up to ten times faster than code from earlier versions.

- *ActionScript 2.0:* This was introduced in 2003 and added new features to ActionScript that made it easier to build larger and more complex applications in Flash.

- *ActionScript 1.0:* This older version is included for backward compatibility with old Flash movies.

Image and sound settings

In this category, you specify the details for compression of your audio and of your bitmap images.

✓ **JPEG Quality:** Sets the compression (size) versus quality of bitmaps, if you have any in your movie. You can set the quality anywhere from 0 (the lowest quality and highest compression) to 100 (the highest quality and lowest compression).

✓ **Enable JPEG Deblocking:** This adds a filter that blends the blocky-looking chunks that can appear if you greatly compress an image in the JPEG file format. This can make low-resolution bitmap images look much better. In some cases, it can make images seem blurry, so enable this option on a case-by-case basis.

✓ **Audio Stream:** Displays and sets the audio compression for *stream sounds* (sounds that use the Stream Sync setting in the Property inspector when a frame with the sound is selected). This setting applies if you haven't set the compression for individual sounds in the Sound Properties dialog box. Also, if you enable the Override Sound Settings check box in the Publish Settings dialog box, this setting overrides the setting in the Sound Properties dialog box. To change the current setting, click Set. The options are the same as in the Sound Properties dialog box. (Turn to Chapter 11 for details on setting sound properties.)

✓ **Audio Event:** Displays and sets the audio compression for event sounds (as set in the Property inspector when a frame with the sound is selected). Otherwise, the compression setting is the same as Audio Stream.

- *Override Sound Settings:* Select this option to override settings in the Sound Properties dialog box. Then the settings here apply to all sounds in your movie.

- *Export Device Sounds:* This gives you the option of exporting sounds in formats suitable for playback on certain mobile phones. To do this, you use proxy sound files, a discussion of which is beyond the scope of this book.

SWF settings

In this category, you specify assorted details of your SWF file.

✓ **Compress Movie:** Compresses your Flash Player file, especially text and ActionScript, so that it can download faster.

✓ **Include Hidden Layers:** This option is set by default. If you deselect this option, Flash won't publish layers (including layers inside movie clips) that are marked as hidden. Deselecting this option can be useful because then you can test different versions of your document simply by hiding layers.

✓ **Include XMP Metadata:** If you enable this option and click the nearby File Info button, a dialog box appears in which you can input information about the contents of your movie, and that information will be embedded in your SWF file, available for other search engines or other software to use. Some of the kinds of information that you can embed include camera data for photos in your SWF file, the frame rate and shot number of video footage, the artist name and song title of music in your movie (as shown in Figure 13-9), and much more.

✓ **Export SWC:** If you're new to Flash, you can safely leave this option disabled. SWC files are packages of precompiled components. Components in Flash can be implemented either in an FLA file or an SWC file. The User Interface components (such as CheckBoxes, ComboBoxes and RadioButtons) are implemented as FLA-based components, and the FLVPlayback and FLVPlaybackCaptioning components are SWC-based.

You can use ActionScript to add SWC-based components while a Flash Player movie is running so that they can be kept in SWC files that are separate from your Flash Player file. Because SWC files contain precompiled components, the components appear faster than ordinary movie clips. If you enable this option, when you publish your file, Flash creates an SWC file that contains your SWC components and an SWF file that uses the SWC file.

Figure 13-9: In an SWF file, embed all kinds of information about the items in your movie.

Advanced settings

In this category, you specify details related to debugging, security, and other advanced stuff.

  ✔ **Generate Size Report:** Creates a TXT file that you can use to troubleshoot problem areas, as shown in Figure 13-10. If you enable the Generate Size Report setting, when you publish your movie Flash creates a very useful report on the size of assorted parts of your movie. The report relates the various parts of your movie to the number of bytes that they require in the SWF file.

```
OUTPUT
Scene                        Shape Bytes   Text Bytes   ActionScript Bytes
-----------------            -----------   ----------   ------------------
Scene 1                               0            0                    16

Symbol                       Shape Bytes   Text Bytes   ActionScript Bytes
-----------------            -----------   ----------   ------------------
NextSlide                           122           35                     0
Slide3                                0            0                     0
Slide2                               73            0                     0
Slide4                               74            0                     0
Slide1                               74            0                     0

Font Name               Bytes      Characters
--------------------    -------    -------------
Arial-BoldMT Bold           418    Netx

ActionScript Bytes      Location
------------------      --------
                 1      Scene 1:actions:1
```

Figure 13-10: Enable the Generate Size Report setting when you publish your movie for a report on the size of movie parts.

The size report can be more useful than the bandwidth profiler in pinpointing the location of the giant-size parts of a movie. It's worth reviewing, and it's interesting (and often surprising) to see the size of the various elements of the SWF file.

✔ **Protect from Import:** Prevents the SWF files from being downloaded from the Web site and imported back into Flash. This feature doesn't provide 100%–guaranteed protection, but it helps keep your work from being "borrowed."

✔ **Omit Trace Actions:** Omits special codes used by programmers. *Trace actions* insert into Flash movies the codes used to record and display technical information about a Flash movie's progress in a special window, named the Flash Debugger. Programmers use this information to *debug* (remove errors from) their ActionScript programming. If you added Trace actions to your Flash movie, select the Omit Trace Actions check box to omit these codes from the SWF file, and your file will be smaller.

✔ **Permit Debugging:** Lets you use the Debugger to debug a Flash movie from another computer. If you permit debugging, you can add a password to protect the movie file. Although this option is useful for ActionScript programmers, discussing it is beyond the scope of this book.

✔ **Password:** Allows you to select a password for debugging, if you enable the Debugging Permitted (or Protect from Import) check box. This option prevents viewers from debugging (or importing) the movie unless they have the password.

✏ **Local Playback Security:** If you select Access Local Files Only, your Flash movie can interact only with files and resources on the computer that it's playing on. If you select Access Network Only, your movie can interact only with files and resources on the network, and not with those on the computer it's playing on. (This separation of local and network access helps make it more difficult for a malicious programmer to create a Flash file that collects data from your computer and transmits it over a network such as the Internet.)

✏ **Hardware Acceleration:** You can enable hardware-accelerated graphics by choosing Level 1 — Direct or Level 2 — GPU from the drop-down list so that Flash uses the computer's graphics card for rendering. However, using these options is tricky. For various technical reasons that are beyond the scope of this book, if you enable one of these hardware-accelerated modes, it will actually slow down your movie in the majority of cases. So if you're just starting out with Flash, you want to leave this option set to None.

✏ **Script Time Limit:** If a Flash movie seems to be stuck in an endless loop, after 15 seconds, the Flash Player will present the user with a dialog box asking whether to continue or quit. Here you can set the limit to a time other than the default of 15 seconds.

If all these settings seem like a bit much, you can always just use the default settings, go with the flow, and check the results.

Publishing to HTML

HTML is the basic language of Web pages. When you publish your Flash movie, Flash creates an HTML file that loads your Flash movie, which you can view in a Web browser. You might want the Flash movie to be the entire Web page (the default), or you might want to make it part of an existing Web page (which we show you how to do later in this chapter).

Specifying Flash Player detection and other HTML settings

To create the HTML file, you can specify the HTML settings on the HTML tab of the Publish Settings dialog box, as shown in Figure 13-11, or you can accept the default settings. In either case, it's good for you to know what those settings are.

Template

The first setting, Template, lets you select a *template,* which determines the format and contents of the HTML file. To keep matters simple, select the default, Flash Only. Table 13-1 explains the other template options, although it's extremely likely that you will never need to use anything other than the default, Flash Only.

Below the Template drop-down list is the Detect Flash Version check box. Select this check box to add browser scripting to detect the Flash Player for the version of Flash you specify on the Flash tab. When this check box is enabled, the Version number text boxes below it are also enabled. If you want to more exactly specify the minimum version required, type revision numbers in the Minor Revision and Incremental Revision text fields there. (*Minor Revision* and *Incremental Revision*

Figure 13-11: Specify how Flash creates HTML code to display your movie.

appear in tooltips when you move the mouse cursor over the text boxes.)

If you select the Detect Flash Version check box, when you publish your Flash file, the resulting HTML code prints the following on your Web page if the Flash Player of the specified version can't be found or if the Web browser doesn't have JavaScript enabled:

```
Alternate HTML content should be placed here. This
content requires the Adobe Flash Player. Get Flash.
```

JavaScript must not be disabled by the Web browser for the Flash Player version detection to work. (A small percentage of people turn off JavaScript on their Web browser as a security precaution.) You can edit the HTML to replace the preceding text with whatever alternative content you want to display when the Flash Player version can't be found. We describe how to edit HTML later in this chapter.

Table 13-1	HTML Template Options
Option	**What It Does**
Flash for Pocket PC 2003	Creates an HTML file with Pocket PC–specific alignment. Can be used with Pocket IE and with desktop IE and Netscape browsers
Flash HTTPS	Creates an HTML file using the HTTPS protocol to specify where to go to download the Flash Player, if necessary. HTTPS is designed to send data over the Web more securely than the standard method (HTTP). It also creates a JavaScript file in your HTML output folder, and this must be uploaded along with the HTML file.
Flash Only (Default)	Creates an HTML file, as we describe in the earlier section "Understanding the HTML code for a movie."
Flash Only — Allow Full Screen	Creates an HTML file and includes support for playing your Flash movie full screen.
Flash with AICC Tracking	Creates an HTML file with support for AICC-HACP tracking when using Adobe Learning Interactions. (AICC is Aviation Industry Computer-Based-Training Committee, and HACP is HTTP AICC Communications Protocol.)
Flash with FSCommand	Used when you have added an FSCommand action to your movie to interface with JavaScript.
Flash with Named Anchors	Creates an HTML file with support for Named Anchors so that viewers can bookmark Flash content in Flash Player 6 and later; thus, it uses the Web browser's Back button effectively while navigating within a Flash movie. This could be a great feature, but many browsers don't support it, so it's fairly useless.
Flash with SCORM 1.2 Tracking	Includes support for SCORM (Sharable Content Object Reference Model) version 1.2 tracking when using Adobe Learning Interactions.
Flash with SCORM 2004 Tracking	Includes support for SCORM 2004 tracking when using Adobe Learning Interactions.
Image Map	(If you don't know what an image map is, don't worry about this option.) Instead of displaying an SWF player file, it uses a GIF, JPEG, or PNG image (which you need to choose on the Formats tab) as a client-side image map coded in your HTML page.

Dimensions

The Dimensions options control the size allotted to your Flash Player movie on your Web page. You have three options:

- ✔ **Match Movie:** Matches the width and height that you set in the Movie Properties dialog box. (Choose Modify➪Document.)

- ✔ **Pixels:** Lets you specify the Width and Height in pixels. Type the desired values in the text boxes.

- ✔ **Percent:** Lets you specify the area used by the Flash Player movie as a percentage of the browser window size. The 100% setting is ideal for pages designed to take up the entire page. Type the desired percentage values in the text boxes labeled Width and Height.

Playback

The Playback section determines the values of parameters in the HTML code. You have four options:

- ✔ **Paused at Start:** Creates a PLAY parameter whose value is FALSE. The person must start the movie by clicking a button in the movie — the button's instance needs to have a Play action in it. Alternatively, viewers can right-click (Windows) or Control-click (Mac) the movie and choose Play in the shortcut menu, but they might not be aware of this. By default, this check box is deselected, so movies start to play automatically.

- ✔ **Loop:** Creates a LOOP parameter whose value is TRUE. The movie repeats over and over. By default, this check box is selected, so make sure to clear it if you don't want to loop your movie!

- ✔ **Display Menu:** Creates a MENU parameter set to TRUE. This option enables viewers to right-click (Windows) or Control-click (Mac) the movie and choose from a menu, as shown in Figure 13-12. The menu options in Flash Player 10 are Zoom In, Zoom Out, Show All, Quality (High, Medium, or Low), Print, and more. Without this option, the only menu items are Settings and About Adobe Flash Player 10. By default, Display Menu is selected.

- ✔ **Device Font:** Applies to Windows playback only. When this check box is selected, the

Figure 13-12: Control whether viewers can bring up the full Flash Player shortcut menu.

HTML file includes a DEVICE FONT parameter set to TRUE, and Flash substitutes *anti-aliased* (smoothly curved) system fonts for fonts not available on the viewer's system. This applies only to static text you create in Flash. By default, this item is not selected.

Quality

The Quality section determines the quality parameter in the <object> and <embed> tags of the HTML code. *Quality* refers to the level of *anti-aliasing*, which is the smoothing of the artwork so that it doesn't have jagged edges. The lower the quality, the faster the playback. Usually, you want to find a good balance between quality and speed. You have six options:

- **Low:** Doesn't use anti-aliasing (and looks awful).

- **Auto Low:** Starts at a low quality but switches to a high quality if the viewer's computer, as detected by the Flash Player, can handle it.

- **Auto High:** Starts at a high quality but switches to a low quality if the viewer's computer can't handle the playback demand. This option should provide good results on all computers.

- **Medium:** Applies some anti-aliasing but doesn't smooth bitmaps. This option is a good middle ground between low and high.

- **High:** Always uses anti-aliasing for vector art. Bitmaps are smoothed only if the file doesn't contain tweens. (See Chapter 9 for the scoop on tweens.) This setting is the default.

- **Best:** Always uses anti-aliasing, including for bitmaps.

Window Mode

Window Mode specifies how the player movie's window interacts with the rest of the page. Here are your options:

- **Window:** Plays your movie as an opaque rectangle within your Web page and does not allow your HTML to render other content in that rectangle. This is the default mode.

- **Opaque Windowless:** Creates an opaque background for the movie so that other elements in the Web page don't show through when they're behind the movie. This setting does allow your HTML to render content in front of the movie.

- **Transparent Windowless:** Makes the Flash background color transparent so that other elements on your Web page show through (or can appear on top of) your Flash content. This setting might slow down playback.

HTML Alignment

The HTML Alignment setting specifies the ALIGN attribute and specifies how the Flash Player movie is aligned within the browser window. You have five options:

- **Default:** Theoretically centers the Flash movie. If the browser window is smaller than the movie, this option theoretically crops the edges of the movie. But in our tests, the default is always left even though it should be center.

- **Left:** Aligns the movie along the left side of the browser window. If the window is too small, this option crops the other sides of the movie.

- **Right:** Aligns the movie along the right side of the browser window. If the window is too small, this option crops the other sides of the movie.

- **Top:** Aligns the movie along the top of the browser window. If the window is too small, this option crops the other sides of the movie.

- **Bottom:** Aligns the movie along the bottom of the browser window. If the window is too small, this option crops the other sides of the movie.

Scale

The Scale setting defines how the movie is placed within the boundaries specified by code in the HTML page when (and only when) you set a width and height different from the movie's original size, using the Pixels or Percent options in the Dimensions section of the Publish Settings dialog box. You have four options:

- **Default (Show All):** Displays the entire movie without distortion but might create borders on two sides of the movie.

  The Show All setting shows all the elements in your Flash movie, even those that you move to the sides, off the Stage.

- **No Border:** Scales the movie to fill the dimensions without distortion but might crop portions of the movie.

- **Exact Fit:** Fits the movie to the dimensions, distorting the movie if necessary.

- **No Scale:** Stops the movie from changing its scale if the viewer resizes the Flash Player window.

Flash Alignment

Flash Alignment determines how the movie fits within the movie window (as opposed to the browser window). It works together with the Scale and Dimensions settings. In other words, it determines how the Flash movie fits within the dimensions you specify. For the Horizontal setting, you can choose Left, Center, or Right. For the Vertical setting, you can choose Top, Center, or Bottom.

Show Warning Messages

At the bottom of the Publish Settings dialog box is the Show Warning Messages check box. When it's selected, you see warning messages during the publishing process. The publishing process continues, but you know that you might have made an error. For example, if you've chosen a template that requires a GIF or JPEG image but you haven't selected either format on the Formats tab, you see a warning message.

After you choose your settings, click OK to return to your movie or click Publish to publish it.

Embedding an SWF file into an existing Web page

You can embed your SWF file into an existing Web page if you want, which is likely. To do this, you need to know a few basics of HTML and how to edit it.

Understanding the HTML code for a movie

Figure 13-13 shows the type of HTML code that Flash generates when you publish your Flash file. This particular code is generated when you enable the Detect Flash Version check box. Flash generates the HTML file, as well as a JavaScript file called `swfobject.js`. To view the HTML code, follow these steps:

1. **Create a Flash movie and choose File⇨Publish Settings.**

   The Publish Settings dialog box appears.

2. **On the HTML tab, select the Detect Flash Version check box. And choose a version or accept the default.**

   You always want to allow the earliest version possible that will run your Flash movie. This allows the maximum number of people access to your movie without having to update their Flash Players — which, of course, is free — but some people don't see updating their Flash Player as the top priority in their lives like we do.

   To find out the earliest version of the Flash Player that will run your Flash movie, choose an earlier version in the Flash tab of the Publish Settings dialog box (choose File⇨Publish Settings). Then click Publish. If Flash doesn't give you any warning, you can try an even earlier Flash Player, until Flash objects to what you chose.

3. **Click Publish.**

   Flash creates a new file with an HTML extension in the same folder as your FLA file. It also creates the `swfobject.js` file that contains JavaScript.

4. **Open your browser and choose File⇨Open File, select the new HTML file that Flash just created, and click Open.**

   Your Flash movie appears in the Web browser.

5. **Right-click (Windows) or Control-click (Mac) outside the Flash movie, and choose View Source (Explorer and Safari) or View Page Source (Firefox).**

   A new window opens with the HTML and JavaScript code automatically generated by Flash, as shown in Figure 13-13.

Figure 13-13: When you publish a movie to a Flash Player file, Flash creates HTML and JavaScript code by default.

If you know some HTML, some parts of this page will look fairly familiar. (And if you don't, you might want to check out *HTML, XHTML, & CSS For Dummies,* 6th Edition, by Ed Tittel and Jeff Noble.) Here's how to understand the code in Figure 13-13:

- ✓ The page starts with the *tags* (codes) that all HTML documents contain: namely, `<html>`, `<head>`, and `<title>`.

- ✓ After `<title>` and `<meta>` tags, along with their `</title>` and `</meta>` closing tags, you see two `<script>` tags, along with their closing tags `</script>`. These script tags are calling the JavaScript file and passing parameters to it, allowing the JavaScript to execute. This JavaScript code creates the HTML code that creates the Web page that you end up seeing.

✔ After the closing `</head>` tag is the `<body>` tag, with the following code. It contains a button and text that appears if the Web browser cannot find the proper Flash version.

```
<body>
<div id="flashContent">
<a href="http://www.adobe.com/go/getflash"><img
        src="http://www.adobe.com/images/shared/
        download_buttons/get_flash_player.gif" alt="Get
        Adobe Flash player" /> </a>
  <p>This page requires Flash Player version (a minimum
        version number here) or higher.</p>
</div>
</body>
```

The `<a...></a>` code creates a button that allows the user to get the latest Flash player.

The text between the `<p>` and `</p>` is what appears below the button.

✔ You see the closing tag that ends every HTML document: `</html>`.

Modifying HTML to include your SWF file

If you want to use the HTML document as is, you can. But if you want to combine your Flash Player file with the elements in another HTML file, you need to combine the code in the two documents.

Fortunately, this is easy to do. You simply copy the code between (and including) the two `<script>` and `</script>` tags in your Flash-generated HTML file and paste it into the HTML code of the other Web page — after the `<head>` tag. Then you copy the code between the `<body>` and `</body>` tags in the Flash-generated HTML file, and paste it where you want it to appear in the HTML code of the other Web page after the `<body>` tag. Where you place it affects its position in the Web page that you see. The instructions for how to do this follow, using a simple editor —TextEdit for the Mac or Notepad for Windows:

1. **After Step 5 in the preceding steps, select all the HTML code and press Ctrl+C (Windows) or ⌘+C (Mac) to copy it.**

2. **Open Notepad (Windows) or TextEdit (Mac). To open Notepad on Windows, click the Accessories folder in your Programs list and click Notepad.**

   If you're using TextEdit, also do the following:

   a. *Choose TextEdit⇨Preferences.*

   b. *From the New Document tab of the Preferences dialog box, select the Plain Text option.*

   c. *From the Open and Save tab of the Preferences dialog box, deselect Add '.txt' Extension to Plain Text Files.*

3. Paste the code from Step 1 into Notepad or TextEdit.

4. Select all the text between (and including) the first `<script>` tag and the last `</script>` closing tag, and press Ctrl+C (Windows) or ⌘+C (Mac) to copy it.

5. Open the HTML code for the Web page to which you want to add the SWF file.

6. Click in the file after `<head>` and press Ctrl+P (Windows) or ⌘+P (Mac) to paste the code into the new Web page.

7. Return to your Flash-generated code in the first file and copy all the text between the `<body>` tag and `</body>`.

8. In the code for your new Web page, decide where you want your Flash movie to be located and then paste it into the body section of the HTML code.

9. Save your new Web page with an `.html` extension (for example, `mywebpage.html`).

   You might also need to place your SWF file and the JavaScript file `swfobject.js` into the same folder as the HTML file for the Web page. To post your masterpiece on the Web, see the upcoming section, "Posting Your Movie to Your Web Site."

 If you usually keep image files in a subfolder and want to also place your SWF file in that subfolder, you can specify that location on the Formats tab of the Publish Settings dialog box. Click the small folder icon to the right of the name of the SWF file and navigate to the subfolder where you want it to be placed.

Publishing to Other Formats

You can use Flash's Publish Settings to generate files in a variety of other formats besides HTML pages and Flash Player movies. These other formats are GIF images, animated GIFs, JPEG images, PNG images, and self-playing Windows and Macintosh projectors.

Even if you use Flash all day, every day, you might never need to generate GIF images or JPEG images from your Flash movies, so we won't clog up your life by describing the Publish Settings for those formats here.

Creating PNG graphic files

PNG files can display millions more colors than GIF files and support transparency. They offer some of the advantages of both GIFs and JPEGs. To create a PNG image, select the PNG Image (.png) check box on the Formats tab of the Publish Settings dialog box. (Refer to Figure 13-7.) Flash creates a PNG tab in the dialog box, as shown in Figure 13-14.

Flash publishes the first frame of your movie unless you label a different frame with the #Static label. (To create a label, click the frame and choose Window⇨Properties to open the Property inspector. If necessary, expand the Label section of the Property inspector to its full size. Type a label name in the Name text box in the Label section of the Property inspector.)

You have the following options:

Figure 13-14: Use the PNG tab to create PNG images.

- ✔ **Dimensions:** Lets you specify your own Width and Height settings if you deselect the Match Movie check box. This could be useful if you want to create a thumbnail image to use on a Web page to link to your movie. By default, Flash matches the dimensions of the movie.

- ✔ **Bit Depth:** Controls the number of bits per pixel, which in turn means how many colors the image contains. You can select 8-bit for 256 colors (like a GIF), 24-bit for 16.7 million colors, or 24-bit with Alpha, which allows for transparency. When you choose 24-bit with Alpha, the image's background becomes transparent. This is one of the things that designers love about PNG files.

- ✔ **Options:** Specifies how the PNG file appears:

  - • *Optimize Colors:* Removes unused colors from the file's color table to reduce the size of the file.

  - • *Interlace:* Causes a static PNG image to load in incremental resolutions, so the image appears first fuzzy and then successively sharper. Some people like this option because viewers may be able to click the image before it fully downloads, thus reducing their waiting time.

  - • *Smooth:* Anti-aliases the artwork. Text usually looks better (and the file size is larger), but occasionally you may get an undesirable halo effect around your art. In that case, turn off smoothing.

- *Dither Solids:* Does just that — dithers solid colors as well as gradients and images. *Dithering* is a way to approximate colors not available on the color palette by using a range of similar colors. This applies only to files with 8-bit color. See the Dither option, which we describe a few paragraphs from now.

- *Remove Gradients:* Turns gradients into solids. Flash uses the first color in the gradient, which may not be the color you want.

✔ **Dither:** Enables dithering for files with 8-bit color, as we define in the Dither Solids bullet in the Options descriptions. Dithering helps to create more accurate-looking colors but increases file size. Choose one of the three options:

- *None:* Disables dithering.

- *Ordered:* Provides a medium amount of dithering and a corresponding medium increase in file size.

- *Diffusion:* Provides the best-quality dithering and increases file size the most. It works only with the Web 216-color palette. (Refer to Chapter 3 for a description of color palettes.)

✔ **Palette Type:** Determines the color palette for the PNG image. This applies only to PNG files with 8-bit color. (Refer to Chapter 3 for a discussion of colors in Flash.) You have four options:

- *Web 216:* Uses the standard 216-color palette, which was developed for old computers that didn't have the capability to show millions of colors.

- *Adaptive:* Creates a unique color table for your file, based on the actual colors present. You get more accurate color, but the file size may be larger. Use this option if an accurate representation of the colors is most important, as in a photographic bitmap image. You can use the Max Colors text box to specify how many colors you want in the table. The default is 255. Use fewer colors to reduce the file size.

- *Web Snap Adaptive:* Works like the Adaptive option but optimizes the color palette for the Web. Colors close to the Web 216 colors are turned into one of the colors on that palette. Other colors function like the Adaptive option. As with the Adaptive option, you can specify the number of colors on the palette in the Max Colors text box.

- *Custom:* Lets you specify a palette in the ACT format. Click the file folder icon near the Palette text field to browse for a color palette file. (Read the section in Chapter 3 on solid colors for an explanation of how to create a color palette and save it in ACT format.)

- **Max Colors:** This option is enabled only when you choose Adaptive or Web Snap Adaptive, and the Palette option is enabled only when you choose Custom.

- **Palette:** You can click the file folder icon beside the text box and browse your files to select a color palette. (See Chapter 3 for more about color palettes.)

- **Filter Options:** Controls how an image is analyzed line by line to compress it. You have these options:

  - *None:* Applies no filtering. The resulting file is larger than with the other options.

  - *Sub:* Filters adjoining pixel bytes (working horizontally). This works best when the image has repeated horizontal information.

  - *Up:* Filters in a vertical direction. This works best when the image has repeated vertical information.

  - *Average:* Uses a mixture of horizontal and vertical comparison; this is a good first-try option.

  - *Paeth:* Invented by Alan Paeth, the Paeth predictor employs a more complex method that uses the three nearest pixels to predict the next one.

  - *Adaptive:* Creates a unique color table for your PNG file based on the actual colors present. You get more accurate color, although these colors might not be Web safe. The file size might also be larger. Use this option if accurate representation of colors is most important, as in a photographic bitmap image.

After you specify your settings, click OK to return to your movie or click Publish to publish your PNG image and create the other files you've chosen.

Creating self-playing movies

You can also create projectors in the Publish Settings dialog box. A *projector* is a self-playing Flash movie that doesn't require the Flash Player. All the interactive and animated features of your Flash movie work in a projector. You can use a projector for a Flash movie that you want to burn to a CD-R or DVD-R. (The projector format isn't compatible with the format of a DVD movie, though.) Projector files tend to have much larger sizes than their corresponding SWF files.

You can create a Windows or Mac version from either platform. But if you create a Mac version in Windows, you need to use a file translator, such as BinHex, so that the Mac Finder recognizes it as an application.

To create a projector, follow these steps:

1. **Choose File⇨Publish Settings.**

   The Publish Settings dialog box opens.

2. **On the Formats tab, select the Windows Projector (.exe) check box or the Macintosh Projector check box, or both.**

3. **Click Publish.**

4. **Click OK or Cancel to close the Publish Settings dialog box.**

Windows creates a folder with your filename with an .app extension as the top folder name. This folder contains the files created. For a Mac, Flash creates a Macintosh Projector application. If you create the Macintosh Projector file in Flash while using a Windows computer, the Macintosh Projector file is stored inside a compressed BinHex file (HQX), which can then be uncompressed on a Mac.

Test your movie after you copy it to a CD or another computer. Try it with a variety of processor speeds if possible.

Using Publish Profiles

You can save all the settings that you configure in the Publish Settings dialog box as a *publish profile.* You can then duplicate, modify, export, import, and delete your publish profiles and trade them with your collaborators. You can create standard publish profiles, which you use to make sure that all your files are published uniformly, and you can create specialized publish profiles specific to a single project. The following sections tell you how.

Creating a publish profile

To create a publish profile, follow these steps:

1. **Choose File⇨Publish Settings.**

   The Publish Settings dialog box appears.

2. **Click the Create New Profile button (the + symbol) in the upper-right part of the dialog box, shown in Figure 13-15.**

   The Create New Profile dialog box appears.

Duplicate

Create New File | Rename

Import/Export | Delete

Publish Settings

Current profile: Profile 1

Formats   Flash   HTML

Type: File:

☑ Flash (.swf)   16.swf

☑ HTML (.html)   16.html

☐ GIF Image (.gif)   16.gif

☐ JPEG Image (.jpg)   16.jpg

☐ PNG Image (.png)   16.png

☐ Windows Projector (.exe)   16.exe

☐ Macintosh Projector   16.app

Use Default Names

Publish   Cancel   OK

Figure 13-15: Create, delete, export, and import your publish profiles and more.

3. **Type a name for your profile and then click OK.**

The Create New Profile dialog box disappears, and the name of your new profile appears in the Current Profile drop-down list of the Publish Settings dialog box.

4. **Specify the publish settings for your document in the Publish Settings dialog box, as we describe in earlier sections of this chapter, and then click OK.**

Duplicating or renaming a publish profile

You might want to duplicate a publish profile to use it as a springboard for new variations.

To duplicate a publish profile, do the following steps:

1. **Choose File⇨Publish Settings.**

   The Publish Settings dialog box appears.

2. **In the Current Profile drop-down list (near the top of the dialog box), select the publish profile that you want to rename (or copy).**

3. **Click the Rename Profile button (or the Duplicate Profile button — the horizontal arrow button) in the upper-right part of the dialog box.**

   The Profile Properties dialog box (or the Duplicate Profile dialog box) appears.

4. **Type a new name for your profile (or the name for your duplicate profile) and then click OK.**

   The dialog box disappears. The name of your renamed profile (or your duplicate profile) appears in the Current Profile drop-down list of the Publish Settings dialog box.

Modifying a publish profile

You might use a particular publish profile as, for example, a standard for your coworkers. As circumstances change, you might want to modify the publish profile, and that's easy to do.

To modify a publish profile, follow these steps:

1. **Choose File⇨Publish Settings.**

   The Publish Settings dialog box appears.

2. **In the Current Profile drop-down list (near the top of the dialog box), select the publish profile that you want to modify.**

3. **Select the publish settings that you want for your document in the Publish Settings dialog box, as we describe in the earlier sections of this chapter, and then click OK.**

Deleting a publish profile

To delete a publish profile, follow these steps:

1. **Choose File⇨Publish Settings.**

   The Publish Settings dialog box appears.

2. **In the Current Profile drop-down list (near the top of the dialog box), select the publish profile that you want to delete.**

3. **Click the Delete Profile button (the trash can) in the upper-right part of the dialog box.**

   A dialog box appears asking you to confirm that you want to delete the profile.

4. **Click OK.**

Exporting and importing publish profiles

To use a publish profile in documents other than the document in which you created it, first you export it from the document in which you created it. Then you import it into the new document.

This makes your work easier if, for example, you're working on a Flash project with a team and need to publish your Flash documents according to a single standard. The entire team can easily share the same publish profile.

To export a publish profile, follow these steps:

1. **Choose File⇨Publish Settings.**

   The Publish Settings dialog box appears.

2. **In the Current Profile drop-down list (near the top of the dialog box), select the publish profile that you want to export.**

3. **Click the Import/Export Profile button (the vertical arrow button in the upper-left part of the dialog box) and select Export in the drop-down list.**

   The Export Profile dialog box appears.

4. **In the dialog box, select a location where you want to save the file and then click Save.**

   The default location is a folder named Publish Profiles, which is located in the Flash CS5 application folder. The file is saved as an XML file.

To import a publish profile, follow these steps:

1. **Choose File➪Publish Settings.**

   The Publish Settings dialog box appears.

2. **Click the Import/Export Profile button (the vertical arrow button in the upper-right part of the dialog box) and then select Import in the drop-down list.**

   The Import Profile dialog box appears.

3. **In the dialog box, browse to find the publish profile that you want to import and then click Open.**

   The name of the imported publish profile appears in the Current Profile drop-down list of the Publish Settings dialog box.

Using Publish Preview

If you want to specify publish settings, see the results, and then go back to tweak your settings, you can use Publish Preview rather than Publish. Publish Preview creates the files specified in the Publish Settings dialog box, just as the Publish command does. The only difference is that Publish Preview automatically displays the requested file, usually the SWF file. The value is in simply saving the steps of manually opening your files in your browser — helpful when you're doing lots of tweaking and going back and forth between your publish settings and your browser to see what works best.

To use Publish Preview, follow these steps:

1. **Specify your settings by using the Publish Settings dialog box (as we explain earlier in this chapter) and then click OK.**

2. **Choose File➪Publish Preview.**

3. **In the Publish Preview submenu, choose the file format that you want to preview.**

4. **When you're finished, close the window or browser.**

Posting Your Movie to Your Web Site

After you finish publishing your movie, you probably want to post your SWF file on your Web site, or place it on a CD-R or other media.

You can make Mac and Windows projectors and copy them onto a CD-R by using CD-burner software. Then you can view your Flash movie independently of a Web browser. Or copy your published HTML and SWF files onto a CD-R along with any external scripts, image files, or text files used by your HTML and SWF files.

Refer to the section "Embedding an SWF file into an existing Web page" earlier in this chapter for instructions on modifying the HTML code if you want to place your SWF file on an existing Web page or place your SWF file in a subfolder.

To post your movie to a Web site, upload both the HTML and the SWF file.

If your HTML or SWF files load data from any image files, text files, or external scripts (such as JavaScript or ActionScript files), you need to upload those, too.

Open your browser and load the Web page that contains your Flash movie. We hope it works perfectly and looks great! If not, check the HTML code, check your publish settings, and make sure that the necessary files are in the proper location on your Web site's server.

Exporting Movies and Images

In addition to publishing, Flash allows you to export image files and QuickTime movies as well as export in the FXG format, which is a common file format for Adobe products such as Illustrator, Fireworks, Catalyst, and more.

Note that when you choose File➪Export➪Export Movie to export a movie to a format such as GIF, JPG, or PNG, you export a sequence of individually numbered images. That might give you some interesting raw material to import into other graphics applications.

To export an image, follow these steps:

1. **Select the frame in the Timeline that you want to export and then choose File➪Export➪Export Image.**

   The Export Image dialog box appears.

2. **Choose one of the following formats:**

   - SWF Movie
   - JPEG Image
   - Bitmap Image (in Windows versions of Flash only)
   - GIF Image
   - Adobe FXG
   - PNG Image

3. **Choose the folder where you want to save the file and then click Save.**

4. **Depending on the format that you selected, a dialog box might appear. If so, specify the settings and then click OK.**

These settings are similar to the kind of settings that we describe earlier in this chapter, in the "Creating PNG graphic files" section.

To export a movie, follow these steps:

1. **Choose File⇨Export⇨Export Movie.**

   The Export Movie dialog box appears.

2. **Choose one of the following formats:**

   - SWF Movie
   - Windows AVI (in Windows versions of Flash only)
   - QuickTime
   - Animated GIF
   - WAV Audio (in Windows versions of Flash only)
   - JPEG Sequence
   - GIF Sequence
   - PNG Sequence

3. **Choose the folder that you want to save the file in and then click Save.**

4. **Depending on the format that you selected, a dialog box might appear. If so, specify the settings and then click OK.**

   The JPEG, GIF, and PNG sequences export a separate image for each frame in the movie. Each image is numbered consecutively. The QuickTime and SWF movie formats export a MOV file and SWF file, respectively.

Part VI
Building Web Sites Fast with Flash Catalyst

The 5th Wave — By Rich Tennant

Where's the dang door?!

C'mon in!

In this part . . .

Adobe Flash Catalyst, a new concept in Web site creation, is perfect for designers. You design the pages in Adobe Photoshop or Illustrator and import them into Catalyst. In Catalyst, you add interactivity and more. The result is a fully Flash-ed Web site — without ever going into Flash!

In Chapter 14, we explain what you can do in Catalyst and how to structure your artwork for best results. Then we show you how to import that artwork so that Catalyst can understand multiple button *states* (various looks for a button) and Web pages. Finally, we explain how to work with buttons and the limited types of animation *(transitions)* that are available in Catalyst.

In Chapter 15, we delve deeper, describing how to add original artwork and text in Catalyst as well as how to add other user interface items, such as check boxes and scrollbars. We tell you how to import sound, video, and SWF files (from Flash) and conclude by showing you how to publish your working Web site.

Working with Flash Catalyst

In This Chapter

▷ Using Flash Catalyst to add interactions to Photoshop or Illustrator files

▷ Setting up your files for importing into Flash Catalyst

▷ Creating pages and buttons from your imported artwork

▷ Adding states to your buttons

▷ Adding navigation and more to your buttons

*W*ould you like to create Flash Web sites or desktop applications the easy way? Flash Catalyst can make that easy. You can start by creating your design in Photoshop or Illustrator and importing the resulting file into Catalyst. Then, you can do the following:

✔ Create buttons that change while the user hovers the mouse cursor over them or clicks them (just like buttons in Flash).

✔ Add buttons, sliders, and other user interface components that link to other locations or perform other marvelous tricks.

✔ Add animation, such as moving components on and off the screen.

✔ Develop an entire site with multiple pages.

✔ Easily add animated transitions, such as resizing, rotating, or moving objects, or fading objects or pages in and out.

HOME   WHITE PAPER   RESOURCES   ABOUT   CC

for Death by PowerPoint!

Learn the steps to turn Death by Power

To download the white paper, enter your name and e-m

You'll receive a confirmation e-mail.

Full Name

In larger projects that might require programming code (such as desktop applications or database-driven Web sites), Catalyst makes it easy for the designer and the developer to interact smoothly. The developer can use the information from Flash Catalyst directly in Adobe *Flash Builder,* a program for adding ActionScript. The designer can then incorporate changes made in Builder back into Flash Catalyst files.

Discovering Flash Catalyst

While Catalyst empowers you as a designer to create a working Web site using your Photoshop or Illustrator files, it also allows designers of large desktop applications to create prototypes of their applications within Flash Catalyst. In this chapter, we assume that you are a Web site designer and not an applications prototyper.

In Figure 14-1, you see Catalyst with an example of a Web site designed in Photoshop and transformed into an interactive Web site. You can find the original site at www.tellnshow.com.

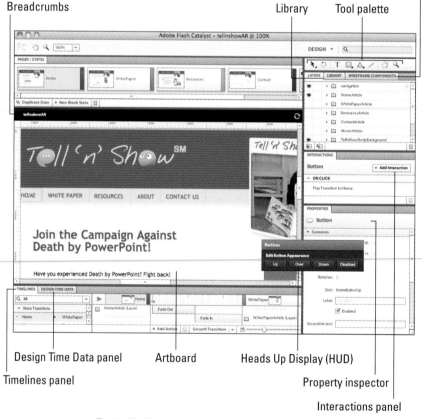

Thanks to Ellen Finkelstein for permission to use her Web site as an example in the chapters on Catalyst. You can find this HTML site at www.tellnshow.com.

Figure 14-1: Exploring the power of Flash Catalyst.

If you're an artist working in Adobe Fireworks, you can also interact with Catalyst using files that are saved in the FXG format. (Choose Commands⇒ Export to FXG from the Fireworks menu.) However, these files do not currently support layers. If you want to use Fireworks files in Catalyst, perhaps the easiest thing to do is to export them into Photoshop format to preserve layers before importing into Catalyst.

The Catalyst screen consists of the following, as shown in Figure 14-1:

- **Artboard:** Like the Stage in Flash: where you do your main designing.

- **Heads-up Display (HUD):** Use this dark floating panel to easily convert objects. It changes based on what you select.

- **Tools palette:** Container for selection tools, basic shapes, zoom, text, and a rotation tool.

- **Layers panel:** Rearrange, view, and lock layers, as well as add and delete layers. It sits below the Tools palette, along with Wireframe Components and Library.

- **Library panel (hidden in Figure 14-1):** For objects that you plan to use more than once, or objects that you import, such as images or SWF files.

- **Wireframe Components panel (hidden in Figure 14-1):** A selection of user-interface components you can add to your Web site.

- **Interactions panel:** Where you define what action to take for button clicks and other interactions.

- **Properties panel:** Set properties for selected objects.

- **Breadcrumbs:** Navigate back from working with button states (or states of other components) to the main Artboard. Figure 14-1 shows only one breadcrumb item.

- **Timelines panel:** Specify movement of objects, rotation, changes in opacity, resizing, and more.

- **Design-Time Data panel (hidden in Figure 14-1):** For applications requiring data, you can add sample data using this panel.

Preparing Your Artwork

Careful preparation of your design in Photoshop or Illustrator is key to getting good results in Catalyst — and not tearing your hair out in frustration! You may have to work a little differently than you're used to so that Catalyst understands the design file.

Creating unique objects

For Catalyst to recognize buttons and other objects, all the artwork that's going to become a button or other component needs to be a unique object that is selectable. (Of course, you can use multiple objects, such as a rectangle and text.)

This is important in Photoshop or Illustrator, where it's easy to ignore this principle. If you create a series of buttons, for example, by adding some text and some dividers over a background, then when you bring the file into Flash Catalyst, you have no unique objects to select. So, be sure that each button can be selected individually or as a group of objects making up that button.

Organizing your layers

If you create your layers in Photoshop or Illustrator the same way that you plan to work with them in Catalyst, you'll have a much easier time creating your project. The idea is to be able to toggle on the visibility of layers to reveal every page in the Web site. Figure 14-2 shows a set of layers in Photoshop that illustrate this principle. We recommend the following:

Figure 14-2: Creating a logical layer structure in Photoshop

- Create a folder for each page of your Web site; and within each folder, place layers with the unique design for each page.

- Create a folder as your top layer, which contains your navigation buttons and anything that doesn't change from page to page, such as your logo. You may want to call this folder something descriptive, such as *Navigation*.

- Assign your background layer a color that appears if you fade out or fade in a page. (Some of it may also appear if your pages don't fully cover the background.)

 Always label each layer as descriptively as possible, especially if you're planning to work with a developer using Flash Builder. The developer may need to use the names of the layers in the code.

Adding the looks for button states

You can create the different looks for your button states (or states of other components) in several ways:

- Stack your button states on individual layers in Photoshop or Illustrator and label the layers carefully to explain what they are. Then you can turn off the visibility of the layers to define the different states in Catalyst, as we describe later in this chapter.

- Add button states in Catalyst (rather than adding the looks in Photoshop or Illustrator), using glows, drop shadows, resizing, or more in Catalyst, which we describe later in this chapter.

- Export a button state from Photoshop or Illustrator as a PNG, JPG, or GIF file, and import it into the new state in Catalyst. We also discuss this method later in this chapter.

Importing Your File into Catalyst

Flash Catalyst allows you to import files in Photoshop format or Illustrator format. When importing from Photoshop, for example, all the layers import intact. The layers of the Photoshop file are in the Layers panel.

You can use Catalyst without importing any file, but its real power for a Web designer lies in its ability to add interactivity to Photoshop or Illustrator files.

To import your file, follow these steps:

1. **Do one of the following:**

    - *Open Catalyst. In the Welcome Screen under Create New Project from Design File, choose either From Adobe Illustrator AI File or From Adobe Photoshop PSD File.*

    - *From within Catalyst, choose File⇨New Project from Design Comp, choose an Adobe Photoshop (psd) or Adobe Illustrator (ai) file, and then click Open.*

2. **Browse to find your PSD or AI file, select it, and click Open.**

    The Photoshop (or Illustrator) Import Options dialog box appears, as shown in Figure 14-3.

3. **To select specific layers to import, click the Advanced button, specify the layers that you want, and then click OK.**

    You may have some layers that you created for temporary use that you don't want to end up in the final Web site file.

Figure 14-3: The Import Options dialog box gives you some choices.

4. **(Optional) Choose a background color for the Artboard.**

   You might have already assigned a background color in your design file.

5. **(Optional) In the Fidelity Options section, change how you import layers by choosing from the Image Layers, Shape Layers, or Text Layers drop-down lists.**

   You can't edit flattened content, such as text. By default, shape layers are flattened so that you can more easily work with them in Catalyst.

6. **Be sure that the Import Non-Visible Layers check box is selected.**

   That way, even if some of your layers are hidden, you import them anyway.

7. **Click OK.**

   A progress bar might appear while Catalyst imports your file.

8. **If you see a message telling you that the file contains a large number of bitmap graphics and/or vector paths (with instructions for optimizing the graphics), click Continue.**

9. **If the Import Issues dialog box appears with messages, such as a list of empty layers that weren't imported or missing fonts, click OK.**

   If you're missing fonts, you may need to install them or use different fonts in the imported file.

Behind the dialog box, your Photoshop file or Illustrator file appears in a Catalyst window.

Defining Pages in Catalyst

After importing your file, the first step is to define pages. After all, most Web sites have more than one page! If you created your layers correctly, defining new pages in Flash Catalyst is simple. Just follow these steps:

1. **Click the Duplicate State button above the Artboard for as many new pages that you want to create.**

   New pages appear in the Pages/States panel, named Page1, Page2, and so on.

2. **For each page, double-click its name, and then type a new name that matches the name of the Web page (no spaces allowed).**

3. **Select the first page and click the Eye icon in the Layers panel for each layer that you want to hide.**

   Hide all layers that you don't want to appear on the first page. The Eye icon disappears for each layer that you hide. The first page appears on the Artboard.

4. **Repeat Step 3 for each page.**

   Each page should appear when you click that page in the Pages/States panel, as shown in Figure 14-4. Here you see the second page, WhitePaper, displayed.

Figure 14-4: Hide layers to define pages.

Working with Buttons

When your layers and pages are set up, it's time to start creating buttons, which are the nuts and bolts of your user interface. First, you convert your artwork into buttons, and then you assign different looks for the different states of the buttons. Catalyst offers so many ways to enhance the design of your buttons through adding filters, animation, or different artwork for their different states — and all without programming.

Converting artwork to buttons

Before you can get fancy with how your button looks when it gets clicked, you first need to convert your artwork into a button. To create a button using Flash Catalyst, follow these steps:

1. **Using the Select tool, press and hold the Shift key, and then click each item in the button (such as the text, the background, and so on) to select all the parts of the button, as shown in Figure 14-5.**

   The Heads-up Display (HUD) appears, if it's not already visible.

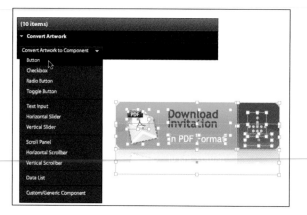

Figure 14-5: Converting artwork to a button.

2. **In the HUD, from the Convert Artwork to Component drop-down list, choose Button.**

   This names the button *Button1* and copies it into the Library. Catalyst switches to Component Editing mode, allowing you to apply different looks to different states of the button, which we describe in the following section.

3. **To rename your button, click the Library tab, expand the Custom Components pane, right click *Button1*, and choose Rename. Then type your new name into the text box that appears.**

Button names cannot contain spaces or hyphens.

Now that your artwork is a button, you can assign the looks for the different states in the following section.

Defining button states

You can create the artwork for the different states of your buttons in Flash Catalyst, or in Photoshop or Illustrator. Catalyst has several filters that you can use to easily add drop shadows or glows to objects. You can use these filters for the different states, or you might want to change the size or color of the button.

To define the states of a button, follow these steps:

1. **Select the button and choose Modify⇨Edit Component.**

   You are now in Component Editing mode, as shown in Figure 14-6. The four states of the button appear in the Pages/States panel.

Figure 14-6: Adding states to a button.

2. **Click any state in the Pages/States panel that you want to edit.**

3. **Edit the button in the Artboard.**

   In the following sections, see instructions for various ways to edit your button, such as adding a filter or resizing a button for a different state.

4. **Exit Component Editing mode by choosing Modify⇨Exit Editing.**

Adding a filter to a different state of a button

To add an inner or outer glow, a drop shadow, an inner shadow, a bevel, or a blur to create a new state for a button, follow these steps:

1. **Select the button and choose Modify➪Edit Component.**

   The four states of the button (Up, Over, Down, and Disabled) appear in the Pages/States panel.

2. **In the Pages/States panel, click the State that you want to edit.**

3. **Click the button again to select it. In the Properties panel, expand the Filters pane (if it's not already open).**

4. **Click the Add Filter button and choose a filter.**

   Filter controls appear in the pane, as shown in Figure 14-7. You might need to scroll down to see them all.

5. **Adjust the look of the filter, using the filter controls that appear in the pane.**

   Each filter is different. For example, the Inner Glow filter lets you specify a color, blur, opacity, strength, *knockout* (hides the fill), and quality.

6. **Test your new button state by clicking the Play button at the top of the Timelines panel, or by choosing File➪Run Project.**

   If you choose File➪Run Project, your Web site opens in your default browser. Check out your new button state with the filter.

7. **Exit the Component Editing mode by choosing Modify➪ Exit Editing or clicking your project name in the Breadcrumbs section above the Artboard.**

Figure 14-7: Filter controls for adding a drop shadow.

Resize the button in a different state

Resizing a button so that it grows when the mouse passes over it is an effective way to bring attention to the button. This can be done with animation so that the button does not jump to a new size, but grows instead. To resize the button that grows using animation, follow these steps:

1. **Select the button and choose Modify➪Edit Component.**

2. **Click the state that you want to edit in the Pages/States panel.**

3. **Click all or part of the button and drag a resizing handle on the button to resize it.**

   In the Timelines panel, a Resize bar appears. If your button has more than one part, you may also see a Move bar, if resizing one part of the button also moved another part.

4. **In the Timelines panel, to adjust the timing of the animation, click and drag the Resize bar's small semicircular thumbtab that appears to the right, as shown in Figure 14-8. Do the same for the Move bar, if you have one.**

   We dragged our Resize bar and Move bar to play the resizing animation for half a second.

Semicircular thumbtab

Figure 14-8: Adding animation when resizing objects between states.

5. **In the State Transitions list of the Timelines panel, notice which state transition is highlighted. Then choose the opposite from the list and drag the tab of the Resize bar on the Timelines panel for the same distance you did in Step 4 and do the same for the Move bar.**

This sets the animation to resize back to its original state.

If you animate the Up > Over states, be sure to select the Over > Up state as well so that it animates back to its normal size when the mouse is off the button.

6. **Test your new button state by clicking the Play button at the top of the Timelines panel, or by choosing File⇨Run Project.**

   If you choose File⇨Run Project, your Web site opens in a browser window. Check out your new button state with the animation.

7. **Exit the Component Editing mode by choosing Modify⇨Exit Editing.**

Importing a new image for a different state

If you created images for each button state in Photoshop or Illustrator, you can import them into Catalyst as long as they are in one of the following formats: PNG, GIF, or JPG. To import an image, follow these steps:

1. **Select the button and choose Modify⇨Edit Component.**

   The four states of the button (Up, Over, Down, and Disabled) appear in the Pages/States panel.

2. **In the Pages/States panel, click the state that you want to edit.**

3. **In the Artboard, delete the button or part of the button.**

4. **Choose File⇨Import⇨Image.**

5. **Select the image file and click Open.**

   The new image replaces the button for the state you selected.

6. **Test your new button state by clicking the Play button at the top of the Timelines panel, or by choosing File⇨Run Project.**

   If you choose File⇨Run Project, your Web site opens in a browser window. Check out your new button state with the animation.

7. **Exit the Component Editing mode; choose Modify⇨Exit Editing.**

Hiding buttons to reveal other button states

You can set up your Photoshop or Illustrator file that you import to include button states that are stacked in layers, similar to how you stack your pages in layers. If you do that, then when you convert your artwork to a button, using the HUD, be sure to select all the different states on the different layers before you convert it. Then select your button, choose Modify⇨Edit Component, and choose a state in the Pages/States panel. You can show the artwork for that state by clicking the Eye in the layers panel, and hide the other layers that you don't want to show.

Assigning Interactions to Components

You can make pretty buttons by defining states, but they won't do anything useful. To get your buttons to do something, you need to add interactions. *Interaction* define a response to a user action. The most typical interaction occurs when you click a button and find yourself on a different Web page.

Before you can add an interaction to a button, you need to make sure that it's really a button. See the section, "Converting artwork to buttons" earlier in this chapter for details.

To add an interaction to a button, follow these steps:

1. **Select the button.**

2. **In the Interactions panel, click the Add Interaction button to open the panel shown in Figure 14-9.**

3. **From the top drop-down list, choose which action initiates the response.**

   The most common choice is On Click, which means that the user has to click the button.

4. **From the second drop-down list, choose the response.**

   To add a link to another page inside your Catalyst project, choose Play Transition to State. (We discuss transitions in the next section.) To add a link to an outside Web page, choose Go to URL, which requires an absolute URL (one with `http://` in it). Other options are to play, pause, or stop a video; or play simple animation that you create in the Catalyst Timelines panel. (We cover video in Chapter 16. For more information on animations, see the end of this chapter.)

Figure 14-9: Add interactivity to buttons to make them work for their pay.

Typically, when you pass the cursor over a link on a Web site, the cursor changes to a hand. If you want your button to display the hand icon, with the button selected, expand the Appearance item in the Properties panel, scroll down, and select the Hand Cursor check box. You need to do this for every button on every page.

5. **Enter the necessary information for the response.**

   If you choose Go to URL, a text box opens, where you need to enter an absolute URL. If you choose Play Transition to State, skip to Step 7.

6. **If you choose Go to URL, in the new drop-down list that appears, choose how you want the link to open.**

   The most common options are Open in Current Window or Open in New Window.

7. **From the Choose State drop-down list, choose the state.**

   If you choose Go to URL in Step 4, choose Any State. If you choose Play Transition to State, choose the page you want to link to.

8. **Click OK.**

9. **Test your button by choosing File⇨Run Project (or by pressing Ctrl+Enter on Windows/⌘+Return on a Mac).**

   When your temporary browser page opens, click the button and see what happens!

Figure 14-10 shows an image that we turned into a button. With a Go to URL interaction, the button links to an Adobe PDF file. Clicking the button opens the PDF file, which users can then save or print.

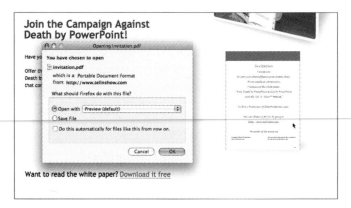

Figure 14-10: The image is a button to download the Invitation, which is a PDF file.

To edit an interaction, select the button and double-click the interaction listed in the Interactions panel. To delete an interaction, select it in the Interactions panel and click the Trash button.

Continue adding interactions to buttons until all your internal and external links work. Congratulations! You have a Web site!

Adding Animation

When you think of animation, you probably think of Flash, and you're right. Catalyst offers a limited number of animations — *transitions* — related to user interface components, pages, and states. And that might be all you need for your Web site. For example, you can move, resize, or rotate a button. You can also fade a page during the transition to another page. In this section, we show you how to add simple animation in Catalyst.

For more advanced animation, use Flash and import the SWF file. We explain how to import SWF files in Chapter 15. Chapter 9 covers animation in Flash.

You create transitions in the Timelines panel, as shown in Figure 14-11. When you work in the Timelines panel, you might want to expand it, which you can do by dragging its top border upward.

Filter drop-down list

Play transition button   Length of transition

Available objects after transition

Available transitions   Available objects before transition   Transition effect   Timing slider

Figure 14-11: Use the Timelines panel for subtle transition effects.

The Timelines panel in Catalyst is quite different from the Timeline in Flash. You won't find any frames, so you can't create keyframes. Instead, you simply specify the length of a transition in seconds.

Assigning beginning and ending states

Although the word *states* properly applies to button variations, Catalyst sometimes uses the word to mean *pages*. On the left side of the Timelines panel is a list of state transitions. In the default view, the list contains every possible pairing of pages. In Component Editing mode, which we discuss in the "Defining button states" section earlier in this chapter, the list contains button states.

To define a transition, follow these steps:

1. **If you want to create a page transition, choose the two pages that you want to work with from the State Transitions list.**

   If you want to create a button transition, double-click the button and choose the two button states you want to work with.

   You can use the Filter drop-down list above the first column to filter the State Transitions list; for example, you can show only transitions that include the Home page.

   In Figure 14-11, we are creating a page transition, and choose Home⇨ WhitePaper.

2. **In the second column of the Timelines panel, select the objects that you want to animate, or select the objects from the Artboard.**

   For a page transition, the second column lists all available objects on the pages. At the top, you can choose the entire page to select everything on the page, which is ideal for a simple page fade. Select specific objects to apply the transition only to those objects.

   For a button transition, select the button from the Artboard. Applying certain transitions to an inappropriate object can provide odd results. For example, as shown in Figure 14-12, we rotated the text as a transition from the WhitePaper page to the Home page. Each click rotates 90 degrees. After two clicks, the text is upside-down!

Figure 14-12: Button transitions can result in odd results.

3. **If the transition that you want isn't listed in the third column, click Add Action at the bottom of that column and then choose the transition you want.**

We're opting for Fade. We explain the available transitions in more detail in the next section.

4. **In the third column of the Timelines panel, pass the cursor over the transition's horizontal block to display the semicircular thumb tab. Then drag to change the time of the transition, as shown in Figure 14-13.**

Figure 14-13: Change the speed of the transition by dragging on the thumb.

Drag to the right to lengthen the time of the transition (make the effect slower) or to the left to shorten it (make the effect faster). Alternatively, you can drag the slider at the bottom of the fourth column to adjust the timing or use the Properties panel to enter a duration.

Make the transition long enough to notice but not so long that your viewers get bored! For example, 1/10th of a second might be too quick, whereas a whole second would seem to drag out forever.

You can test the animation in the Timelines panel. Just click the Play button at the top of the second column. For example, if you added a fade between pages, when you click to go from the first page to the second page, you'll see the fade effect.

To delete a transition, select the transition in the third column of the Timelines panel, and click the Trash can (Delete) button.

Defining the transition

In the previous section, we explain the steps for adding transitions. Here, we delve a little deeper into the available transitions and how to configure them. In all cases, you work in the Timelines panel. To add a transition to a component, such as a button, first double-click the component to enter Component Editing mode.

Adding a Fade transition

When you add a Fade transition, your objects fade in or out as you change states. For example, an entire page can fade out when you click a button to go to another page on the side. The fade usually lasts only about half a second, so it just provides a soft transition between pages. You can fade individual objects, including buttons, as well.

In many cases, after you select the state transition in the Timelines panel's first column, the Fade transition automatically appears in the third column. (If you don't see it, choose it from the Add Actions pop-up list at the bottom of the third column.) Just drag the semicircular thumbtab to adjust the length of the fade. We found that half a second was a good length. Click the Play button (refer to Figure 14-11) to view the transition.

For more controls, go to the Properties panel, where you can set the opacity, duration, delay, and easing. Easing effects control how the transition starts and ends.

Rotating an object

You can rotate an object while moving from one page to another. Why would you do that? We showed you some funny results with this effect in Figure 14-12. However, if you also include a fade out and the timing of the rotation is shorter than the fade out, you'll see the object rotating before the new page appears. Think of it as a whirling, disappearing act. You can also rotate a button when you hover over or click it.

To add a rotation transition, click Add Action and choose Rotate from the pop-up list. In the Properties panel, you can set the angle, duration, and delay.You can also choose an *easing* effect, which determines how the rotation starts and ends.

Rotating an object in 3D

The Rotate transition rotates in 2D, but the Rotate 3D transition adds a new dimension to your transitions. Figure 14-14 shows the states of an image's 3D rotation. At the end, you can see that the image of the next page is starting to fade in.

To add a rotation transition, click Add Action and choose Rotate 3D from the pop-up list. In the Properties panel, you can set the From and To angles in three directions, the duration, and a delay. For Figure 14-14, we use the default From and To angles.

Moving an object

You can move an object during a transition. As we described for rotation, if you add the Move effect to a page transition, you won't see the movement until you return to the page unless you also have a fade transition. On the other hand, it could be pretty funny to move the object without a fade so that when viewers return to the page, the object has mysteriously moved! (Well, if that's your kind of humor.)

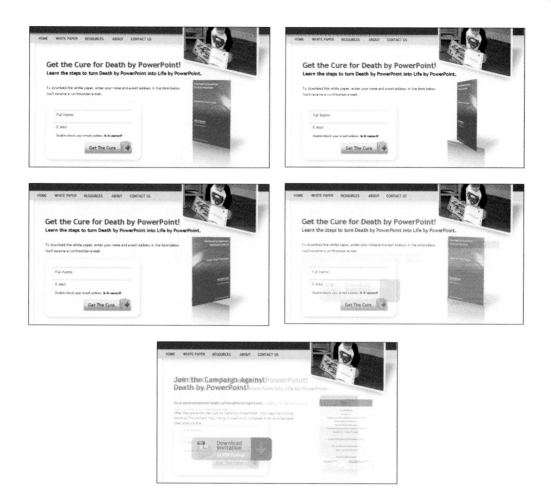

Figure 14-14: It's a whirling image!

To add a Move transition, click Add Action and choose Move from the pop-up list. In the Properties panel, you can set the X (horizontal) and Y (vertical) distance of the move, the duration, delay, and easing effects.

Resizing an object

Resizing an object is just like rotating it. Select the object, choose Resize from the Add Action pop-up menu, and set its properties. You specify the new size in pixels.

Adding a sound effect

Why be silent? You can add a sound effect and make noise! After selecting an object, follow these steps:

1. **Click the Add Action pop-up menu and choose Sound Effect.**

2. **In the Select a Visual Asset dialog box (Catalyst thinks sounds are visual?), click the Import button.**

3. **In the Open dialog box, choose an MP3 file, and click Open.**

4. **Expand the Media item and choose the MP3 file you selected.**

5. **Click OK.**

In the Properties panel, you can adjust the duration, set a delay, and choose to repeat the sound. (Please don't!)

Setting object properties

You can set some specific properties that apply to certain types of objects. After selecting an object, choose Set Property from the Add Action pop-up menu. In the Properties panel, choose one of the following from the Property drop-down list:

- **Text:** For a component that includes text, such as a check box's label, you can specify text, which animates a change in the text content. (We cover components in Chapter 15.) This option isn't available for all objects.

- **Alpha:** Click to the right to display a text box, where you can enter an Alpha value. *Alpha* is equivalent to opacity. A setting of 25% dims an object so that it's only 25% opaque. You could use this setting to make a button appear unavailable.

- **Enabled:** Choose True or False. This setting is available only for components that you converted to buttons. By selecting False, you deactivate the button.

Adding Components, Audio, Video, and More to Catalyst

atalyst's power is greatest when you import files that you designed in Photoshop or Illustrator, but we bet that you'd be surprised at what you can do in Catalyst itself. In this chapter, we show you how you can create artwork and text, add user interface components, import sound and video, and finally put it all together into a cool Web site.

Creating Artwork and Adding Text

Catalyst has its own tools for creating artwork and text on the Artboard. In fact, Catalyst has some unexpected offerings. For example, even Flash doesn't have a triangle, a hexagon, or an octagon tool!

You use the Tools panel to add vector (line) art and text, as shown in Figure 15-1. It doesn't look like much, but when you take into account the modifications you can make in the Properties panel, you have some capable tools.

For more information about the difference between vector and bitmap art, see "Understanding vectors and bitmaps" in Chapter 2.

0:00 /0.5

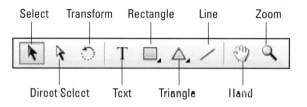

Figure 15-1: The Tools panel is your entryway into drawing and creating text in Catalyst.

Viewing and selecting objects

Before you start drawing, you'll find it helpful to know Catalyst's tools for viewing and selecting objects:

- ✓ **Select:** Select entire objects.

- ✓ **Direct Select:** Selects a component of a grouped object.

- ✓ **Hand:** Pans the view. You can also use the Hand tool at the upper-left corner of the screen.

- ✓ **Zoom:** Zoom in the view, making everything look larger. You can also use the Zoom tool at the upper-left corner of the screen, where you'll also find a Zoom drop-down list. There you can choose from a list of magnifications. Alt+Zoom (Windows)/Option+Zoom (Mac) zooms you back out again.

Drawing paths

Catalyst calls the line art you draw *paths*.

Before you draw a path, make sure that you're in the right place! That means you should choose the page you want to be on from the Pages/States panel and the folder you want the path to be in from the Layers panel. We explain more about the Pages/States and Layers panel in Chapter 14.

You can draw the following paths:

- ✓ **Rectangle:** Click the Rectangle button on the Tools panel. Click in the Artboard and drag to specify the opposite corner. Press Shift while you drag to draw a square.

The Rectangle, Rounded Rectangle, and Ellipse buttons are part of a drop-down list, so you might not see the tool you're looking for. If necessary, click and hold the visible button to display the drop-down list; then click the one you want.

- ✓ **Rounded Rectangle:** Click the Rounded Rectangle button on the Tools panel. Click in the Artboard and drag to specify the opposite corner. Press Shift while you drag to draw a rounded square.

✔ **Ellipse:** Click the Ellipse button on the Tools panel. Click in the Artboard and drag to specify the diagonally opposite corner of the ellipse. Press Shift while you drag to draw a circle.

✔ **Triangle:** Click the Triangle button on the Tools panel. Click in the Artboard to specify the middle of one side and drag to specify the opposite point of the triangle. While you drag, you can move the cursor to rotate the triangle. Press Shift to constrain the rotation to 45-degree increments.

TIP

The Triangle, Hexagon, Octagon, and Star buttons are part of a drop-down list, so you might not see the tool you're looking for. If necessary, click and hold the visible button to display the drop-down list, then click the one you want.

✔ **Hexagon:** Click the Hexagon button on the Tools panel. Click in the Artboard to specify one point and drag to specify the opposite point of the hexagon. While you drag, you can move the cursor to rotate the hexagon. Press Shift to constrain the rotation to 45-degree increments. Figure 15-2 shows a formatted hexagon.

✔ **Octagon:** Click the Octagon button on the Tools panel. Click in the Artboard to specify one point and drag to specify the opposite point of the octagon. As you drag, you can move the cursor to rotate the octagon.

Figure 15-2: Unlike Flash, Catalyst has a hexagon tool.

✔ **Star:** Click the Star button on the Tools panel. Click in the Artboard to specify a corner of its bounding box and drag to specify the opposite point of the star. While you drag, you can move the cursor to rotate the star. Press Shift to constrain the rotation to 45-degree increments.

✔ **Line:** Click the Line button on the Tools panel. Click in the Artboard to specify one end of the line and drag to specify the other end. Press Shift to constrain the rotation to 45-degree increments.

When you draw a path, Catalyst automatically creates a new layer for that path, named for the type of path, or simply named Path. As we explain in the "Defining Pages in Catalyst" section in Chapter 14, you use layers to define pages of your Web site. In this way, you can assign the path to one or more pages.

Formatting paths

When you select a path, it displays a bounding box, square handles on the bounding box, and a center square, as shown in Figure 15-3. Use the square handles on the bounding box to change the path's size. Drag on the center square to move the path.

 To rotate a path, use the Transform button on the Tools panel. Drag the cursor over one of the handles in a circular motion. You can also set the exact rotation in the Common section of the Property inspector.

Figure 15-3: A selected path is easy to move or resize.

When you draw a path, the Properties panel appears, shown in Figure 15-4. You use the Property inspector to change the path's location and size more precisely than with dragging. You can also change the stroke, fill, and other properties.

Format a path's position, size, and rotation in the Common section of the Property inspector as follows:

- Click in the X and Y values and type a new value to change the path's horizontal and vertical location, respectively, measured from the upper-left corner of the Artboard. Then press Enter/Return. Alternatively, drag the value up or down.

- Click in the W (Width) value to change the width and in the H (Height) value to change the height of the path and press Enter/Return, or drag up or down.

- Click in the Rotation value, type a new value, and press Enter/Return, or drag up or down.

Figure 15-4: Use the Property inspector to make beautiful paths.

Formatting a path's stroke and fill

To change the path's stroke (the outline), use the Stroke section of the Property inspector, shown in the upcoming Figure 15-6. Click the right-facing arrow to expand this section. You have three choices for strokes:

Figure 15-5: Specify a color in the color gallery.

- **Solid:** Click the left-most of the three boxes and then click the color swatch on the right to choose a color, as shown in Figure 15-5. You can also enter a hexadecimal number value.

- **Gradient:** Click the middle box for a linear gradient. To define the gradient, use the gradient bar, as shown in Figure 15-6. Click the bar to add a color marker. Click inside a color marker to open the color box and choose a color. Drag a color marker to adjust where the gradient changes colors.

- **No stroke:** Click the right-most box and remove a stroke.

Figure 15-6: You can create linear gradients in Catalyst for both strokes and fills.

For solid and gradient strokes, you can also set additional properties:

- **Weight (thickness):** Next to the Width item, click and enter a new value.

- **Opacity:** Click and enter a new value.

- **Rotation:** For gradients only, you can set a rotation. Drag the rotation circle's radius or click in the current value, enter a new value, and then press Enter/Return.

- **End Caps:** Choose None, Round, or Square from the drop-down list. *End caps* define how ends of lines and open paths look. You can see the effect more clearly with heavier weights.

- **Joints:** Choose Miter, Round, or Bevel from the drop-down list. Joints define how corners work, for example, in hexagons. You can see the effect more clearly with heavier weights. For miter joints, you can set a limit; a higher value helps to create a sharp corner, rather than a bevel look, at the corner.

You format a path's fill in the same way that you format the stroke. You can specify a solid or gradient fill, or choose no fill. You can likewise set the opacity and rotation.

Formatting a path's blend mode

Blend modes affect how a path looks when it overlaps another object. In the Appearance section of the Property inspector, you can choose a blend mode. We discuss these same blend modes as they relate to Flash in the "Adding filters and blends" section of Chapter 7.

Adding filters to a path

Filters are special effects. You can make a boring path look special with a filter. To add a filter, expand the Filters section of the Property inspector and click the Add Filter button. Then choose the filter you want from the drop-down list. You can add the following filters:

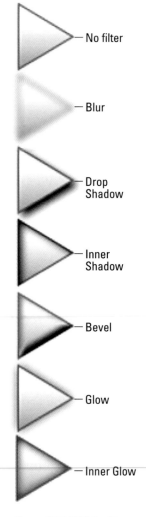

- **Blur:** Blurs the path, including its fill. You can even apply the blur to text. You can change the width of the blur by clicking the Radius item, entering a new value, and clicking Enter/Return. You can also choose Low, Normal, or High from the Quality drop-down list. Figure 15-7 shows a clear and a blurred play button.

- **Drop Shadow:** Adds an outer shadow. To change the color, click the Color swatch and choose a color. You can also change the values for distance, blur, angle, and opacity. Select the Knockout check box to see the background through the object. Select the Hide Object check box to make it invisible; you see only the shadow. Finally, choose Low, Normal, or High from the Quality drop-down list.

Figure 15-7: Will the blurry play button play blurry sound?

- **Inner Shadow:** Adds the shadow color just within the boundaries of the path. It can make a button look raised. The settings are the same as for the drop shadow.

- **Bevel:** A 3D edging effect that can also make a button look raised. You can choose both highlight and shadow colors. Like the drop-shadow filter, you can set the distance, blur, and angle. You can also specify a knockout and set the quality.

- **Glow:** Adds color around the outside of the path. You can set the color, blur, opacity, strength, and quality. You can also specify a knockout, as described for the drop-shadow filter.

- **Inner Glow:** Adds color along the inside of the path's border. It has the same settings as the glow filter and makes your art look enlightened!

Creating text

T You can easily add text in Catalyst. Click the Text tool on the Tools panel, click in the Artboard, and start typing.

To format the text, select it and use the following options in the Property inspector:

- **Font:** Select the font you want from the Font drop-down list. You can also choose the font style (Regular, Italic, Bold, and Bold Italic) from the drop-down list to the right.

- **Size:** Click the font size, enter a new value, and press Enter/Return.

- **Color:** Click the color swatch and choose a new color.

- **Line Height:** Click the line height value, enter a new value, and press Enter. From the drop-down list, choose to specify by percent (%) or pixels (px).

- **Tracking:** Tracking is the spacing between the letters. Click, type a new value, and press Enter/Return. You can choose to specify by percent (%) or pixels (px).

- **Opacity:** Click, enter a new value, and press Enter/Return.

To underline text, select the Underline check box. To strike through text, select the Strikethrough check box.

Importing images

Although you usually create images in Photoshop or Illustrator (or perhaps Fireworks) and import them to create a project, you might have an image, such as a photograph, that you want to import separately. You can easily do so. You can just display the image or you can convert it to a component, as we explain in the "Converting artwork to buttons" section of Chapter 14. To import an image file, follow these steps:

1. **Choose the page or state where you want the image file to go from the Pages/States panel.**

2. **Choose File➪Import➪Image.**

   You can import PNG, GIF, JPG, JPE, or JPEG files.

3. **Navigate to the image file and double-click it.**

   The image appears on the Artboard.

4. **Click and drag the file on the Artboard to the desired location.**

   You can also drag a handle and resize the image. If you later need the image on another page, drag it from the Library panel.

5. **In the Property inspector, set the properties of the image.**

   Most of these are similar to the settings we describe in the "Formatting wireframe components" section, later in this chapter.

To reduce your final project size, you can compress images. Right-click the image in the Library panel and choose Compression Options. In the Compress Image dialog box, choose a quality and then click OK.

Editing in Adobe Illustrator

Say that you imported all your graphics from Illustrator and have done quite a bit of work in Catalyst. You created pages, turned artwork into buttons, and more. Now you decide that you want to change the way a button looks, but Catalyst's tools are not precise enough for you. What do you do?

You're in luck. Just select the item, right-click, and choose Edit in Adobe Illustrator CS5. In Illustrator, make your changes and close the document. Flash Catalyst will prompt you to accept the changes. You're all done! This process is called *round-trip editing*.

Adding Interface Components

In Chapter 14, we explain how to create buttons from artwork that you import from Photoshop or Illustrator. Buttons are the most common user interface component, but you can create other components as well. If you imported the artwork or drew it in Catalyst, you can select it, choose Convert Artwork to Component from the HUD, and then choose the component you want from the drop-down list. (You can read about Heads-up Display — HUD — in Chapter 14.)

Catalyst also offers wireframe components that you can insert onto the Artboard. Wireframe components don't contain much formatting but include the necessary parts to make the component work. For example, a check box include both the box and a label.

Inserting wireframe components

REMEMBER

Before you insert a component, choose the page you want to be on from the Pages/States panel and the folder that you want from the Layers panel. We explain more about the Pages/States and Layers panels in Chapter 14.

Drag the component that you want from the Wireframe Components panel to the Artboard. You can add the following components:

- ✔ Button
- ✔ Checkbox (see Figure 15-8 for an example)
- ✔ Data List (which we discuss briefly in the "Adding a data list" sidebar, later in this chapter)
- ✔ Horizontal Scrollbar
- ✔ Horizontal Slider
- ✔ Radio Button
- ✔ Text Input
- ✔ Toggle Button
- ✔ Vertical Scrollbar
- ✔ Vertical Slider

What sports do you enjoy watching?

☐ Baseball   ☐ Soccer
☐ Basketball   ☐ Hockey
☐ Football   ☐ Other

Figure 15-8: Collect information with check boxes; these use default formatting.

TECHNICAL STUFF

Most of the components require some ActionScript programming to make them useful. Pretty check boxes don't help much if you can't gather data from them. You add ActionScript in Adobe Flash Builder. We don't cover Builder in this book, but we discuss it briefly at the end of this chapter.

Formatting wireframe components

You format wireframe components in the Property inspector. The settings available vary with the component. Start by selecting the component.

In the Common section of the Property inspector (refer to Figure 15-4), you specify some general settings. Some of the settings apply to all the components. For example, you can use the X and Y settings to specify the location and the W and H settings to specify the size of the component. We discuss these settings in the "Formatting paths" section, earlier in this chapter. You can also set the opacity and rotation. We cover these settings in the "Formatting a path's stroke and fill" section, also earlier in this chapter.

When you drag a component to the Artboard, it has a generic label. For example, a radio button is labeled Radio Button. Quite creative, yes? To change the label, so that your visitors know which radio button is which, enter a new label in the Label text box.

Other components have one or both of the following settings:

✔ **Selected:** When you check the Selected check box, the component is already filled in. You can use this option for a default setting.

✔ **Enabled:** Components are enabled by default. Deselect the Enabled check box to make the component unavailable. You might then add ActionScript that enabled the component under certain conditions.

In the Component section of the Property inspector, shown in Figure 15-9 for a check box, you specify how the component functions. Some of these settings are unique for each component.

Some of the common settings are as follows:

✔ **Accepts Mouse Events:** By default, components accept clicking, but you could deselect the Accepts Mouse Events check box to require keyboard navigation.

✔ **Repeat If Held:** Repeats an action if the user holds down the mouse button. You could use this for an arrow on a scrollbar, for example, so that repeated clicking isn't necessary.

✔ **Tab Index:** The tab index, which is –1 by default, controls the order of focus with which a user presses the Tab key on the keyboard. For example, you might want the tabbing order of a two-column list of check boxes, like the one in Figure 15-8, to be in three rows rather than in two columns.

Figure 15-9: Use the Component section of the Property inspector to make your components more functional.

✔ **Tab to Focus:** Select this option to allow users to tab from one component to another, such as a set of check boxes or radio buttons.

✔ **Tooltip:** By default, the *tooltip* (a pop-up label) is the same as the label that you specify in the Common section of the Property inspector, but you can change it. You might want to add a more complete explanation, as shown in Figure 15-10.

Sliders and scrollbars have additional settings that allow you to specify minimum and maximum values, the snap interval, and step size.

In the Appearance section of the Property inspector (refer to Figure 15-9), you can set other properties, depending on the component:

☐ Baseball	☐ Soccer
☐ Basketball	☐ Hockey
☐ Football	☐ Ot... What the rest of the world calls football

Figure 15-10: A tooltip can help your audience understand the meaning of a label.

✔ **Blend Mode:** Affects the component when it overlaps other objects. We cover the blend modes in Flash in Chapter 7. They are the same in Catalyst.

✔ **Focus Ring:** A kind of halo around the component that you see when you tab through the components, as shown in Figure 15-11. You can change the color by clicking the color swatch and choosing a new color.

✔ **Hand Cursor:** Display a hand cursor (indicating a hyperlink) when the user passes the cursor over the component. Usually, you use a hand cursor for buttons that hyperlink to another location.

☐ Baseball	☐ Soccer
☐ Basketball	☐ Hockey
☐ Football	☑ Other

Figure 15-11: The focus is on hockey!

In the Filters section of the Property inspector, you can add filters, which we discuss earlier in this chapter in the "Adding filters to a path" section.

Adding a data list

A data list is an advanced type of component. A data list is an interface for choosing an item from a list. For example, you could choose your favorite color from a list of colors, including color swatches. You can define not only the text list, but images — in our example, the color swatches. The data can be stored in your Catalyst project or externally. For a basic tutorial on creating a data list, go to tv.adobe.com/watch/discover-flash-catalyst/create-a-data-list-in-flash-catalyst.

After adding a component, you might want to copy it to other pages or states. Components can have states, just like buttons (which we explain in Chapter 14). However, states are most common for buttons; check boxes and radio boxes don't usually change appearance when you hover the mouse cursor over them or click them (except that they're selected when you click them).

Adding Sound

You can add sound to your Web sites in Catalyst. Turn it up, turn it up! You can import MP3 files. (The only alternative is to import an FLV or F4V file with sound only: that is, no video.) To import the sound, choose File⇨Import⇨Video/Sounds. Navigate to the sound file and double-click it.

You're now ready to use the sound. You attach the sound as an action to a state in the Timelines panel.

We cover the Timelines panel in more depth in the "Adding Animation" section of Chapter 14.

You can add a sound to a page state or any component state. The most common situation is probably playing a sound when you click a button. In the following steps, we explain the process to follow so that a sound plays when you click a button, assuming that you already created a button:

1. **Click the Page where you want the button to play the sound from the Pages/States panel.**

2. **Choose File⇨Import⇨Video/Sound File.**

3. **Navigate to the MP3 sound and double-click it.**

   You can now see the sound in the Media section of the Library panel.

You need to know how long the sound is so that you can set the duration of the animation effect. In Windows Explorer, right-click the sound, choose Properties, and then click the Details tab to see its length. On a Mac, Control-click the file and choose Get Info. Also, you can usually find the length of a sound in a media player.

4. **Double-click the button to enter Component Editing mode.**

   We explain Component Editing mode in the "Defining button states" section of Chapter 14.

5. **In the Timelines panel, select the state that you want to use.**

   We chose Up ⁊ Down to start with.

6. **Select the button on the Artboard.**

   Be sure to select all its subcomponents.

7. **From the bottom of the Timelines panel, choose Add Action⇨Sound Effect.**

8. **From the Select a Visual Asset dialog box, expand the Media item, select the MP3 that you imported, and then click OK.**

   You see the Sound Effect animation in the third column of the Timelines panel for each subcomponent of the button, as shown in Figure 15-12. In this example, both the rectangle and the label that make up the button contain a sound effect.

Figure 15-12: Sound effect animations.

9. **Select the Sound Effect bar in the third column. In the Property inspector, click the Duration value, enter the length of the sound (or a little extra) that you found in Step 3, and then press Enter/Return, as shown in Figure 15-13.**

   You can also specify a delay or repeat the sound. Repeat this step for other Sound Effect animations if your button has more than one object.

10. **Repeat Steps 4–8 for the other states of the button.**

   We opt for Over > Down, Down > Up, and Down > Over because we want the sound to start when someone clicks the button (from either the Up or Over state) and to continue after someone releases the mouse button. Our sound, an invitation to sign up for a newsletter, lasts 57 seconds. (If we choose just the first two options, the sound will stop when we release the mouse button.)

Figure 15-13: Adjust sound duration.

Test your site (Ctrl+Enter in Windows/⌘+Return on a Mac) and click your button. Your sound should play, loud and clear!

Adding Video

You can add video to your Web site by importing FLV or F4V video files. FLV and F4V (a later variation of FLV) are Flash video files that are highly compressed.

In the "Converting your video with Adobe Media Encoder" section of Chapter 11, we explain how to convert other video formats to FLV or F4V using Adobe Media Encoder.

To add a video to your Web site, follow these steps:

1. **Click the Page where you want the video to appear from the Pages/ States panel.**

2. **Choose File⇨Import⇨Video/Sound File.**

3. **Navigate to the FLV or F4V file and double-click it.**

   You can now see the video file on the Artboard, complete with a control frame that includes a Play button. You can also find the video in the Media section of the Library panel. If you select the video file there, Rewind, Play, and Pause buttons appear, which you can use to preview the video.

4. **Click and drag the video on the Artboard to the desired location.**

   If you later need the video on another page, you can drag it from the Library panel.

5. **In the Property inspector, set the properties of the video.**

   Most of these are similar to the settings we describe in the "Formatting wireframe components" section earlier in this chapter. You can also choose Wireframe or Standard controls from the Video Controls drop-down list — or none. You can choose to autoplay or loop the video. In the Component section of the Property inspector, you can specify a volume.

Test your site (Ctrl+Enter in Windows/⌘+Return on a Mac) and click the video Play button, as shown in Figure 15-14. Enjoy the show!

Figure 15-14: Catalyst automatically adds player controls to your video.

Using SWF Files

You can import SWF files that you create in Flash. What's so cool about this feature is that you don't have to convert or otherwise set up the SWF file. You just import the file and it works! Follow these steps:

1. **Choose the page or state where you want the SWF file to go from the Pages/States panel.**

2. **Choose File⇨Import⇨SWF File.**

3. **Navigate to the SWF file and double-click it.**

   The file appears on the Artboard.

4. **Click and drag the SWF file on the Artboard to the desired location.**

   If you later need the video on another page, you can drag it from the Library panel.

5. **In the Property inspector, set the properties of the SWF file.**

   Most of these are similar to the settings we describe in the "Formatting wireframe components" section earlier in this chapter.

Test your site (Ctrl+Enter in Windows/⌘+Return on a Mac). The SWF animation plays. In Figure 15-15, you see the flower power button that we introduce in Chapter 8.

Figure 15-15: Plop in an SWF file, and its animation immediately works.

Integrating with Flash Builder

Adobe Flash Builder, a companion to Flash Catalyst, allows developers to add serious programming code to Web design. After all, most interactive features of Web sites require some programming. Of course, if you need a back-end database to accept customer orders, for example, you'll also need to add code. Adding the code is the business of Flash Builder.

Because both Catalyst and Builder (as well as Flash Professional) use the same code (called *Flex* code) the designer and developer can work together.

After you bring your Catalyst file into Builder, you can't make design changes, so make sure that the design is complete before opening the file in Builder.

Publishing Your Web Site

You had a blast and created a great Web site. You tested the project locally in your browser a zillion times, and it looks perfect. Time to get it up on the Web already! Follow these steps:

1. **Choose File⇨Publish to SWF to open the Publish to SWF dialog box, shown in Figure 15-16.**

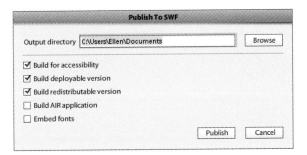

Figure 15-16: You're about to be published!

2. **Click the Browse button to specify a folder for your Web site.**

   Catalyst creates a subfolder named after your project and two folders inside that subfolder: one to store on your computer (run-local) and one to upload to the Web server (deploy-to-web).

3. **Make choices for the following options:**

   - *Build for Accessibility:* Adds features that allow people with disabilities to view your site.

   - *Build Deployable Version:* Includes a copy to deploy to your Web server. Of course, you want this option!

   - *Build Redistributable Version:* Includes a copy to store on your computer that you can send to others for storing or deploying.

   - *Build AIR Application:* Creates a stand-alone application that works outside a browser.

   - *Embed Fonts:* Embeds the fonts in case you used some unusual fonts that viewers might not have available. Careful, though, because embedding fonts adds to the size of your project.

4. **Click Publish.**

   You don't see anything in Catalyst, so go and check that the new folders are where you specified.

5. **Upload the entire `deploy-to-web` folder to your Web server.**

   The main page is called Main.html. (You can change its name, of course.) So browse to www.*yoursite*.com/Main.html and test your new site. Congratulations!

We think Catalyst is a great tool and will soon become very popular, especially for simple Web sites. We hope you have fun with it!

Part VII
The Part of Tens

The 5th Wave — By Rich Tennant

GOLF WORLD

"I can't really explain it, but every time I animate someone swinging a golf club, a little divot of code comes up missing on the home page."

In this part . . .

In the famous *For Dummies* Part of Tens, we
answer the ten most-asked questions — or at
least the ten questions we most wanted to answer.
In the chapter on the ten best Flash resources, we
manage to give you dozens of Flash resources,
such as the many Flash resource Web sites (while
convincing our publisher that only ten exist).
Finally, to top off the book, we give you our votes
for ten great Flash designers. Surf to see the work
of all ten and be amazed and inspired by the
possibilities!

16

Ten Frequently Asked Questions

- How do I combine two Flash movies?
- How can I sync sound with motion?
- What is the best way to import bitmaps?
- How do I rescale my movie's size?
- What are the best tips for creating movies?
- Can Flash do real 3D?
- How do I center a Flash movie in a Web page?
- What are the size limits for a Flash movie?
- How do I export Flash movies for use in video editing software?
- What are the top tips for Web design with Flash?

I n this chapter, we answer some frequently asked questions about Flash while explaining how to create some cool effects and streamline the process of creating Flash movies.

How Do I Combine Two Flash Movies?

Merging two Flash movies isn't difficult. You simply copy all the frames in each scene in your first movie to new scenes that you create in your second movie. To merge two Flash movies into one, follow these steps:

1. **Choose File⇨Open. In the Open dialog box that appears, navigate to and select the Flash movie you want to copy from.**

   The Flash movie you select appears on the Stage.

2. **Click the Edit Scene button near the top right of the Stage (shown in Figure 16-1). In the drop-down list that appears, choose the scene you want to copy.**

Edit Scene button

Figure 16-1: Use the Edit Scene button to choose your scene.

The scene you select appears on the Stage.

3. **Unlock all the layers in the scene.**

See Chapter 6 for information on unlocking layers.

4. **Choose Edit⇨Timeline⇨Select All Frames.**

This selects all keyframes and tweens in all layers in the scene.

5. **Choose Edit⇨Timeline⇨Copy Frames.**

This copies all the keyframes and tweens in your scene.

6. **Choose File⇨Open. In the Open dialog box that appears, navigate to and select the Flash movie you want to copy to.**

The Flash movie you select appears on the Stage.

7. **Choose Insert⇨Scene.**

An empty scene appears on the Stage.

8. **Click the first frame in the Timeline and then choose Edit⇨Timeline⇨ Paste Frames.**

This pastes the scene you copied from your first movie into your new scene in your second movie.

9. **Repeat Steps 1–8 for each scene you want to copy from your first movie.**

10. **Choose Control⇨Test Movie⇨In Flash Professional.**

Your second movie now includes all the scenes you copied from your first movie.

How Can I Sync Sound with Motion?

Suppose you want certain parts of your animation synchronized with specific sounds. For example, you want a bouncing ball to synchronize with the beat of music you imported into Flash. If you don't synchronize the sounds, the sound and the animation might play at different speeds. For example, a faster computer might play the animation faster but won't adjust the length of the sound. Or a slow computer might take its time displaying a transparent ball bouncing, and the synchronization with sound will drift. (For basic information on adding sound to Flash, refer to Chapter 11.)

To synchronize animation with sound, you need to use a *stream sound*. When you add the sound file to a frame, choose Stream from the Sync drop-down list in the Property inspector. Then adjust the keyframes so that the animation and the sound end at the same time.

To be even more precise, you can synchronize your animation with specific parts of the sound. Choose Modify⇨Timeline⇨Layer Properties, and then choose 200% or 300% from the Layer Height drop-down list. You can also choose Medium or Large for the size of the frames from the drop-down menu in the upper-right corner of the Timeline. Now, as shown in Figure 16-2, you can see the shape of your sound wave more clearly so that you can adjust the keyframes of your animation to match certain parts of the sound.

Figure 16-2: Increase layer height in the Timeline to see your sound wave shape more clearly.

One way to pinpoint which frame to use for placing an animation event is to drag the playhead (the red rectangle) just above the Timeline. This technique lets you control the speed of the animation. You can drag left or right until you find the exact frame that you want to work with. You can then move a keyframe to that frame, for example, to move an animation event to a frame that contains a specific portion of your sound.

What's the Best Way to Import Bitmaps?

Maybe you're working on an animation, and you need to include your boss' photograph or a photo of the product that you sell. Or maybe you want an effect in your Flash movie that you can create only in Photoshop. So you need to use a bitmap image. What bitmap format do you use?

You might not have a choice of format. If your information systems department hands you a logo with a solid white background in JPEG format, you probably have to use it.

At other times, you can choose your format. For example, when you scan a photo, most scanner software lets you choose from among several formats. A digital camera might also let you choose the format. Of course, if you create the bitmap in an image-editing program, you can choose from any format that the program supports. (Turn to Chapter 3 for instructions on importing bitmap images. ***Hint:*** Choose File⇨Import⇨Import to Stage or File⇨Import⇨Import to Library.)

Here are some commonly used bitmap formats as well as their pros and cons:

- **GIF:** The GIF file format can't have more than 256 colors. You can use the GIF format for simple drawings with a limited color palette, but you might be better off using the PNG format, described later in this list.

- **JPEG:** Because JPEG files can display many more colors than GIF files, they produce more realistic photos and other complex drawings. However, although JPEG graphics can be highly compressed to reduce file size, they might lose some detail or color fidelity as a result, depending on how much you choose to compress them.

- **BMP:** BMP doesn't lose quality when compressed, but the BMP format results in larger file sizes than GIF or JPEG.

- **PNG:** PNG is a nice compromise between file size and image quality. The PNG format doesn't lose quality when compressed and allows also many more colors than the GIF format. And it provides the capability for transparency. If you want the smallest file size but don't want to compromise quality, the PNG format is a good choice. The Flash image compressor works best and most efficiently with images that haven't been compressed by using techniques that can lose some image quality.

Your final result is the SWF file that you publish. Flash compresses bitmaps (as well as the entire movie) when the movie is exported to a SWF Flash Player file. Therefore, you need to think about the entire round-trip journey that your bitmap will make. You might have to test varying bitmap formats and publish the movie for each one to see the exact results.

When you export, you can set the JPEG quality on the Flash tab of the Publish Settings dialog box. You also set the overall quality on the HTML tab. For that quality setting, only the High and Best settings *smooth* (anti-alias) the bitmaps in the movie. (Refer to Chapter 13 for more information about publishing your Flash movie.)

When you import a bitmap image into Flash, you can take the following steps to ensure good-looking results:

✔ **Save your graphics in the highest quality possible.** If you have a photograph, don't import it as a GIF file.

✔ **Don't overcompress your original bitmaps.** Find a happy medium. Try saving an image at several compression levels to see the difference in quality and size.

✔ **Set the compression type and quality in the Bitmap Properties dialog box.** After you import the image, open the Library (choose Window➪ Library), right-click (Windows) or Control-click (Mac) the image, and then choose Properties to open the Bitmap Properties dialog box, as shown in Figure 16-3.

![Bitmap Properties dialog box showing skateboarder.BMP settings]

Bitmap Properties

skateboarder.BMP

.\skateboarder.BMP

Wednesday, December 22, 1999 12:41 PM
400 x 400 pixels at 32 bits per pixel

☑ Allow smoothing

Compression: Photo (JPEG)

Quality: ⦿ Use publish setting: 80

○ Custom: 50   (100=highest)

☐ Enable deblocking

Will use JPEG setting from Export Movie

OK   Cancel   Update   Import...   Test   Advanced

Figure 16-3: Use the Bitmap Properties dialog box to fiddle with your bitmaps.

How Do I Rescale My Movie's Size?

You create a beautiful Flash movie that takes up the entire page. But then your boss says that you need to fit it into an existing HTML page, which translates into reducing the size of the whole thing by 25 percent. What do you do? Get a new boss, if possible. Barring that, you can rescale the size of the movie.

1. **Decide the amount of the reduction you need to achieve, such as 25%.**

2. **If you have any locked layers, unlock them.**

   See Chapter 6 for all the info on locking and unlocking layers.

3. **If you have any hidden layers, right-click (Windows) or Control-click (Mac) the name of any layer and then choose Show All.**

   This step ensures that all layers are considered in the reduction.

4. **Click the Edit Multiple Frames button (just below the Timeline).**

5. **Drag the onion skin markers to the beginning and ending frames of your animation.**

   See Chapter 9 for more information on how to use onion skin markers.

6. **Choose Edit⇨Select All.**

7. **Choose Window⇨Transform to open the Transform panel (shown in Figure 16-4).**

8. **In the Transform panel, select the Constrain icon so that the graphic of the chain link is unbroken.**

9. **In the Scale Width or Scale Height input box, type the new number for your reduction percentage, and then press Enter (Windows) or Return (Mac).**

   Flash scales your animations by the reduction percentage.

TRANSFORM

⟷ 100.0 % ↕ 100.0 %

⊙ Rotate
   △ 0.0 °
○ Skew
   ⬚ _ °   ⬚ _ °

3D Rotation
   X: 0.0 °   Y: 0.0 °   Z: 0.0 °

3D Center point
   X: 96.0   Y: 213.0   Z: 0.0

Figure 16-4: Rescale everything here.

10. **Choose Modify⇨Document.**

11. **In the Width and Height boxes of the Document Properties dialog box that appears, type new numbers reflecting the reduction percentage size, as shown in Figure 16-5.**

Document Settings

Dimensions: 300 px (width) x 200 px (height)   OK

☑ Adjust 3D Perspective Angle to preserve current stage projection   Cancel

Ruler units: Pixels ▼   Match: ⊙ Default
                                ○ Contents
                                ○ Printer

Background color: ☐

Frame rate: 24.00

Make Default

Figure 16-5: Type in your new Width and Height.

Here, you'll have to first do a little math, multiplying the old Width and Height by the reduction percentage to come up with the new numbers you type in.

You're done! Flash scales your entire movie as you specified. You might have to drag everything so that it fits appropriately within your smaller-sized movie.

Size requirements are key pieces of information to nail down before building a Flash movie to avoid rescaling your movie's size.

What Are the Best Tips for Creating Movies?

Every Flash user collects a number of techniques that make creating a Flash movie easier. Following are a few ideas to help you get started:

- ✓ **Save multiple versions of your movie** by choosing File➪Save As. If a problem arises, you can always go back to a previous version and start again.

- ✓ As soon as you have an overall structure, **test your movie in a variety of browsers** (for example, Internet Explorer; Mozilla Firefox; Google Chrome; and Safari) and at various resolutions, if possible. It's easier to correct problems early, before your project becomes too complex. Choose Control➪Test Movie➪In Flash Professional as soon as you develop your animation and continue to test it in this way for each new significant change. It's also a good idea to keep testing your movie with Publish Preview (press F12) to see how it will work in a browser.

- ✓ **Use consistent names for symbols.** Many Flash users add the type of symbol after the name: for example, a button called Contact_btn and a movie clip called Intro_mc. When you start creating movie clips inside buttons, you might get confused if you don't name your symbols intelligently.

- ✓ **Use meaningful names for your instances.** If you have three instances of a button symbol, you need to be able to distinguish which is which. You can name them by their purpose, such as Email, Services, and Clients.

- ✓ When you complete work on a layer, **lock the layer** to avoid making unwanted changes.

- ✓ **Give layers meaningful names.**

- ✓ **Place related elements in layers that are near each other,** and then put the layers in layer folders to group them.

✔ **If you have ActionScript on a layer, don't put anything else on that layer.** This avoids potential conflicts between items you might have on the Stage and your ActionScript code that references them.

✔ **If your ActionScript code references particular frames, reference them with frame labels rather than frame numbers.** Then if you later move those frames on the Timeline, you don't have to change any frame numbers in your code.

✔ **Organize similar assets in your Library with library folders,** and give your Library folders meaningful names, as shown in Figure 16-6.

Figure 16-6: Organize Library assets in folders with meaningful names.

✔ For longer presentations, **use several SWF files in sequence** rather than a series of scenes. Then your audience can download your presentation more quickly in small pieces, one SWF file at a time, rather than having to download the entire SWF file that contains many scenes all at once. On the other hand, if you create lengthy animations, you might want to use scenes in a single, big SWF file so that your audience downloads everything at the beginning, and can then view the lengthy animation without interruption.

Can Flash Do Full 3D?

As you see in Chapter 9, it's really cool that you can use Flash's new 3D transformation tools to animate 2D Flash objects in 3D space. But is there any way to create and animate fully 3D objects in your Flash worlds? Yes, but you need to resort to additional software packages to do so — or do some pretty fancy ActionScript programming.

Software-wise, check out Electric Rain's Swift 3D (Figure 16-7), which is specifically designed for creating 3D animation for Flash. It's also fairly easy to use compared with other 3D software packages. Electric Rain also sells software plug-ins that you can use to export 3D animation from the 3D animation software packages 3ds Max and Lightwave 3D into Flash.

Figure 16-7: Create 3D animations in Swift 3D and import them into Flash.

Those with a high level of programming skill can choose from several increasingly popular, free software programming frameworks to create 3D animation with ActionScript. Papervision3D is one such framework, and you can see an example of its capabilities at www.papervision3d.org, shown in Figure 16-8. To learn more about Papervision3D and to see more demonstrations of its capabilities, check out http://blog.papervision3d.org.

Figure 16-8: An interesting example of what Papervision3D can do.

Other popular 3D programming frameworks for Flash include the Go ActionScript Animation Platform (www.goasap.org), Away3D (away3d. com), and the Sandy 3D Engine (www.flashsandy.org; see Figure 16-9).

Figure 16-9: Sandy 3D Engine demos, tutorials, forum, and blog are online.

How Do I Center a Flash Movie in a Web Page?

As we discuss in Chapter 13, you can make your Flash movie appear in a Web page by choosing both the Flash and HTML formats in your Publish Settings and then publishing your movie. Flash then generates the HTML code (like the code in Figure 13-13) for a Web page. This Web page appears to contain your Flash movie when you view the Web page in a browser. To make the Flash movie centered in that Web page, you just need to add a little bit of extra code to the HTML page, which you can do with a text editor.

To add the code for centering your Flash movie in the Web page, follow these steps:

1. **After choosing the Publish Settings for Flash and HTML (using the Flash Only or Flash HTTPS template in the HTML tab of the Publish Settings dialog box, as we describe in Chapter 13), choose File⇨Publish.**

   Flash creates a Flash Player (SWF) file and a Web page (HTML) file.

2. **Start a text editor or an HTML editor, and open the HTML page within the editor.**

   You can use an HTML editor (such as Dreamweaver) or a text editor (such as Notepad in Windows; or TextEdit on a Mac).

   In TextEdit, choose TextEdit➪Preferences. In the Preferences window, on the New Document tab, select Plain Text rather than Rich Text in the Format section. On the Open and Save tab of the Preferences window, deselect the Add '.txt' Extension to Plain Text Files check box in the When Saving a File section.

3. **Find `</head>` in the file and insert this code before it:**

```
<style type="text/css" media="screen">
    body {text-align: center; }
    div#flashContent {width: 550px; margin: 0px auto;
    text-align: left; }
</style>
```

   Be sure you find `</head>`, not `<head>`.

   This code defines some Cascading Style Sheet (or CSS) styles that your Web browser will use to dynamically create margins on the left and right of a Flash movie, 550 pixels (px) wide, so that the movie is automatically centered on the page. If your Flash movie is a different width — say, 200 pixels — just change `550px` in the preceding code to `200px`.

   In HTML lingo, `<div>` and `<style>` (and any other words starting with a bracket [`<`]) are called *tags*. The `<div>` tag defines the beginning of a division or section of a Web page, and the `</div>` tag defines the end of it. The `<div>` containing the `id` equal to `flashContent` is where the Flash movie will appear, and the Web browser uses the style that you define for `flashContent` in Step 3 and applies it to everything between the `<div>` and `</div>` tags that will contain the Flash movie.

   Figure 16-10 shows an example of an HTML file with all the code added. This is the code shown in Figure 13-13, revised with `<style>`, `</style>`, `<div>`, and `</div>` tags, which center the movie in the Web page.

4. **In the editor, save the file with the changes you made.**

   Now when you view the HTML page in a Web browser (assuming it's not an ancient version of a Web browser), your Flash movie appears centered in the Web page.

```
●○○                    Movie of the Year Centered.html
<!DOCTYPE html PUBLIC "-//W3C//DTD XHTML 1.0 Strict//EN" "http://www.w3.org/TR/xhtml1/DTD/xhtml1-strict.dtd">
<html xmlns="http://www.w3.org/1999/xhtml" lang="en" xml:lang="en">
        <head>
                <title>Movie of the Year Centered</title>
                <meta http-equiv="Content-Type" content="text/html; charset=utf-8" />
                <script type="text/javascript" src="swfobject.js"></script>
                <script type="text/javascript">
                        <!-- Adobe recommends that developers use SWFObject2 for Flash Player detection. -->
                        <!-- For more information see the SWFObject page at Google code (http://code.google.com/p/swfobject/). -->
                        <!-- Information is also available on the Adobe Developer Connection Under "Detecting Flash Player versions and
embedding SWF files with SWFObject 2" -->
                        <!-- Set to minimum required Flash Player version or 0 for no version detection -->
                        var swfVersionStr = "10.1.0";
                        <!-- xiSwfUrlStr can be used to define an express installer SWF. -->
                        var xiSwfUrlStr = "";
                        var flashvars = {};
                        var params = {};
                        params.quality = "high";
                        params.bgcolor = "#ffffff";
                        params.play = "true";
                        params.loop = "true";
                        params.wmode = "window";
                        params.scale = "showall";
                        params.menu = "true";
                        params.devicefont = "false";
                        params.salign = "";
                        params.allowscriptaccess = "sameDomain";
                        var attributes = {};
                        attributes.id = "Movie of the Year Centered";
                        attributes.name = "Movie of the Year Centered";
                        attributes.align = "middle";
                        swfobject.createCSS("html", "height:100%; background-color: #ffffff;");
                        swfobject.createCSS("body", "margin:0; padding:0; overflow:hidden; height:100%;");
                        swfobject.embedSWF(
                                "Movie of the Year Centered.swf", "flashContent",
                                "550", "400",
                                swfVersionStr, xiSwfUrlStr,
                                flashvars, params, attributes);
                </script>
                <style type="text/css" media="screen">
                        body {text-align: center; }
                        div#flashContent {width: 550px; margin: 0px auto; text-align: left; }
                </style>
        </head>
        <body>
                <!-- SWFObject's dynamic embed method replaces this alternative HTML content for Flash content when enough JavaScript and
Flash plug-in support is available. -->
                <div id="flashContent">
                        <a href="http://www.adobe.com/go/getflash">
                                <img src="http://www.adobe.com/images/shared/download_buttons/get_flash_player.gif" alt="Get Adobe Flash
player" />
                        </a>
                        <p>This page requires Flash Player version 10.1.0 or higher.</p>
                </div>
        </body>
</html>
```

Figure 16-10: This code centers the movie on the Web page.

What Are the Size Limits for a Flash Movie?

Usually, you won't be too concerned about how big of a movie you can create with Flash, because one of the reasons to use Flash is that it employs vector graphics, tweening, and other methods to create small files that download quickly over the Web. If you're using Flash to create gigantic projects, that can be great fun and even workable in some cases. Just keep in mind that Flash wasn't primarily designed to do that. On the other hand, more and more studios are using Flash for production animation (including broadcast TV shows), and video is now an important feature of Flash.

In any case, it's interesting to know that other than limits imposed by your computer's RAM, CPU, hard drive, video card, browser, and operating system, there are few limits to the size and complexity of a Flash movie. However, here are at least two limits:

✏ The minimum size of your Stage is 1 pixel wide and 1 pixel high.

✏ The maximum Stage size is 2880 pixels wide x 2880 pixels wide.

How Do I Export Flash Movies for Use in Video Editing Software?

One way is to export your Flash movie as a QuickTime movie. To do that, choose File➪Export➪Export Movie. In the File dialog box that appears, choose QuickTime from the Save as Type drop-down list. Then type in a name for your movie and choose Save.

This should render all the animation in your Flash movie, including movie clip and ActionScript animations — if you have a superfast computer with loads of RAM. If you don't, it's not likely that you'll get all the frames at the correct duration. Adobe is aware of this shortcoming, but as of this writing, no better solution is available.

In any case, hope for the best, open the QuickTime movie of your Flash project in your video editing software, and have fun editing it in with your other video footage.

What Are the Top Tips for Web Design with Flash?

The vast majority of Flash movies end up on Web sites. Here are some tips to help ensure that your Web site is as attractive and useful as possible.

Set your goal

Know why you have a Web site. Write out one main goal and perhaps one or two secondary goals. For example, the main goal of your site might be to sell used music CDs. A secondary goal might be to provide viewers with music reviews so that they can decide which CDs they want to buy. Another secondary goal could be to attract viewers to your site (so that they can buy your CDs). Avoid putting material on your site that doesn't help you reach your goal.

How does your Flash movie help you attain your Web site's goal? Perhaps your movie displays the covers of your most widely sold CDs and plays some of the music, giving viewers an instant understanding of your site's purpose.

Make thumbnail sketches first

This might be the most radical, life-altering advice in this book: After you articulate the goals for your Web site, try out several different designs for each type of page in your site by drawing small sketches of them. For your home page, try out at least a dozen designs.

Keep the sketches really small, so they're the size of a postage stamp. This makes it easier for you to try a lot of different designs quickly. It also forces you to think of the overall design of your site before you jump into the details. This gives you a chance to pick a strong overall design that graphically supports your goals for the site.

Connect the parts to the whole

You can find a compelling overall graphic design by drawing your thumbnail sketches, as we describe in the preceding section. Now while you fill in the details of your page, see how you can organize the details of your page so that they fit well into its main graphic theme as captured in your thumbnail sketch. This will help you avoid clutter and will make your pages easier to understand, more powerful, and more attractive.

Clutter and complex structures are usually counterproductive. You can use Flash to create a simple, compelling navigational system that connects the user to every page effortlessly.

Use fewer than four fonts

For maximum coherence and impact, you should probably restrict your Web page design to use two or three fonts at most. It might make visual sense to use one font for the body of your text and one font for the headlines. You could perhaps use a third font for a logo or for some other special item, but this will probably look best if it has some kind of strong visual harmony with the other fonts that you're using.

Test and test again

As we describe in Chapter 13, you undoubtedly need to test your Web site with several browsers, not just the latest version of Internet Explorer. Testing at various screen resolutions (probably at least 800 x 600 and 1024 x 768) is also extremely important. Then have a few friends review your site and navigate through it. Ask them to tell you about their impressions, moments of confusion, questions, comments, and praise as they explore your site — so that you can view your site from a fresh perspective.

Ten Best Flash Resources

*F*lash is such a flexible program that you'll never stop discovering what it can do. In this chapter, we point you to the many resources you can turn to when you want to increase your knowledge about Flash.

We (of course) think that this book is a great resource on Flash. But much more about Flash is out there, readily available to help you become a great Flash designer and animator.

Caffe Fibonacci - Episode 3 Learn about Tim's own favorite recipes using nested styles in Adobe InDesign, a truly life changing productivity ingredient that will transform the way you cook together your layouts forever.

Flash in a
Victor Vec
and graph
sound. Ho
the speed

Check Out Award-Winning Movies

It's both inspiring and instructive to see what the best Flash movies can do, and you can find the best Flash movies on a couple of sites. The Best Flash Animation Site archive (at www.bestflash animationsite.com/archive, of course) showcases Flash sites that have been voted the best each week by viewers. This is a good place to find top-notch examples of Flash in a variety of categories, including Applications, Corporate, Experimental, Technical Merit, and Video.

Look on the Flash Web Pages

Adobe maintains large resources for Flash users on its Web site. Go to www. adobe.com/support/flash and www.adobe.com/devnet/flash, where you can find tips, tutorials, support, technical notes, news, and updates.

Another great resource is Adobe TV (at http://tv.adobe.com, shown in Figure 17-1), which features many high-quality videos on Flash and other Adobe software.

Figure 17-1: Adobe TV features many insightful and inspiring online videos about Flash.

Visit Our Site

Check out the *Flash Professional CS5 and Flash Catalyst CS5 For Dummies* page on the Wiley Web site. You can find the site by surfing to www.dummies.com/ go/flashcs5fd. It contains sample files from the book, tips, and updates. We hope that you find the site helpful!

Take a Course

Many colleges and universities offer courses in Flash. Sometimes these courses are part of a Web design or graphic arts course, or they might stand alone. To find these courses, call local educational institutions and ask.

The advantage of a course led by a teacher is that you have a chance to ask questions — and receive answers. A teacher also guides the learning process and possibly even gives you lots of tips and hints!

You might also consider taking self-paced courses in Flash offered by Adobe or instructor-led courses at an Adobe Authorized Training Center. Visit `www.adobe.com/training` for more information, including free sample lessons.

Lynda.com also offers high-quality video-based online training courses on Flash for a monthly fee. You can find out more at `www.lynda.com`.

Join a Flash Discussion Group

Adobe maintains active Flash support forums, where anyone can ask questions and get answers from other members of the Flash community. To read messages from and send messages to these discussion forums, point your Web browser to `http://forums.adobe.com/community/flash`.

Several other excellent active discussion groups reside on Web sites. The best way to tell whether a discussion group is active is to see how many messages have been posted in the past one or two days. You can also check out how many different people are participating. See the following section in this chapter.

You can also subscribe to electronic mailing lists for ongoing discussions sent by e-mail. With more than 3,000 members, the Yahoo! FLASHmacromedia list is one of the largest lists specifically for users who want to discuss Flash techniques. You can ask questions and get answers from the community of Flash users. To sign up or to view the Web archive of messages, go to

```
http://tech.groups.yahoo.com/group/FLASHmacromedia
```

You can find more than 1,000 other Flash e-mail discussion groups at Yahoo! alone. Find them by surfing to

```
http://tech.dir.groups.yahoo.com/dir/Computers___Internet/
        Software/Multimedia/Macromedia_Flash
```

That's three underscores between *Computers* and *Internet.*

Check Out Flash Resource Sites

A huge Flash community is on the Internet — so vast, in fact, that you'll probably never be able to participate in all its offerings. These Web sites offer news, tutorials, discussion groups, tips, and links to other Flash resources.

Some of these sites are more up to date, lively, and complete than others. The quality of the tips and tutorials varies widely. Some specialize in tips for beginners; others are geared toward advanced users. The following list briefly reviews the ones that we find most useful, in alphabetical order:

- www.actionscript.org: This site is a well-designed, comprehensive resource on ActionScript. It includes extremely active discussion forums (with more than 100,000 discussions); more than 400 tutorials on ActionScript at beginning, intermediate, and advanced levels; a library with more than 700 ActionScripts, and more than 1,000 Flash movies; links; and an employment section.

- www.flashandmath.com: This site features many interesting, high quality tutorials on ActionScript 3.0.

- www.flashkit.com: Flash Kit is probably the largest Flash site, and it's up to date, having Flash CS5 material within days after it shipped. You can find more than 10,000 FLA files to download and study, more than 1,100 tutorials, dozens of active discussion forums (some with hundreds of thousands of discussions), links, thousands of sounds, more than 1,500 downloadable fonts — if you can think of it, you can find it here.

- www.flashgoddess.com: FlashGoddess is an informative site showcasing women who do brilliant work with Flash. It includes profiles of and articles on terrific Flash designers, a gallery of work by featured artists, links, and more.

- www.flashmagazine.com: This site features news and reviews of Flash and Flash-related products.

- www.gotoandlearn.com: This site contains dozens of terrific, free Flash tutorials on video, developed by Lee Brimelow, a Platform Evangelist at Adobe. The site also includes a forum with thousands of discussions. Lee's blog at http://theflashblog.com is a good place to find out what's new at Gotoandlearn.com. See Figure 17-2.

- www.kirupa.com: This is Kirupa Chinnathambi's site about Flash and other Web technologies. It contains hundreds of tutorials (many of them on video) and discussion forums with hundreds of thousands of posts.

- www.ultrashock.com: This site includes discussion forums on Flash with more than 600,000 posts

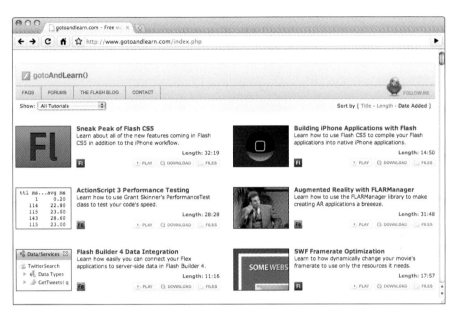

Figure 17-2: Find dozens of terrific, free Flash tutorials on video here.

Check Out Sites That Use Flash

You can get ideas by looking at what others do. (It's interesting, for instance, that simple Flash sites are sometimes the most beautiful and practical.) In Chapter 18, we list sites by ten great designers that use Flash.

Attend a Flash Conference

Attending a conference on Flash is an exciting way to find out much more about Flash from an array of experts, see award-winning Flash movies, participate in workshops and seminars, hear the latest news from Adobe, make contacts with others interested in Flash, and generally immerse yourself in the world of Flash. Even just visiting the Web sites of some of these conferences can be instructive. Conferences you might consider attending include the following:

- **FlashBelt Conference:** A four-day conference in Minneapolis in June. For information, visit www.flashbelt.com.

- **Adobe MAX:** A four-day conference in Los Angeles in October, sponsored by Adobe. This conference for designers, developers, and industry leaders features presentations on the entire range of Adobe software, not just Flash. For information, visit http://max.adobe.com.

Collect Flash Movies

Many Flash resource Web sites let you download FLA files. You can also trade FLA files with others who you know use Flash. Analyzing FLA files is one of the best ways to see how effects are created. In Chapter 12, we explain how to use the Movie Explorer to ferret out all the hidden details of an FLA file.

Be sure to check out the Library of an FLA file — many of the secrets lie there. And you can use the Movie Explorer to find and study all the actions in an FLA file. You'll soon be on your way to adapting the techniques that you see to your own projects.

Reuse Your Best Stuff

After you create some great Flash movies, you can reuse your best stuff. *Fadeouts* (changing transparency), *glows* (soft edges), and masks are simple effects that you can use again and again. You can also reuse ActionScript on new objects. After you get a technique down, you don't need to reinvent the wheel. If you've created an animated logo, you can have an entirely new animation by merely swapping a symbol.

You can import items from the Library of any movie into your current movie. Choose File⇨Import⇨Open External Library and then choose the Flash file that contains the Library you want to use. Then drag the items that you want from the imported movie Library onto the Stage or into the Library of your current movie. This is a really nifty Flash feature.

Ten Flash Designers to Watch

Trying to choose ten of the best designers who use Flash is almost absurd — so many brilliant designers are out there. Nevertheless, in this chapter, we give you a shortcut to finding some of the most innovative and skilled Flash designers so that you can check out their work, get ideas, and see the possibilities.

Note that some of the sites they've designed can take a really long time to load if you don't have a broadband connection to the Web.

Joshua Davis

Joshua Davis is one of the most relentless explorers of Flash's capabilities. His legendary PrayStation site, an archive that you may see at http://ps3.praystation.com/pound/v2, originally went online in 1997 as a spoof of PlayStation graphics, but it soon morphed into one of the most aggressively experimental Flash sites on the Web. He then moved on to create Once Upon A Forest (which you may see at www.once-upon-a-forest.com), a visually poetic series of computer-generated imagery that is easier to experience than describe. (He likes to bury his links, so you may have to search to find anything clickable.) You can see his current work at www.joshuadavis.com. Benek Lisefski's essay on Joshua Davis, at www.pixelinspectors.com/reviews/joshua-davis.html, can help you understand his mysterious work a little more clearly.

Anthony Eden

Australian designer Anthony Eden showcases a fascinating group of Flash experiments at his site, www.arseiam.com, shown in Figure 18-1.

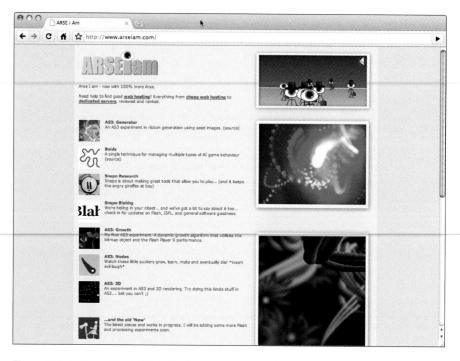

Figure 18-1: Anthony Eden's Web site features numerous interesting Flash experiments.

Andy Foulds

Andy Foulds' clients includes Nike, Miramax Films, Mercedes-Benz, Microsoft, and Yahoo!. His Flash portfolio, on view at `www.andyfoulds.co.uk`, is tremendously inventive and visually intriguing.

Freedom & Partners

Mark Ferdman, Vas Sloutchevsky, Robert Forras, and Shea Gonyo lead a design firm and advertising agency that makes bold, highly effective use of Flash to connect their clients to the public. You can see their work at `www.freedomandpartners.com`.

Chris Georgenes

Chris Georgenes is a freelance artist and animator whose clients include Cartoon Network, Dreamworks, ABC, NBC, FX, Comedy Central, PBS, and UPN. Check out his online portfolio of many charming animations at `www.mudbubble.com` (shown in Figure 18-2) and his blog at `www.keyframer.com`.

Figure 18-2: Chris Georgenes portfolio at Mudbubble.com is jammed with charming animated characters.

Ben Hantoot

Ben Hantoot is one of the most, as he says, "over-the-top" animators on the planet. Other Flash sites look positively motionless compared with the site of his studio, www.slickmill.com. The incessant inventiveness of his work is outrageously delightful

Seb Lee-Delisle and Dominic Minns

Seb Lee-Delisle is a Flash 3D innovator who has pushed Flash's boundaries in games, physics simulations, and interactive 3D animation. You can see some of his handiwork at his company's site at www.pluginmedia.net (shown in Figure 18-3), which also features charming graphic design by creative director Dominic Minns. Be sure to check out the lab there. His blog (www.sebleedelisle.com) presents lots of interesting and useful material on 3D techniques in Flash.

Figure 18-3: You can see the work of Dominic Minns and Seb Lee-Delisle work at their company's site, which features crazed Flash wizards from beyond the stars.

Erik Natzke

Interactive designer Erik Natzke presents some truly spectacular animation at `http://play.natzke.com`. Erik's online journal at `http://jot.eriknatzke.com` is also worth visiting.

Micaël Reynaud

At `www.dunun.com`, the award-winning French Flash designer Micaël Reynaud has created a site full of surprises that, like several of the sites in this chapter, is difficult to describe but charming to experience. For example, his work at `www.dunun.com/2002` (shown in Figure 18-4), combines music, imagery, and unusual user-interface techniques to showcase a panoramic view of this artist's multiple skills.

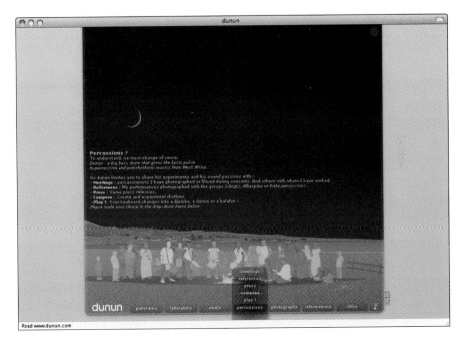

Figure 18-4: Micaël Reynaud uses Flash to create fascinating virtual environments such as the one shown here.

Jared Tarbell

Jared Tarbell uses ActionScript to generate beautiful imagery. Interestingly, his mathematical explorations in Flash often end up in commercial projects. You can see his work (and download his ActionScript code) at www.levitated.net.

Index